Dan Gookin's

Naked
Windows® XP

Dan Gookin

SYBEX® San Francisco · London

Associate Publisher: Joel Fugazzotto

Acquisitions and Developmental Editor: Ellen Dendy

Editor: Colleen Wheeler Strand

Production Editor: Dennis Fitzgerald

Technical Editor: Mark Chambers

Book Designer and Compositor: Owen Wolfson

Proofreaders: Nanette Duffy, Emily Hsuan, Nelson Kim, Laurie O'Connell, Dave Nash, Yariv Rabinovitch, Suzanne Stein, Sarah Tannehill

Indexer: John S. Lewis

Cover Designer: Richard Miller, Calyx Design

Cover Illustrator: Richard Miller, Calyx Design

CONTENTS

PART 1
Windows XP from Desktop to bottom   1

4   Halting Desktop Madness (Part II) 46

5   Taming the Taskbar 64

6   Betcha Didn't Know All This Stuff About the Start Panel 78

7   Learn About the Quick Launch Bar So You Look Better Than Your Co-Workers Who Are Clueless 94

PART 2

All the Intermediate-Level, Good Stuff about Disks, Files, and Stuff Like That 155

PART 3

Nifty Audio and Graphics Information That No One Shares 221

PART 4

There's More Internet Out There Than You Know — 291

To be Naked is to be Exposed, Vulnerable.

To be nude is to be without clothes.

"Oh! Naked lady!" the school kid shouts on the bus. Everyone turns to look, but the poor woman is just standing on the street. She may feel cold, helpless, and lacking all support—kind of like the typical Windows user waiting on a tech support line—but she's fully clothed. Naked, yet fully clothed.

This book's object is not to strip Windows nude, but rather to show you more of Windows than you would expect from a typical computer book. In the pages that follow, you will be exposed to some of Windows inner workings and finer details. The end result is that you'll become a more efficient, productive, and clever Windows XP user. So instead of your feeling cold, exposed, and unsupported, it will be Windows itself that's been rendered naked.

About This Book

I did not write this book to apologize for the shortcomings of the Windows operating system. Quite honestly, I'm on *your* side. I get frustrated just like anyone else using Windows. For example, why does Windows have several different and confusing ways to do something simple, such as start a program or copy a file? Why do we put up with such multiple inconsistencies? And why do other computer books excuse this and show you *all* the ways to do something instead of showing you the best way?

What poppycock!

Yes, this book has *attitude*! I am not going to sit here and justify why Windows does things in the silly and awkward that way it does. Rather than bore you with that information—most of which you've already figured out on your own—I though that I would write this book with the intention of exposing you to the best and most useful parts of Windows. The nifty stuff. The handy and useful things. The quick commands. The keyboard shortcuts. All that stuff that propels you from being a typical ho-hum Windows user to a more advanced, at-ease and in-charge Windows user.

Oh, and this book's readers generally lose weight and become smarter and more attractive after applying the tips and tricks described in these pages!

What's Covered Here

This book covers the Windows XP operating system, both the Home and Professional editions.

This is *not* a beginner's book. Instead, this book assumes that you already know basic Windows operations and techniques. For example, this book may direct you to "Open the Control Panel." It's assumed that you know how to do that, so I won't waste your time going over trivial, introductory steps.

This is not an advanced Windows book. There is nothing overly technical here. In fact, my research has shown that anyone who's familiar with Windows can grasp the concepts and ideas here. The text doesn't float off into advanced configuration options or networking nonsense that only the die-hard geek needs to know. Instead, the material here covers a broad variety of information for the intermediate user.

Specifically, this book dwells on topics that those other Windows books just don't have time to cover (or that they cover in only one paragraph or as an aside). Because this book skips over all the beginner material, there are ample pages to dwell upon intermediate topics, such as:

- Arranging the Start menu
- Messing with toolbars
- Configuring the Control Panel
- Managing your disk drives
- Storing graphics files
- Creating CD-ROM disks
- Organizing your Internet Favorites
- Managing your e-mail address book
- And many more!

What You Won't Find in This Book

This book does not touch upon the basics. If you are new to Windows or find it confusing, then you should be able to find several books that cover Windows XP in easy, step-by-step tutorials or references.

Specifically, this book does not cover:

- Basic anything (file operations, configuration, operation, and so on)
- Connecting to the Internet for the first time
- Composing your first e-mail message
- Adding new hardware
- Installing new software
- Adding or managing users
- Networking
- Computer nerd recipes
- Autopsy photos

All of these subjects are typically covered by a beginner's book, so there's no point in repeating them here. Some topics, such as Networking, are best left to Those Who Know What They're Doing. (Besides, in Windows XP the Networking Wizard is a pretty good source for anyone wanting to get started—no point in repeating that information in a book.)

On the advanced side, this book does not cover scripting, connecting to a Windows NT/2000 Server, interfacing Windows to an android, creating negative psion singularities in an inverted gravity matrix, or any of that nonsense.

This book does not cover Microsoft Office, Works, or generally any productivity software. Only programs that are included with Windows XP are used in this book's examples.

Conventions

This book refers to both Windows XP Home and Professional Editions as "Windows." Specific differences between Windows XP Home and Windows XP Pro are noted in the text. Older versions of Windows may be referenced from time to time, and if so their version number (Windows 2000, Windows 98, and so on) will be specified, along with humorous reasons why those operating systems no longer exist.

This is an active book with many steps and tutorials that show you how things get done. The steps are numbered, often with comments (or even sub-steps) between them:

1. Pick up the telephone handset.

2. Dial 1234.

Press the numbers 1, then 2, then 3, then 4 on the telephone keypad.

3. Wait for someone to answer.

The stuff you need to type (Step 2) appears in `bold text like this`.

Key combinations are specified using the plus symbol (+). Ctrl+D means to press the Ctrl (control) key and type a D, just as you would use Shift+D to get a capital letter D in a standard typing operation.

The Windows key on your keyboard is labeled "Win" in this book. So if I tell you to press Win+D, it means to press the Windows key, tap the D key, then release both keys. (Older computers with keyboards that lack the Windows key cannot run Windows XP. And if you're using an older keyboard just because you love it, then I trust you'll be able to figure out the various alternatives for the Windows key combinations.)

There are three icons used in the books:

Note icons flag information that needs to be, well, noted. Notes are asides or supplemental information to what's already written in the text.

While I like to say that everything in the book is a tip, some tips are more important than others. You'll find them flagged with this icon.

Finally, the warning is for something not to do or something to avoid. Such as, "Don't run around the house with scissors."

Various sidebars highlight specific information. Two types of sidebars appear most often:

The "Nerd's Corner" sidebars contains trivial or aside information that computer nerds might find interesting. (I just can't help myself sometimes and must lapse into computer trivia or by-the-way information that only the nerdiest readers will find appealing.)

The "Keyboard Master" sidebars contain keyboard "accelerators" or methods of accomplishing common tasks in Windows by using the keyboard alone. You'll find that using these Keyboard Master techniques are faster than using the mouse. And anyone watching you perform a keyboard accelerator will be very impressed—useful stuff!

About You!

Greetings, gentle reader! To get the most out of this book I am assuming the following things about you. Let me put on my Computer Book Author Psychic Turban and describe you:

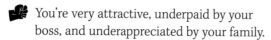 You're very attractive, underpaid by your boss, and underappreciated by your family.

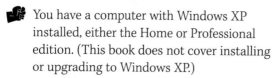 You have a computer with Windows XP installed, either the Home or Professional edition. (This book does not cover installing or upgrading to Windows XP.)

Your account is set up as an Administrative user, not a guest or limited account. This is the case for most single-person computers.

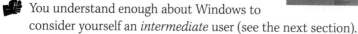 You understand enough about Windows to consider yourself an *intermediate* user (see the next section).

You're willing to learn more about your operating system so that you can become a more efficient and impressive computer user, at least better than the dweebs you work with.

You have some secret talent, such as you're double-jointed or you can whistle through your nose.

You live within ten miles of a large body of water: a lake, river, or ocean.

I can see by the Three of Cups that your previous romantic interest was a scoundrel and should probably be serving time in jail.

Okay! Okay! Time to remove the Psychic Turban!

So What Is an "Intermediate User"?

I wrote a book on Advanced DOS about 15 years ago. In the book, I defined an *advanced* DOS user as someone who knew what the MODE command did. For this book, I'll define an intermediate user as someone who accidentally deletes a swath of icons, then says "Oh, no!" (or something privately similar), and tries to get them back on their own *for at least ten minutes* before consulting with another source. That's an intermediate user.

You know how to do the following:

- Open windows and move them around
- Start programs
- Install programs
- Whack the computer's monitor when you feel frustrated and not be afraid that you've "hurt the computer's feelings"
- Be comfortable in front of a computer without having an irrational fear that it's laughing at you each time you turn away
- And you don't desire to have someone of greater computer knowledge nearby, or (put another way) you can work well enough on your own without feeling that empty pain when your computer guru flies off to Puerto Vallarta for a well-deserved week's vacation.

While this is all good for you—after all, you're not a pathetic and hopeless newbie (at least not any more)—you're most likely aware that there are certain things that the computer can do, stuff that you'd like to know more about, but for which you have yet to find a competent book or reliable source. For example, you would like to:

- Learn how to set things up and configure Windows just the way you like
- Explore alternative and possibly better (but not obvious) ways to do things
- Use keyboard "accelerators" to quickly summon windows or activate commands
- Discover powerful commands that make you more productive than the typical PC user
- Understand how Windows thinks so that you can anticipate its actions and be one step ahead of it
- Eat right and exercise more
- Learn a few witty sayings in Estonian

This book takes full advantage of those assumptions. For example, I won't waste your time with excess steps on stuff you're already familiar with. There's no sense in telling you to close this or that window, when you've probably jumped ahead on those steps anyway.

Most importantly, this book respects whatever knowledge you have about the computer. No babying, but yet no rude condescension or arrogant assumptions either. I assume that you don't know everything but are eager to learn that which you don't know.

Assumptions about Your PC

This book concentrates on Windows XP and the applications that come with it, such as Media Player or the Printer and Fax Viewer program. It's assumed, for example, that you use Internet Explorer as your web browser and Outlook Express as your e-mail program. These are the most common programs for doing the Internet, and they come "free" with Windows, which is why they're covered here.

 Please do note that there is a definite difference between Outlook and Outlook Express. Outlook is a part of the Microsoft Office suite and a more complex and capable program than Outlook Express. This book covers only Outlook Express.

Further, I don't assume that your computer is on a network. Networking is a big nut to crack, and I just didn't have the space in this book to cover it adequately. Chances are, however, that if you're on a network you can get whatever support or help you need from your network administrator.

What Now?

Now you're ready to start reading the book!

Where to Start Reading

There is no need to read this book in order. For example, you do not have to complete the tutorials in the early chapters to work the tutorials in later chapters. Feel free to dive in and start reading anywhere.

This book is divided into five parts, each of which is geared to a specific area of Windows:

 Windows XP from Desktop to Bottom

All the Intermediate-Level, Good Stuff about Disks, Files, and Stuff Like That

Nifty Audio and Graphics Information That No One Shares

There's More Internet Out There Than You Know

All the Random Tidbits about Configuring Your Computer That You'll Want to Ignore but You Shouldn't

Each part has various chapters that present specific issues based on that part's subject. You can start reading in any chapter in any order. The book is cross-referenced so if something is covered in an earlier chapter, you'll know where to look.

Where You Can Get More Information

As a computer book author it's my duty to provide you with as complete and accurate information as possible. If anything appears confusing or if you require additional information, then I feel I owe it to you to give you that information. Therefore I'm offering my e-mail address should you have any further questions regarding this book or its subject:

dgookin@wambooli.com

I do promise to reply to every e-mail sent to me. However, I cannot troubleshoot your PC, nor can I provide answers to questions on topics not directly covered by this book.

I also offer a free weekly newsletter that contains tips, how-tos, bonus lessons, and Q&A for this and all my books. You can read more information about my free "Weekly Wambooli Salad" newsletter at:

http://www.wambooli.com/newsletter/weekly/

In addition to the newsletter, supplemental information specific to this book can be found at:

http://www.wambooli.com/help/Windows/XP/

Any errors, omissions or additional information—including bonus chapters and special how-tos—can be found on that page.

And for general information about me, fun quizzes, trivia, and a list of other books I've written and stuff, go visit:

http://www.wambooli.com

Now you're ready to go forth, read, and enjoy your Naked Windows XP!

PART 1

Windows XP from Desktop to bottom

1

Who Could Believe That There's a Harder Way to Log Into Windows?

I'll bet you didn't know that there are *two* welcome screens in Windows. Two of them! I'd rather have four, but two is all they gave us. They are "Simple and Way Too Cute" and "Serious beyond All Grim Reality."

I'd like to see two other logon screens. The first would be "Terrify You out of Your Wits," where an evil guardian (which you can select between Turn-You-to-Stone Gorgon, Three-Headed Snake, or Mother-in-Law in the Users part of the Control Panel) taunts you for your password. That I would enjoy. And, of course, the fourth option would be—HELLO!—no welcome screen at all, thank you very much.

Unfortunately, Windows XP gives us the options we're stuck with. You must log in because the computer really, *really* needs to know who you are. And you have only the two options to choose from, which I'll review in this chapter, along with the various settings and other whatnot about logging in that you probably don't already know.

Secrets Hidden and Mysteries Unraveled:

- Welcome screen tour, passwords, and other basic stuff
- Info on recovering from a forgotten password
- Quickly locking the computer
- Locking the computer after a given period of inactivity
- Using the rude logon screen
- Determining just how many accounts you need

The Cheap-Ass Tour of the Traditional, Silly Welcome Screen

Figure 1.1 illustrates the traditional silly welcome screen, which Windows XP starts up with unless you tell it otherwise. You should already know these things referred to in the figure.

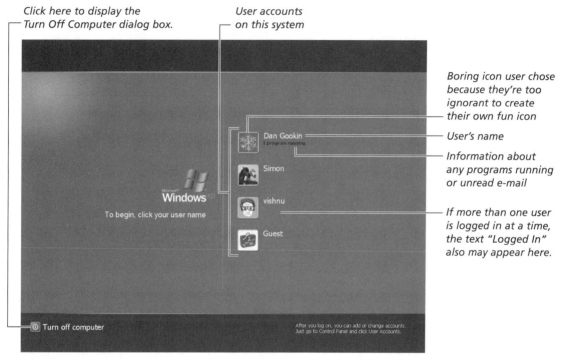

Figure 1.1 The ever-familiar and lackluster Welcome screen

The User Was Smart Enough to Apply a Password

Passwords on accounts are optional things, but only the dopiest user wouldn't have one. When you open a password-protected account, you get the login bubble, shown in Figure 1.2. Again, this is simple stuff you know or can figure out:

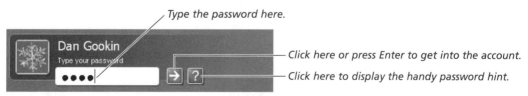

Figure 1.2 Typing your password is more fun when it's in a graphical bubble.

I Was Dumb and Didn't Create a Password

It's easier not to have a password. If so, then you can log in simply by clicking your name on the Welcome screen. To hell with security! In addition living on the edge security-wise, in such a state Windows won't "remember" your Internet password or other passwords used on your computer; you'll be denied access to features like the Task Scheduler and other unpleasant things that Windows won't let password-less users do. Better slap a password on your account:

1. Open the Control Panel.

2. Choose "User Accounts."

3. Choose the "Create a Password" item.

4. Follow the Instructions on the "Create a Password for Your Account" screen.

Be sure to type the password hint! That's your clue to getting the password back should you forget it. (See Figure 1.2.)

5. Click the Create Password button to slap that password down on your account.

6. Do not forget the password!

 With your password fresh in your memory, now would be a good time to create a Forgotten Password Disk. See the next section.

Don't Be Dumb! Password Hints

 Keep your passwords short and memorable, like your first kiss.

 Use a combination of numbers and letters.

 I recommend typing the password all lowercase. The Windows help system recommends mixing upper- and lowercase, but that can be confusing and frustrating. Mixing up letters and numbers is generally good enough.

Use the hint, but ensure that it's accurate enough for you to understand which password to use, but not for other people to do so.

As an example, a good password might be "bmw2056" which is the make of your car and the last four digits on the tag. A good hint would be "auto" which will remind you of your car password but is still vague enough to mislead others. A bad hint would be "my car and its tag number." Bad, bad, bad.

 Don't use the same password over and over. Use different passwords for different computers, websites, and so on.

 Change your password frequently, especially if you're in a high-security environment, such as a day care center.

I Fear That One Day I Shall Forget My Password. Is There Anything I Can Do?

Of course! Windows recognizes that people forget passwords. After all, people forget physical objects like car keys, eyeglasses, and plutonium. Passwords are no different.

Rather than give yourself a silly, easy password and pray you don't forget it, follow these steps:

1. Open the Control Panel.

2. Choose "User Accounts."

3. Click to select your account.

4. Under "Related Tasks," choose "Prevent a Forgotten Password."

   Behold! It's the Forgotten Password Wizard! A program that creates a disk (floppy or Zip) you can use to start the computer when you forget your password. How handy. (I'd put a picture of it in here, but you've seen one Wizard and you've seen them all.)

5. Mind the Wizard, working through its steps. The end result is a disk (floppy or Zip) that you can use when you forget your password.

 Yes, you must already know your account's password to make the disk. If you don't know the password, then you're just really screwed.

When the Wizard is done, remove the floppy disk (or Zip disk, if you used one of them instead) from the drive, label it, and *store it in a safe place*. If you forget where you put the disk, then consider removing the password from your account (see the next section).

To use the disk from the Welcome screen (Figure 1.1), follow these steps:

1. With the password field blank, click the green arrow.

2. Click "Use Your Password Reset Disk."

3. Insert your password disk.

4. Follow the steps for Password Reset Wizard.

5. Eventually you'll be asked to enter a new password, confirm that new password and, optionally, type a hint—just as when you first set up your account. (Or just as you were *supposed* to do when you first set up your account.)

   The disk basically says, "It's okay to change this fool's password." It does not automatically enter the password for you.

6. After entering the new password (and hint), click the wizard's Finish button.

7. *Now* enter your password to get into Windows.

8. Remember to remove the disk from the floppy (or Zip) drive and store it back in its safe place.

KEYBOARD MASTER

Getting to the Control Panel's Users Accounts Window

You'll often be visiting the Users icon in the Control Panel for various tasks in this chapter. Here's your keyboard master trick to get to the Control Panel ➢ Users icon quickly:

Win+E, F4, "control panel\user accounts"

 Pressing Win+E brings up a Windows Explorer window.

 F4 activates the Address Bar

 Typing control panel\user accounts *displays the User Accounts window from the Control Panel.*

Passwords Are a Waste of Time!

No you don't really need to specify a password. But read the earlier section "I Was Dumb and Didn't Create a Password" before you commit to getting rid of it. Then comply with these steps:

1. Open the Control Panel.

2. Choose "User Accounts."

3. Click to select your account.

4. Choose "Remove My Password" from the list of choices under "What Do You Want to Change about Your Account."

That's it. Go ahead and log off and try logging in again. You'll find that you can do so simply by choosing your name from the list. It's a lot faster. Well, granted it's not secure. Any random wino off the street can now access your account and look up your sensitive financial data and find out where you put your filthy Internet pictures. But I suppose you want to live dangerously.

The Fastest Way to Lock the Computer
and Hide What You're Doing

If you need to break away from your computer for a moment, but want to ensure no one else peeks in and sees what you're doing, press Win+L. (That's the Windows key plus the L key.) That instantly pops up the Welcome screen. Ta-da! The computer is locked and only the users listed on the Welcome screen can unlock it—providing that they have a proper password.

 The Win+L key command is easy to remember because L stands for lock.

Is Locking the Same as Logging Out?

No, you don't log yourself off by locking the computer. In fact, any programs you've been running continue to run while the computer is locked; open windows stay open and—unfortunately—any files you haven't saved to disk remain unsaved. In effect, it's just as if you walked away from the keyboard, but more secure.

Note that others can log in while the computer is locked. This doesn't affect your programs or data, which is securely password-protected from access by others—unless they elect to disconnect you. See the section about how to rudely log other people off in Chapter 27. (For that reason, it's a good idea to save your stuff before you lock the computer—unless you're the only one who has an account on that computer.)

What's the Difference between Locking and Switching Users?

One is slower than the other. To lock you press Win+L. At that point you can switch users by clicking on another account and logging in as that user. The slower way is to choose "Log Off" from the Start menu then click the Switch User button in the Log Off Windows dialog box. That's essentially the same thing as pressing Win+L, but it takes more time. And, of course, it also ensures that you don't have any programs running that may be interrupted should another user elect to turn off the computer.

I Can't Switch Users! There Is No Option

Switching users (or the fast way to get to the Welcome screen) is an option. When it's turned off, the Switch User commands don't appear and Win+L does something different. To turn the option on, do this:

1. Open the Control Panel.

2. Choose "User Accounts."

3. Choose "Change the Way Users Log On or Off."

4. Remove the check mark by "Use Fast User Switching."

   Note that "Use the Welcome Screen" must also be checked for this option to be available. (More on un-checking that option in the later section, "Is There a More Serious Way to Log into Windows?")

5. Click the Apply Options button and you're set.

Now when you click the Start menu's Log Off button, the dialog box just says "Are You Sure You Want to Log Off?" No more user switching. Boring. But you asked for it.

By the way, Win+L still works here; pressing Win+L locks the computer all nice and tight. But what you see is the boring logon Window, as shown in Figure 1.4 later on.

But, okay, say that you're a wise guy and you're thinking, "Golly! I can still type Win+L to lock the computer and get to the Logon window, so what's to stop me from entering another user's name and logging on with them!" Ha! Nice try. But it won't work: Windows will log off the original user, causing them to lose any unsaved data. No, Smarty Pants, if you want to use Fast User Switching, then enable it by putting the check mark back in Step 4 above.

Can I Lock the Computer after a Period of Inactivity?

Certainly! Use the screen saver for that.

1. Open the Display Properties dialog box.

    (Right-click the Desktop and choose Properties from the shortcut menu.)

2. Click the Screen Saver tab. Figure 1.3 illustrates this, (mostly because it's been a while since I've put an illustration in this chapter and I'm running short of space.)

    You must first select a screen saver from the drop-down list if one isn't already selected (otherwise the next two options are dimmed and unavailable).

3. Enter your desired period of inactivity in the "Wait" box.

4. Put a check mark in the "On Resume, Display Welcome Screen." Or if you have the rude startup screen, it says, "On Resume, Password Protect." Same thing, basically. (See the next section for more information on the rude logon screen.)

5. Click OK, and the inactivity lock-up is set.

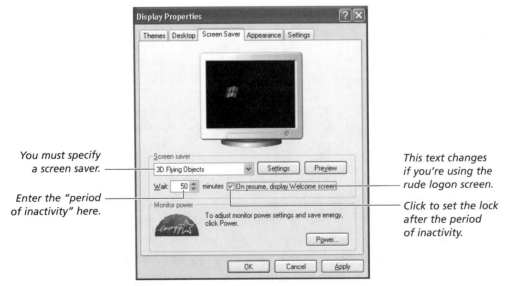

Figure 1.3 Locking the computer via the screen saver.

Is There a More Serious Way to Log into Windows?

The Welcome screen may just be too graphical, fun, and reminiscent of preschool for you. That's understandable. Why would you want such a thing when you're a *serious* computer user? No, you demand cold respect from your computer's operating system. You want the serious logon screen, the rude one former Windows NT and Windows 2000 users will feel comfortable with. Pursue these steps:

1. Open the Control Panel.

2. Choose "User Accounts."

3. Choose "Change the Way Users Log On or Off."

4. Remove the check mark by "Use the Welcome Screen."

5. Click the Apply Options button.

Now log out. The new, serious logon screen appears in Figure 1.4. You'll notice that the figure is blank. That's because I haven't figured out how to "capture" the serious logon screen. (Yes, it's that boorish!) However, if you haven't seen it, then just imagine one of the most horrible dialog boxes you've ever seen in the space provided.

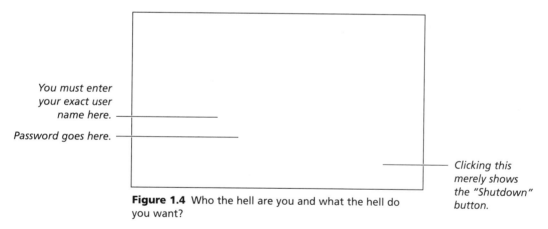

You must enter
your exact user
name here.

Password goes here.

Clicking this
merely shows
the "Shutdown"
button.

Figure 1.4 Who the hell are you and what the hell do you want?

 You may not be able to change to the serious logon screen if other users are logged into your computer. See Chapter 27 for information on logging those users off.

How Do I Know Who the Users Are with the Serious Logon Window?

You don't! Providing you haven't deleted the Guest account, you can still log in using it. I recommend keeping the Guest password set to nothing so that you can get onto the computer that way. But because the Guest account is typically a "Limited" account, there's not much you can do there (such as, you can't check to see which other accounts exist on the computer).

Indeed, the serious logon window is ideal for higher security, where guessing account names could be a liability. After all, serious computer users don't guess. Mr. Spock would never guess. He'd estimate.

How Will Using the Serious Logon Window Affect Things?

There are a few subtle differences the serious logon window option presents over using the Welcome screen. For example, pressing Ctrl+Alt+Delete brings up the Windows Security dialog box when you use the serious logon. If you have the Welcome screen logon selected instead, then pressing Ctrl+Atl+Delete brings up the Task Manager window. A minor detail, but important if you were expecting one and not the other

This book was written assuming that the friendly, happy, bubbly, graphical, madness that is the Welcome window is the one you use. That's the way Windows XP is configured by Microsoft out of the box, so that's the option I chose for this book.

Be aware that other books, manuals, and references may also assume the Welcome screen is being used and not the serious logon screen. (This book does note the differences between the two, but other references may not.)

Hey! I'm Just One Person! Do I Really Need All These Accounts?

No, you don't. There must be one "Owner" account for the computer, which needs to be an Administrator-type of account. You can delete all the rest, but that one account has to stay. No way around it.

I do recommend, however, keeping the Guest account. You never know when someone else will need to use your computer. For example, I had a friend visit who *just had* to check his AOL mail while he was away from home. Having him use the Guest account was great; he had no way to venture off into my stuff while he was (supposedly) reading his e-mail. Now I had never anticipated anyone else using my Windows XP system, but I was thankful that I kept the Guest account "just in case."

For a household where you have several people using one computer (whether they've been told not to or not), then obviously making up individual accounts for everyone is a blessing. Nothing is more relaxing than knowing your 6-year-old is using his own account and, God bless him, he just loves changing the Desktop colors to hot-pink-on-green. But that's his account and you'll never have to see your Desktop look that way.

For individuals, there really isn't any point in having more than two accounts, the "Owner" and a guest. I originally thought, "Hey! I can have one account for all my graphics work, then another for when I do web publishing," and so on, but that never worked out; it's too much of a pain to "share" the files as opposed to having access to them all from the same account.

Also, because there are only two account security levels, Administrator and Limited, there isn't any point in being anything other than an Administrator if you're the only user on the computer. Had Windows an account type between the two, then there might be an argument for using that account most of the time and only using Administrator for system chores. But there isn't, so there.

Startup Options, Situations, and Programs

Along its cheerful journey to the Desktop, Windows XP takes several detours. You see, for some reason whistling down the merry path of life is full of distractions for Windows. Some of these diversions are voluntary. For example, if you're having problems (like that would ever happen), you can elect to start the machine in Safe Mode or use the Last Known Good Configuration—two handy options, providing you know when to use them and how to get at them.

As Windows creeps further into existence, there are points in the process where you can add your own startup programs. For example, if Word is the only program you use, then why not have the stupid computer start Word automatically for you? Duh. Or if you do e-mail first, why not have Outlook Express pop into being? It can all be done, and this chapter shows you where the levers are hidden and options are buried.

Hidden Levers and Options Unburied Here:

- Everything you don't know about Safe Mode
- Hidden startup options
- MSCONFIG, or the "System Configuration Utility"
- Muddling through the Notification Area
- Starting specific programs
- DOS trivia

When and How to Use Safe Mode

So if they call it "Safe Mode" then is a normal startup "Unsafe Mode?" Or perhaps "Dangerous Mode?" If you don't start the computer in Safe Mode are you in "Living on the Edge Mode?" Oh, I could go on all day...and I will!

How about the "Break" key? Why isn't it the "Brake" key instead? After all, what fool would want to "break" anything on-purpose on a computer? And have you tried using the Break key? You can't, because on most keyboards it's shacking up with the Pause key, neither of which do anything in Windows as far as I know.

Why are there so many keys on the keyboard with the word "Lock" on them?

"Print Screen" doesn't.

"SysRq" is the only key that's its own typo.

Windows has had a Start button for over six years now, but still no Stop button. If there were a Windows automobile, would it have an accelerator and no brake? Or perhaps a "Break" instead?

Enough silliness!

Why Should I Care about Safe Mode?

Safe Mode isn't really safe. It's just limited. You see, where you (as a human) would want to be safe by putting on more and more protective layers of clothing, Windows does the safe thing by undressing itself. That's right, Safe Mode is Nude Windows.

When the computer starts in Safe Mode, either automatically or under your command (see the section "Can I Force the Computer into Safe Mode?"), Windows refuses to load most of itself into memory. Specifically, Windows doesn't activate various device drivers. These device drivers, or the hardware they control, are usually the source of problems in the computer. So by not loading them, Safe Mode makes it easier for you to track down trouble.

For example, suppose the CD-ROM drive is failing. Who knows why! It could be the hardware itself, a loose cable, or the device driver (the software that controls the CD-ROM drive) may be corrupted or incompatible with other software recently installed. In that case, starting in Safe Mode prevents the device driver from loading, which means that you can track down the problem without having the problem present.

Why Not Run in Safe Mode All the Time?

Well, first of all, because Safe Mode looks really stupid on the screen. That's because Safe Mode doesn't load all your computer's needed device drivers, so you cannot use all your hardware. Forget about using the network, advanced abilities of your video adapter, external devices (scanners,

CD-Rs, DVD drives), and other fun toys. If you want to use all the computer you paid for, then don't run in Safe Mode.

If your computer can only start in Safe Mode, then something definitely needs attention. While you can work somewhat in Safe Mode, and the computer may behave normally, having Save Mode start all the time is a potential sign of trouble. Better check things out. (Also see two sections later in this chapter, "Can I Force the Computer into Safe Mode?" and "My Computer Always Starts in Safe Mode! How Can I Get It Back to Normal?")

Can't I Just Start Windows in Safe Mode?

You can force Windows to start in Safe Mode whenever you suspect a problem and other means have failed to produce a result. Here's how:

1. Restart Windows.

2. Just after the screen clears, clearing away all the text screen information (BIOS and other startup messages), press the F8 key. Better still, stab repeatedly at the F8 key just incase the computer isn't paying attention. On some computers, the screen says, "Please Select the Operating System to Start." When you see that message, press the F8 key.

Pressing F8 displays the Windows Advanced Options Menu, which is illustrated in Figure 2.1. The menu has several options, most of which are geared toward troubleshooting.

3. Choose "Safe Mode" from the menu.

Use the arrow keys to select and highlight "Safe Mode."

4. Press the Enter key.

Windows continues to start, but in Safe Mode.

5. Login.

A warning dialog box appears, telling you that you're in Safe Mode and that some things may not work. Also, the message reminds you that Safe Mode is for troubleshooting and repair, not for getting work done.

Don't be surprised when the Desktop finally appears. Because your system's display drivers were not loaded, the Desktop is set to a low resolution. Don't fret! This is done on purpose. Remember: troubleshoot and repair.

6. Fix whatever's wrong.

For example, if you chose an all-green color scheme and can't see any text when you use Windows, then Safe Mode is the place where you can reset your color scheme back to "Windows Standard" or whatever you selected before.

7. Restart Windows when you're done messing around.

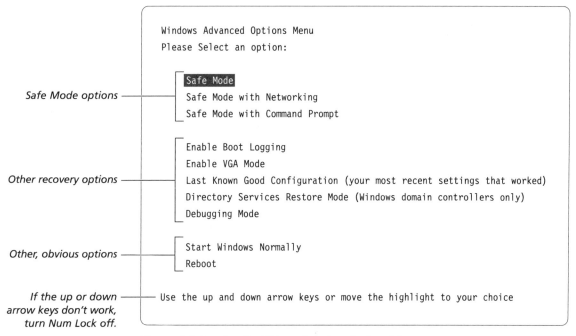

Figure 2.1 Pressing the F8 key at startup displays this menu.

  Hardware problems can easily be found by checking the Device Manager. Right-click the My Computer icon and choose Properties from the pop-up shortcut menu. Click on the Hardware tab. Click the Device Manager button. Look at the hardware listed in the Device Manager window for any failures or malfunctions. A yellow circle with an exclamation point (!) flags failing hardware. Double-click to open any malfunctioning hardware; the dialog box displayed tells you exactly what the problem is and, hopefully, how to fix it.

What is the Last Known Good Configuration Startup Option?

Another option on the Windows Advanced Options Menu is Last Known Good Configuration. This is a great option to choose if you've just installed some new hardware doohickey or software program (such as an old game you weren't certain was Windows XP compatible) and the system won't start up properly or at all. Or when anything else "bad" happens, restart Windows, press the F8 key at the proper time, and then choose the "Last Known Good Configuration" option.

After Windows starts, *immediately* undo whatever you last did: uninstall software or remove hardware. Double-check to ensure that the software or hardware is Windows XP compatible. Then visit the developer's web page to see if there are any support notes about the software, something that may have suggested similar problems with other computers. Finally, as a last resort, phone up the developer's tech support to see what the issue is.

Is There a Place Where These Startup Options are Hidden?

The Startup and Recovery dialog box is where you can find some settings affecting the Windows Advanced Options Menu, though there's nothing really secret or hidden there. And if you don't have multiple operating systems installed on the computer, then there really isn't anything to do here:

1. Right-click the My Computer icon on the Desktop.

2. Choose Properties from the pop-up shortcut menu.

3. In the System Properties dialog box, click the Advanced tab.

4. In the Startup and Recovery area, click the Settings button. This brings up the Startup and Recovery dialog box, shown in Figure 2.2. The top part of the dialog box contains settings that affect how the computer starts, as illustrated in the figure.

Other options are available only if you have multiple operating systems on the computer.

Items that control the "Please Select the Operating System to Start" menu

Allows you to edit the BOOT.INI file

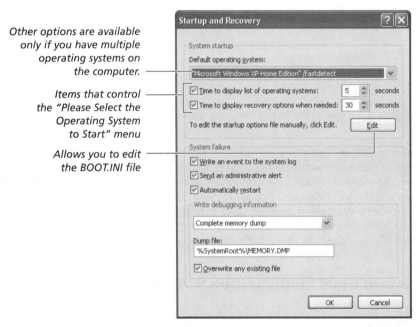

Figure 2.2 Where some startup options can be found

By the way, certain BOOT.INI file options can be set using the System Configuration Utility, which is covered in the next section. In fact, the System Configuration Utility is a far more interesting place for setting startup options than the silly Startup and Recovery dialog box.

 I use Windows XP on a computer with several operating systems, but I use the System Commander 2000 utility to switch operating systems, not the silly Windows method. If you plan on installing more than one operating system on your computer, such as keeping a copy of the very stable Windows 98 around for compatibility with older programs, then I highly recommend System Commander (www.v-com.com).

The System Configuration Utility Is Truly a Buried Treasure You Must Know

The System Configuration Utility is mostly a troubleshooting tool, though it does contain options that affect how you start your computer.

You know, that seems to be a theme here in this startup chapter; supposedly a lot that can go wrong with the computer occurs when you first turn the computer on. So, in a way, I suppose the only truly "safe mode" for the computer is when it's turned off.

To get to the System Configuration Utility you must follow these steps:

1. Press Win+R to bring up the Run dialog box.

2. Type MSCONFIG into the box.

   Hey! Do you already see MSCONFIG written there? Then there's no need to re-type it.

3. Click OK to run the System Configuration Utility, shown in Figure 2.3.

   (The next several sections assume that this dialog box is open.)

 Memorize these instructions or dog-ear this page; the System Configuration Utility is something you'll be visiting a lot in this and other chapters.

Older Windows files you can edit (included here for compatibility)

Other startup files are listed here, a nifty place to know.

Startup options

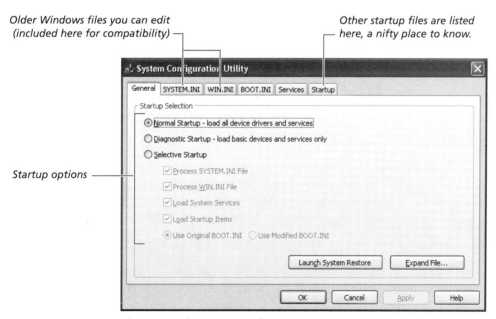

Figure 2.3 The System Configuration Utility dialog box

Certain Peril Loomed Until Percy Activated Safe Mode

The feeling of dread and panic swelled like a balloon, filling the room from wall to wall. Both Eunice and Lyle were frozen with fear, unable to move or even scream! Just then, Percy dashed in. Slicing through the darkness like a lighthouse beacon, he deftly pulled the plug and the computer went dead. "There," he intoned, "we're all safe now." He then added ominously, "Unless, of course, this is merely the first act."

KEYBOARD MASTER

Bringing up the Run Dialog Box

The Run dialog box is where you can type in various commands to directly run certain programs and utilities—a handy thing to use. To pop it open, hit this key combination:

Win+R

If your keyboard lacks the Windows key, then you'll have to access the Run command from the Start menu.

Can I Force the Computer into Safe Mode?

Certainly, which is one of the purposes of the General tab in the System Configuration Utility (see Figure 2.3). To force the computer to start in Safe Mode, select the "Diagnostic Startup - Blah, Blah, Blah..." option and click OK. This forces Windows to start in Safe Mode for troubleshooting help and whatnot.

(Again, it's generally *not* a good idea to use Safe Mode unless you're troubleshooting.)

My Computer Always Starts in Safe Mode! How Can I Get It Back to Normal?

First, if the computer always starts in Safe Mode, then something is probably wrong. You should fix whatever that is so that the computer does *not* start in Safe Mode. However, there may be times when the computer is forced into Safe Mode by setting an option in the System Configuration Utility. In that case, it's easy to reset the computer to startup in "Normal" mode once again:

1. Summon the System Configuration Utility as described earlier in this chapter.

2. In the General tab, select "Normal Startup - Blah, Blah, Blah ..." (And if either of the other options were selected, then that explains why the computer started in Safe Mode.)

3. Click OK and you're set.

What's the Point of the Selective Startup Option?

Troubleshooting is what Selective Startup is all about. It's something you'll be directed to use by tech support people and not something to be messed with. Therefore, while you can see the option there on your screen, and it just looks like it's brimming with help, you're not supposed to mess with it unless you're told to do so.

So, say someday you're lucky enough to get through to tech support and get someone who really, *really* wants to help you and isn't under the threat of being fired if the call isn't completed in 12 minutes. In that rare and precious instance, you may be directed to use Selective Startup to help diagnose your problem.

Or, then again, after 11 minutes the tech support employee (who also works part time at Starbucks) may just tell you to reformat your hard drive and reinstall Windows, which works but is an awful and inappropriate solution to many problems that can otherwise be solved without reformatting and reinstalling.

Oh...

Selective Startup allows you to restart the computer in a quasi-Safe Mode. For example, instead of disabling *all* the device drivers and whatnot, Selective Startup lets you pick and choose what you want disabled. And, of course, what you want has nothing to do with it; it's up to tech support to tell you which options to select. If you live that long.

 Rarely is there a need to reinstall Windows or reformat your computer's hard drive. Yet tech support people offer these catastrophic solutions all the time (mostly because tech support is under pressure to dump calls after an average 12 minutes). Most problems can be fixed without reinstalling Windows or reformatting the hard drive. If you're ever given that as a solution, then try getting another tech support person or a tech support supervisor.

How Do the Icons in the Notification Area Get There and Can I Get Rid of Them?

The Notification Area (once known as the "System Tray") is truly one of the most remarkable mysteries of Windows. It's one of those things that was created way back with Windows 95 that started out with one original purpose and has since then morphed into something that has multiple purposes, none of which make any sense. Of course, the original purpose didn't make any sense either, mostly because no one back then seemed to know why the System Tray was needed or what should or should not go there.

I suppose that, in a way, the Notification Area is like the glove box in your car. How many people *really* put gloves in there? Huh? So, anyway, we're stuck with the System Notification Area Tray Thing. At least it's collapsible and can be hidden (just like you can close the door to your car's glove box, so you don't see the old gum wrappers, straws, melted caramels, and used Kleenex).

The System Notifixation Area is a really story for another chapter (5, to be exact). For this chapter, the topic centers on how those icons—or programs —get into the System Tray Area Novocain thing in the first place.

The Secret Behind the Icons in the Notification Arena

The secret is that each icon in the Nontoxification Area is actually a program that runs when the computer starts. Because the icon is a program, and because Windows must be told to start that program, it's possible to turn the icons off.

Now some of the icons are not programs but merely extensions of various things Windows does. For example, the Volume Control icon is an extension of Windows internal sound programs. The Internet Connection icon is an extension of Windows Dial-Up Networking. Those icons are controlled through various settings in Windows itself. But the other icons, the programs, are started when Windows first starts.

The Aha! Section: Checking the Startup Tab in the System Configuration Utility for Even More Programs That Start, Some of Which End up in the Nonfiction Area

I trust that you'll enjoy digging up this treasure:

1. Bring forth the System Configuration Utility, aka MSCONFIG.

(Remember that I told you to dog-ear that page! Okay: Win+R ➤ type MSCONFIG ➤ press Enter)

2. Click the Startup tab.

3. Say, "Aha!"

The list of programs you see (similar to Figure 2.4) are those that are run sneakily by Windows when it first starts. I say "sneakily" because the programs installed themselves to run this way; they are not like the programs you would put in the Startup menu (covered later in this chapter).

For example, the "America Online" item in Figure 2.4 was placed there by AOL when it was first installed. It coincidentally controls an icon in the Notification Area. It's the thing that insists that I start AOL every time I log onto the Internet, just so I can visit my e-mail box and view all the lovely free offers and discounts that await me there.

Can I Disable a Program in the Startup Tab?

To disable any startup program in the System Configuration Utility, just click to remove its check mark. That seems easy enough. But the real question is, "Should you?" I would answer, "Never!" to that question. Only if you're directed by tech support or you absolutely know that you want to disable some start up program, should you go clickin' and removin' here to disable a startup program.

By the by, clicking to disable a program in the Startup tab is not *the same as deleting that program. No, you're merely directing the program not to run; removing the check mark does not blast the program to smithereens.*

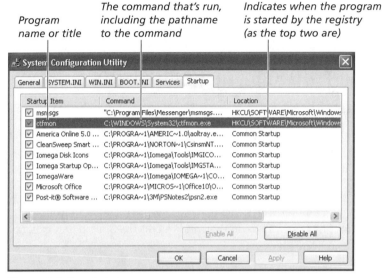

Program name or title

The command that's run, including the pathname to the command

Indicates when the program is started by the registry (as the top two are)

Figure 2.4 Secret startup programs

Can I add a program to the Startup tab?

No. If you want to automatically start a program, then use the Startup menu, as described later in this chapter.

How Can I Disable Some of the Programs that Put Themselves into the Notification Area?

The easiest way is to find the control that put the program there in the first place. To do that, right-click the icon in the Notification Area. A pop-up menu appears, from which you can select a command that may disable the icon or at least lead you to a dialog box where the icon can be disabled.

For example, right-clicking on the AOL icon displays a menu with several options, two of which are "Subscribe to this Magazine" and "You May Already Be a Winner," but the one you want is called "Exit." Choosing that option displays a dialog box that asks, "Do You Want the AOL Tray Icon to Appear the Next Time You Start Your Computer?" Click the No button, and the icon is gone from the Notfixation Area.

For some icons, you must choose the Properties command from their pop-up shortcut menu, then visit the Properties dialog box to look for the option that displays the tiny icon in the Notification Area (or "System Tray").

What? No "Exit" item on the menu? Or no right-click menu at all? Then there's probably some other way to remove the program. Alas, you're gonna have to hunt for it.

I Want to Get a Leg up on My Competition

and Need to Start Word Fast, Like Right When the Computer Starts

The final thing Windows does when it starts is to look for programs in the Startup menu, which it then starts automatically for you. So if you want to start Word or Outlook or whatever your desired first program is, have Windows do it for you.

Each of your programs appears as a menu item on the Start menu's All Programs menu. To have a particular program start when the computer starts, you need to *copy* its menu item from wherever it is now to the Startup submenu. The best way to do that, and to edit the Start menu generally, is to use Windows Explorer instead. Here's how:

1. Right-click the Start button.

2. Choose "Open" from the pop-up shortcut menu.

The Start menu's items now appear as folders and shortcut icons inside a standard Windows Explorer window. This is the best way to prune and graft the various menus.

3. It helps to view things in the Folder view; click the Folders button or press Alt+V, E, O if you don't see the Folders panel on the left side of the window, as shown in Figure 2.5.

And now the rub: you'll notice on your screen that you *do not* see many of the items on the Start menu. Instead, what you see are only those items custom to your user account. For example, in Figure 2.5, you see only the Accessories and Startup folders. And the other shortcuts that appear there are "top menu" items, which appear at the top of the All Programs menu. Gone and missing are the various Microsoft Office applications as well as the Games submenu and other submenus. Ohmigosh!

KEYBOARD MASTER

Display the Folder Tree

Switches between the Folder tree and the Task pane on the left side of a file window.

Alt+V, E, O
Press it once to display the folder tree, again to hide the folder tree.

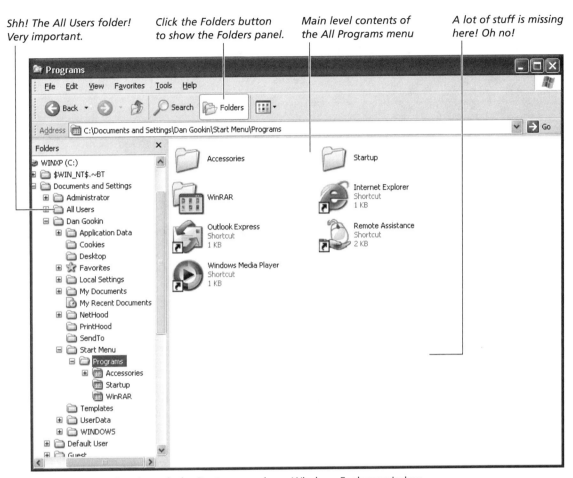

Figure 2.5 Hunting through the Start menu using a Windows Explorer window

But I Can't Find the Program I'm Looking For!

Keep in mind that Windows XP is geared toward multiple users. You are only one user in the computer's eye—yes, even if you're the only person who uses the computer at all. So if you look at the Address bar (see Figure 2.5), you'll see that the Start menu items you're looking at are specific to your account ("Dan Gookin" in the figure). The rest of the Start menu items are deemed *common* and available to all users.

To get to a specific program to startup, you'll have to locate it on the common Start menu. More hunting.

You Must Know This: Copying and Pasting an Icon

After selecting the icon, you can do any of the following to copy the icon:

- *Press Ctrl+C.*
- *Choose Edit ➤ Copy.*
- *Right-click the icon and choose Copy from the pop-up shortcut menu.*
- *After the icon has been copied, choose one of these steps to paste it:*
- *Press Ctrl+V.*
- *Choose Edit ➤ Paste.*
- *Right-click the folder window and choose Paste from the pop-up shortcut menu.*

OK, now we're ready to proceed with our earlier attempt at getting Windows to launch your desired program. Continuing from the previous section:

4. Scroll up in the list of folders until you find the All Users folder.

5. Display the All Users branch by clicking its + sign.

6. Display the Start menu branch by clicking its + sign.

7. Click to select the Programs folder. Now you'll see all the Start menu hoo-haw displayed, all the menus/folders and menu items/shortcut icons.

8. Locate the program you want to automatically start. For example, Word may be right there in the All Programs folder or perhaps in a Microsoft Office folder. For games, you'll have to open the Games folder.

Keep hunting until you find your program's icon!

9. Copy the icon.

Now you need to paste that icon back into the shortcut menu.

Providing that you've been following my steps exactly, you can quickly return to your account's Start menu by pressing the Back button on the toolbar. (You may have to do this several times if you've been sifting through the folders.)

You're ready to continue when you're back in your own account's Start Menu ➤ Programs folder.

10. Open the Startup folder.

11. Paste.

If the icon is named "blah-blah-*shortcut*" then you can edit the name to remove the "short-cut" part (keep *blah-blah*); press the F2 key after selecting the icon to rename it. Just hit the End key, then the Backspace key to erase "shortcut."

The Program Isn't on Any of the Start Menus!

Well, then you're gonna have to hunt for it, partner! How do you normally start the program? If it's from an icon on the Desktop, copy the icon from there and paste it into your Startup folder. If you open various folders to get to the file, then open them, find the file, copy it, then paste it as described in the previous section.

If you still cannot find the program, use the Search command to locate it. When the program is found, copy it from the Search Results window.

Show Me a Clever Way to Disable Automatically Started up Programs

Oh, a "clever" way. I assume that the un-clever way is simply to delete the shortcut icon. That works; any program that's *not* in the Startup folder doesn't start up automatically. There's some logic there. And there's also some logic in the following:

1. Open your account's Startup folder window as described earlier in this chapter.

2. Click the Go Up button to get to the Programs folder window.

3. Choose File ➤ New ➤ Folder.

4. Name the folder "Not Startup."

5. Copy the programs you no longer want to automatically startup into the Not Startup folder.

This clever approach has two effects. First, it removes startup programs from the Startup folder, which is what you want. But second, it keeps track of programs that were once in the Startup folder but are now no longer. That way, should you change your mind, it's a simple matter to move the icons back out of the Not Startup folder and into the Startup folder in the future.

KEYBOARD MASTER

The Go Up Button

To "go up" one folder in the folder hierarchy, you click the Go Up button, or you use this handy keyboard equivalent.

Backspace

Can I Start the Computer in DOS Mode?

Of course you can start the computer in DOS mode. You can also shave your face in such a manner that gives you four eyebrows. The real question with both issues is *why the hell would you want to?*

Are you nuts? DOS cannot access half the power in your computer. But I suppose you have your reasons, such as the computer cannot or will not run your DOS program otherwise. This questions why you would have a Windows XP computer in the first place. Why not go pick up a cheap 486 or Pentium I computer on eBay and use it for your DOS stuff?

Oh, bother...

The best way to start in DOS mode is to go out and buy a fresh new copy of DOS. IBM still sells PC-DOS, so you can get a copy of that. Or you can try finding one of the many free DOS knock-offs available on the Internet for downloading.

My best advice would be to use System Commander or some such similar disk partitioning/multiple-operating system program to create a special DOS partition on your hard drive. (DOS doesn't need much, maybe 1GB of disk space.) Then use the disk-partitioning program to simply start your computer in DOS mode. That's the best approach.

In Windows XP you can create a DOS boot disk, for whatever random times you would want to start your computer in Windows Me (yes, Windows Me) DOS mode—which is a waste of time, but I'm on a roll and can't stop so I have to write about it anyway. Follow these steps:

1. Shove a blank floppy disk into Drive A. It doesn't have to be blank, but the process of creating a DOS boot disk will erase anything already on the disk.

2. Open the My Computer icon.

3. Right-click the floppy disk icon.

4. Choose Format from the shortcut menu.

5. Click "Create an MS-DOS Startup Disk."

   You'll notice that choosing that option disables everything else in the dialog box, as shown in Figure 2.6.

6. Click the Start button.

7. Click OK in the Warning dialog box.

   If the disk is bad (which happens a lot), throw it away and try with another disk.

8. Oh happy day! Click OK in the Format complete dialog box.

   The disk is now ready to use. Well...barely. You can start the computer with it; go ahead and restart the computer, keeping the floppy disk in Drive A. That will show you the horrid days of DOS.

Your only choice

Something to watch while it happens

Figure 2.6
Creating an
MS-DOS boot disk

Technically, the disk is a Windows Me boot disk, not a Windows XP disk at all. And you cannot access any CD-ROM drives or even your Windows XP hard drive in some cases using the disk. And people will laugh at you if they see you try this. So don't hold me responsible (though I am available for group therapy at some really cheap rates).

To restart the computer without DOS, remove the floppy disk from the drive and press the Ctrl+Alt+Delete keys.

Be sure to label the DOS boot disk as a boot disk. In fact, you should label all your floppy disks. Look at your desk! It's full of *unlabeled* disks! What a sloppy thing to have going on! I am so ashamed...

 Remove that DOS boot floppy! If you don't, then the computer will always start from the floppy disk, which is probably not what you want.

27

3

Halting Desktop Madness (Part I)

The field upon which Windows plays is the Desktop. It's a peculiar name, which we take for granted. It could just as well be called the "splash back" or the "muggy stuffing" or the "thick scribble truffle," because it really has nothing to do with a real Desktop at all.

The original graphical user interface computer (developed by a company once known as "Xerox") actually had a true Desktop image. There was a graphical pad of paper, a clipboard, a phone, a calendar, tape, scissors, and other common Desktop tool images. You would use the mouse to grab these tool images and do things. Compared to that simple-to-understand and use metaphor, Windows XP Desktop more closely resembles a Las Vegas slot machine gone awry than anything on the top of your actual desk.

The Desktop is important only because it's the first thing you see when you actually get into Windows. It has several purposes and many more vital doohickeys, the more essential of which are all covered in this chapter.

Important Doohickeys and Desktop Purposes:

- Fussing over icons
- Worrying over windows
- Cleaning and primping the Desktop
- Buried Desktop treasure

There's lots of Desktop information to offer, so the Desktop information has been split between this chapter and the next. Also refer to Chapter 8, which covers more Desktop fun and frivolity (geared to starting programs from the Desktop).

Desktop Stuff You Should Already Know

Windows XP presents you with the same Desktop metaphor that's been hanging around since Windows 95. You should be able recognize the three basic parts of the Desktop, illustrated in Figure 3.1—icons, background, and the Taskbar.

 This chapter covers the icons and the background image you see on the Desktop, as well as some other trivia about the screen. The Taskbar is a big deal (or at least it thinks it's a big deal), so it gets Chapter 5 all to itself.

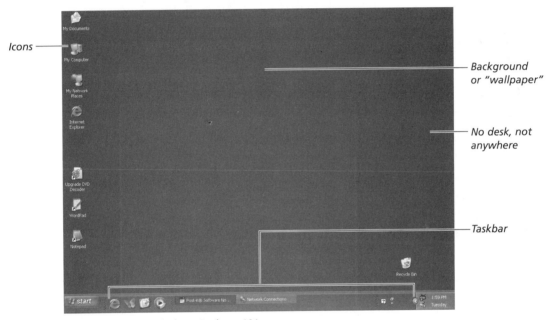

Figure 3.1 Basic Windows Desktop 101

Icons Can Be Desktop Beauty Marks or Ugly Moles,
Depending on How You Look at Them

The first thing I notice about the Desktop are its icons. I'm an icon snob myself. I enjoy and employ them. I have program icons lining the left side of my Desktop and folder shortcuts marching down the right side. Drag-and-drop icons, such as Notepad and Paint, are on the bottom edge. That's the way I like things.

Some people are icon gluttons; they keep dozens and dozens of icons on the screen. I blanched once when looking at this guy's laptop screen because it was so filled with icons I couldn't see the nude background image. Amazing to me, but that's the way he liked to work.

And then there is the icon austere. They'd have no icons on the Desktop if they could. And they can! With Windows XP, any icon fetish can be dutifully served, providing you know some tidbits about how the Desktop deals with its icons.

What Kind of Icons Can Live on the Desktop?

Windows XP comes pre-configured to display a slate of icons on the Desktop, supposedly to help you better use Windows and never, never, under any circumstances, are the icons placed there because of some favorable back-room deal made between Microsoft and some other company. No way! This is America, where stuff like that just doesn't happen.

Anyway, the traditional Desktop icons used by Windows are:

My Documents

My Computer

My Network Places

Recycle Bin

The Desktop may also contain an Internet Explorer or Outlook Express (or Outlook) icon, which again is (supposedly) tightly integrated into the fabric of Windows XP.

Beyond those core icons, you can stick any number of shortcut icons on the Desktop that you wish. And you can also save documents and create folders directly onto the Desktop. No problem there.

Why Are Shortcut Icons Handy to Have on the Desktop?

A shortcut icon is merely a ghostly placeholder for the original file. So if you're a super organized person, you probably have all your files and folders—the stuff you create—saved in the My Documents folder. If so, then a quick and handy way to get at that stuff is to place shortcuts to those files (and even folders) directly on the Desktop.

For example, I pasted a shortcut to this book's folder on my Desktop. I have shortcuts to all my project folders. But I also have shortcuts to programs I occasionally use, such as FreeCell, Paint, Notepad, the Calculator, and so on.

Wait, did I say "FreeCell?" No, I meant, "FinancialCalc." Yeah. That's better.

The advantage to having a shortcut to, say, Notepad, on the Desktop is that you can use the shortcut icon for a drag-and-drop. For example:

1. Locate a mysterious or unknown file in a folder.

2. Drag and drop that file's icon onto the Notepad shortcut icon on the Desktop.

This opens the file in Notepad, allowing you to view its contents. If the file is a text file, it shows up just grand. If the file contains junk, then the junk shows up grand, but junky.

3. Close Notepad.

Do not save the document if you're prompted to save! You're merely using Notepad here to view the file. If you attempt to save it, you may change the file, which would be a Bad Thing.

By using drag-and-drop with a shortcut icon on the Desktop, you can quickly force a specific program (Notepad, for example) to open any type of file. This is quicker than right-clicking the file and messing with the Open With submenu.

I like to keep shortcut icons for the following types of files on my Desktop:

- Project folders

- Occasionally popular documents (wish lists, honey-do lists, shopping lists, and so on)

- Notepad (for viewing file's contents)

- Paint or a graphics program (for viewing graphics files in specific programs)

- Shortcuts to removable disk drives (floppy or Zip) for quickly copying programs

To put these shortcuts on the Desktop, first locate the original icon for the program, file, folder, or disk drive. Right-click the icon and choose Copy from the pop-up shortcut menu. Then right-click the Desktop and choose Paste Shortcut from the menu. Ta-Da. There's your shortcut. Or if you need detailed steps, here is how you would put a shortcut to a Zip drive on the Desktop:

1. Open the My Computer icon.

2. Using the *right* mouse button, drag the Zip drive icon over to the Desktop.

   If you cannot see the Desktop, then resize the My Computer window so that you can see some Desktop real estate.

   Remember to use the *right* button, not the left button you normally use to drag an icon.

3. When you release the mouse button (to "drop" the icon), choose Create Shortcuts Here from the pop-up menu.

   And there is your shortcut.

 If you're not a very organized person, refer to Chapter 9 on the My Documents folder.

Do I Really Need All Those Windows Icons on the Desktop?

No. Icons are like warts; you can lethally burn them with acid if you detest them. (Or you could change your diet to get rid of your warts, which worked for my warts. Alas, there is no handy Windows XP equivalent for changing your diet, unlike burning icons with acid, which I find a more satisfying image anyway.)

You can have as many or few icons on the Desktop as you want. Some people have a whole screen full of icons. Some people are very organized and put program shortcuts on one edge of the screen, shortcuts to documents and folders along another edge, and still other icons along another edge of the screen.

If the icon is a shortcut icon and you don't want it displayed, then feel free to delete it. Deleting a shortcut icon does not delete the original; feel free to be merciless.

The core Windows icons can also be slain, but you must do so from the proper dialog box:

1. Right-click the Desktop to display the pop-up shortcut menu.

2. Choose Properties to beckon forth the Display Properties dialog box.

3. Click the Desktop tab.

4. Click the Customize Desktop button.

   Ah, the Desktop Items dialog box, a fun place to remember. (See Figure 3.2.)

5. Remove the check mark by whichever standard icon you don't want to see on the Desktop.

   You have four choices: My Documents, My Computer, My Network Places, or Internet Explorer. Note that you cannot remove the Recycle Bin icon. It stays there no matter what.

6. Click the OK button to close the Desktop Items dialog box.

7. Click the Apply button to see how the Desktop looks.

   If you don't like what you see, start over at Step 4 and restore the check marks by the items you want to keep.

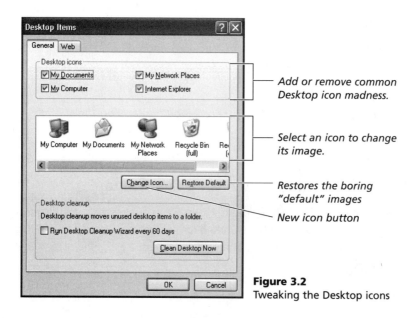

Figure 3.2
Tweaking the Desktop icons

Wow! I Can Change the Look of the Dorky Windows Icons?

An interesting place to visit in the Desktop Items dialog box is the spot where you can change the look of the standard Desktop icons—including the Trash. Oh, I'm sorry, I mean Recycle Bin. (Like somehow the bits and bytes from your garbage files will somehow be recycled into a new park bench or snow jacket.)

Normally these standard Desktop icons are tweaked with if you mess with a "theme" in Windows. The Themes tab in the Display Properties dialog box is where you dink with Themes. Using this, you can gear the display of the windows, menus, fonts, mouse pointers, as well as the standard Desktop icons, toward some amusing or distracting theme. Sample themes include Outer Space, Sports, Nostalgia, Nature, and so on. (Note that no nudity or sacrilegious themes are available with the standard Windows XP releases.)

To change the appearance of just one of the standard icons without buying into a whole theme, comply with these steps:

1. Right-click the Desktop to display the pop-up shortcut menu.

2. Choose Properties to beckon forth the Display Properties dialog box.

3. Click the Desktop tab.

4. Click the Customize Desktop button.

5. Click to select an icon to change: My Computer, My Documents, My Network Places, Recycle Bin (full) or Recycle Bin (empty). (Refer to Figure 3.2.)

6. Click the Change Icon button.

A Change Icon dialog box appears (Figure 3.3), showing a palette of icons you can view or choose from.

You can also use the Browse button to go out and hunt down more icons, including those you create yourself!

7. Choose a new icon.

8. Click OK to replace the original, stuffy Windows icon with the new one of your choosing.

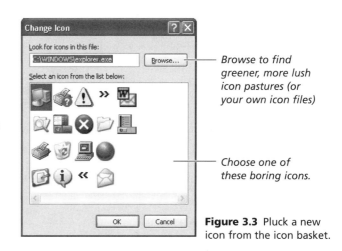

Browse to find greener, more lush icon pastures (or your own icon files)

Choose one of these boring icons.

Figure 3.3 Pluck a new icon from the icon basket.

Your best resource for changing icons is Chapter 19 in this book, which covers where icons can be found in Windows and how you can create your own. That way you can use the Browse button in the Change Icon dialog box to hunt down more interesting icons than those you might have found in Step 6 above.

Quickly Whisk Away All Your Desktop Icons

For a fast Desktop flush, try this:

1. Right-click the Desktop.

2. Choose Arrange Icons By ➤ Show Desktop Items.

There is probably a check mark by "Show Desktop Items," so what you're doing here is removing the check mark, which dumps all icons and stuff off the Desktop.

Everything goes! Icons! Shortcuts! Even the Recycle Bin! Gone! Any windows or programs you have open remain, but that's because this is a Desktop icon cleanup trick and not a Windows cleanup trick. (Press Win+D to minimize all your open windows.)

Of course, to get the Desktop icons back, reverse the above steps; restore the check mark by "Show Desktop Items," and you'll be back to whatever you believe "normal" to be. (Remember, it's normal to be different.)

I Can't Move My Desktop Icons!

The most annoying instance of Desktop icon paralysis comes when you have the Auto Arrange option on. In that mode, your Desktop icons line up like soldiers, top-to-bottom, left-to-right. Hut-ho! Dragging them doesn't help; they all snap back at attention when you release the mouse button.

To deactivate Auto Arrange, proceed as follows:

1. Right-click the Desktop.

2. Choose Arrange Icons By ➤ Auto Arrange.

This removes the check mark by that menu item, and allows your icons to wander freely across the Desktop.

Or, of course, if you really like having your icons yanked into an orderly detention center, then choose the Auto Arrange item to force them to snap-to.

Auto Arrange lines up the icons by Name, Size, Type, or the date they were last Modified or created. This option is chosen in the top of the "Arrange Icons By" submenu, as shown in Figure 3.4.

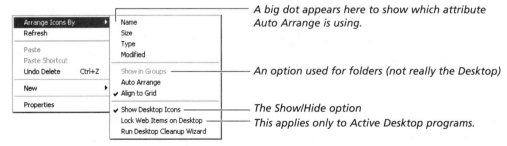

Figure 3.4 The good-to-know "Arrange Icons By" submenu

The Desktop Icon Gridiron Solution (or Frustration)

The second most annoying aspect of icon freeze is when you have the Align to Grid option selected (see Figure 3.4). When that item is checked, the icons line up to an invisible pixel grid for each icon on the Desktop. A must for neat-nicks. But for slop-nicks, removing the check mark from the menu item can turn it off.

How to Avoid "Window Slop"

Beyond icons, the Desktop is occasionally populated with windows. Unlike icons, however, these windows are transients. Windows open, minimize, maximize, and close. And if you have more than one of them open at a time, you can use the *power of the Desktop* to arrange how they appear on the screen.

You Must Know This: Basic Window Arrangements

A single window, whether it's a program window, document window, or file folder, can appear on the screen in three ways:

Minimized *The window appears as a button on the Taskbar*

Maximized *The window covers the entire Desktop (and cannot be made larger or moved)*

Restored *The window "floats" on the Desktop, and can be moved or resized.*

When you have more than one window open, you can arrange them in several patterns:

Random *How windows normally appear, which is in whichever location and size you last used them*

Cascaded *The windows are arranged in an overlapping manner from the upper right corner of the screen to the lower left. You can see the windows' title bars, but only the top window (on the bottom right) has its contents visible.*

Tiled horizontally *All windows are arranged from top to bottom so that you can view a portion of each window.*

Tiled vertically *All windows are arranged left to right so that you can view a portion of each window*

35

The Interesting Window Manipulation Shortcut Tutorial

I assume that moving windows around is a basic operation that most Windows users are familiar with. But how to do that using keyboard shortcuts and options you may not be familiar with is also worth knowing. This tutorial guides you through some window arrangement skills you probably don't already know.

First, you need to have two windows open on the screen. If you already have two windows open, great. If you have more than two windows open, close all but two. And if you don't have two windows open, then open the My Documents icon on the Desktop, then open the My Computer icon. That gives you two windows to work with.

 Second, ensure that neither window is maximized, e.g., filling the entire screen. (If a window is maximized, then you'll see the Restore button on the window's title bar. If so, click that button.)

Third, follow these steps:

1. Right-click the Taskbar to display its pop-up menu.

You must be careful where you click; do not click on a button! Click on any blank part of the Taskbar, as shown in Figure 3.5.

2. Choose "Cascade Windows."

I use this mode when I'm reviewing documents. I open them all up, then I cascade them. That way I can work through them one at a time—just as I would work through a stack of papers.

3. Right-click the Taskbar and choose "Tile Windows Horizontally."

This is my favorite mode for copying files between two folders, or checking the contents of one document verses another.

 If the menu bars and button bars take up too much room when comparing documents tiled horizontally, then check out the View menu. Often the View menu has items that can hide the various toolbars, status bars, and whatnot, which lets you see more of the window's contents.

4. Right-click the Taskbar and choose Tile Windows Vertically.

Again, this is a great way to compare documents, but in a side-by-side manner.

Commands for arranging the windows

| Toolbars ▶ |
| Cascade Windows |
| Tile Windows Horizontally |
| Tile Windows Vertically |
| Show the Desktop |
| Undo Minimize All |
| Task Manager |
| Lock the Taskbar |
| Properties |

Click on a blank part of the Taskbar.

start | Post-it® Software No... | 2 Windows Explorer | Thursday

Figure 3.5 Clicking the Taskbar

5. Press Win+M.

The windows are minimized. Each has become its own button on the Taskbar. Or the windows may be stacked onto a single button on the Taskbar.

6. Click the My Documents button to restore that window.

If the two windows were stacked onto one Windows Explorer button, then click that button and choose My Documents from the pop-up list.

You'll notice that the window restores itself in the same position it lived in when it was last tiled. I usually rearrange and resize the window at this point.

7. Drag the window to a new position on the screen (click and hold down on the window's title bar to drag).

8. Resize the window to something pleasing to you.

Point the mouse at the window's lower right corner and drag up, down, left, or right to resize the window accordingly.

9. Now maximize the window: double-click on the title bar.

10. Now restore the window: double-click on the title bar.

11. You can also use the control menu to manipulate the window: Press Alt+Spacebar, X to maximize the window.

12. Press Alt+Spacebar, R to restore the window.

13. Press Alt+Spacebar, M to go into move mode.

A four-way arrow appears in the window's title bar, which indicates that you're in *Move mode*.

14. Use the left, right, up, and down arrows on the keyboard to move the window.

 Using the keyboard to access "Move mode" (Alt+Spacebar, M) is the best way to restore a window that has wandered off the Desktop. Just press Alt+Spacebar, M and use the arrow keys to walk the window back to where you can manipulate it with the mouse.

15. Press the Enter key when the window is back to where you want it.

16. Press Alt+F4 to close the window.

The My Computer window should remain, time to switch to it using what Microsoft calls the "cool switch."

17. Press Alt+Tab.

This should open (restore) the My Computer window, provided that it's the only other window open (or program running).

If you have more than one window open, keep pressing Alt+Tab until the My Computer window appears on the screen.

The windows on the screen can also be controlled from the Task Manager. Refer to Chapter 27, which has more information on the Task Manager.

18. Press Ctrl+Alt+Delete to conjure the Task Manager's window.

19. Click the Applications tab (if you need to).

This is the place, shown in Figure 3.6, where you can manipulate running programs and do other fun stuff, such as control the Windows on the screen. That's done in the Windows menu.

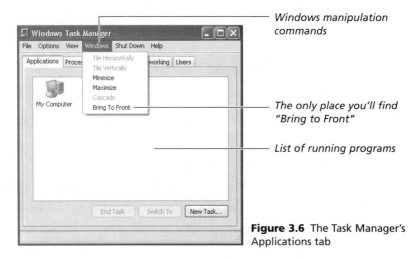

Figure 3.6 The Task Manager's Applications tab

20. Click to select the My Computer icon.

21. Choose Windows ➢ Minimize.

22. Choose Windows ➢ Bring to Front (which is like "Restore").

23. Click on the Windows Task Manager window.

24. Click the My Computer icon to select it.

25. Click the End Task button.

And it's gone.

26. Close the Task Manager.

Now you're well versed in the art of window manipulation. For dinking with two windows, it's not such a big deal. But when you have dozens of windows open or you are switching madly from window to window to finish up some project, knowing how to beat your windows into submission can really help.

KEYBOARD MASTER

Window Manipulation Commands

Here is a slew of commands you can use to futz with windows on the Desktop.

Alt+Spacebar
Activates a window's Control menu.

Alt+Spacebar, R
Restores a window.

Alt+Spacebar, M
Uses the keyboard's arrow keys to move a window.

Alt+Spacebar, N
Minimizes a window.

Alt+Spacebar, X
Maximizes a window.

Alt+F4
Closes a window.

Ctrl+W
Also closes a window (but may not work with all Windows programs).

Win+M
Minimizes all open windows.

Win+Shift+M
Restores all windows minimized by Win+M.

Alt+Tab
Switches to the "next" window or program.

Ctrl+Alt+Delete
Displays the Task Manager window.

Ctrl+Tab
Cycles through the tabs in a window (such as the Task Manager).

I Have More Than Two Windows Open and Need to See Only Two of Them Tiled Horizontally

For a fun time, try this: open about a dozen windows and then tile them! Horizontally or vertically, it doesn't matter because you'll never be able to see the windows' contents. What a mess! Figure 3.7 shows only six windows tiled horizontally, which is next to useless.

If you have lots of windows open and would like to see only two tiled, then minimize all the unwanted windows. Leave only the two windows you want to tile open on the Desktop. Then right-click the Taskbar and choose Tile Windows Horizontally (or Tile Windows Vertically) from the menu.

Figure 3.7 Trying to tile too many windows

39

You can also pull this trick from the Task Manager window, which may be more orderly:

1. Press Win+M to minimize all the windows and get them down to tame little buttons on the Taskbar.

2. Press Ctrl+Alt+Delete to bring forth the Windows Task Manager window.

3. Click to select the Applications tab (if necessary).

4. Ctrl-click the icons of the two windows that you want to tile.

(Pressing the Ctrl key while clicking allows you to select more than one icon.)

5. Choose Windows ➢ Tile Horizontally (or Tile Vertically). And there you have it.

Any Quick Way to Close a Ton of Open Windows?

Certainly! But understand that the slow and inefficient way to do this is to click on the Close button of each window individually. Boring!

1. Press Ctrl+Alt+Delete to bring out your pal the Windows Task Manager.

2. Click on the Applications tab (if necessary)

3. Use the mouse to drag over and select all the windows and applications listed.

Or if you just want to shut down specific windows, Ctrl-click to select them.

4. Click the End Task button. The windows are closed!

 If any applications had unsaved files, then you'll be prompted by that application to save the files. But note that this prompt (a dialog box) often appears behind the Windows Task Manager window. Watch out for it.

The Taskbar Is Too Busy a Place to Talk About in This Chapter Alone

If the Desktop is the face of Windows, then the Taskbar is its bowtie. Refer to Chapter 5 for more information on the Taskbar.

The Desktop Cleanup Wizard

One of the first new—and completely annoying—things that former Windows users noticed about Windows XP was the Desktop Cleanup Wizard. That program was the first to bombard you with warning messages and pop-up balloons from the System Notification Area. So it's generally the first duty of the experienced Windows user to turn that sucker off before you go insane.

What the Desktop Cleanup Wizard Does

For some reason, I suppose, Windows must hate your Desktop shortcut icons. I don't know why. I enjoy having mine around, even the ones I rarely or even never use. So it's none of Windows damn business whether or not my Desktop needs "cleaning." Hey! Why not clean some of the gibberish out of the Windows "help" messages, huh? Now there would be a Wizard I wouldn't mind running from time-to-time.

Anyway...

Basically the Desktop Cleanup Wizard looks for old or seldom-used icons on the Desktop. Any it finds are copied into the Unused Desktop Shortcuts folder, which oddly enough is also stored right there on the Desktop.

If you tell Windows to run the Desktop Cleanup Wizard automatically, then you get that funky pop-up message from the Notification Area. But, hey, I don't know; maybe you like such intrusions. Whatever. I turn the sucker off.

Turning That Stupid Wizard Off

No point in wasting time here:

1. Right-click the Desktop.

2. Choose Properties from the pop-up shortcut menu.

3. Click the Desktop tab.

4. Click the Customize Desktop button.

    Hey! Déjà vu! See Figure 3.2. The bottom part of the Desktop Items dialog box is where you can beat the Desktop Cleanup Wizard into submission.

5. Remove the check mark next to "Run Desktop Cleanup Wizard Every 60 Days."

Supposedly that disables the wizard from automatically crouching into being. But there's another place you should still check, and that's the Scheduled Tasks window:

1. Open the My Computer icon on the Desktop.

2. Press the F4 key.

3. Type `Control Panel\Scheduled Tasks` into the Address box, then press Enter.

    Look through the list for any Desktop Cleanup tasks. There are two of them shown in Figure 3.8, one for "Dan Gookin" and the other for "Vishnu" (both users of my XP computer).

4. Right-click a Desktop Cleanup task.

5. Choose Properties from the pop-up menu.

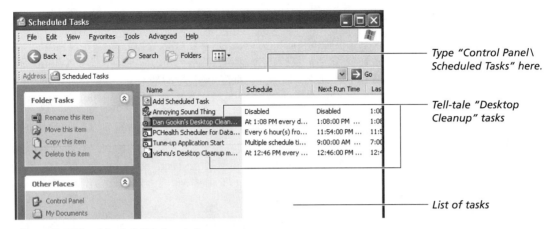

Figure 3.8 The Scheduled Tasks window

6. In the task's Properties dialog box, click the Task tab (if necessary).

7. Remove the check mark next to "Enabled (Scheduled Task Runs at Specified Time)."

This prevents the task from running, but doesn't delete the task, which makes it easier to restore in the future, should you be so gullible as to do so.

8. Click OK to close the task's Properties window.

(You can close the Scheduled Tasks window as well.)

Running the Desktop Cleanup Wizard Manually

Without risking repetitive mental stress injury by having the Desktop Cleanup Wizard run manually, you can run it on-purposefully by taking these steps:

1. Right-click the Desktop.

2. Choose Properties from the pop-up shortcut menu.

3. Click the Desktop tab.

4. Click the Customize Desktop button.

5. Click the Clean Desktop Now button.

And there runs the Wizard.

Oh, read the propaganda if you like; it's just telling you what a swell utility this is without explaining why you would possibly want to keep an icon on the Desktop that you—yes, you!—put there at some time in the past. On purpose.

6. Click the Next button.

The summary screen tells you which icons on the Desktop have been loitering and for how long, according to Figure 3.9.

Windows cleans up the check-marked icons.

I never Work.

Figure 3.9 The Desktop Cleanup Wizard tattles on lingering icons.

7. Click the Next button.

8. Click the Finish button.

If you're quick, you'll see the ne'er-do-well icons vanish in the background.

9. Close the Desktop Items and Display Properties dialog boxes.

 Now there's a folder on the Desktop called Unused Desktop Shortcuts. So the question I really have is this: If cleaning up is done by replacing one "unused" shortcut icon with a folder called "Unused Desktop Shortcuts," is anything really saved?

Well, of course! The shortcuts are all saved.

10. Open the Unused Desktop Shortcuts folder.

And there are the shortcuts.

If you want to restore them back to the Desktop, ensure that the Unused Desktop Shortcuts folder isn't maximized, then select and drag the shortcut icons out of that folder and back onto the Desktop.

And if you really don't need the Unused Desktop Shortcuts folder any more, feel free to delete it. The Desktop Cleanup Wizard stupidly creates another one the next time it runs.

Is It Important to Know Where the Desktop *Really* Is?

No, you do not need to know the details to use your computer. There's no reason for you to know anything more than the millions of other ignorant people out plodding away with the keyboard and timidly poking with the mouse and blaming themselves any time the computer does something unexpected. So you never really need to know more than what you can myopically see on the screen. And besides, clever people hate competition.

Accepting all that, bear in mind that you're an *intermediate* user, which means to know more about your computer you should understand how things work beyond the basic level. While this information may not seem useful now, in the future it may come in handy, especially when your competition at work *does not* know this and you do! That's what getting a leg up on your rivals is all about.

If you can understand a wee bit of what goes on "behind the scenes" in Windows, then you won't be so frustrated the next time something weird happens.

Desktop Mystery Revealed

So now the mystery can be revealed: the Desktop is really just a folder. That's all! Windows takes the contents of that folder —icons, folders, shortcuts, everything—and displays them on the background (Desktop) you see when you use Windows.

With older versions of Windows, the Desktop folder could be found right inside the Windows folder itself. So the path to the Desktop was `C:\Windows\Desktop`. Because Windows XP handles more than one user, plus there are security issues in that many users don't want others to know what's on their Desktop, the secret Desktop folder is now stored elsewhere on the hard drive.

1. Open the My Computer window.

2. Open Drive C.

3. Open the Documents and Settings folder.

Here you'll see a list of all the users on your computer, or just your name if you're the only user, plus the Guest, Administrator, Default User, and All Users folders (Figure 3.10). Each of these folders represents an account or a type of account in Windows XP. And each folder contains its own Desktop folder, which is where the icons on the Desktop really live.

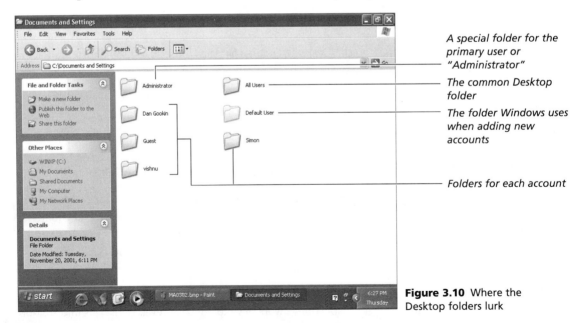

A special folder for the primary user or "Administrator"

The common Desktop folder

The folder Windows uses when adding new accounts

Folders for each account

Figure 3.10 Where the Desktop folders lurk

To prove this, open the folder that bears your name (or your account name). You'll see more folders inside of that folder, each of which contains personal information for your account.

Find and open the Desktop folder, and therein you'll see your Desktop shortcuts and folders and anything that lives on your Desktop.

Using the Common Desktop Folder

Suppose you have several people using your computer or several accounts you use, and you'd like to have a common item installed on everyone's Desktop. If so, just paste that icon into the All Users\Desktop folder.

For example, I enjoy having a shortcut icon to my Zip drive on the Desktop. To make that icon available to all the accounts on my computer, I took these steps:

1. Open the My Computer window.

2. Open Drive C.

3. Open the Documents and Settings folder.

4. Open my account's folder ("Dan Gookin").

5. Open the Desktop folder.

6. Select the Zip drive shortcut icon and press Ctrl+C to copy.

7. Press Backspace twice to return to the Documents and Setting folder.

8. Open the All Users folder.

9. Open the Desktop folder.

10. Press Ctrl+V to paste a copy of the Zip drive shortcut icon.

And now everyone has that shortcut icon on their Desktop.

 KEYBOARD MASTER

The "Go Up" Key

To go "up" one level in the folder tree.

Backspace
This is the same as clicking the Go Up button in any folder window.

Halting Desktop Madness (Part II)

Welcome to the Valley Beyond the Desktop, which is that tract of land upon which dwells the icons, windows, and Taskbar. It's the background picture! The wallpaper! But it's also the frame in which that picture hangs, which is the display.

This chapter continues the discussion of the Desktop from Chapter 3, but here the discussion centers on the background, effects, and display options of the Desktop. Specifically, the information here covers points you may be unfamiliar with, as well as the things you can do with the Desktop that make you a far superior Windows user over that doofus in the next cubicle over. Hey! Is he sleeping? Again?

Mysteries Unveiled and Madness Restrained:

- Controlling the background image
- Putting two images on the Desktop at once
- Putting a custom message on the Desktop
- Using the screen saver to lock the computer
- Perfecting resolution and color
- Creating custom Desktop settings

The Furtive Boundary between Desktop and Display

The Desktop is more *top* than *desk*. There's nothing desk-like about it. When I think of a desk, a really impressive desk, I think of this huge, green marble–topped, aircraft carrier–sized desk of the Master of the Universe. There's a lamp. A technical-looking phone. Some papers. A cigar box. And a $500 pen. That's a desk.

I once believed: the more important you were, the bigger your desk. The Barons of Industry would have these desks you could park a Winnebago on. But that was just a silly pipe dream of my youth. Now I recognize that having the largest LCD monitor in the office is the key to ruling the universe, which brings me right back to the Windows Desktop!

In Windows, the Desktop is the top of your computer's hierarchy. You can prove this easily. Open the My Computer window, or really any folder window. Drop-down the Address bar's list by pressing the F4 key. Then scroll up to the top of that list, or just press the Home key. See? It's the Desktop.

It's the top!

It's the tower of Pizza!

But lurking behind the Desktop top is the background, which can be a solid color, an image, or even a web page (if you dare)—but rarely is it a desk. I suppose you could put the picture of a desk there, but I doubt if any Windows user ever thinks about a desk when they use the Desktop—unless it's to wonder where their real desk went because, I mean, aren't computers supposed to help keep you organized? And look at all that junk on your desk. Sheesh.

KEYBOARD MASTER

Get to the Desktop Level in Any Folder Window

The Desktop is the top, and to get to the top from any folder window you must practice the following key commands:

F4, Home, Enter
The F4 key drops down the Address bar list; Home moves you to the top of the list, the Desktop; and Enter sends you there, displaying the Desktop's contents in the window.

Use this if you want to see the Desktop.

Win+D
Remember: On a Win-D day, you can see the Desktop.

Dare to Be Uncreative and Not Have Any Background Image at All!

The ancient graphical operating system ancestor of Windows didn't have a desktop image at all. That was back before color monitors were affordable (even by the research groups), so the background image was just a gray splotch. A solid color. A picture of the fog at dawn.

I prefer solid colors to images as my Desktop background. First, solid colors make it easier to see the icons. Second, it's not distracting; don't expect me to sit here and work when I can see Miss March sunning herself on Martinique in the background. Third, background images consume more resources and take longer to load. A minor quibble, but I love minor quibbles. Especially with cheese.

To set the background as a solid color, do this:

1. Right-click the Desktop and choose Properties from the shortcut menu.

2. Click the Desktop tab.

First step is to get rid of any background image you may have.

3. Ensure that "(None)" is chosen from the list.

If you've just removed a background image, then you'll notice that the background does have a color. It's shown in the Color button in the bottom right corner of the dialog box.

4. Click the Color button.

A palette of 20 colors appears, from which you can choose a new Desktop color. Figure 4.1 shows the colors, but because this is a black-and-white book, you'll have to trust me on them.

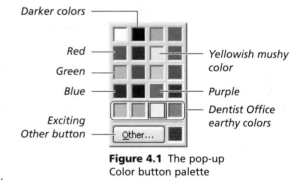

Figure 4.1 The pop-up Color button palette

5. Choose a color from the palette.

The background color on the preview monitor changes to match. But notice that your Desktop hasn't yet changed color. That's good because you're not just limited to 20 colors.

No, say all those pop-up colors stink and you want more. No, you *demand* more!

6. Click the Color button.

7. Click the Other button.

Ah-ha! That's what I'm talking about. A much larger color palette to choose from, plus a handy color picker tool to let you pluck out the prettiest and bestest color for your monitor. Now *that* is choice!

8. Mess with the colors to select a nice, custom color for your background.

Refer to Figure 4.2 for some brief instructions, though it's easy to play with the color palettes and type in strange numbers to see what comes up.

 If you do manage to get a custom color you like, click to select a new "square" in the Custom Colors area, then click the Add to Custom Colors button. That places your color in to the Custom Colors palette so that you don't have to re-create it should something unexpected happen in the future.

9. Click to choose the color you want, either one of the "Basic Colors," one you selected manually, or even one from the "Custom Colors" list.

10. Click OK.

11. Click OK in the Display Properties dialog box to set your background color.

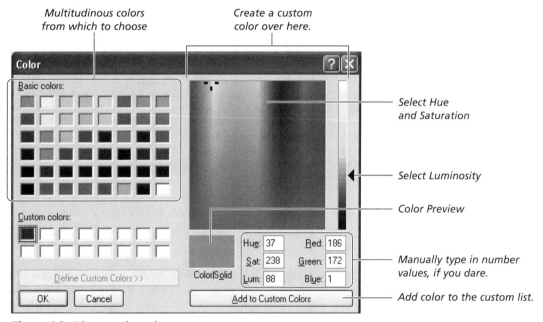

Figure 4.2 labels:
- *Multitudinous colors from which to choose*
- *Create a custom color over here.*
- *Select Hue and Saturation*
- *Select Luminosity*
- *Color Preview*
- *Manually type in number values, if you dare.*
- *Add color to the custom list.*

Figure 4.2 A better color palette

Background Image Stuff You May Not Know

To set a background image for the Desktop, you use the Display Properties dialog box ➢ Desktop tab. Or, to be brief, the Display Properties/Desktop dialog box. In that dialog box, you'll see a list of *all* the graphics files on your computer, any of which you may pick as the background image. But you most likely knew that. But did you also know...?

If you choose an animated GIF image, such as a movie or cartoon, then that image also becomes the background image—an animated wallpaper? Funky. (But note that not every type of animated GIF file will do that; you have to just keep trying them until you find one that animates on the Desktop.)

The Position drop-down list lets you set how the image appears on the Desktop. Stretch to make the image fill the screen (but it's often distorted); Tile to fill the screen with a repeating pattern of the image; and Center to just center the image, un-distorted. Note, however, that animated GIF images always appear full-screen. If it's an animated image, "Stretch" is possibly the best option. For smaller images, "Tile" is a good option.

You can slap down any image from the Internet onto the Desktop. From your web browser, right-click the image and choose "Set as Background" from the pop-up menu. This image then becomes known as "Internet Explorer Wallpaper" in the scrolling list of the Display Properties/Desktop dialog box.

By the way, you can have only one "Internet Explorer Wallpaper" at a time. Each time you choose an image using "Set as Background," the new image replaces any existing image you may have. (Remember that you can always save an image from the Internet to disk; just choose "Save Picture As" when you right-click the image.)

 If you accidentally add an image from the Internet that you don't want your wife or kids (or coworkers) to see on the Desktop, then open the Display Properties dialog box ➢ Desktop tab. Select the "Internet Explorer Wallpaper" item in the scrolling list, then click the Browse button. In the Browse dialog box, locate the "Internet Explorer Wallpaper" file, select it, and then press the Delete key. Or press Shift+Delete if you really want to delete it for good.

Forget About Automatically Changing Background Images at Random Times

Alas, Windows has no built-in way to randomly show different backgrounds, either changing every time you boot or after a given time interval. The only official way to change background images is as documented here; use the Display Properties dialog box ➢ Desktop tab.

 Beware of third-party programs, utilities, and shareware on the Internet that claim to shift background images! I've messed with a few of them and they were all very disappointing. The majority of them are advertisements; sure they change the background image, but every other image is an ad. Many of them turned out to be almost virus-like in their ability to take over your computer. One I had just would not uninstall no matter what I tried. So beware of those "easy solutions."

Why Bother Putting a Web Page on the Background?

Via the Active Desktop, you can place a web page on the background, either all of the web page or merely one part of it (such as a picture). The problem here is that the Desktop-Web relationship works best only if you have a high-speed Internet connection, one that's hopefully on all the time. Otherwise the web page appears as a static image on the background, which I don't find all that exciting and, in fact, can become distracting.

Unlike prior versions of Windows, you have to dig a little to summon the Active Desktop dialog box:

1. Right-click the Desktop and choose Properties from the shortcut menu.

2. Click the Desktop tab.

3. Click the Customize Desktop button.

4. Click the web tab.

Ah, you're finally there. Figure 4.3 shows some of the highlights, though it's pretty plain to make out:

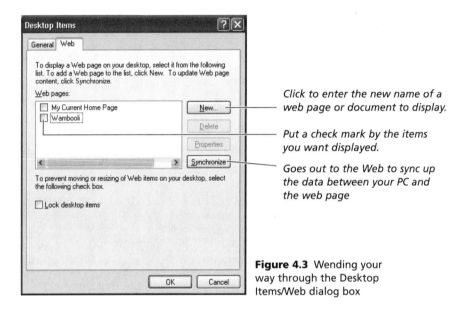

Click to enter the new name of a web page or document to display.

Put a check mark by the items you want displayed.

Goes out to the Web to sync up the data between your PC and the web page

Figure 4.3 Wending your way through the Desktop Items/Web dialog box

5. Click the "New" button to add a web page or Active Desktop gizmo to the Desktop.
The New Desktop Item dialog box becomes visible.

6. Enter the URL of the web page into the Location text box.
You know, like `http://www.wambooli.com`—like that.

Or you can click the Visit Gallery button to get on the Web and see what kind of Active Desktop doohickeys Microsoft has to share.

Or you can click the Browse button to add an HTML document, link, or any old picture to the Active Desktop. (More on this in the next section.)

7. Click OK to add your Active Desktop item.

8. Close various dialog boxes and you'll see your Active Desktop web page or item on the Desktop.

Active Desktop items appear in their own funky window. If you point the mouse at the Active Desktop item, then its toolbar appears and you can use the buttons on the toolbar to adjust the item, close it, and so on. The down-pointing triangle on the left side of the title bar contains a control menu that has even more options, including the handy "Customize My Desktop" command, which flings you immediately back into the Desktop Items dialog box.

You Must Know This:
Active Desktop Item/Window Controls

×   *Close the Active Desktop item (you must reopen it from the Desktop Items/Web dialog box)*

☐   *Maximize the item's window, save for a strip along the left side for displaying icons*

☐   *Maximize the item's window to full screen (distorts pictures)*

▾   *Display control menu*

◪   *Restore maximized window*

Can I Put Two Different Images on the Desktop at the Same Time?

Certainly, and this is how the Active Desktop can pay off: you can use it to display a whole scrapbook of pictures, even custom web pages or HTML documents you create yourself, right there on the Desktop. This is kind of a nifty thing to do, and few people know about it:

1. Right-click the Desktop and choose Properties from the shortcut menu.

2. Click the Desktop tab.

3. Click the Customize Desktop button.

4. Click the Web tab.

5. Click the New button.

6. Click the Browse button.

   Use the Browse dialog box to hunt down an image file on your computer.

    Click the My Documents shortcut on the left side of the Browse dialog box, then open the My Pictures folder. That should give you a buncha images to choose from.

7. Select the image and click Open.

   The image's path is placed into the Location text box in the New Desktop Item's dialog box. You're all set!

8. Click OK to close the New Desktop Item dialog box.

   You won't see the image displayed until you close the other two dialog boxes as well.

9. Click OK.

10. Click OK.

    And there's the image, wrapped in an Active Desktop item window.

If you point the mouse at this image, the item's frame appears and you can drag the image or resize it. Resizing is tricky, though, because the image doesn't resize proportionally. So you'll have to mess around to get what you want—or just put up with the funhouse effect.

Anything Else I Can Do with Active Desktop That My Coworkers Would Be Jealous Of?

The final trick you can pull with Active Desktop is to create your own custom HTML document and stick it on the Desktop. This requires knowledge of HTML, the formatting language used to create web pages. However, I can show you one or two tricks in just a few steps. Be patient and type carefully!

1. Open Notepad.

2. Type in the following text exactly:

```
<html>
<head></head>
<body text="white" bgcolor="green">
<h1>
All Work and No Play Makes Jack a Dull Boy!
</h1>
</body>
</html>
```

   Don't bother with the details, just obey! (Well, most of this is basic HTML. The codes are contained in angle brackets and typically have a starting code and an ending code. The ending code is the same as the starting code, but with a slash before the code name, as in <h1> and </h1>, the "Heading Level One" style.)

   You must be careful to save the file as an HTML document, which is doable in Notepad, but tricky:

3. Choose File ➢ Save As.

4. From the "Save as Type" drop-down list, choose "All Files."

   This allows you to save the document using the HTML extension, instead of the .txt (text file) extension.

53

5. Type `Admonishment.html` into the File Name text box.

6. Double-check to ensure that you're saving the file in the My Documents folder.

If not, use the Save As dialog box to wiggle your way to that folder.

7. Close Notepad.

Now you need to set your HTML document as an Active Desktop item.

8. Right-click the Desktop and choose Properties from the shortcut menu.

9. Click the Desktop tab.

10. Click the Customize Desktop button.

11. Click the Web tab.

12. Click the New button.

13. Use the Browse button to hunt down your file.

Remember, it's named `Admonishment.html` and it can be found in the My Documents folder. Use the Browse dialog box to select that file.

14. Click OK to close the New Desktop Item dialog box.

Your HTML document now appears in the list of web pages in the Desktop Items/Web dialog box. The item is already checked, so all you need to do is return to the Desktop to see it.

15. Click OK.

16. Click OK.

You may need to move or resize the item's window, but eventually it shows up right on the screen, boasting your message for all to see, as shown in Figure 4.4.

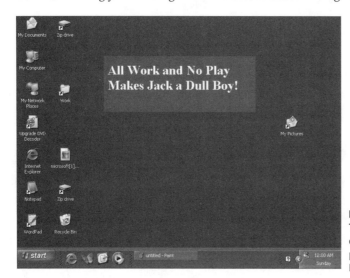

Figure 4.4
The final HTML document displayed as an Active Desktop item

Now for the suggestions!

Your HTML document is very simple, but can be used to display a variety of messages in a bunch of interesting colors. Here are the things that you can change in the document:

```
<body text="white" bgcolor="green">
```

You can change the color of the text by putting a new color word in the `text="white"` part of the HTML document. So `text="yellow"` would give you yellow colored text.

The background color is set by `bgcolor="green"`. To set a new background color, specify it between the quotes, as in `bgcolor="red"` or `bgcolor="black"` or whatever common color name you can think of.

You can change the text displayed by typing any next between the `<h1>` and `</h1>` lines.

```
<h1>
Don't mess with my computer, Bill!
</h1>
```

For more help, you'll need to refer to an HTML manual. Simple HTML documents are easy to create once you know a few of the codes. And Notepad is an entirely valid way to type in the HTML codes and create your own custom screen messages, or even more complex web page documents.

For example, with a proper knowledge of HTML, you could create a document that would display a different image every day of the week, or an image that changes every hour.

I Hate Trying to Move the Active Desktop Items Around

That's why there is a Lock Active Desktop items command available, which effectively glues the items down on the Desktop, removing the funky window-border they frustratingly sport:

1. Right-click the Desktop.

2. Choose Arrange Icons By ➤ Lock Web Items on Desktop.

That does it!

Saving the Screen from Certain Boredom

You probably have heard the screen saver story over and over, but I'm going to tell it again anyway. Way back in the early days of computers, people would often leave their PCs on all day, running the same program: WordPerfect, Lotus 1-2-3, dBASE, whatever. When they turned the computer off at the end of the day, a ghost image of the program would appear on the monitor—even with the computer off. That was known as *phosphor burn-in*. It was a real problem.

 Some ATMs, or cash machines, often have phosphor burn-in; you can see the menu on the screen even when the machine is turned off.

The solution to phosphor burn-in was to run a screen saver program. That would, after a given interval or based on a certain keystroke, blank the screen to save it from being burned. Lo, the screen saver was born.

Eventually screen savers did more than blank the screen, they would display flying toasters, Disney characters, animations, or games. The strange thing is that at that time, the monitors had improved so much that phosphor burn-in was no longer a serious problem, but the screen saver continued and is still used today.

Any Fool Can Choose a Screen Saver, So Tell Me Something I Don't Know

Screen savers are actually special programs that live in the Windows\System32 folder. That's where you would save a screen saver that you downloaded from the Internet (unless the screen saver has its own installation utility). That's also where you would remove a screen saver that you didn't want.

Here's how to see the bunch of screen savers "in the raw" on your system:

1. Open the My Computer icon on the Desktop.

2. Open Drive C.

3. Open the Windows folder.

4. Open the System32 folder.

5. Choose View ➤ Details from the menu.

6. Choose View ➤ Arrange icons by type.

7. Scroll through the list until you see the group of "Screen Saver" files in the list, as shown in Figure 4.5.

    And there they are.

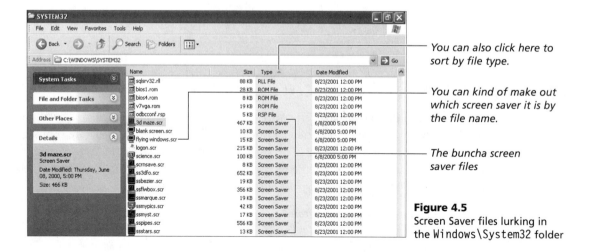

You can also click here to sort by file type.

You can kind of make out which screen saver it is by the file name.

The buncha screen saver files

Figure 4.5
Screen Saver files lurking in the Windows\System32 folder

I Can Get Other Screen Savers?

Certainly. The Windows Update utility (found at the top of the Start button's All Programs menu) lists new screen savers from time to time. Some can be found on the Internet, and there are third-party companies that sell screen savers. Sometimes you may even get a new screen saver with new software or hardware that you buy.

 Beware of shareware screen savers that you download from the Internet! Some are only part-time screen savers and full time advertisements—and they're hard as ticks to pull out of your PC. Only download a screen saver from the Internet if it has a full uninstall utility, or if the screen saver is a single *.scr *file that you merely copy to the* Windows\System32 *folder.*

Can I Use the Screen Saver to Lock My Computer?

Certainly. This replaces the password-protected screen savers with older versions of Windows. Now Windows can lock the computer when you do the following to your screen saver.

1. Right-click the Desktop and choose Properties from the shortcut menu.

2. Click the Screen Saver tab.

Note that you must have a screen saver chosen. In Figure 4.6, the Windows XP screen saver is selected.

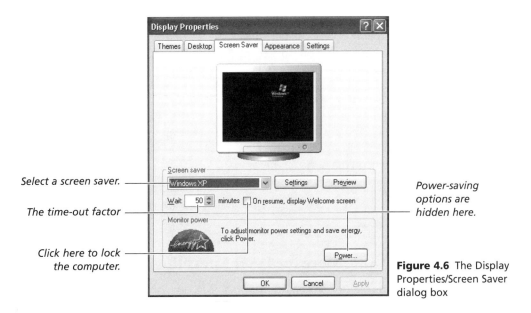

Figure 4.6 The Display Properties/Screen Saver dialog box

3. Put a check mark by "On Resume, Display Welcome Screen."

Or if you're using the serious logon window, the option is "On Resume, Password Protect."

4. Click OK.

Now when the screen saver fires off, the computer is essentially locked. When the mouse is moved or a key is clicked, the Welcome or Logon screen is displayed. And if all the accounts are password-protected, then you'll need to know one of the passwords to get back into the computer.

The key to this operation is really the idle time to wait for the screen saver to kick in. If you have the time set to something like 10 minutes (or less), then you can be assured that the screen saver lock will work to keep others out of your computer. But if the time is set too high, it may not kick in soon enough to prevent unauthorized access. In that case, just lock the computer by pressing Win+L.

Which Is Better, the Screen Saver or "Sleeping" the Monitor?

I read once that you shouldn't use screen savers on LCD monitors, but use the sleep feature instead. Or was it the other way around? Well, anyway, I have LCD monitors in my office and I use both techniques. I have the screen saver come on after a given interval, depending on the computer. Then after about two hours, I have the monitor enter sleep mode.

Sleep mode is accessed by clicking the Power button in the Display Properties dialog box ➤ Screen Saver tab (see Figure 4.6). Click that button to display the Power Options Properties dialog box. You can set the monitor time-out by using the "Turn Off Monitor" drop-down list, as Figure 4.7 illustrates.

By the way, I like to keep my computers on all the time, even to the point of not sleeping (or hibernating) the system or the hard drives. I just prefer to have a system handy and warm when I'm ready to type, as opposed to waiting for something to start or come out of Coma Mode.

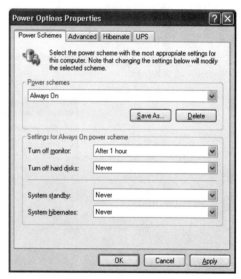

Figure 4.7 Setting monitor sleeping options

Making the Screen More (or Less) Appealing

The Desktop, plus the items on the screen, can be as big or as tiny as you want it. Of course, it does have to fit within the confines of the monitor. So if you have a 19-inch monitor, then 19-inches of Desktop is all that you're going to see. But within that 19-inches you can display things really big, teensy tiny, or somewhere in between.

How Can I Select the Best Resolution for My Monitor?

The monitor's resolution is set in the Display Properties dialog box ➤ Settings tab, which is shown in Figure 4.8. The best way to set the resolution is to use the slider to move it up as high as it can go and still look good on your monitor.

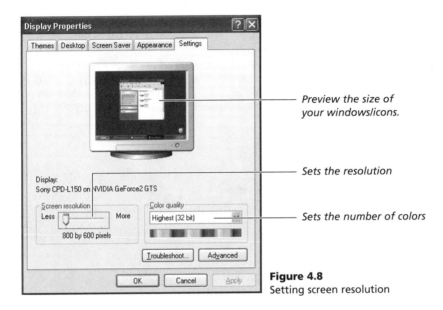

Preview the size of your windows/icons.

Sets the resolution

Sets the number of colors

Figure 4.8
Setting screen resolution

Low resolution modes, such as 800 by 600, don't give you much Desktop real estate, but they're easier to see.

A typical resolution is 1024 by 768. Most 15-inch LCD monitors are configured to work best in this mode. Other monitors also look good in this mode, though the icons may be rather small.

Higher resolution values depend on your video hardware, so the upper limit you have is based on the video adapter (not the monitor or Windows itself).

Also note that at higher resolutions, fewer colors may be available. I have a system that can go to 1600 by 1200 resolution, but with only 16-bit stupid colors.

Note that the monitor itself will adjust any scan rates or frequencies. This isn't something you need to mess with. And if you do need to mess with it, you must use your monitor's controls to set the values, not Windows.

Bring on the High Resolution and Big Icons!

Set the resolution high in the Display Properties dialog box ➤ Settings tab. Then do this:

1. Click the Appearance tab.

2. Click the Effects button.

3. Click to put a check mark by "Use Large Icons."

4. Click OK.

Note that some systems may actually reset the resolution here. But in most cases all that happens is that the icons get bigger.

Another setting to consider is the font size setting, which is found in the Display Properties dialog box ➢ Appearance tab. You can use that drop-down list to choose Large or Extra Large fonts, which makes some of the higher resolutions easier to view.

 You can also use the Zoom command in many applications to view your stuff in a larger size than the screen displays. For example, I'm using high resolution (1280 by 1024) on my monitor, but I've set the Zoom command in Microsoft Word to 125 percent.

That "Fade Effect" Is Driving Me Nuts

Ever notice how some menus seem to "fade" into existence? They appear faintly, then more solid, then completely opaque. Slowly. Just like a computer, right? Yes, I hate fading-in things myself...

Effects are handled by the Effects button in the Appearance tab of the Display Properties dialog box:

1. Right-click the Desktop and choose Properties from the menu.

2. Click the Appearance tab.

3. Click the Effects button.

Removing the check mark from the top item (Figure 4.9) eliminates the fade effect.

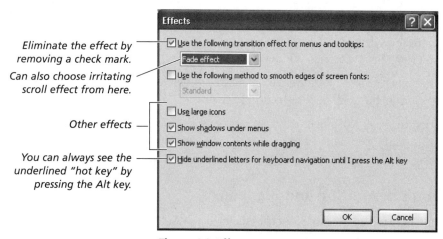

Figure 4.9 Effects accepts and rejects

Anyway to Make the Monitor Display Colors More Accurately?

One of Windows' hidden treasures is its ability to adjust the colors on your monitor to more accurately reflect the colors available in the images you display or edit. This is really a part of tinkering that's mostly done by photographic professionals and graphic artists who require their monitors to display colors accurately. If that's not you, then you can merrily skip this!

To get to the buried Color Management tab, follow these steps:

1. Right-click the Desktop and choose Properties from the menu.

2. Click the Settings tab.

3. Click the Advanced button.

   A dialog box appears for your display adapter. You should know that the display adapter hardware is really what controls what you see on the screen; the monitor is just the end result of all that video hardware.

4. Click the Color Management tab.

   Here is where you can choose a color profile for your monitor. Windows comes with a few of them, but you'll be better off using the color profile that came with your monitor on a CD or floppy disk. Or, sometimes the profile is available from the photo editing software developer.

5. Click the Add button.

   Use the Add Profile Association dialog box to browse for a new color profile. Windows lists a bunch of them, but like I said earlier you'll probably find a perfect one among your hardware or software disks.

6. Choose a profile and click OK.

   The profile appears in the list in the Color Management tab.

7. Click the Apply button.

   And there you go. If you're not into photo editing or having realistic colors, then you may not notice any difference. Then again, these are not options for people who aren't into that kind of stuff.

8. Click OK.

9. Click OK.

I Need the Monitor to Display Perfect Dimensions!

Another fussy thing to set for Those Who Want Things Perfect is the DPI setting. Normally Windows displays information on the screen with 96 pixels in one inch. However, as you may guess, with all the different resolutions available on the screen, 96 pixels don't always add up to equal one inch. If you need to be exact, then you must follow these steps:

1. Right-click the Desktop and choose Properties from the pop-up menu.

2. Click the Settings tab.

3. Click the Advanced button.

   Your video display adapter's Properties dialog box pops up.

4. Ensure that the General tab is up front.

5. Choose "Custom Setting" from the DPI Setting drop-down list.

   The Custom DPI Setting dialog box appears (Figure 4.10).

6. Hold a ruler up to the screen.

   I'm serious! Use your left hand.

7. Use the mouse to drag the on-screen ruler to match the real world ruler you're holding in your left hand.

8. Click OK.

9. Click OK to close the warning dialog box.

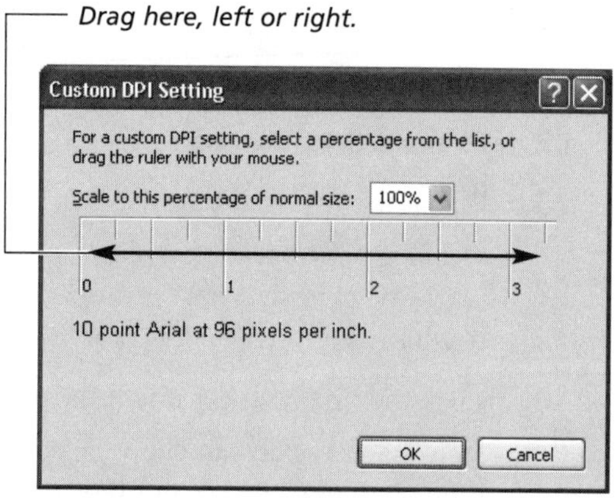

Figure 4.10 Setting the exact Desktop dimensions

10. Click OK to close the adapter's Properties dialog box.

    Another warning dialog box appears. The files needed are most likely already on the hard drive, so you can click Yes. Otherwise follow the instructions in the dialog box.

    Eventually, you'll click the Close button on the Display Properties dialog box. You may be asked to restart the computer. Do so.

If you don't like the new settings, then you can repeat these steps and choose the standard 96 DPI setting from your display adapter's Properties dialog box.

I Prefer a Fancier Desktop, Something Really Showy

This is easy to do—a great time waster—but it gives you a screen utterly different from your friends and co-workers. It's creating your own theme, and it's just too much fun to be in Windows:

1. Right-click the Desktop and choose Properties from the menu.

2. Click the Appearance tab.

3. Click the misnamed Advanced button.

   There's nothing advanced about the dialog box you see (Figure 4.11). It just lets you control the colors, fonts, sizes, and styles of 18 different Desktop or Windows elements.

   Each element is listed in the Item drop-down list. Choose the item from that list, or just click the mouse on the item in the window (see Figure 4.11).

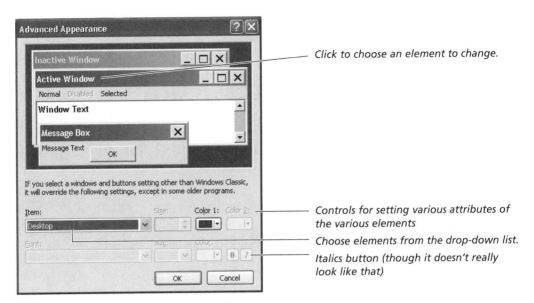

Click to choose an element to change.

Controls for setting various attributes of the various elements

Choose elements from the drop-down list.

Italics button (though it doesn't really look like that)

Figure 4.11 Create new, custom Desktop themes here.

Use the controls on the bottom and right sides of the dialog box to set the individual elements. (Not all the controls are available with each element; some elements are manipulated with only one or two of the controls.)

4. When you're done, click the OK button.

Wait! Don't do anything yet! First, you need to save your settings in case something screws up. Then you can preview things.

5. Click the Themes tab.

6. Click the Save As button.

A Save As dialog box appears. Work it like any Save As dialog box, giving your theme a name and location on the hard drive. (The My Documents folder is okay for saving themes, unless you have a lot of them in which case creating a Personal Themes folder would be in order.)

7. Save your theme.

8. Click OK.

And your theme takes over the Desktop.

With your custom theme saved, you can easily restore it from the Display Properties/Themes dialog box. Just use the drop-down list to pluck your custom theme any time you want it. Or you can use the Advanced Appearance dialog box (Figure 4.11) to tweak specific elements, then resave the theme back to disk.

 The "Windows XP" theme is the one Windows XP uses out of the box. If you ever want to return to use that theme, then choose it from the drop-down list in the Display Properties/Themes dialog box.

5

Taming the Taskbar

Down Taskbar! Down! Down! Back, back!

Do you talk to your Taskbar? I sometimes do. I wonder why it's so fat all of the sudden. What did it eat? Or why it disappears. Where did it go? And I know there are some people whose Taskbars have a tendency to jump to the right edge of the screen, which may or may not be a political statement. I still find the mere fact that the Taskbar is capable of jumping anywhere at all rather alarming.

For some reason, the Taskbar just looks good and feels right on the bottom of the screen. For some other reason, Windows allows you to move the Taskbar to any edge of the screen, resize it, junk it up with other Taskbars, plus a whole lotta other nonsense all carefully covered here in this chapter.

Meddlesome Moving Taskbars and Other Nonsense

 Getting something more from the Start button

Moving, hiding, wrangling, and dinking with the Taskbar

Increasing screen space

Overloading on toolbars

Crushing the Notification Area

The Taskbar, from Left to Right

Assuming (of course) that the Taskbar sits merrily on the bottom of the screen, you will find the following Taskbar pieces parts, also shown in Figure 5.1. This is basic stuff you should already know:

- The Start button, which powers the pop-up Start panel full of interesting things to do or see.

- The Taskbar itself, which is where buttons appear representing the various programs you're running or windows that are open (though that's not entirely true, but I'll write more about that later).

- The Notification Area, which is a hodge-podge, "junk drawer" of a place, and not even Bill Gates knows what it's for.

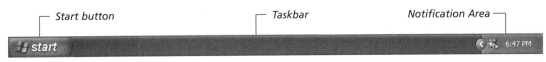

Figure 5.1 The Taskbar, undressed

Yes, There Are a Few Unknown Things About the
Start Button

Honestly, beyond popping up the Start button, there's really nothing else much that goes on with the left side of the Taskbar. Chapter 6 covers the Start panel in particular, but until then, there's always the right-click: Right-clicking the Start button displays a pop-up menu that helps you deal with the Start panel's options and settings. Figure 5.2 illustrates what's what on the menu.

The only items worth noting are the Open and Explore commands. There are two sets. The top two Open and Explore commands open your account's Start menu. This contains only those Start menu items that are private to your account. (Also see Chapter 3; like the Desktop, there are personal Start menus.)

The bottom two Open and Explore commands open the Start menu that contains the commands shared by all the computer's users. That's the one you'll most likely choose if you want to do any major Start menu pruning.

The Properties option gets you to the Taskbar and Start Menu Properties dialog box, the relevant points of which are covered later in this Chapter and in the next.

Finally, many third-party programs may add custom items to the Start button's shortcut menu. In Figure 5.2, you see two items that let you interact with a third-party program called WinRAR. I've also seen graphics programs add shortcut items to the Start button's pop-up menu. This isn't unusual, so don't freak out when you see other things on that menu.

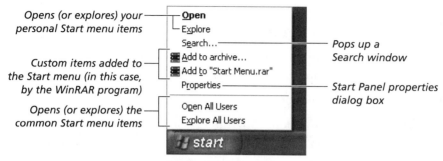

Opens (or explores) your personal Start menu items

Custom items added to the Start menu (in this case, by the WinRAR program)

Opens (or explores) the common Start menu items

Pops up a Search window

Start Panel properties dialog box

Figure 5.2 What's what on the Start button's shortcut menu.

KEYBOARD MASTER

Start Button Keystrokes Galore!

Win

Pressing the Windows key by itself pops up the Start panel. This the one they teach in kindergarten.

Ctrl+Esc

To pop up the Start button's shortcut menu you normally right-click on the Start button.

Win, Esc, Context

Pressing the Windows key pops up the Start Panel; the Esc key pops it back down, but keeps the Start button selected. Pressing the Context key (that's the funny key between the Windows key and the Ctrl key on the left side of the spacebar) then displays the shortcut menu.

Why Use the Open All Users Command on the Start Button?

It's easier to edit the Start panel when you open it up in a window. Well, technically you don't open the Start panel; you're opening the All Programs menu, which contains all the programs you've installed on your computer.

1. Right-click the Start button.

2. Choose Open All Users.

A window appears listing menu items that appear at the top of the All Programs menu. For example, you may see a shortcut icon to the Windows Update. That icon, plus any others you see, represents items at the top of the All Programs menu.

3. Click the Start button and choose All Programs.

   Look at the top of the menu. See the programs listed above the line? They are represented by the shortcut icons in the Start Menu folder.

4. Click the Start Menu folder on the Taskbar.

5. Open the Programs folder.

   This folder contains the menu items and submenus that appear on all users' All Programs menu. Folders are submenus. Shortcut icons are menu items.

   You'll notice that not all the programs are listed there. That's because the others come from the private account's Start Menu folder. More on that in a minute.

6. Close the Programs window.

The point to all this is that it's easier to edit the menu when the menu items and such appear as folders and shortcut icons. So, say if you want to copy a menu item from one menu to another, use the folder windows to copy (or cut) and paste items.

 If you're doing a lot of "pruning and grafting" of the menus, then choose the Explore option instead of Open. That way you can see the folder tree when you work with the menus, which makes it easier to drag and drop menu items between the folders.

What's the Point of the Open (All by Itself) Command?

If you're editing the All Programs menu and you don't find what you're looking for, then it's probably an item personal to your account and not something on the All Users menu. Right-click the Start button and choose the Open (or Explore) command to find the menu or shortcut icon.

Why Is This So Screwy?

Because several people may be using your computer, each of whom has customized commands. Some large organizations may go to the trouble to really edit the All Users menu and keep the personal menus short. For an individual using Windows XP, it really makes no difference whether the commands are in the All Users or an individual account's folder.

So the point really isn't that it's screwy. Many things are screwy. Hey! It's Windows! Were you expecting logic or something? Get real! Just know the difference between Open and Open All Users, and you'll be okay.

The Taskbar Here, There, and Everywhere

After I-don't-know-how-many versions of Windows, we have finally been blessed with a lockable Taskbar. No more will the damn thing wander all around the Desktop. Now that could, at one time, have been an interesting option. But so few people use it and so many more are confused by the peripatetic Taskbar, that it makes you wonder why locking the thing down wasn't an option with Windows 95?

Ah! But I'm getting ahead of myself. The following sections cover the Taskbar, locks and all, plus various tidbits and options you won't find in any beginner computer book.

Know Your Taskbar

Figure 5.3 illustrates the visual differences between a locked and an unlocked Taskbar. There are two big differences you should already know:

- The unlocked Taskbar has an extra strip of flesh along its inner edge.

- The unlocked Taskbar shows the dimple area, which is how you drag the Taskbar around. Also, if you have other toolbars on the Taskbar, each will sport its own dimple area.

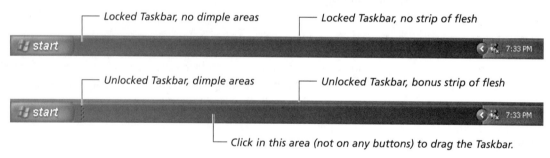

Locked Taskbar, no dimple areas — Locked Taskbar, no strip of flesh

Unlocked Taskbar, dimple areas — Unlocked Taskbar, bonus strip of flesh

Click in this area (not on any buttons) to drag the Taskbar.

Figure 5.3 Differences between a locked and unlocked Taskbar

The other difference not shown in the image is that an unlocked Taskbar can wander. It can be on the top, left, or right sides of the screen. When you lock the Taskbar, it cannot move.

Lock That Puppy Down

To lock the Taskbar, right-click on its dimple area and choose "Lock the Taskbar" from the pop-up menu.

To unlock the Taskbar, right-click on any blank part of the Taskbar and choose "Lock the Taskbar" from the pop-up menu. This removes the check mark by "Lock the Taskbar" and allows you to fling the Taskbar wildly around the screen.

There's also a slower way to unlock the Taskbar:

1. Right-click the Start button.

2. Choose Properties from the pop-up menu.

3. Click the Taskbar tab in the Taskbar and Start Menu Properties dialog box.

4. Remove the check mark by "Lock the Taskbar."

5. Click OK.

Note how the Taskbar preview window in the dialog box changes to reflect a locked or unlocked Taskbar.

Visually confirm that you have a locked Taskbar, using Figure 5.3 as your guide.

 If you have trouble finding the proper place to right-click the Taskbar, then click on the time display in the Notification Area.

The "Yes I Can," Moving a Taskbar Tutorial

Most people have no problem moving the Taskbar around the screen. No, the problem is moving it back. To solve that problem, you need to work through a dragging the Taskbar tutorial, which will exercise your flabby Taskbar-moving muscles and get you into ready shape.

1. Unlock the Taskbar.

2. Close all open windows.

It doesn't matter if there are windows open or not, but with windows open there are buttons on the Taskbar, which makes it harder to drag the Taskbar with the mouse. Besides, if your Taskbar is hopelessly glued to the left side of the screen, it shouldn't matter to you whether you have windows open or not.

3. Point the mouse at the center of the Taskbar.

4. Drag the mouse over to the right edge of the screen.

When you get close to the right edge of the screen, the Taskbar snaps up, snuggling close to your monitor's starboard side.

The Start button may not show the word "Start," which simply means that the Taskbar is too narrow. Fatten it up a bit:

5. Point the mouse at the Taskbar's inside (left) edge. The mouse pointer changes to a left-right arrow thing.

6. Drag the mouse toward the center of the screen, which fattens the Taskbar.

See Figure 5.4 for what it looks like on my screen.

Figure 5.4
Messing with
the Taskbar

7. Click the Start button.

See? It still works. In fact, the reason Windows gave us a kinetic Taskbar was that someone somewhere could possibly enjoy and use their Taskbar this way. (And if we can find that person....)

8. Press Esc to hide the Start panel.

9. Drag the Taskbar to the top of the screen.

Again, point the mouse at the center of the Taskbar and drag the mouse to the top center of the screen.

You'll notice that the Taskbar appears more "normal," albeit a bit high. Also, did you see how any Desktop icons wiggled out of the way to make room for the Taskbar? Handy.

10. Drag the Taskbar to the left side of the screen.

Now if you like the Taskbar there—or on the top or right side of the screenóyou can lock it into position. The Lock command works no matter which side of the screen the Taskbar is on.

11. Drag the Taskbar back to the bottom of the screen.

And there you goófour sides of the screen in less than five minutes.

By the way, you can mess with the Taskbar's thickness even when it's horizontal:

12. Point the mouse at the Taskbar's inside (top) edge.

13. Drag the mouse up to increase the Taskbar's thickness.

You can drag it as high as almost halfway up the screen—though that's a bit ridiculous.

14. Resize the Taskbar so that it's as thin as it can be.

Drag the Taskbar's inner edge all the way down to the bottom of the screen. Now it appears as only a thin blue line. You can't see the Start button or Notification Area, nor any buttons on the Taskbar. This is the closest you can come to getting rid of the Taskbar entirely.

15. Restore the Taskbar to its original thickness (and optionally locked) condition.

Will Hiding the Taskbar Give Me More Screen Space?

Certainly. The Taskbar eats up a chunk of the screen and if you need that space, then you can resize the Taskbar to nothing, as described in the previous section. Or you can choose to Auto-hide the Taskbar, which may come in handier:

1. Right-click the Taskbar and choose Properties from the pop-up menu.

If you don't see the Properties item, then you're clicking on the wrong part of the Taskbar; close all the windows and then click in the middle of the Taskbar.

2. In the Taskbar and Start Menu Properties/Taskbar dialog box (Figure 5.5), click to select "Auto-Hide the Taskbar."

3. Click the Apply button.

And the Taskbar drops out of site like a bad actor through a trapdoor. But it's not always gone, just hiding:

4. Point the mouse at the bottom of the screen, where the Taskbar was.

And it pops right back up.

5. Click OK to close the Taskbar and Start Menu Properties dialog box.

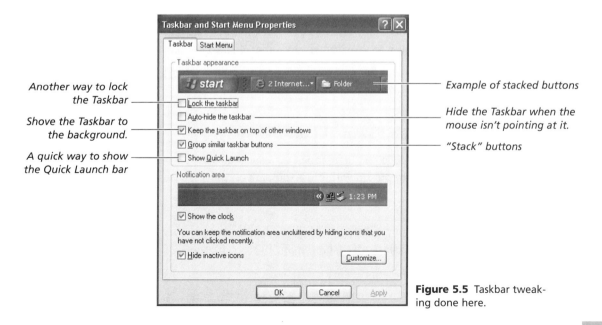

Figure 5.5 Taskbar tweaking done here.

I'm not a big fan of the drop-out Taskbar. I like my graphics to stand still until I need them. But there is another option that shoves the Taskbar out of the way when you maximize a window:

1. Right-click the Taskbar and choose Properties from the menu.

2. Click to remove the check mark next to "Keep the Taskbar on Top of Other Windows."

3. Click OK.

Now the Taskbar will no longer appear "in front" of other windows on the screen. Indeed, it's now gone to the background, like the icons or Active Desktop things on the Desktop. Prove it:

4. Open the My Documents window.

5. Maximize the My Documents window.

See? Bye-bye Taskbar. Even pointing the mouse at the bottom of the screen doesn't help.

6. Restore the My Documents window.

7. Move the window around to see how it floats over the Taskbar.

Nifty, huh?

8. Close the My Documents window when you're done with it.

You may also return to the Taskbar and Start Menu Properties dialog box to restore or reset any options you'd like.

Other Toolbars Invading the Taskbar!

The list of silly things you can put on the Taskbar is endless, endless! There are other toolbars you can add. Some of them are handy, such as the Quick Launch bar. Some of the options are questionable, such as the ability to shove an entire web page into a toolbar on the Taskbar. As if.

 The Quick Launch bar is so dern important that it's covered all by itself in Chapter 7.

So If I See a Toolbar I Don't Want, I Can Delete It?

There are no rules about the Taskbar. Remember: you can hide the Taskbar completely if it ticks you off. So there's no reason to put up with more toolbars on the Taskbar than necessary.

To remove a toolbar, follow these steps:

1. Right-click the Taskbar to display the pop-up shortcut menu.

You must click on the Taskbar itself, not on any buttons on the Taskbar or any toolbar.

2. Choose the Toolbars submenu.

Figure 5.6 shows what you should see, as well as which items do what.

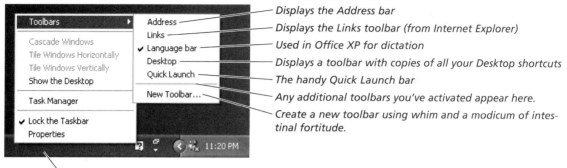

Click on a spot not occupied by any buttons.

Figure 5.6 The Toolbars submenu

3. Choose Address.

This places the Address bar on the Taskbar.

Chances are, however, that you cannot see all of the Address bar. That's because Windows tends to scrunch up the toolbars, making them look ugly and hard to use. I'll show you how to fix that problem later in the chapter. For now, here's how you would delete that item:

4. Right-click the Taskbar and choose Toolbars ➢ Address from the menu.

That removes the check mark by that item, which removes the toolbar.

You can also remove a toolbar by right-clicking on it and choosing "Close Toolbar" from the pop-up menu. If the toolbar isn't locked, then click on the toolbar's dimple area. Otherwise, you have to click on the toolbar as best you can, without right-clicking on any toolbar buttons.

 Scrunched up toolbars typically have a "show more" arrow (or chevron) you can click that displays a pop-up menu of the hidden toolbar buttons.

Some Toolbars Have Names, Others Do Not

To get a toolbar to cough up its name, right-click on the toolbar and choose "Show Name" from the pop-up menu.

It is duly noted, however, that the pop-up menu for each toolbar is subtly different. Some have the Show Name command, others do not. They may also sport commands such as Show Text or Show Title, or even have a View submenu where you can elect to see the toolbar's icons in Large or Small sizes.

Because there seems to be no logic to any of this, I simply recommend clicking on a toolbar to see what kind of goodies its pop-up menu holds.

 If you're having trouble clicking on a toolbar, then unlock the Taskbar so that you can see the toolbar's dimple area. You can right-click on the dimple area to get that specific toolbar's pop-up menu. (Remember, the dimple area is to the left of the toolbar.)

What's the Language Bar Doing Here?

If your computer has Microsoft Office XP or Word 2002 installed, then the Language bar is configured to automatically show up on the Taskbar (or often floating near the upper right corner of the screen). No problem; this is a feature of Office/Word. To remove the Language bar, right-click on it and choose "Close Toolbar" from the pop-up menu.

The "I Can Arrange Toolbars" Tutorial

Toolbars are more slippery than eels, and yet they are stackable… like…snakes. You can get used to arranging them if you practice through the following tutorial.

1. Unlock the Taskbar.

2. You need at least three toolbars to make this tutorial sing; ensure that the Quick Launch bar and Address bar are both available.

   Right-click the Taskbar and choose the Toolbars submenu. There need to be check marks by both the Quick Launch and Address items in that submenu. If not, select those items. If other items have check marks, then remove them. You need to work with just two other toolbars, and I don't have the patience to put up with readers who do not obey my specific instructions. So there.

   As it stands now (or lies now), the Taskbar has three toolbars: Quick Launch, the Taskbar itself, and the Address bar. Figure 5.7 shows how they line up on my screen.

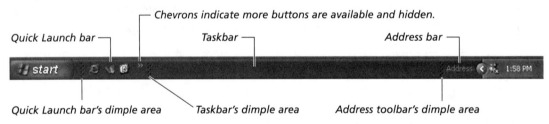

Figure 5.7 Three toolbars on the Taskbar

3. Grab the Address bar's dimple area and drag it just a wee bit to the left.

   As you drag the mouse left, the Address bar expands until you can see the text input box.

4. Drag the Address bar down a bit, below the Taskbar and Quick Launch bars.

   Be delicate! Don't jerk the mouse; just drag gently. This moves the Address bar to its own level, beneath the Quick Launch and Taskbar.

   Now the Taskbar has two levels; the Address bar is on the bottom by itself, and the Quick Launch bar and Taskbar share the top level, left to right respectively.

5. Drag the Quick Launch bar's dimple area to the right until the Quick Launch bar and Taskbar change places.

This is how you can swap two toolbars on one level; just keep dragging one over until it slides beneath and to the other side of the first toolbar.

6. Drag the Quick Launch bar down.

The Quick Launch bar is now on the bottom half of the Taskbar, along with the Address bar.

7. Drag the Quick Launch bar down even further.

Eventually the Quick Launch bar becomes its own level, below the Address bar. Now you have three toolbars, each on its own level, which Figure 5.8 illustrates.

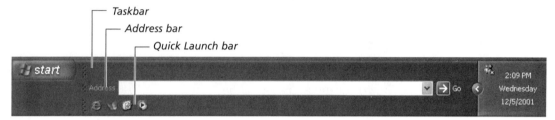

Figure 5.8 The triplex Taskbar

Suppose you prefer to have the Quick Launch bar on top:

8. Grab the Quick Launch bar's dimple area with the mouse, then carefully drag it up until the other two toolbars slide beneath it.

Drag slowly! If you drag too high, then the toolbar "floats" off the Taskbar. Just drag it back down to the Taskbar if that happens.

9. Right-click the Address bar's dimple area and choose "Close Toolbar" from the pop-up menu.

A warning dialog box appears. If you grasp the concept, then remember to put a check mark in the "In the Future Do Not Show Me this Dialog Box" dialog box.

10. Click OK to close the Confirm Toolbar Close dialog box.

11. Now arrange the Quick Launch bar and Taskbar so that the Quick Launch bar is to the left of the Taskbar on the same line.

If you just drag up a bit, then they both move to the same line.

You may notice that the Taskbar remains fat. If you don't like this, then resize the Taskbar; point the mouse at the Taskbar's inside edge and drag toward the outside edge of the screen.

There is more information on using the Quick Launch bar in Chapter 7.

 Yes, if you drag a toolbar too high then it becomes a floating palette and no longer a toolbar. You can drag the palette back to the Taskbar if you like. Also refer to Chapter 8, which covers using this technique to your advantage.

The Notification Area

The Notification Area is the mystery place where Windows keeps all its junk—random annoying warnings, teensy icons, and other miscellaneous things that don't seem to have any real function in life. Heck, one day I suppose I'll find an old pair of socks there, or those cool Opera glasses I had (and lost) when I was a kid.

Can I Get Rid of the Notification Area?

Alas, no. Figure 5.9 shows the teensiest you can get the Notification Area, which isn't all gone, but at least it's mostly not there.

Here's how to get there:

This wee li'l button is all that remains.

Figure 5.9 The almost-gone Notification Area

1. Right-click on the Show/Hide dot to the left of the Notification Area.

2. Choose Customize Notifications from the pop-up menu.

   This opens the Customize Notifications dialog box. (You can also get there by clicking the Customize button in the Taskbar and Start Menu Properties/Taskbar dialog box.)

   In Figure 5.10, you see all the dang doodle items that dwell on my computer's Notification Area. The key to disabling them is the "Behavior" column in the list.

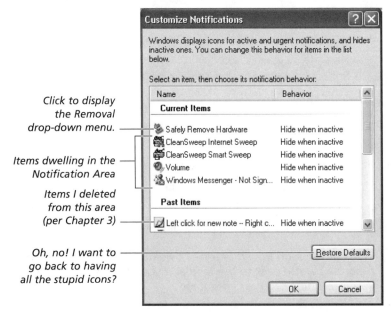

Click to display the Removal drop-down menu.

Items dwelling in the Notification Area

Items I deleted from this area (per Chapter 3)

Oh, no! I want to go back to having all the stupid icons?

Figure 5.10 The secret to a less crowded Notification Area

3. Click to select an item.

   Like, say, Windows Messenger (which appears on all new Windows XP systems).

   After clicking, you'll notice that the behavior column changes to a drop-down list:

   "Hide When Inactive" merely slides the icon out of the Notification Area for now, but it returns later when it's used.

   "Always Hide" hides the sucker no matter what (my favorite).

   "Always Show" is for those people who I suppose think that having more icons in the Notification Area makes them look busier. Whatever.

4. Choose "Always Hide" from the list.

5. Repeat this action for every stupid item in the list.

   I suppose Microsoft didn't think that we'd want to hide everything like this, otherwise there would be a "Hide Everything" button, dontcha think?

6. When you're done, click OK.

   This returns you to the Taskbar and Start Menu Properties dialog box. The bottom half deals with the Notification Area, and you can return to the Customize Notifications dialog box by clicking the Customize button. But not now.

7. Click Apply.

   There. Almost everything is gone. Everything but the time, and that goes in the next section!

 Keep an eye on that "Hide Inactive Icons" check box in the Taskbar and Start Menu Properties dialog box! If you uncheck that item, then all your icon-hiding work is undone! That removes the wee li'l button and unzips the Notification Area wide open.

What About Getting Rid of the Clock?

The clock is the last thing to go, providing that you've followed the steps in the previous section:

1. Right-click on the Show/Hide dot to the left of the Notification Area.

2. Choose Properties from the pop-up menu.

3. Remove the check mark by "Show the Clock."

4. Click OK.

   Conversely, if you wanted the clock back, you would repeat these steps to put a check mark back in the box.

6

Betcha Didn't Know All This Stuff About the Start Panel

The Start panel boggles me. It's entrancing, yet bewildering. It's remarkable how the thing is neither lovely nor elegant. It's intuitive, certainly; point the mouse and things are highlighted or pop-up. That makes sense. But why are there are icons plus text? Aren't icons supposed to be obvious enough that you don't need the text? Apparently Microsoft just can't break with its DOS past

The Start panel is, obviously, the place you go to start programs. As such, it serves its purpose well. But it's also one of the many places in Windows that can be over-customized. There are many, many options you can use to create your own personal Start menu. Icons can appear, disappear, or even appear differently. Knowing which options are most useful propels you on the road to being a more efficient computer user. That's what this chapter is all about.

Useful Options and Motivational Settings Revealed:

- Revealing ugly truths about the Start panel
- Rearranging the options
- Hiding and showing options
- Forgoing the Start panel for the old Start menu
- Taming the All Programs menu
- Rearranging and alphabetizing the menus
- Fixing, pruning and grafting menus

I Detest the Start Panel, So Why Should I Bother with It?

Agreed. The Start panel is yet another computer abomination you can truly live without. Oh, but let me not be too harsh. It's not like bad Canadian opera, or anything that would make your teeth rattle.

Unlike the Notification Area (see Chapter 5), the Start panel does have a purpose in life. It was born to be the root from which you start your programs, as well as starting other activities for adjusting and maintaining Windows. Then again, the problem with tossing in so many options (menus, icons, and so on) is that you end up with the Windows equivalent of an all-toppings pizza: The Works! It has something for everyone that pleases no one.

 Hey old fogy Windows user! It's called the Start panel now; apparently they burdened it with more options than a mere mortal menu could bear. What's next? The 3D pop-up Start pamphlet with pull-out sliders. Call it Windows OBNX for "obnoxious."

Know Your Start Panel

Figure 6.1 illustrates the typical Start panel, noting the common areas and whatnot. The terms mentioned there are used in this chapter as well as in on-screen menus. Know them. Live them. Be them.

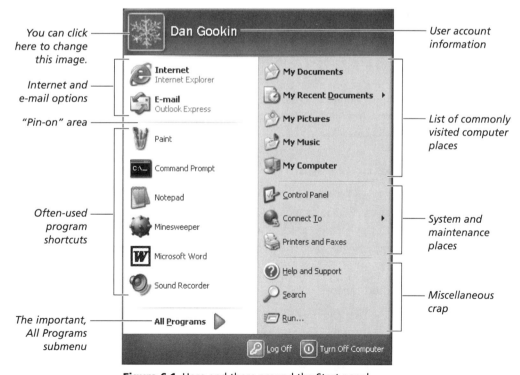

Figure 6.1 Here and there around the Start panel

79

KEYBOARD MASTER

Starting Programs

I firmly believe that it was easier to start programs in the old days of DOS than with anything Windows has to offer. Sure, you can configure Windows to start programs with a single click of the mouse—but not all your programs.

So if you want to be really quick about starting programs, you can use the Run dialog box and type in the program's name. For example, to start Word you need to run the "Winword" program. Here are the keystrokes to do that:

Win+R, WINWORD, Enter
Pressing Win+R brings up the Run dialog box. From there, you type WINWORD *and press Enter to start Microsoft Word. Here are the command line names of other Windows programs, which you can easily type from the Run dialog box:*

NOTEPAD   SOL *(Solitaire)*

WORDPAD   FREECELL

MSPAINT *(runs the Paint program)*   IEXPLORE *(Internet Explorer)*

AOL   MSIMN *(Outlook Express—go figure)*

CALC *(Calculator)*

Instructions in the sidebar "Finding the Programs to Type in the Run Dialog Box" tell you how to find the names of other programs you run, so that you can take advantage of the Win+R/"Run" dialog box and get to them faster.

And even faster still: Keep in mind that the Run dialog box sports a drop-down list of the last several things you've typed. Oftentimes you need only type the first few letters of the command, then press the down-arrow key and enter to instantly run that program. Nifty.

Can I Get Rid of the Internet and E-Mail Options?

Yes. I too have noticed that Internet and e-mail options often tend to be duplicated directly on the Desktop as well as the Quick Launch bar. Of course, eliminating these options does not fully remove the top part of the left side of the Start panel; that continues to become the "pin-on area" for just about any program you wish. (More on that in the section, "What Does 'Pin to Start Menu' Mean?" later in this chapter.)

1. Right-click the Start button.

2. Choose Properties from the pop-up menu.

The Taskbar and Start Menu Properties dialog box appears, which is just too incredibly dull for me to include an illustration of it here. (Though it's remarkable that the "Preview Window" shows most everything on the Start panel clearly except for the user's name, which appears blurry. If I squint hard enough, however, I can kind of make out "Bill Gates," but that may just wishful thinking on my part.)

3. Click the Customize button by Start menu.

This is one of several places in Windows XP where they still call it the Start menu, though elsewhere it's referred to as the Start panel. The Customize Start Menu (again with the Start menu) dialog box appears, as illustrated in Figure 6.2. (The next several sections also have you working in this dialog box.)

4. Remove the check marks by "Internet" and "E-mail."

5. Click OK.

6. Click OK.

7. Pop-up the Start panel.

Hmmm. The Internet and E-mail options are gone, but the recently used programs list remains—and on my screen at least, it's bigger! Egads! But you can get rid of that list as well, as covered in the next section.

 This book assumes that the Internet and E-mail options are present in the pin-on area in the Start Panel. I do prefer having them there, and they will show up that way in the various illustrations of the Start Panel.

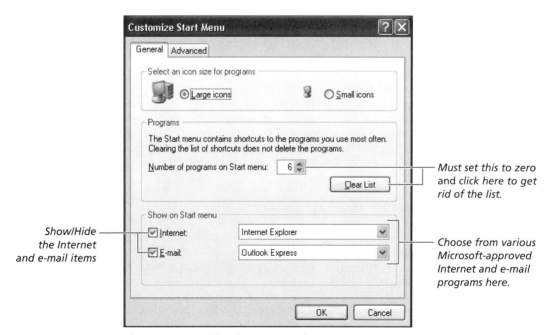

Figure 6.2 Tweaking the Start panel, Part A

Finding the Programs to Type in the Run Dialog Box

This is a sidebar to the Keyboard Master sidebar—a sidebar to a sidebar, because you're probably itching to find out how to know what command name to type for which program. It's actually quite easy, but it takes some training:

First, find a shortcut icon to the program you want to run. Shortcut icons live on the Desktop, the Quick Launch bar, or can be plentifully found on the All Programs menu in the Start Panel.

Second, right-click the icon and choose Properties from the pop-up menu. This displays the shortcut icon's Properties dialog box, which lists information about the original program, the "Target."

Third, look at the text box by "Target" in the Properties dialog box. The program's name is the last bit of text after the last backslash. For example:

```
C:\Program Files\Messenger\msmsgs.exe
```

The last part of that text is MSMSGS.EXE, *which is the name of the Windows Messenger program. You need to type in only the first part— not the ".exe". So, to start the Windows Messenger program from the Run dialog box, type* MSMSGS.

Can I Do Away with the Recent List of Program Shortcuts?

Certainly, the list of recently used programs can either be gotten rid of entirely, or reduced in number if you like. Note that this does not completely remove the left side of the Start panel; it just leaves it blank.

 Some people view the listing of recently used programs as a security risk. For example, you don't want people to know that you're using a certain encryption tool or special e-mail sending program. Even so, keep in mind that everyone using the computer in Windows XP should have their own, password-protected account, which makes such concerns less essential. However, if you feel like yanking the recently used program list, then go ahead.

1. Right-click the Start button.

2. Choose Properties from the pop-up menu.

You can also right-click the Start panel itself and choose the only item that appears in that pop-up menu, Properties. (Ensure that you're clicking on a blank part of the Start panel, not on any menu items or icons.)

3. Click the Customize button by Start menu.

4. Enter 0 (zero) for the "Number of Programs on the Start Menu."

And, most importantly:

5. Click the Clear List button.

That removes the items already on the list. Setting the "Number of Programs..." value to zero prevents any further items from being added.

6. Click OK.

7. Click OK.

8. Pop-up the Start menu.

And you'll see that the list is empty. In fact, if you've also removed the Internet items, then the only thing remaining on the left side of the Start panel is the All Programs menu button.

What Does "Pin to Start Menu" Mean?

The top part of the Start panel's left side is the Pin-on area. It can contain two Internet items, but also whatever other program shortcuts you want. Unlike the list of recently used programs, items pinned to the Start menu do not go away (well, unless you un-pin them).

You can pin any program to the Start panel. It must be a program, not a folder or a regular file. Simply right-click on the program's icon (or a shortcut icon) and choose "Pin to Start Menu" from the pop-up menu (see Figure 6.3).

The programs appear at the top of the Start panel, just beneath the Internet program items.

You can pin as many programs as you like to the Start panel. I do recommend, however, you keep the number small; the more items you pin to the Start panel, the taller it gets. Also, the idea here is convenience. Only pin items you use often. On my system, I pinned Adobe GoLive, my web page publishing program, to the Start menu. That way it's handy with my other Internet programs.

Figure 6.3 Pinning a program to the Start menu

To un-pin an item, pop up the Start panel and right-click a pinned item. Choose "Unpin from Start Menu" from the pop-up menu, and it's gone.

 A good way to find your programs is to use the All Programs menu; surf through the menu, then right-click any menu item you want pinned to the main Start panel. Choose "Pin to Start Menu" from the pop-up menu, and a copy of the program's shortcut is placed directly on the Start panel.

Isn't the Link to My Recent Documents a Security Risk?

The list of recently opened documents is only a security risk if your Windows XP account isn't password-protected. If so, then anyone can pop up the Start panel and snoop around to see which programs you've last been editing or viewing.

The My Recent Documents submenu lists the last 15 documents you've opened in Windows. (It does not list documents opened by some older Windows or DOS programs—presuming you got such programs to work on Windows XP in the first place!)

Windows comes pre-configured to display the list, which I personally find quite handy. The list lets me get back and edit some of the stuff I've been working on recently without having to wade through folders or hunt for documents in an Open dialog box. But if you don't feel you need such an option, or feel it might blemish your reputation, then you can pull that menu off of the Start panel:

1. Right-click the Start button.

2. Choose Properties from the pop-up menu.

3. Click the Customize button by the Start menu option.

4. Click the Advanced tab.

Ah, the more interesting half of the Customize Start Menu dialog box, which Figure 6.4 illustrates for your benefit.

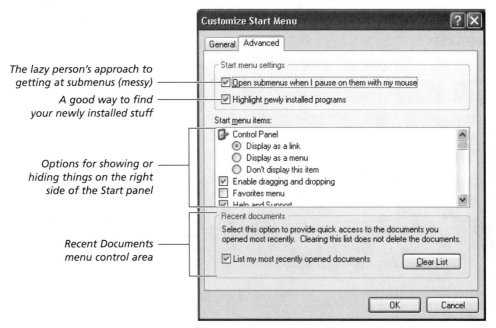

Figure 6.4 Tweaking the Start panel, part B

5. Remove the check mark by "List My Most Recently Opened Documents."

Likewise, you could merely click the Clear List button, which doesn't remove the list but may remove some compromising documents from the list. (Actually, it removes all documents from the list, compromising or not.)

6. Click OK twice to get out of Dialog Box Hell, then check the Start panel again to assure that the Recent Documents list is gone, gone, gone.

KEYBOARD MASTER

Quickly Get to the Recent Documents Submenu

If you're like me and you use the Recent Documents submenu, then take advantage of the following keyboard accelerators to get there quickly:

Win, D
Press the Win key to pop up the Start menu, the press the D key to display the My Recent Documents list. You can then scroll through the list, which displays your most recently accessed documents alphabetically.

Remember that's Win and then D, not Win+D, which displays the Desktop.

Which Is More Useful, a Link or a Menu?

Windows lets you display up to six items on the right side of the Start panel, either as links, as menus, or not at all. The six items can also be accessed from other parts of Windows, but it's often useful to have their links or menus on the Start panel. Here's the list.

- Control Panel
- My Computer
- My Documents
- My Music
- My Pictures
- Network Connections

Displaying the item as a link means that the items name and icon (why both I'll never know) are displayed on the right side of the Start panel; click the item and a window opens up displaying the relevant bits.

Display the item as a menu means that its relevant bits (the contents of the item's folder) are displayed as a submenu from which you can choose various things.

I feel that the menu option works only for three of these items: Control Panel, Network Connections, and System Administrative Tools. I have each of these configured to display as a menu on my personal Start panel.

I also have the My Computer and My Documents icons display as links. The rest (My Music and My Pictures), I elect not to display at all.

You make these choices from the scrolling list found in the Customize Start Menu dialog box ➤ Advanced tab (refer back to Figure 6.4).

Note that there are other on/off display items to be found in that scrolling list as well. They are:

- Favorites Menu
- Printers and Faxes
- Help and Support
- Run command
- My Network Places
- Search

You can just turn these options on or off. For example, if you'd rather be a power user and press Win+R to get at the Run command, then you don't need to junk up the Start Panel with the Run command. Likewise, the Printers and Faxes folder can be reached from the Control Panel. So on my system I have Help and Support and My Network Places. The rest of the commands I can get to from other places.

Also, there are Administrative Tools I use from time to time, so I have that item displayed as a menu both on the Start panel as well as in the All Programs submenu.

Finally—as if this isn't all confusing enough already—there are two options scattered through the scrolling list like breadcrumbs on the way to the evil witch's house:

- Enable Dragging and Dropping
- Scroll Programs

Figure 6.5 My recommended options for the Start panel

You want "Enable Dragging and Dropping" on if you plan on using the mouse to rearrange your All Programs menu items on the fly. If not, or if you find that you accidentally drag items off of submenus hither, thither, and yon, then do yourself a favor and disable this item!

You want the Scroll Programs option off all the time. If you turn it on, then the All Programs menus will scroll up or down when they get taller than the screen. This is perhaps the most annoying thing that Windows can do.

Figure 6.5 shows how a Start panel configured using my recommendations would look.

Why Are Some Programs on the All Programs Menu Highlighted?

Whenever you install new software, Windows lets you know where it's been hidden on the All Programs menu by highlighting the new program(s) and submenus. On my screen, they appear with an orangish tint. This is to help you locate your new stuff—an entirely welcome thing.

If you notice that your new programs do not highlight themselves on the All Programs menu, then take these steps to change that:

1. Right-click the Start button.

2. Choose Properties from the pop-up menu.

3. Click the Customize button by Start menu.

4. Click the Advanced tab.

5. Put a check mark by "Highlight Newly Installed Programs."
   And there you have it.

How about Sending the Start Panel to Hell and Using the Good Old Start Menu from My Favorite, Windows 98?

There is absolutely nothing wrong with "going retro." If that's what you're more comfortable with, then bless you 10,000 times! Keep in mind, however, that this book as well as other material on Windows XP, assumes that you're using the new Start panel instead of the old Start menu:

1. Right-click the Start button.

2. Choose Properties from the pop-up menu.

3. Click "Classic Start Menu."

4. Click OK.

5. Pop-up the Start menu.
   It looks just like it used to in other versions of Windows, as show in Figure 6.6.

To make modifications to the retro Start menu, use the Customize button by that option in the Taskbar and Start Menu Properties dialog box ➤ Start Menu tab. I'll assume that you're desperate enough to figure out those options on your own.

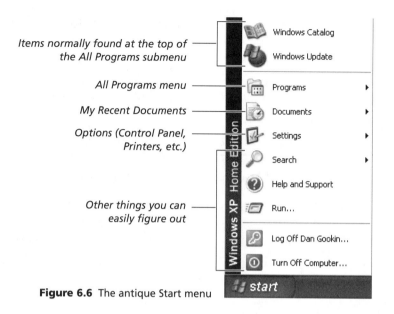

Figure 6.6 The antique Start menu

The All Programs Menu Just Begs to Be Fixed

My Windows philosophy is that every program you can run on your computer should have a menu item somewhere on the All Programs menu. That way you can run any old program without having to hunt for it, which saves time. This philosophy is reinforced by most installation programs, which automatically create menus and shortcut icons for their installed applications. And so the world can continue spinning its merry dance.

When you choose the All Programs menu from the Start panel, a huge pop-up menu appears. If you have a typical PC, you'll see dozens of submenus plus menu items. Ugly!

> ## You Must Know This: Things on the All Programs Menu Are Not What They Seem
>
> *Remember from Chapter 5 that the submenus you see on the All Programs menu are really folders stored elsewhere on the hard drive. The menu items themselves are actually short-cut icons held in the special folders.*
>
> *There are several groups of All Programs folders that merge to create the list you see on your screen. One is the common All Users menu, another is a specific menu for your own account. Review Chapter 5 for more information on how to find these folders.*

I don't recommend using the All Programs menu for the stuff you start every day. No, there are better, quicker options. First, you have the Quick Launch bar, then there are shortcuts you can paste on the Desktop, items you can pin on the Start panel, the recently started programs list on the Start panel, and there's even the Run dialog box. But the All Programs menu? It's a mess! I only use it for things I don't want to hunt for using the Search command.

The All Programs Menu Scrolls About Wildly and Makes Me Want to Puke!

I hate the scrolling menu; when it's too tall to display all at once on the screen, Windows puts little "up" or "down" arrows at the top or bottom of the menu, letting you scroll the turkey up or down. Hey! If I want a thrill ride I'll visit an amusement park.

1. Right-click the Start menu and choose Properties from the pop-up menu.

2. Click the Customize button.

3. Click the Advanced tab.

4. Scroll through the list of Start menu items and remove the check mark by "Scroll Programs."

5. Click OK twice, and you're back out of hell.

Do I Need All These Dumb Folders?

No.

Can I Rearrange Things on the Menus?

Yes, you can do this with the mouse. But be careful! If you screw up, you get in worse trouble than just having sloppy menus.

After displaying the All Progams menu, you can move any visible menu item around as follows:

1. Point the mouse at the item to move.

It can be a submenu or a menu item.

2. Drag the item to a new location.

Press and hold the mouse button down for a few moments before you start to drag. This ensures that you really have a hold of the item.

As you drag the item, an insertion bar appears, indicating the exact position where the item will be inserted or moved to (refer to Figure 6.7).

3. Release the mouse button to move the item.

And there it is in a new spot.

I recommend this technique for rearranging any All Programs menu. However, if you need to move items between submenus or remove submenus, it's best not to use the mouse; the mouse can get slippery when moving between menus and it's easy to lose your grip and drop something where it's not supposed to go. See the section "How Can I Merge Folders or Rearrange Them in a More Orderly Manner?" later in this chapter for another menu rearranging technique that isn't as sloppy as using the mouse.

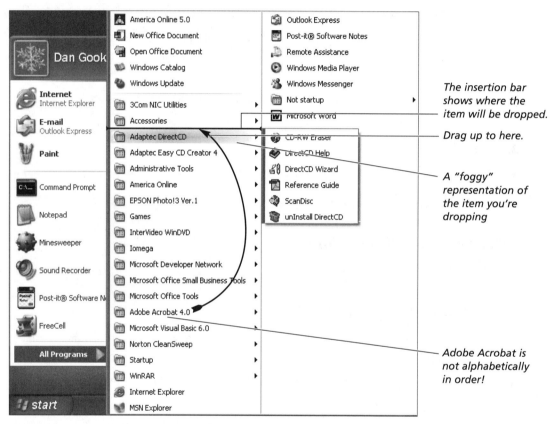

Figure 6.7 Dragging around on the All Programs menu

It Seems Rather Tedious to Use the Mouse to Rearrange the Items Alphabetically

Yes, it does. Using the mouse is good for moving new items (which Windows places at the end of the menu for some reason) around the menu. But there is a shortcut: Right-click on any item in the menu. Then choose "Sort by Name" from the pop-up menu. Thwoop! All the items are alphabetized, folders first.

I Cant' Move the Menu Items with the Mouse! They're Stuck!

You need to enable drag and dropping on the menu. Heed these steps:

1. Right-click the Start button and choose Properties from the shortcut menu.

2. Click the Customize button.

3. Click the Advanced tab in the Customize Start Menu dialog box.

4. Scroll through the list of Start menu items and put a check mark by "Enable Dragging and Dropping."

5. Click OK twice and the mouse is free to wreck havoc on the All Programs menu.

 You can also drag and drop items from the Start panel itself, such as dragging a recently used program up to the pin-on area for long-term keeping.

I Used the Mouse to Drag Items Around in the All Programs Menu and Now I'm Really Screwed!

First, try to move the items back using the mouse; just drag and drop.

Second, if you accidentally dragged an item to the Desktop, immediately press the Ctrl+Z (undo) key command. That brings it right back. (If not, then you can drag the item from the Desktop to the Start button, then use the mouse to drag it through the menus back to where it belongs.)

Third, you can follow my advice in the next section and use a Windows Explorer window for editing the Start menu.

Finally, if you tire of this happening, you can switch off drag-and-drop editing on the All Programs menu: follow the instructions in the previous section, but remove the check mark by "Enable Dragging and Dropping."

How Can I Merge Folders or Rearrange Them in a More Orderly Manner?

If you really need to do major pruning, then I recommend opening up the All Programs folder and working with the menus and menu items as folders and shortcut icons in a Windows Explorer window.

Suppose that every utility you installed on your computer creates its own submenu off the main All Programs menu. For example, back in Figure 6.7, you see menus for 3Com NIC Utilities, Iomega, Norton CleanSweep, and WinRAR, all of which are utilities. What a mess! It's better just to have one main Utility menu with each of the other utilities placed inside that menu. That seems more logical.

Here is how I cleaned up those items and placed them into a general Utilities menu:

1. Right-click on the Start button and choose "Open All Users."

2. Open the Programs folder.

3. Choose File ➤ New ➤ Folder to create a new folder (menu).

4. Rename the folder to Utilities.

   You can rename the folder by typing its new name right after it's created. Otherwise, select the folder and press the F2 key to rename it.

5. Drag the other utility folders into the new Utilities folder.

   On my screen, I drag 3Com NIC Utilities, Iomega, Norton CleanSweep and WinRAR.

 If you have trouble seeing all the folders for your drag-and-drop activities, then choose View ➤ Icons from the menu.

You can continue to create and organize folders like this. If you have a swath of Games folders, move them all into the one Games folder that Windows has already placed on the All Programs menu.

If you have scads of graphics programs, then create a general Graphics menu (folder) then cut and paste your graphics applications into it.

 If there are any programs missing from the folder, then they might be specific to your account. Repeat these steps, but choose "Open" in Step 1, instead of "Open All Users."

When you're done, close the Programs window. Then pop-up the Start panel to look at your newer, leaner menu. Figure 6.8 shows the results of my pruning and grafting to the menu that was originally shown in Figure 6.7.

Can I Delete Programs or Menus?

Certainly. This can be done directly with the mouse: Just pop up the Start panel, choose All Programs, then right-click any unwanted submenu or menu item. Choose "Delete" from the pop-up menu, and that item is gone.

(Well, actually it's moved to the Recycle Bin, so it can be restored if you like.)

Figure 6.8 A more organized, sane, even nifty All Programs menu

KEYBOARD MASTER

Pruning and Grafting Keys

Alt+F, W, F
Creates a new folder (menu)

F2
Renames selected folder

Ctrl+X
Prunes (cut) selected folders

Ctrl+V
Grafts (paste) selected folders
(Of course, I feel that dragging and dropping is far more efficient.)

7 Learn About the Quick Launch Bar So You Look Better Than Your Co-Workers Who Are Clueless

Oh how often the Quick Launch bar sits avoided or unused! Or sometimes people become annoyed with it, gobbling up space on the Taskbar and seeming to grab vital territory from those nifty buttons. Alas, people are really missing out on the power and the handiness of the Quick Launch bar, something that I hope this chapter instills in you.

Power Revealed and Hope Instilled:

- Ruminating on the Quick Launch bar
- Eliminating unwanted icons
- Adding useful icons to the Quick Launch bar
- Customizing the Quick Launch bar

Why Do I Need the Quick Launch Bar?

No one needs the Quick Launch bar. In fact, many astute users turn it off. But that's sad, because the Quick Launch bar can really help you get into those programs you use most often. Having it sitting there on the Taskbar can be a tremendous boon to your productivity.

My philosophy on the subject works like this: On the Quick Launch bar I put the five or six programs I use the most, for example, Word, Internet Explorer, Outlook Express, the Command Prompt, and maybe a game. That's it! A nice, short list. That way I can start those programs with a single click any time. (I always keep the Taskbar visible.)

I put other program shortcuts that don't make the Quick Launch cut on the Desktop (Chapter 3), along with shortcuts to my work folders and projects. Everything else is located on the All Programs menu. So it breaks down like this:

 Quick Launch bar for your most used programs

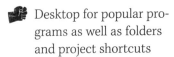 Desktop for popular programs as well as folders and project shortcuts

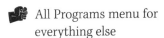 All Programs menu for everything else

Of course, you can also pin programs to the top of the Start panel (see Chapter 6), but nothing is quite as handy as having the programs on the Quick Launch bar.

NERD'S CORNER

Cocktail Party Trivia, Part I

JOHN: Of course I use the Quick Launch bar. You don't see me slogging along like Mervin over there, fumbling with his mouse.

EVERYONE: Ha-ha!

PHIL: But, say, the Quick Launch bar has been around a long time, John. You think that people would be familiar with it enough to partake of its goodness.

JOHN: That's true, Phil. But did you know that the Quick Launch bar wasn't a part of the original Windows 95?

EVERYONE: Say it isn't so!

JOHN: True. Back in Windows 95, the Taskbar was just...well, a taskbar!

PHIL: Then the Quick Launch bar was added with Windows 98. (He sips some of his bourbon.)

JOHN: That's not entirely correct, Phil. (Phil gags.) While Windows 98 did launch what I jokingly call "Taskbar craziness," it was really Internet Explorer 5 that brought the Quick Launch bar to Windows. You see, anyone using Windows 95 who upgraded his or her copy of Internet Explorer, also got the Quick Launch bar.

PHIL: Oooo. So then I was wrong about that.

JOHN: You certainly were, Phil. (Smiles.)

EVERYONE: Ha-ha!

Summoning the Quick Launch Bar

To show the Quick Launch bar (if it's not already visible), right-click on the Taskbar and choose Toolbars ➤ Quick Launch from the menu. The Quick Launch bar typically shows up on the left edge of the Taskbar, right next to the Start button, as shown in Figure 7.1.

If you're having trouble right-clicking on the Taskbar, try these steps:

1. Right-click on the Start button and choose Properties.

2. In the Taskbar and Start Menu Properties dialog box, click on the Taskbar tab.

3. Put a check mark by "Show Quick Launch."

4. Click OK.

It helps if you unlock the Taskbar when working with the Quick Launch bar. After setting up the Quick Launch bar in this chapter, feel free to relock the Taskbar. (See Chapter 5 for Taskbar locking instructions.)

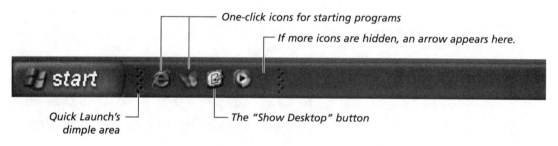

One-click icons for starting programs

If more icons are hidden, an arrow appears here.

Quick Launch's dimple area

The "Show Desktop" button

Figure 7.1 The Quick Launch bar (before messing with it)

Do I Really Need the Stupid Icons Microsoft Put on the Quick Launch Bar?

No. I find the icons Microsoft puts on the Quick Launch bar to be redundant. For example, the Internet Explorer icon is not only on the Quick Launch bar, it's at the top of the Start panel plus it's on the Desktop. You would think that the big blue "E" is really a bolt holding everything down on your monitor!

Ditto for the Media Player icon. In fact, Media Player is so dutiful about popping up, that I've never once had to start it by myself. Ugh.

I've no idea which icons your computer manufacturer may have preset on your Quick Launch bar. On the various versions of Windows XP I have there are typically three icons already there:

Internet Explorer

Show Desktop

Media Player

One of my systems also has the MSN Explorer. Whatever. My point is that you didn't put those icons there, so if you don't need them, delete them.

To remove an icon from the Quick Launch bar, right-click it and choose "Delete" from the pop-up menu.

Don't fret! You're merely deleting a shortcut, which is shoveled off into the Recycle Bin anyway, so you can restore it later if you like. And you don't have to delete things you want to keep; by all means, if you feel you'll use that big blue "E" down there, then keep it!

(And if you don't know the Win+D keyboard shortcut, then you can keep the Show Desktop icon; otherwise it can go as well.)

So with the preset icons all gone, you can start stacking the Quick Launch bar with your own useful stuff.

So Tell Me What I Do Need on the Quick Launch Bar?

Place on the Quick Launch bar any program you use regularly, anything you start every day. After all, you bought your computer to do something. Whatever that something is, that icon (or those icons) should be on the Quick Launch bar.

Try to limit the number of icons to five or six. Any more and then you're most likely stacking the Quick Launch bar with programs you don't use every day. (Unless you're nuts, in which case, by all means!)

The best way to add an icon to the Quick Launch bar is to drag and drop it. Like any mouse operation, this can be tricky. So I've created the following steps to try and make it easy.

Because the All Programs menu is a repository for all programs on your computer, it's best if you copy your program icons from there to the Quick Launch bar. Here's an effective way to do that:

1. Find the program you want to copy.

    For example, Microsoft Word. On my computer I can find Word right there on the main All Programs menu.

2. Right-click the desired program.

3. Choose Send To ➤ Desktop (Create Shortcut).

4. Press Esc a few times to hide the All Programs menu and Start panel.

    And there, on the Desktop, you'll see your program's shortcut icon.

5. Drag and drop the shortcut icon down to the Quick Launch bar.

    When you find the "sweet spot," a large I-beam insertion pointer appears on the Quick Launch bar. That's your signal to release the mouse button.

Keep adding programs that you use every day.

What Are Those Dorky Arrows on the Left Edge of the Quick Launch Bar?

If the Quick Launch bar contains more icons than it can show, you'll now see a little chevron pointing east, telling you that there are more icons to display; resize the Taskbar so that you can see all of the Quick Launch bar. Figure 7.2 illustrates this.

To avoid this, first ensure that you're not stacking the Quick Launch bar up with more than half a dozen buttons. Ugh.

Second, resize the Taskbar (see Figure 7.2) so that all the buttons can be shown. (Also see Chapter 5 for Taskbar rearrangement information.) Make sure that the Taskbar is unlocked, or you won't be able to resize anything!

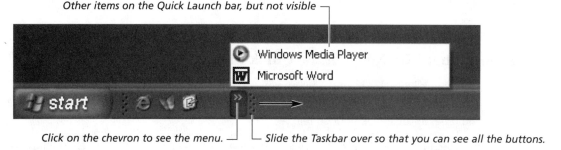

Other items on the Quick Launch bar, but not visible

Click on the chevron to see the menu. — Slide the Taskbar over so that you can see all the buttons.

Figure 7.2 The annoying chevron (You must get rid of it!)

Those Icons Are Soooo Tiny!

I agree. I like big icons myself, so I switch my Quick Launch bar over to Large Icon view: Right-click the Quick Launch bar and choose View ➢ Large Icons from the menu. (Right-click on the Quick Launch bar's dimple area.)

Before

After

Figure 7.3 Before and after big icons on the Quick Launch bar

Immediately you'll notice bigger icons. Plus the Taskbar will be resized to fit the larger icons. Plus you'll probably have to rearrange the Taskbar to see all the icons on the Quick Launch bar. Figure 7.3 shows the before and after shots.

(And, likewise, if you detest the larger icons, then just choose View ➢ Small Icons from the menu.)

Where Did All That Junky Text Come From?

If you notice that your beautiful Quick Launch bar has suddenly become burdened with unnecessary text, don't set fire to the monitor! Instead, right-click the Quick Launch bar's dimple area and ensure that there are no check marks by the "Show Title" and "Show Text" items.

When those items are checked, the Quick Launch bar feels obligated to tell you about each of the icons, which I find uncalled-for.

Anything Else Interesting or Useful That You Can Tell Me About Quick Launch?

Oh secret of secrets! The Quick Launch bar, like other types of toolbars you can have on the Taskbar, is really a secret folder out on your computer's hard drive. That's where the shortcuts you see on the Quick Launch bar are really stored.

To see this folder, right-click the Quick Launch bar's dimple area and choose "Open Folder" from the pop-up menu. You'll see a folder window display, showing the shortcut icons you can find on the Quick Launch bar.

Take a look at the folder location using the Address bar. See how the folder is customized for each user? On my screen the pathname reads:

```
C:\Documents and Settings\Dan Gookin\Application Data\Microsoft\
Internet Explorer\Quick Launch
```

I bring this up because it's possible to "save" icons in the Quick Launch bar and then easily restore them later. For example, you can save the Show Desktop icon (or any icon) as follows:

1. Click the Show Desktop icon to select it.

Or click whichever icon you want to temporarily remove from the Quick Launch bar.

2. Press Ctrl+X.

The Cut command.

3. Press the Backspace key.

Backspace is the equivalent of the "Go Up" button in a folder window.

You're now in the Internet Explorer folder, where certain options are kept (nothing worth fussing over).

4. Press Ctrl+V to paste.

Now the Show Desktop icon has been disabled, removed from the Quick Launch bar. You can even see this down at the bottom of your screen. It's gone!

But this is only an exercise. You can easily restore the icon at this point:

5. Press Ctrl+Z.

The Undo command restores the icon (though it may not show up on the Quick Launch bar until you log in again).

You can use this technique to temporarily disable some of the items you put on the Quick Launch bar. To get them back, just follow Steps 1 and 3 above to get to the Internet Explorer folder, then cut and paste the icon back to the Quick Launch folder.

Show Desktop Mystery Icon

The Show Desktop icon on the Quick Launch bar is not a program. No, it's actually an option in Windows Explorer—the program that displays the Desktop on the screen.

The actual file itself is a plain text file. Here are its contents:

```
[shell]
Command=2
IconFile=explorer.exe,3
[Taskbar]
Command=ToggleDesktop
```

Boring. Let me just say that it does the same thing as pressing the Win+D key combination. Anyway, the file is saved to disk as SHOW DESKTOP.SCF (not SHOW DESKTOP.TXT). The dot-SCF part of the filename tells Windows that it's a Windows Explorer Command and not just a dumb text file.

By the way, don't worry about recreating this file should you lose it or delete it. There is a spare copy kept in the C:\Windows\System folder. You can just copy that back over to your Quick Launch folder, and you'll be fine.

8

Other Creative and Useful

(But Not Too Bizarre) Ways to

Start your Stuff

I love those tension-filled scenes in movies when they're about to launch a rocket. It could be a missile launched in a war movie or a spaceship blasting off into the deep part of the sky, but no matter what the projectile is or where it's headed, there is that scene with the guy holding his finger over the button. When the countdown reaches zero, he pushes the button and the rocket rides a pillar of flame up into some future plot twist.

Of course, we always assume that there is only one button. That helps build the dramatic tension. If there were three buttons, then it wouldn't be as exciting. Suppose one guy is on one button—the Big Red Button. Then there is another guy somewhere else who has a handy throw switch. Then there is a guy in an office building who just has to pick up the telephone and say "boom" and the rocket blasts off. That wouldn't be as exciting, just like starting a program in Windows isn't that exciting.

Windows just gives you too many options for starting your stuff. Way too many. There's the Start button, which could be dramatic, but then you have the Recent Programs list, the Pin-on menu, and the All Programs menu. Then there's the Run dialog box, the Desktop, even the Taskbar. It makes starting things more convenient, but it utterly wrecks the dramatic tension.

Conveniences Revealed and Dramatic Tensions Resolved:

- Finding programs not on the Start panel
- Creating Desktop shortcut items
- Putting useful things into the Send To menu
- Building a custom toolbar
- Floating a palette of commands

The Starting a Program Philosophy

To review, here is how I feel you can best use the tools Windows provides for starting programs:

- Put the programs you use all the time on the Quick Launch bar (five or six icons max).

- Put other programs or project folders on the Desktop as shortcuts.

- Access all other programs from the All Programs menu, which should list every available program and application on your computer.

You can also take advantage of the "Pin-on" area in the Start panel for certain applications, though I find the Quick Launch bar is a better alternative in most cases.

The list of recent programs is also a handy place to look for things to start. If you're like most computer users, then you probably use your applications in a cyclical manner: you work for a few days on a single project so you return to the same application for a spell. For example, it may be the end of the year and you're using TurboTax more often than normal. It's at those times when the recently used program list on the Start panel comes in handy.

How Can I Find Programs That Are Not on the All Programs Menu?

The All Programs menu lists all the applications that were installed on your computer, but not all of the programs on your hard drive. That's because many of the programs are specific tools Windows itself uses. Some of them may be command-line utilities. And others may be troubleshooting or support programs. Oh, what the heck, why not find them all?

1. Press Win+F to bring up a Search window.

There is no need to connect to the Internet for this activity, so if you're prompted to go online, just click Cancel or close those dialog boxes.

 The Search window is one part of Windows that's been getting progressively worse with each release. In a feeble attempt to make searching more friendly, Windows XP's rendition of the Search window utterly fails. Come on! I want the advanced options staring at me in the face. I know what I'm looking for and I don't need to pussyfoot around with "files and documents" or "paintings and dances" or whatever the stupid options are. Give me power! Give me advanced user controls! But enough ranting...

2. Choose "All Files and Folders."

3. Choose Drive C only.

There's no point in searching other hard drives; most of the hidden stuff will be on your main hard drive.

4. Choose "More Advanced Options."

5. Choose "Application" from the "Type of File" drop-down list.

6. Put a check by "Search System Folders."

(You want to look everywhere.)

7. Click the Search button.

In a few tense moments the window fills with a list of all the program files on your computer. Figure 8.1 shows the files found on my computer. You're going to find a lot of files on your computer as well.

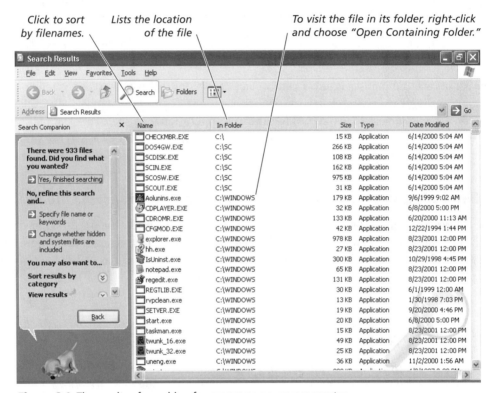

Figure 8.1 The results of searching for programs on your computer

Most of the files are, as I've said, support files. Anything truly worthy exists on the All Programs menu. You may find a few that do not, however. Or, perhaps you're searching for one program in particular and want to add it to the All Programs menu now. For example, suppose you want to add the old Windows 3.1 Program Manager (an antique, but still around) to the All Programs menu. Here's how you would go about that:

8. Scroll through the list of found programs until you find PROGMAN.EXE.

To find this program more quickly, click on the Name header in the Search Results window, then type a P. That scrolls you right away to all the programs that start with P. From there, you can search for PROGMAN.EXE more quickly.

9. Right-click the `PROGMAN.EXE` file.

10. Choose Send To ➤ Desktop (Create Shortcut).

Now there is a shortcut to the program on the Desktop, which may be what you want. In this case, however, you want the shortcut on the All Programs menu. You're almost there!

11. Close the Search Results window.

Look for the icon on the Desktop. If it's named "Shortcut to `PROGMAN.EXE`," then feel free to rename the icon: Select it, then press F2 and type "`Program Manager`" as the new name.

12. Right-click the icon and choose Cut from the shortcut menu.

Snip!

13. Right-click the Start button and choose Open.

Or, if you want to add the Registry Editor command to everyone's All Programs menu, then choose "Open All Users" instead.

14. Open the Programs folder.

15. Open the Accessories folder.

16. Open the System Tools folder.

If you don't see the System Tools folder, then close the window and start over in Step 13 by choosing "Open All Users" instead.

17. Choose Edit ➤ Paste.

Now your new icon has been added to the menu.

18. Close the System Tools window.

Time to test it to see if it worked:

19. Pop up the Start panel.

20. Choose All Programs ➤ Accessories ➤ System Tools.

Check to see if the Registry Editor is there, and it is. You're done!

KEYBOARD MASTER

Searching for Files

Like starting a program in Windows, there are many ways to bring up a Search window. The quickest one I use is this:

Win+F

Yes, it's the F key and not S. That's the only thing you need to remember; think "Find" and not "Search."

If the Quick Launch Bar Is So Handy, Why Bother Pinning Any Programs to the Start Panel?

I view the pin-on thing as temporary myself. Unlike the Quick Launch bar, which is something I don't regularly like to edit, the pin-on part of the Start panel seems to be something I can pin programs to, then un-pin them later when they may not be on my normal plate of applications.

For example, to add a program to the Quick Launch bar, you have to find the program, create its shortcut, and then drag the shortcut to the Quick Launch bar. But to pin something to the Start panel, you right-click it and choose "Pin to Start Menu." Simple.

To unpin, you right-click a pinned icon and choose "Unpin" from the menu. Again, it's simple.

 Also see Chapter 7 for more information on the Quick Launch bar, as well as Chapter 6 for information on pinning items to the Start panel.

And Some Folks Prefer to Use the Desktop

Instead of the Start Panel

The Desktop is one heck of a playground. It's also a handy place on which to hang shortcuts to your favorite programs or folders. I do this all the time, despite the redundancy of having those same items available elsewhere. Sometimes it's just quicker to get to a location from the Desktop, rather than having to fish for it from some other location.

Getting Stuff on the Desktop Is Easy, Providing That You Know This Trick

The easiest way to get something onto the Desktop is to right-click it and choose Send To ➤ Desktop (Create Shortcut) from the pop-up menu (Figure 8.2). You can right-click folders, icons, programs in the All Programs menu, just about anything. That gets you the shortcut icon pasted to the Desktop in no time flat. In fact, it's so convenient I won't even waste your time showing you the other ways of creating shortcut icons on the Desktop.

Figure 8.2 The handy Send To ➤ Desktop (Create Shortcut) menu command

Oh, Come On! Show Me a Time-Wasting Method of Getting My Files to Be Shortcut Icons on the Desktop!

No.

How Do I Stick a Shortcut to a Disk Drive on the Desktop?

Oh, you *would* have to ask that! So now I suppose I'll *have* to show you the time-wasting method:

1. Locate the item you want to place on the Desktop as a shortcut.

Suppose it's a disk drive. Disk drive shortcuts are nice to have on the Desktop. Open the My Computer window to see your computer's selection of disk drives.

2. Right-click the disk drive icon you want to copy—CD-ROM, DVD, floppy, or Zip drive—whatever you feel is most handy.

3. Choose Copy from the Shortcut menu.

And, so far, this is how you would create a shortcut for any icon as opposed to using Send To ➤ Desktop (Create Shortcut); you start by copying the icon.

4. Close the (My Computer or whatever) window from which you copied the icon.

5. Right-click the Desktop and choose "Paste Shortcut" from the menu.

And there is your Desktop shortcut.

What If I Need to Create Desktop Shortcut Icons for All the Computer's Users?

When you paste a shortcut icon on the Desktop, you paste it only in your personal account's Desktop. If others use the same computer, they will not see the new shortcut you created—unless you place the shortcut in the All Users Desktop folder instead of the one for your personal account.

Assume that you've already pasted the shortcut to the Desktop. If so, then this is one way you can create the same shortcut for all the accounts on your computer:

1. Right-click the Shortcut icon.

2. Choose Cut from the pop-up menu.

The icon has been cut from your own personal Desktop. Now you need to repaste it into the All Users\Desktop. Here's a shortcut for getting there:

3. Right-click the Start button.

4. Choose "Open All Users."

This displays the Start panel's menu for all the accounts on your system, so you're close to where you want to end up, but not quite there yet!

5. Click the Up button on the toolbar.

Now you're in the All Users folder.

6. Open the Desktop folder.

7. Choose Edit ➤ Paste.

And now your icon is on everyone's Desktop.

8. Close the Desktop window.

 If you plan on doing a lot with the All Users folders, then consider putting a shortcut to that folder on your personal Desktop: after Step 5 in this section, click the Up button one more time to visit the Documents and Settings folder. Right-click the All Users folder and choose Send To ➤ Desktop (Create Shortcut) from the menu. And there you go! (You may want to rename the icon after it's created; something more clever than "Shortcut to All Users."

How About Getting Something from the Desktop Back to the Start Menu?

No problem here, though there isn't a shortcut. Basically you cut the icon from the Desktop, then paste it back into the Start panel's folder. Refer to the section "How Can I Find Programs That Are Not on the All Programs Menu?" earlier in this chapter, Steps 12 through 20.

Is There Any Way I Can Add a Command Like "Send To ➤ Start Menu" to the Pop-up Menu?

Yes, you can add anything to the "Send To" submenu: a folder, a program, a disk drive, or a network location. Unfortunately, in its wisdom, Microsoft saw fit to hide the "Send To" menu's folder, which means that they probably don't want you messing with this. So I'll show you how it's done anyway.

First, you need to make a shortcut to the All Programs folder:

1. Right-click the Start button.

2. Choose Open.

3. Right-click the Programs folder.

This is your own account's Programs folder. While you could make such modifications for all the accounts on your computer, it's best just to stick with your own account for now.

4. Choose Copy.

Now you have a copy of that folder, which you'll paste as a shortcut icon elsewhere.

Second, you need to get to your account's SendTo folder:

5. Click the Up button.

The items on the "Send To" menu are kept in your account's SendTo folder. This folder is hidden, so if you cannot see it displayed, you'll need to direct Windows to show the hidden files:

a. Choose Tools ➤ Folder options.

b. In the Folder Options dialog box, click the View tab.

    c. In the scrolling list of "Advanced Settings," locate the "Hidden Files and Folders" section.

    d. Choose "Show Hidden Files and Folders."

    e. Click OK.

Now you can see the SendTo folder.

6. Open the SendTo folder.

Third, you paste the shortcut.

7. Choose Edit ➤ Paste Shortcut

Windows gives it the stupid name "Shortcut to Programs." Press the F2 key and rename it "All Programs Menu." That way the command will read "Send To ➤ All Programs Menu."

8. Close the SendTo folder.

Or, if you prefer *not* to have hidden files and folders show up in Windows, then repeat Steps a through e (above) to restore Windows to the way it was.

Fourth, you test!

9. Right-click a shortcut icon on the Desktop.

Or you can choose any shortcut icon anywhere.

 You must choose a shortcut icon! Otherwise Windows copies the entire file, program, or folder to the All Programs menu.

10. Choose Send To ➤ All Programs Menu.

And the shortcut icon is copied to the All Programs menu. Pretty nifty. You can confirm this by popping up the Start Menu button and choosing All Programs. Your newly added item will be on the bottom of the list.

KEYBOARD MASTER

The Up Button

To go "up" one level in the folder "tree structure" you can click the Up button or use this handy keyboard shortcut:

Backspace

How "backspace" equals "up" is beyond me, but it works.

Be Even More Awesome: Create a Custom Palette of Programs

If you're a project-oriented person, then it might behoove you to create program palettes you can use and exchange for your various projects. This may be easier than managing multiple Quick Launch bars or Pin-on menu configurations.

A custom palette is really just another toolbar on the Taskbar, though one that you detach and "float" on top of the Desktop. There are lots of interesting and fun things you can do with such a tool, more than enough to impress the neighbors—or at least the in-laws!

The first step to creating the custom palette is to build a special folder full of program shortcuts.

The second step is to add that folder as a toolbar on the Taskbar.

The final step is to float the toolbar off the Taskbar, either creating the custom palette or a secondary toolbar you can use all the time.

And You Probably Thought Having Yet Another Toolbar on the Taskbar Was a Big FAT Waste of Time

If you're like me, then you probably have several operating modes when you use the computer. For example, I have:

- Financial mode, when I use programs like Quicken and TurboTax, as well as Excel and Word and the Windows Calculator.

- Web design mode, where I use a web page designer, graphic arts program, photo editing and scanning programs, plus the web browser and an FTP program.

- Document production mode, where I use desktop publishing software, Word, an image converter, and a drawing program.

- Oh, and there's even Game mode, but I need not go into that (at least not until I'm ahead on my deadlines for writing this book).

For each mode you need to gather icons and place them into a special folder:

1. Open the My Documents folder.

2. Create a subfolder named Toolbars.

   This is the folder that will contain the various toolbars you're about to create.

3. Open the Toolbars folder.

   For this example, you'll create a toolbar full of graphics tools in Windows. In practice, however, you would create a toolbar full of whichever common tools you use when you're working on specific projects (as discussed above).

4. Create a new folder named Graphics.

5. Open the Graphics folder.

Now you need to gather various graphics applications and paste their shortcut icons into this folder. This chapter discusses several methods for finding programs, but the easiest spot is on the All Programs menu.

6. Click the Start button.

7. Choose All Programs.

8. Choose Accessories.

9. Right-click the Paint menu item.

10. Choose Copy from the pop-up menu.

This copies the shortcut to the Paint program from the All Programs menu.

11. Return to the Graphics folder.

12. Chose Edit ➤ Paste Shortcut.

13. Repeat Steps 6 through 12 for all the various shortcuts you want to place on your toolbar.

For example, copy the Windows MovieMaker program from the Accessories menu into the Graphics folder. Also copy the Calculator and Notepad shortcuts as well. That gives you four icons that you can play with for this tutorial.

14. When you're done pasting in the shortcut icons, close the window.

Now it's time to add that window to the Taskbar:

15. Right-click the Taskbar.

16. Choose Toolbars ➤ New Toolbar from the menu.

17. Use the New Toolbar dialog box to navigate to your Toolbar folder.

If you've followed my directions, then open the My Documents folder, then the Toolbar folder, and there will be your Graphics folder.

18. Select your folder and click OK to close the New Toolbar dialog box.

And your new toolbar appears on the Taskbar, looking something like Figure 8.3. Well, looking ugly, too. How about some clean-up?

19. Right-click on the new toolbar's dimple area.

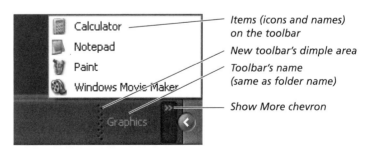

Figure 8.3 Your new toolbar on the Taskbar

20. Remove the check mark by "Show Text," then repeat Step 19 and remove the check mark by "Show Title."

Now you'll see a toolbar with just icons, which I think is more appropriate.

You could just live with the toolbar if you want. Refer to Chapter 5 for information on arranging the new toolbar along with the Taskbar and the Quick Launch bar if you're using that. Otherwise, the next section covers converting this toolbar into a floating palette—and then liberating it to becoming its own free-will toolbar. Amazing stuff.

KEYBOARD MASTER

Some Tips for Creating the New Toolbar

Creating a new folder is done with the File ➤ New ➤ Folder command:

Alt+F, W, F
Type the new folder's name after pressing the last F key.

F2
Renames a selected icon

Enter
Opens a selected folder

Alt+E, S
Pastes an icon as a shortcut

Look, It Floats!

Even though a toolbar lives on the Taskbar, it's not imprisoned there. Toolbars are free to roam, either as floating palettes—special windows that seem to float in front of all other windows on the Desktop— or as independent toolbars. Follow these steps to fun and frolic with the Graphics toolbar created in the previous section:

1. Drag the Graphics toolbar up and onto the Desktop.

Grab the toolbar by its dimple area, then drag it to the Desktop. Release the mouse pointer and you have a floating palette, as shown in Figure 8.4.

Drag the palette around with this title bar.

Closes the palette

Right-click in here to get the toolbar's pop-up menu.

Resize by dragging here.

Figure 8.4 The floating palette

Floating palettes are like mini-windows. They can be resized and moved like windows, but unlike windows they can float "on top" of everything else on the Desktop.

2. Move the palette around.

Drag it hither and thither.

3. Open the My Documents icon on the Desktop.

See how the My Documents window is behind the floating palette? What? It's not? You can fix that:

4. Minimize the My Documents window.

5. Right-click the Graphics floating palette.

6. Choose "Always on Top" from the pop-up menu.

7. Restore the My Documents window.

And there you go.

You can toggle the floating palette to either float on top of all other windows or to stay in the background. Now for another adjustment.

8. Right-click in the Graphics floating palette.

9. Choose View ➤ Large Icons from the menu.

I'm a big fan of big icons.

10. Resize the floating palette so that it's just big enough to show all the icons.

Figure 8.5 shows how it looks on my screen.

Always some room over here to right-click

Figure 8.5 The resized and larger icon view of the floating palette

Note that if you make the palette too narrow, then all the icons stack up and down. Otherwise, they arrange themselves left-to-right. Also, see how there's always some space to the right of the icons? That's so you can always right-click on the floating palette to get at the pop-up menu.

11. Press Win+D to minimize all open windows and show the Desktop.

12. Drag the Graphics palette all the way over to the right edge of the screen.

Thwoop! It becomes a toolbar. Amazing. Figure 8.6 shows how it looks on my screen. (If you can't get the floating palette to transmogrify into a toolbar, then you aren't dragging the mouse far enough to the edge of the screen.)

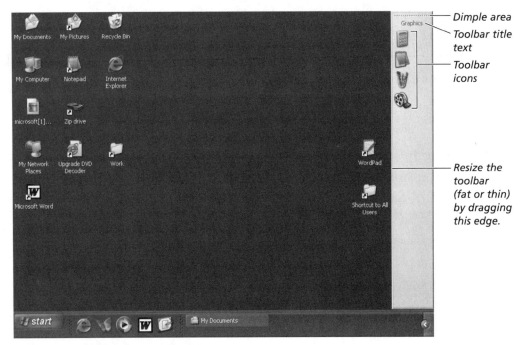

Figure 8.6 Behold the new toolbar!

13. Restore the My Documents window.

Did it cover up the new toolbar? That can be fixed:

14. Minimize the My Documents window.

15. Right-click in the Graphics toolbar.

16. Choose "Always on Top" from the shortcut menu.

 Try not to choose the "Auto Hide" option. It doesn't seem to work properly and makes getting at the toolbar exceedingly difficult.

17. Restore the My Documents window.

There. Now it's more like a "real" toolbar.

18. Close the My Documents window.

Imagine the possibilities this entails for your custom projects or for conjuring up specific toolbars for your specific projects!

You can do anything with the Graphics toolbar that you can with the Taskbar: You can move it to the top or left sides of the screen as well. Or you can drag it (using the dimple area) back out to a floating palette. If you drag it back to the Taskbar, however, it once again becomes a toolbar on the Taskbar, which is a lot less dramatic.

Can I Pull the Same Type of Stunts with the Quick Launch Bar?

Certainly. This trick works with any toolbar on the Taskbar.

How Do You Properly Get Rid of Any Bonus Toolbars?

As usual, there are several ways, from closing the floating palette's window to right-clicking the toolbar and choosing the "Close Toolbar" command. Doing so does display a Confirm Toolbar Close dialog box. Boring! Be sure to put a check mark next to "In the Future, Do Not Show Me this Dialog Box," and then click the OK button.

Stuff You Should Know About Your Documents and My Documents

My Documents is the folder where you put your stuff, the things you create, when you use Windows. You should know this. In fact, you're probably sitting there shaking your head, saying, "Dan! This is but kindergarten computer stuff. Everyone knows about the My Documents folder."

Silly as it may seem, some people do not know about the My Documents folder. They don't create subfolders to keep their stuff organized. They don't take advantage of the My Pictures or My Music folders. No, they save their stuff in stupid places, like on a floppy disk or on Drive C's root directory. These people should be shunned. But you don't need to worry about that because you know just about everything there is to know about the My Documents folder, save for the informative and enlightening tidbits held in this chapter.

Informative Tids and Enlightening Bits:

 Understanding My Documents (beyond the basics)

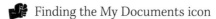 Finding the My Documents icon

 Using subfolders in My Documents

 Finding the real My Documents folder

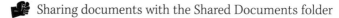 Sharing documents with the Shared Documents folder

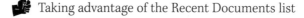 Taking advantage of the Recent Documents list

The Basic My Documents Folder Stuff You Already Know

The My Documents folder is where you put all the things you create in Windows. Put them there and no where else. Even those wicked graphics programs that create "galleries" for you in god-knows-where on the hard drive, attempt to compel such miscreant applications to behave and use the My Documents folder like everything else.

Some Bad Places You Shouldn't Save Your Data

Never save your stuff on a floppy disk. Floppy disks are great for transporting files between computers, mailing, or (occasionally) for backup. But floppy disks are just too unreliable and have such a low capacity that it makes them highly unsuited for anything else. You'd think this would be common sense information, but I still encounter people who use floppy disks instead of the hard drive or My Documents folder. (Some moron in some magazine once said to use floppy disks to prevent viruses. Uh-huh.)

Zip disks have the ability to be just as flaky as floppy disks, though they tend to be moderately more reliable. Still, use them for backup or transportation, not as your main storage source.

CD-Rs and CD-RWs are also good for backup but, again, use the hard drive as your main storage place. (Though it's perfectly fine to create a CD using data from the hard drive, then erase it from the hard drive; more on this in Chapter 15.)

No, just be a good computer user and stick with the hard drive. That's why the manufacturer stuck a hard drive inside your computer.

And while you're on the hard drive, avoid storing data in the root folder, which has a limited capacity. Avoid storing the stuff you create in the Windows folder or Program Files folder or anywhere else but the My Documents folder.

What About Using Hard Drive D?

If you have a hard drive D (or E or whatever), then you can feel free to use it for storing extra programs as well as your documents. There are no rules or specific folders you need to create for drive D. However, I do recommend that if you use Drive D (or any other hard drive), that you create unique names for the folders there; do not use "Program Files" or "My Documents," as this may confuse you or Windows when looking for files.

For example, on my Drive D I have a folder called Archives, which is where I copy older files. I also store all my programming applications (Microsoft Visual C, Visual Basic, and so on) on Drive D, so I use that for my programming files.

Many people devote Drive D to games.

Drive D can also be used to store spare copies of all your files.

So use drive D if you have one!

NERD'S CORNER

Cocktail Party Trivia, Part II

JOHN: Ha-ha, Phil. You are such a cut-up. Who would have thought there was such humor about the boring old My Documents folder?

EVERYONE: Ha-ha.

PHIL: Well, actually, John, I'll bet that you didn't know the My Documents folder wasn't always a part of Windows.

JOHN: What? Where did the ancient computer users store their data files?

PHIL: No one knows for certain. Computer archeologists have determined that most beginners stored their data files in the root folder.

EVERYONE: Gasp!

PHIL: Some intrepid users, mostly those who read early books by Dan Gookin, created "Home" directories for their data files. Very clever. But it wasn't until Microsoft Office 95 debuted that the My Documents folder first appeared.

JOHN: (Laughing) You mean to tell me that even Windows 95 didn't come with a My Documents folder?

PHIL: I'm afraid not, John.

JOHN: Wow. I just consider myself lucky that Windows XP comes with the My Documents folder, and that so many applications anticipate its use. Not only that, I'm fully taking advantage of subdirectories and various organizational skills that will propel me far beyond the rest of you in the job market!

PHIL: And I think I'll have another chug of Mad Dog 20/20.

JOHN: As long as you're buying.

EVERYONE: Ha-ha.

Getting to My Documents, the Very Slow and Oh-So-Fast Ways

The My Documents folder exists in only one place on your computer. Yet it's so important that there are many paths you can beat to its door. Mostly, however, you'll be getting there through various Open or Save As dialog boxes. But the My Documents icon itself can be found in a number of places:

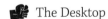 The Desktop

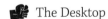 The Start panel

 The Address bar's drop-down list

 The "Other Places" part of a folder's task pane

You can elect whether or not to show the My Documents icon on the Desktop or Start panel, though I recommend that you do so. Information in Chapter 3 covers showing the My Documents icon on the Desktop; see Chapter 6 for information on showing or hiding the icon on the Start panel.

Here Is the Fastest Way to Open the My Documents Folder

Try these keystrokes: Win+D, Home, Enter. As long as there is a My Documents icon firmly fixed in the top left corner of your Desktop, those keystrokes will open the My Documents folder:

1. Win+D displays the Desktop.

2. Home selects the icon in the upper left corner of the screen, which is usually My Documents.

3. Enter opens that icon.

KEYBOARD MASTER

Opening the My Documents folder

Here's that keystroke again in case you missed it in the main text:

Win+D, Home, Enter

A quick way to open the My Documents folder, as long as it's in the upper right-hand corner of your Desktop screen.

Getting to My Documents from an Open or Save As Dialog Box

Because you use applications more than you use stupid old Windows, you'll most likely be visiting the My Documents folder through the Open or Save As dialog boxes. With few exceptions, the Open or Save As dialog box naturally opens to display the contents of the My Documents folder. (The exceptions are graphics programs, which use the My Pictures folder, and other applications that may preselect specific folders that you've used before.)

But no matter where the Open or Save As dialog box takes you, you can easily return to the My Documents folder by clicking that big dumb My Documents button on the left side of the dialog box, as shown in Figure 9.1.

If the dialog box lacks the buttons on its left side, then you can choose My Documents from the "Look In" drop-down list.

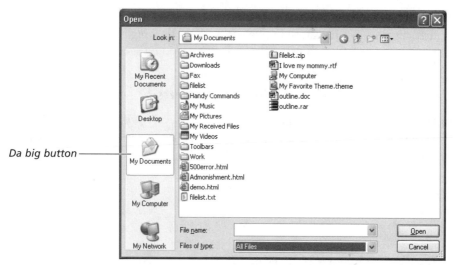

Figure 9.1 Use da big button to get to the My Documents folder.

What's Important and What's Not

in the My Documents Folder

Everything is important in the My Documents folder. That's where all your stuff lives!

What's most important is being able to *organize* your stuff. While Windows will let you have hundreds if not thousands of files in the My Documents folder, it's best to keep things organized. The My Pictures, My Music, and other "My" folders various applications create are but a first step. You, on your own, should create other folders for your work and organize your stuff into them.

Everything in the My Documents folder should represent something that you created yourself. As such, you can do whatever you want with it: move it, copy it, edit it, delete it, whatever. It's *your* stuff.

My Pictures, My Music, My Goodness!

Windows gets you started on the My Documents organizational binge by giving you two sample folders: My Pictures and My Music.

My Pictures is for your graphics files. It's the spot where most of the Windows XP–aware applications will go to save your graphics. It's also where you should start saving graphics files.

My Music is used by the Windows Media Player to help you organize your music and sound files. Now you can work in there if you like, but it's best to organize and work with your music files— and therefore the My Music folder—from within the Media Player program itself. Chapter 20 discusses this in detail.

I've seen two other folders that Windows has created: My Received Files, which sounds like where Internet downloads go, but the folder is actually empty on my computer; and My Videos, which the Windows MovieMaker program uses.

Be Creative and Make Your Own Folders!

The more folders you have, the more organized you can be, and the easier it will be to find things. Here is a smattering of folders I typically create whenever I get a new computer. All of these live in the My Documents folder:

- Work
- Play
- Junk
- Downloads
- Toolbars
- Web Pages
- Programming

Each of these is a major category for the things I do on the computer. So, for example, in Web Pages there is a folder titled "Wambooli," which is where I keep all the data and support files for my web page, www.wambooli.com.

Organization! Rah! Rah! Rah!

As an example, why not create a Downloads folder? This would be the spot where you store any files or programs you download from the Internet:

1. Open the My Documents folder.

2. Choose File ➢ New ➢ Folder.

   You know, I really wish Microsoft would make this command a handy shortcut. While you can do it from the keyboard (see the Keyboard Master sidebar), why not just make Ctrl+N, the traditional "New" command, the keyboard shortcut for making a new folder? Or is that too "Macintosh" for the boys and girls in Redmond?

3. Rename the folder `Downloads`.

   The folder is ready for renaming right after you create it. If not, select the folder and press the F2 key.

   There's no need to open the folder just yet. Instead, try some *customizing*!

4. Right-click the Downloads folder.

5. Choose Properties from the shortcut menu.

   The Downloads Properties menu appears (though "Downloads" in this case is merely the name of the folder). Figure 9.2 tells what's going on, though most of the options don't apply for a Downloads folder.

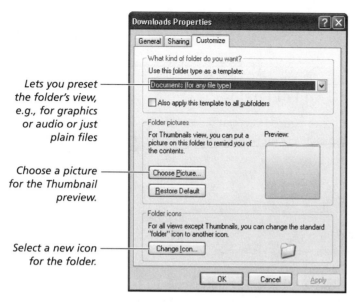

Lets you preset the folder's view, e.g., for graphics or audio or just plain files

Choose a picture for the Thumbnail preview.

Select a new icon for the folder.

Figure 9.2 Where folders are customized

6. Click the Change Icon button.

Now you need to pick an icon that represents the folder's task, storing downloaded files. You can use any icon in this list, though if you gander at Figure 9.3, you'll see which one is my favorite. (Also refer to Chapter 19, which covers icons specifically.)

7. Select an icon.

8. Click OK.

Now the Downloads folder has its own custom icon. You can see how this icon holds up in the different folder views.

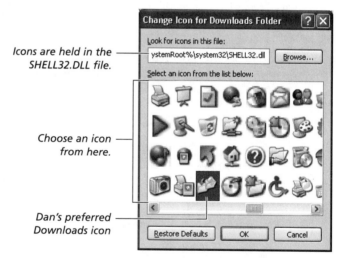

Icons are held in the SHELL32.DLL file.

Choose an icon from here.

Dan's preferred Downloads icon

Figure 9.3 Pluck an icon from this huge archive.

9. Switch to Thumbnail view: Choose View ➢ Thumbnails.

10. Switch to Tiles view: Choose View ➢ Tiles.

11. Switch to Icons view: Choose View ➢ Icons.

12. Switch to List view: Choose View ➢ List

13. Switch to Details view: Choose View ➢ Details.

And, when you're done, after proving that the icon sticks no matter what, switch back to your favorite view. (Mine is still Icons.)

Don't forget that you can make subfolders within the folders you create. For example, a folder full of correspondence can have subfolders categorizing who the correspondence is to, what it's about, or the dates on which the correspondence took place. The more organized you are, the easier it is to find things or at least know where to look.

KEYBOARD MASTER

Creating a New Folder

To conjure up a new folder, use this key combination:

Alt+F, W, F

This is the same as choosing File ➢ New ➢ Folder from the menu, but much faster!

Switching the Folder Views

Here's how to switch to the folder view that gives you the most pleasure.

Alt+V, H
Switches to Thumbnail view

Alt+V, L
Changes over to List view

Alt+V, S
Peruse your files in Tiles view

Alt+V, D
For Details view

Alt+V, N
Converts to Icons view

Why Do I Need a "Junk" Folder?

I love Junk folders, also "Sto" and "Temp" folders. That's where I keep stuff I don't want to keep; stuff that's okay to delete later. If you can't possibly think of a folder to create, then create one and name it Junk. You'll find it filling up in no time.

Deleting stuff in a Junk folder is also a keen way to save on disk space. Of course, the amount of space saved depends on the pile of junk in that folder.

Don't Be Dumb: Using the Folder Tree

When you get way into this organizational stuff, you may find that the opening of file folders and browsing around that way takes too much time. I have a rule: Any time I know that I have to dive down more than three folders, I use the folder tree.

To see the Folder tree, click on the Folders button. Figure 9.4 shows a folder tree I have on one of my computers. You can use it to see the organization; there are lots of project folders under the main Work folder.

Working the Folder tree is basic Windows stuff:

- Use the + button by a folder to open a folder branch

- Use the − button by a folder to close that branch

- Select a folder by clicking on it; the folder's contents appear on the right side of the window

Also, using the Folder tree makes it easier to drag and drop files when you go on an organizational binge.

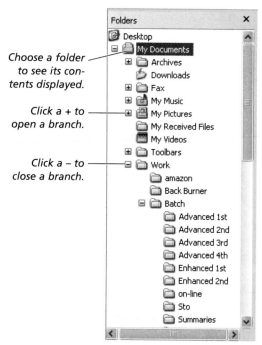

Choose a folder to see its contents displayed.

Click a + to open a branch.

Click a − to close a branch.

Figure 9.4 The Folders list

KEYBOARD MASTER

Manipulating the Folders List

Alt+V, E, O
Toggle the Folder tree from the keyboard

Here are the keys you can use to crawl all over the folders tree—without fear of falling!

Up arrow key	**+**	*****
Move up the tree	Open a branch	Open all branches

Down arrow key	**−**	
Move down the tree	Close a branch	

(The +, −, and * keys are on the numeric keypad.)

Brutal Secrets About My Documents

Windows XP is designed for multiple users, so what you see on the screen as the My Documents folder is really a specific folder for your account only. This is true whether you are the only person using the computer or not.

The good news is that Windows keeps everything sorted out. So that when you access the My Documents folder, you always get *your* My Documents folder and not some other user's.

The bad news is that the folder isn't static. So if you save something to the My Documents folder, then another user on the same computer cannot get at it. No, all they see in the My Documents folder is their own account's stuff.

Or, for example, suppose you're in the habit of sharing the contents of the My Documents folder on your network. In that case, you have to be specific about which folder to share. (Or you can take advantage of the Shared Documents folder, covered in the next section.)

So, to break the truth to you—the My Documents folder is really kept in the following location:

1. Open the My Computer icon on the Desktop.

2. Open Drive C.

3. Open the Documents and Settings folder.

    This is the "branch" in which information for all the various accounts on your computer is kept. You'll see a folder for every account, plus a general All Users folder.

4. Open your account's folder.

    On my computer it's named "Dan Gookin."

5. Open the My Documents folder.

    And there it is.

Of course, getting there this way is rather obtuse, which is why Windows handles things the way it does; it's much easier to use all the various My Documents folders littered around Windows than to stomp through the orchard to get to the "real" folder.

 Don't fret over security! Your account is completely safe. Even "limited" accounts have their data hidden from other users who are smart enough to know where the My Documents folder really lives.

What's the Purpose of the Shared Documents Folders?

The Shared Documents folder provides a way for several users on a single computer to share files that would otherwise be inaccessible. It's not meant as a substitute for My Documents; you should use My Documents for all your stuff and only use the Shared Documents folder for the stuff you want to share with other accounts on the same computer.

For example, if everyone using the same computer were working off the same database, it would be best to keep that database in the Shared Documents folder as opposed to keeping it in only one account's folder.

Or, say that everyone who uses the computer updates the same web page. Then keeping that web page's data in the Shared Documents folder would make a heck of a lot of sense.

 The Shared Documents folder is accessible from all accounts on the same computer. But to make the folder available on the network, you must share it.

No, They Don't Really Hide the Shared Documents Folder

All Windows XP computers have a Shared Documents folder, whether you're the only person using the computer or not:

1. Open the My Documents icon on the Desktop.

2. In the Other Places task pane (on the left side of the window), choose "Shared Documents."

If you see the Folders list instead of the task pane, then click the Folders button.

You'll see a list of folders predefined for sharing, typically a Shared Music and a Shared Pictures folder. Anything else in there is stuff designed to be shared by all users. For example, in Figure 9.5, you see that I'm also sharing the WRAR280.EXE program (which I downloaded from the Internet), plus I've also created a Shared Videos folder.

Any Other Ways to Get to the Shared Documents Folder?

If you don't see the Shared Documents folder listed in the task pane, then you can get to it from any drop-down Address list, shown in Figure 9.6: Click the down-arrow and choose "Shared Documents" from the list. (It's listed after the last disk drive, after the Control Panel.)

Standard shared folders created by Windows ⎯

Task pane ⎯

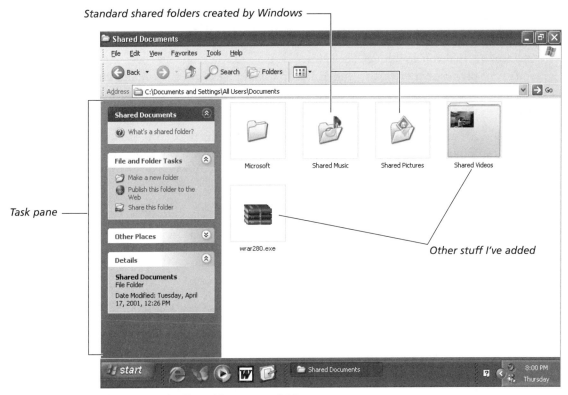

Figure 9.5 The Shared Documents folder

Here it is! ⎯

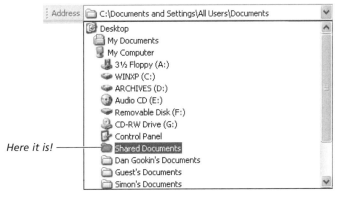

Figure 9.6 Yet another way to get to the Shared Documents folder

How Would a List of Recent Documents Save My Butt?

Chances are that you go through spells where you access the same files over and over. Unless you're one of those wunderkinds who can whip something out in a few hours, chances are that you'll go through a time where you're working with the same group of documents over and over. If so, then the My Recent Documents list is for you.

Chapter 6 covers how to display the list of My Recent Documents on the Start panel. I know that I don't recommend using it there, but suppose you're one of the few who really like it. If so, then turn it on:

1. Right-click the Start button.

2. Choose Properties from the pop-up menu.

3. Click the Customize button.

4. Click the Advanced tab.

There, on the bottom of the dialog box, is the spot you're looking for.

5. Click to put a check mark by "List My Most Recently Opened Documents."

6. Click OK.

7. Click OK.

You're out of dialog box hell.

8. Click the Start button.

9. Click to choose the My Recent Documents submenu.

And there are your recently accessed files and documents.

If you had the list turned off, then you're probably amazed that Windows still remembers the last 15 documents that you opened. But don't let that put a chill into your heart; Windows remembers a lot more than that!

Obviously, if your purpose is to start a recently used document, you would pluck it from the list and get on your way. Simple. Efficient. (But I still think it's a security risk.)

 If you want to be part of the "in" crowd, then refer to the My Recent Documents list as an MRU, Most Recently Used. MRU is internal Microsoft slang for any list of most recently used documents. Very trendy.

Where Else Can I Muster the My Recent Documents List?

Another handy, yet not as well known, place for the My Recent Documents list is in the Open dialog box.

1. Start WordPad.

Or it could be any Windows application (though some older programs may not sport this feature).

2. Choose File ➢ Open.

And there's the Open dialog box, which is also shown back in Figure 9.1.

3. Click the My Recent Documents button on the left side of the dialog box.

And there is yet another list of documents you've recently opened. Note that this list appears whether or not you have the My Recent Documents submenu visible in the Start panel. Also, this list is limited to the items you've opened by using the Open dialog box. So in many cases, this list is utterly different from the one displayed by the Start panel.

4. Go ahead and close the dialog box and quit WordPad.

Or, if you were really working, you would continue working here. My purpose is merely to show you that oh-so-keen list of recently opened programs.

 Windows displays only the most recent 15 documents you saved or opened on the My Recent Documents list on the Start panel. However, the list of documents displayed when you click the My Recent Documents button in an Open dialog box is much, much longer.

How Do I Clean the List?

It's easy to zap the list of recent programs:

1. Right-click the Start button.

2. Choose Properties from the pop-up menu.

3. Click the Customize button.

4. Click the Advanced tab.

5. Click the Clear List button.

And everything in the My Recent Documents list on the Start panel is utterly gone.

Also, much to your relief, all the files listed when you click My Recent Documents in an Open dialog box are gone as well.

No, I Mean, How Do I Really Clean the List?

Believe it or not, the Clear List button does do a good job. If you really don't like having the list available, then don't display it! (See Chapter 6.) But if you want to know where the information is really kept, then you have to dig deeper.

Like other things in your account, the list of recent documents is stored in your personal area on the hard drive. In this case, the folder is named Recent and it lives in your account's folder in the Documents and Settings folder:

1. Open the My Computer icon on the Desktop.

2. Open Drive C.

3. Open the Documents and Settings folder.

4. Open your account's folder.

 The Recent folder is the one that contains items you've recently opened or saved to disk. This is a hidden folder, so if you've trained Windows to display hidden folders, it appears rather ghostly on the screen (see Figure 9.7).

 If you cannot see the hidden folder, then follow these sub-steps to display hidden folders in Windows:

 a. Choose Tools ➤ Folder Options.
 b. Click the View tab in the Folder Options dialog box.
 c. Scroll through the list of Advanced settings and select "Show Hidden Files and Folders."
 d. Click OK.

And now the bad news: Windows keeps stuffing any document you open or save (or any folder you open) into the My Recent Documents folder. This holds true whether you have the list displayed on the Start menu or not! There is, unfortunately, no known way to turn it off.

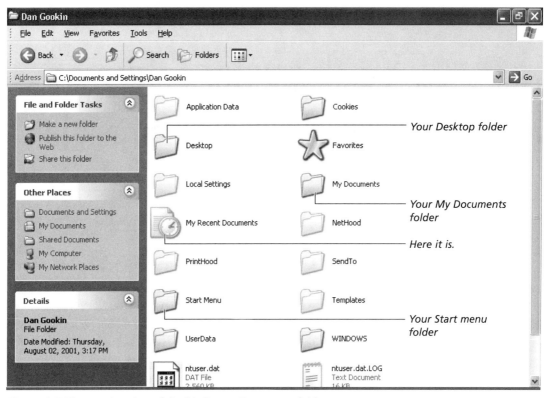

Figure 9.7 The true location of the My Recent Documents folder

10

The My Computer Folder: Not as Important as My Documents, but Vital Nonetheless

I find the My Computer icon amusing. First, I think it should be called "This Computer" and not "My Computer." As my eighth grade English teacher would say, "Who is the 'my' here?" If the "my" is really the computer itself, then the icon should be named "Myself."

Second, the My Computer icon doesn't really contain what I would expect it to. I would imagine that you'd open the My Computer icon and there would be a snapshot of your computer's dusty guts. But no. It's just disk drives and a smattering of folders.

Third, though vital enough to be slapped down on the Desktop (or on the Start panel), there really isn't much you can do with the My Computer icon. It's more like a door to your computer's disk drives, plus a few other useful locations you may visit from time-to-time. But it really isn't one of those central places, not like the My Documents folder or the Desktop itself.

Anyway, despite there not being much oomph behind the My Computer icon, I still thought it worthy to devote a handful of pages to the subject. This short, to-the-point chapter takes a look at the various things you might not be aware of or tricks that you can use on the My Computer icon.

Various Things, Tricks, and Occasional Oomph

- Discovering useful things about the My Computer folder
- Using the handy \ and .. shortcuts
- Opening the My Computer folder from just about anywhere
- Knowing some handy commands from the shortcut menu
- Evaluating used disk space
- Ejecting disks

Why is My Computer Necessary?

Oh, I suppose your computer isn't necessary at all. But *mine* is very necessary of course! Or are you talking about the My Computer icon on the Desktop? In that case, it's yet another necessary thing in Windows, though not as *ne plus ultra* as one would think.

What Does "Parent of the Root" Mean?

I suppose that the My Computer window is necessary because everything in Windows must have a parent. It's not that "family" is a big thing in Windows. No, it's just that all folders require a parent or owner.

For example, the root folder of Drive C owns the Windows folder. That's written as a pathname like this: C:\Windows

C: is the disk drive, \ is the root folder, and Windows is a folder itself. The root folder (represented by the backslash) is the parent of the Windows folder. (C:\Windows is a *pathname*, which is discussed in Chapter 13.) If you create a Magic Tricks folder in the My Documents folder, then My Documents is Magic Tricks' parent.

Subfolders don't have a family name per se. While you can call them "child" folders if you like, it's not common. No, they're just "subfolders."

So this all begs the question, if everything in Windows has a parent folder, what is the parent folder for Drive C? What folder does the root on Drive C call "Daddy"? Why, it's the My Computer folder! And that's how My Computer comes into play; it's the parent folder for all the other parent folders on your hard drive (the root directories on all your disk drives), plus it's the parent folder for the My Documents folder.

(And what is the apex of all, the parent of the parents? The Lord High Folder itself? Why, it's the Desktop itself! Wow. Now you've found PC nirvana.)

So rather than have a bunch of disk drives floating out there in the ether (or have them sloppily attached to the Desktop), mad scientists working late hours in castles high on craggy rocks (and during thunderstorms) developed the My Computer folder.

The My Computer Folder Window (Which You Should Know Well)

Figure 10.1 shows the My Computer folder window. It contains items that would otherwise be parentless. The top part of the window lists the various My Documents folders that belong to all the computer's accounts. (Or if you're the only one using the computer, then you'll see your account and the Shared Documents folder, which belongs to the All Users account.)

Next come the hard disk drives. Then come any removable disk drives.

The following sections cover the few interesting things you can do here. Mostly, however, the My Computer window is a starting point for exploring or maintaining your disk drives.

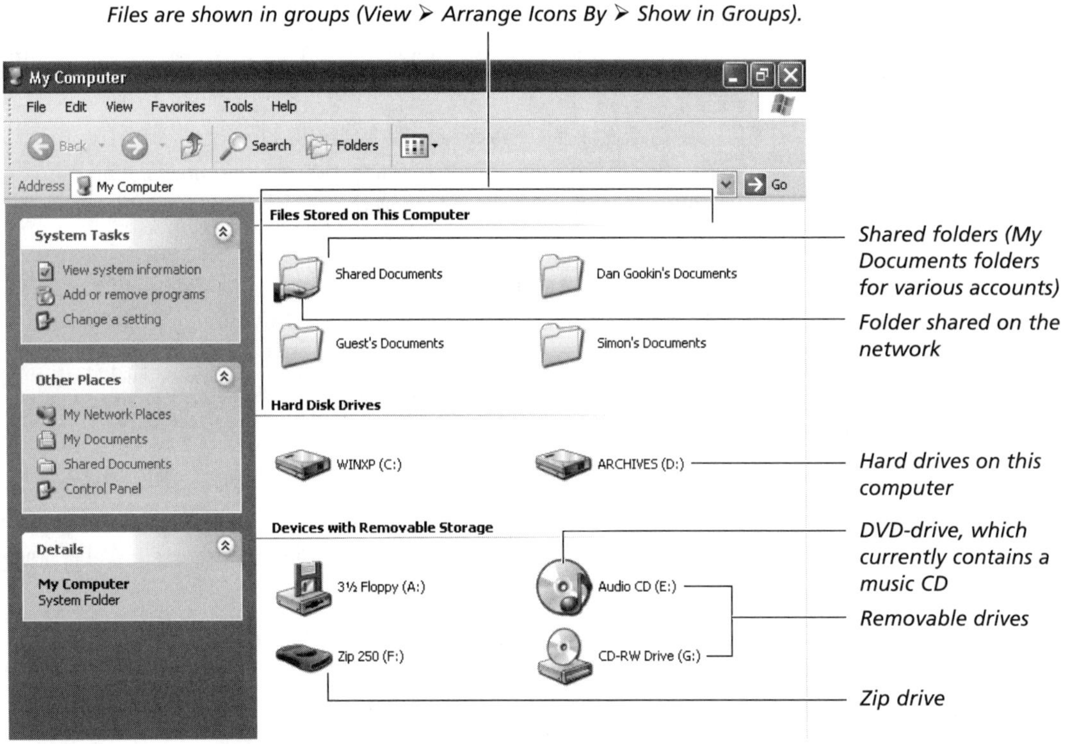

Files are shown in groups (View ➤ Arrange Icons By ➤ Show in Groups).

Figure 10.1 Fun things in My Computer

How to Visit a Root Folder

The My Computer window is just a-brimmin' with root folders. Remember, the root folder is the main folder on any hard drive:

1. Open the My Computer icon on the Desktop.

2. Open Drive C.

You'll see the contents of the root folder on Drive C displayed. There are three basic folders on all Windows XP computers:

Documents and Settings
customized folders for each account

Program Files
where applications are installed

Windows
for Windows XP itself

Any other folders you see in Drive C's root were most likely placed there by other applications or utilities. No problem!

What's with the Weird \ and .. Symbols? Can They Come in Handy?

The weird \ (backslash) symbol is a shortcut for the root directory. The .. (dot-dot) symbol is a shortcut for the current folder's parent directory. Remember how I said parent directories are important? Try this little demonstration:

1. Open the My Computer icon on the Desktop.

Or just keep using the My Computer window already open from the previous section.

2. Open Drive C.

3. Open the Program Files folder.

4. Open the Accessories folder.

Now go back to the root folder.

5. Press the F4 key.

This activates the Address bar, which will drop down to display a list of places you've been. That's okay. Ignore the drop-down list.

6. Press the backslash key.

The "root" folder shortcut.

7. Press Enter.

And there you are back at the root of Drive C.

8. Open the Program Files folder.

9. Open the Accessories folder.

10. Press F4.

11. Type .. (two periods) and press Enter.

Remember that dot-dot is the "parent" directory symbol. After typing dot-dot and pressing Enter you'll find yourself at the Accessories folder's parent, which is the Program Files folder.

Also note that the Address bar is still selected, meaning that you can continue to type there:

12. Type .. and press Enter.

Now you're back at the root folder, which is the Program Files folder's parent.

13. Type .. and press Enter.

And the parent of the root folder is...the My Computer folder! Keep going up!

14. Type .. and press Enter.

Nirvana: The Desktop. Try it again, what the heck:

15. Type .. and press Enter.

Oh, no! The Internet! I suppose this is Microsoft's way of telling us that all computers are "owned" by the Internet (which Microsoft itself is trying desperately to own).

Seriously, what you've done is typed an address into the Address bar and because there is no parent for the Desktop, Windows dutifully went out to the Internet to look for the dot-dot Web page—which it won't find, but that's the end of the story.

 ## KEYBOARD MASTER

Display the Root Folder

You can quickly zoom to the root folder of any drive in any folder window:

F4, \, Enter

The F4 key activates the Address bar; \ (backslash) is the shortcut to the root, and pressing the Enter key takes you there.

Getting at My Computer from Just About Anywhere (Plus the Fastest Way in the Universe to Summon the My Computer Folder)

Like many other vital locations, you can get to the My Computer window from a number of interesting places. Its icon can appear in the following vacation spots located throughout Windows:

- The Desktop
- The Start panel
- In the Other Places task pane (on any folder's window)
- In the panel on the left side of any Open or Save As dialog box
- From the drop-down list on any Address bar

If you want to show the My Computer icon on the Desktop and it's not there, or you want to hide the My Computer icon on the Desktop, then see Chapter 3.

If you want to show or hide the My Computer icon on the Start panel, refer to Chapter 6.

Of course, the best way to whip up the My Computer window is with the Win+E keystroke. Win+E summons the Windows Explorer, complete with the Folder list open and, well, pointing right at the My Computer folder.

Now if you don't like having the Folders list open, you can hide it by clicking the Folders button, or press Alt+V, E, O.

KEYBOARD MASTER

Quickly Bringing Forth the My Computer Window

*This is the command that starts the Windows Explorer, though it always opens on the My Computer folder: **Win+E***

Strange and Occasionally Useful Things
to Do with My Computer

The My Computer folder isn't really a destination. No, it's more like a launching pad for you to get to common places in your computer—disk drives and special folders. But it has other uses too, if you're clever. Here are some you may not be familiar with:

Good-To-Know My Computer Icon Shortcuts

I recommend keeping a copy of the My Computer icon on the Desktop simply because its shortcut menu is so handy.

There are three commands in the My Computer icon's pop-up menu that allow you to get to key places in Windows quickly. Figure 10.2 shows what I believe you'll find to be useful commands on the My Computer shortcut menu:

Explore brings up a Windows Explorer window.

Manage displays the techy (though handy) Computer Management window.

Properties summons the System Properties dialog box.

The other commands are more-or-less obvious, however I recommend against renaming the My Computer icon. And the Delete command doesn't seem to make sense; who would want to delete all their computer files? But no, it merely removes the icon from the Desktop; see Chapter 3 for information on restoring it, should you accidentally delete the My Computer icon.

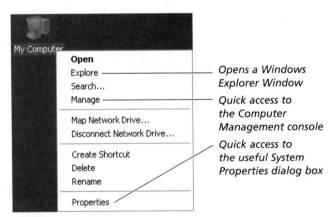

Figure 10.2 Useful commands on the My Computer shortcut menu

How Much Space Is Left on That Disk?

Because the My Computer window illustrates your computer's disk drives, it's the first place you'll go when you need more disk information. And one of the most basic bits of information you need to know about any disk drive is "How full is it?" Follow these steps:

1. Open the My Computer icon on the Desktop.

2. Click to select Drive C.

Observe the Details portion of the task pane (it's near the bottom). That shows you information about the disk, as detailed in Figure 10.3. (This information is displayed only when the Folders list is not visible.)

Of course, better information can be displayed by viewing the disk's Properties dialog box:

3. Press Alt+Enter.

Pressing Alt+Enter displays the Properties dialog box for a selected disk drive, file, or folder in Windows. The information you see is far more detailed than what is offered in the Details panel; compare Figures 10.3 and 10.4. I prefer the "disk pie" for seeing how much space is available.

4. Click OK to close the disk's Properties dialog box.

Don't fret over disk storage space just yet.

 Windows also has a program called the Low Disk Space Notification Tool. When free disk storage space drops below a certain level, you'll see a warning dialog box. So you don't have to fret every day over your PC's disk storage.

Figure 10.3 Oh the details, details...

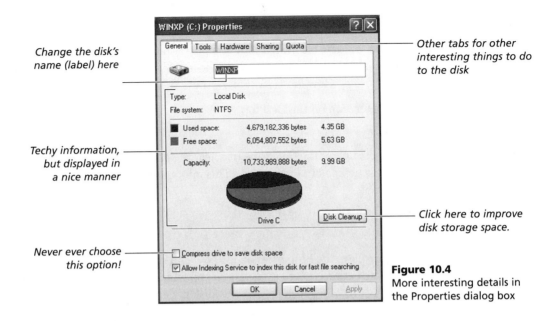

Change the disk's name (label) here

Other tabs for other interesting things to do to the disk

Techy information, but displayed in a nice manner

Click here to improve disk storage space.

Never ever choose this option!

Figure 10.4
More interesting details in the Properties dialog box

Displaying the Properties Dialog Box

Rather than right-click and choose Properties from an icon's shortcut menu, just do this:

Alt+Enter

Remember that the icon must be selected.

Ejecting a Disk

The My Computer window is also the place where I wind up ejecting disks more often than not. While it's true that Windows Media Player has its own Eject command (as do other movie and CD players), you can also eject a disk directly from the My Computer window:

1. Choose the removable disk from the list.

2. Choose "Eject this Disk" from the System Tasks task pane.

    And the disk spits out.

You can also eject a disk by right-clicking on the disk's icon and choosing Eject from the pop-up menu.

 Do not eject any disk you're working on, especially a disk with open files. If you do, Windows has a veritable heart attack.

If you dislike having to wade through the My Computer folder to eject your disks, then a clever shortcut is to place a clever shortcut to the disk drive on the Desktop:

1. Select the disk you want.

2. Press Ctrl+C to copy the disk's icon.

    This copies the disk's icon and not the entire disk.

3. Press Win+D to see the Desktop.

4. Right-click the Desktop and choose Paste Shortcut from the menu.

And there is your disk drive shortcut. You can now right-click it and choose the Eject command instead of having to open the My Computer window.

There Must Be a Better Way to Get to the Control Panel

I like the Control Panel because it's a central place where I can mess with just about any and every option in Windows. You name it, you can change it, modify it, fiddle with it, or fix it using the Control Panel. It's handy.

What isn't handy, however, is how badly Windows obscures the Control Panel. This has been getting worse and worse with each release of Windows; in Windows 3.1, the Control Panel was an icon right there on the screen (in the "Main" folder), but with Windows 95 up through Windows 2000, the Control Panel moved to the Start menu's Settings submenu. Now with Windows XP, the Control Panel is again on the Start panel, but where are all of its little buttons? How come things that took me two clicks to get to before now take six or seven? Aghghgh! It's Control Panel cartoon hell! But fortunately, this chapter is here to rescue you.

If you're like me, you probably visit the Control Panel more often than you should. As such, you may have noticed how tough it is sometimes to get from here to there in the Control Panel. This frustration fills me with such fire and pepper that I've written this entire chapter—nay, diatribe—on how to better tame that necessary beast, the Control Panel.

Fire Doused and Pepper Un-Spiced:

 Getting to the Control Panel

Changing the Control Panel's look

 Making Control Panel shortcuts

 Making shortcuts to Control Panel icons

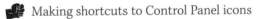 Building a Control Panel toolbar

Using the keyboard to do Control Panel things

Getting to the Control Panel in one keystroke

Show Me the Most Bitchin' Way to Get to the Control Panel

There is no single most bitchin' way to get to the Control Panel, but rather some useful alternatives. First, let me entertain you with the standard way Windows XP displays the Control Panel, which isn't really the Control Panel at all but rather a goofy-looking wrapper around more useful options. Figure 11.1 shows the sins of the standard Control Panel.

 This book assumes that the Control Panel is accessible from the Start menu, as described in Chapter 6.

I was going to provide a list here of which of the traditional options (which made more sense) are located under the newer mushy categories in the Control Panel. But why bother doing that when I can just show you other ways to get at them directly? Yeah. That's a better idea.

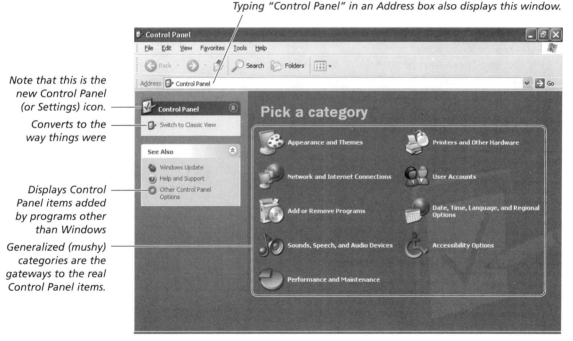

Figure 11.1 The Control Panel in all its dorkiness

I Much Rather Enjoyed the Old Style Control Panel

Mem'ries. Like a teeny bit of RAM...

If you were fond of the old way the Control Panel looked, restore it: choose "Switch to Classic View" from the Control Panel task pane (see Figure 11.1). This brings up the Control Panel as shown in Figure 11.2, which I think you'll agree is a lot more straightforward. I mean, dinking is *serious stuff*. Why wade through Fantasyland to get there?

 By making the change to the Classic View, the Control Panel will always appear that way when summoned. To change back to the Fun House view, choose "Switch to Category View" from the Control Panel's task pane.

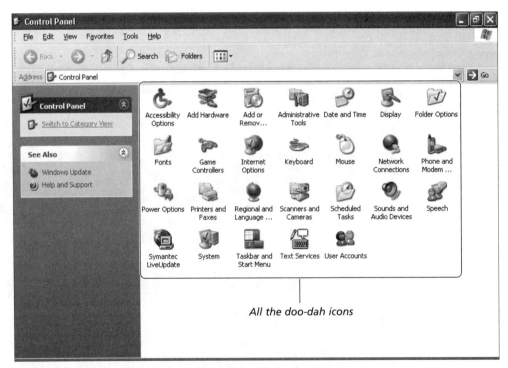

All the doo-dah icons

Figure 11.2 The Classic View of the Control Panel (better)

 If you elect to use the Classic View or have the Control Panel appear as a menu on the Start panel, understand that most books, manuals, and tech support folk will assume the Control Panel is in the Category View, the same stupid way it comes pre-packaged in Windows XP.

The Most Effective Way to Get to the Control Panel Options

Personally, I feel the best way to view the Control Panel is as a menu on the Start panel. That way I can get at the icons there more quickly than in either the Classic or Category View:

1. Right-click the Start button.

2. Choose Properties from the pop-up menu.

3. Click the Customize button.

4. Click the Advanced tab.

5. Under the Control Panel section in the scrolling list, choose "Display As a Menu."

If this item is already chosen, then great!

6. Click OK twice to back out of those dialog boxes.

Now try it to see if you like it:

7. Click the Start button.

8. Display the Control Panel submenu.

Figure 11.3 shows what it looks like on my screen. I find plucking specific items from this menu to be ideal.

Note that some Control Panel items appear as submenus themselves. Again, this is handy; most of the submenus in the Control Panel menu are items you'd choose otherwise in the course of opening an icon or folder. So it all makes sense.

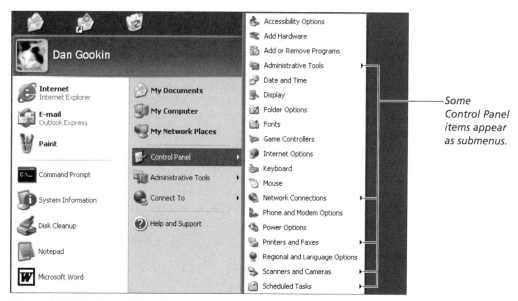

Some Control Panel items appear as submenus.

Figure 11.3 The Control Panel as a menu on the Start panel

Is There Any Reason to Keep the Silly-Looking Control Panel?

Certainly. That view—the Category View—is okay if you don't really know what you're looking for. In my travels, however, I've always known exactly where to go in the Control Panel, either because of my own experience or from being directed to open a specific icon by some manual or tech support person.

Another reason to keep the silly-looking Control Panel is that many common activities are often highlighted and presented right in the window. For example, the Appearance and Themes category lists common tasks such as "Choose a Screen Saver" or "Change the Screen Resolution," which are the most frequently chosen tasks when opening a particular Control Panel icon.

Also, in the Silly view, related tasks, items, and helpful information appear in the window's task pane. *Hey boys and girls! Windows can be oogly-googly fun!*

(*Sound of the author clearing his throat.*)

Still, if you really know what you're doing, then all that seems rather silly.

Why Not Just Type "Control Panel"?

Yet another way to get to the Control Panel is to type "Control Panel" into the Address bar:

1. Open the My Documents icon on the Desktop.

2. Press F4 to activate the Address bar.

3. Type `Control Panel` and press Enter.

And there you are.

You can also run the Control Panel from the Run dialog box:

1. Press Win+R to summon the Run dialog box.

2. Type `Control Panel` and press Enter.

And there you are again.

Wasn't There Once a Shortcut Link to the Control Panel from the My Computer Window?

Technically there still is one, though it may be hidden:

1. Open the Control Panel window using one of the techniques mentioned in the previous section.

Or if the Control Panel window is still open, then you're okay.

2. Type **..** (dot-dot) into the Address bar.

3. Press Enter.

You're taken to the "parent" folder of the Control Panel, which is the My Computer folder. (See Chapter 10 for more information on the My Computer folder.)

Something must have gotten messed up in the adoption papers, however, because you cannot get back to the Control Panel from the My Computer window by clicking an icon; there's no icon to be found. Abandonment! What an issue for the Control Panel to shoulder? No wonder it's returned to a rather cartoon-like, childhood existence.

Oh, well, yes, there is the Control Panel link in the Other Places task pane (on the left side of the My Documents window), but there is no *real* icon alongside the disk drives and special folders icons. What to do. What to do…

4. Press Alt+← (left arrow) to return to the Control Panel.

This is the same as choosing the Back button from the toolbar.

5. Open the Folder Options icon.

Now, I'm assuming that you have the Classic View up. If not, here are the alternative steps you must take:

   a. Open the Control Panel (Category View).
   b. Choose "Appearance and Themes."
   c. Choose "Folder Options" (near the bottom of the window).

See? Much better to be direct. (And just how would one know that Folder Options is in "Appearance and Themes"? Ugh.)

6. In the Folder Options dialog box, click the View tab.

7. In the scrolling list, locate "Show Control Panel in My Computer" and put a check mark there.

8. Click OK.

9. Back in the window, choose "My Computer" from the Address drop-down list.

And there you should see the Control Panel list. Figure 11.4 shows how it looks on my screen.

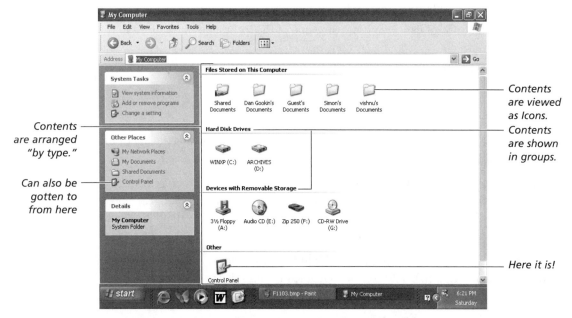

Contents are arranged "by type."

Can also be gotten to from here

Contents are viewed as Icons.

Contents are shown in groups.

Here it is!

Figure 11.4 Now the Control Panel lives in the My Computer folder.

Other Interesting and Useful Control Panel Stuff

The following sections list a bunch of Control Panel tricks I've pulled out of my sleeve.

Creating a Shortcut to the Control Panel

If you're obsessed with the Control Panel, then why not create a shortcut to it? This is easiest to do if you have the Control Panel sitting in the My Computer folder; refer to the section "Wasn't There Once a Shortcut Link to the Control Panel from the My Computer Window?" earlier in this chapter for the details.

Once the icon can be found, follow these steps:

1. Right-click the Control Panel icon.

2. Choose "Create Shortcut" from the menu.

Windows bemoans that it cannot create a shortcut where you want one, but will instead put it on the Desktop. Excellent! This works in your scheme most prodigiously.

3. Type Y for Yes.

4. Close the My Computer window.

And there on the Desktop is your shortcut. Now you've completed the first step to easy Control Panel access.

(You can rename the icon from "Shortcut to Control Panel" to something else now if you like; F2 is the Rename key command.)

If you're a Big Desktop User, then you can continue by just keeping the icon on the Desktop. Or, if you're that much of a Control Panel Nut, you could copy it down to the Quick Launch bar. See Chapter 7 for more information on that. Or you could copy it to a special Toolbar folder for creating a Control Panel toolbar. (See Chapter 8.) Whatever. You have your shortcut.

Creating Shortcuts to Your Favorite Control Panel Icons

Every icon in the Control Panel can be its own shortcut if you like. To create a shortcut, first find the icon you want to create a shortcut to. (It helps if you're viewing the Control Panel in the classic view.) Right-click the icon and choose Create Shortcut from the pop-up menu. Windows will balk about this and suggest that the shortcut be placed on the Desktop. That's okay; whatever. You can collect all the shortcut icons on the Desktop and then put them elsewhere for long-term storage if you like.

The Control Panel icons I feel are most handy are:

- Add or Remove Programs
- Date and time
- Display
- Internet Options
- System
- User Accounts

I tend to use these more than others. (Date and time specifically because my computer keeps lousy track of the time; more on that in Chapter 28.)

Another icon worthy of having a shortcut is the Scheduled Tasks folder. In older versions of Windows, this folder was a real folder you could get to either from the Start menu or the My Computer window. If you plan on messing with Scheduled Tasks at all, do consider creating a shortcut for it on the Desktop.

Building a Control Panel Toolbar

This is cinchy—and quite handy. Following the instructions in the previous two sections, create a group of some Control Panel icons you plan on using often. Then refer to Chapter 8 for information on creating a floating palette or toolbar. The end result can be your own Control Panel toolbar, similar to the one I've created in Figure 11.5.

Here are a few things to remember or take advantage of if you're doing this:

 Collect all the shortcut icons on the Desktop.

Cut them from the Desktop and paste them to a special Control Panel toolbars folder. (I used My Documents\Toolbars\Control Panel on my computer.)

Rename them, if necessary, so they don't all start with "Shortcut To."

Rearrange the Taskbar so that the Control Panel toolbar shows up well (see Figure 11.5).

You might also want to hide the text and title on the toolbar, as well as show the icons in large view (as shown in the figure).

You can rearrange the icons on the toolbar by dragging them with the mouse. Otherwise they appear in alphabetical order.

I got the Control Panel shortcut to show up first by renaming it "_Control Panel." Because the underscore sorts higher alphabetically than an "A," the "_Control Panel" icon appears first in the list. Nifty trick.

Remember that this toolbar can also be a floating palette of tools or a toolbar on the left, right, or top sides of the Desktop; Chapter 8 has all the details.

Now use the toolbar! I believe you'll find it extremely handy, especially if you're as much of a Control Panel maniac as myself.

I have a special Toolbars folder in the My Documents folder. The Control Panel folder inside the Toolbars folder is where I keep my popular Control Panel shortcut icons.

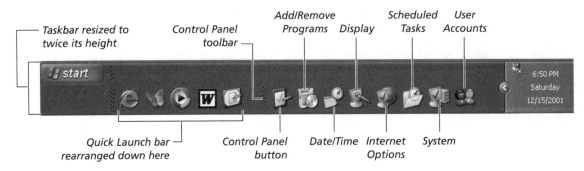

Figure 11.5 An example of a Control Panel toolbar

Keyboard and Other Shortcuts to Popular Control Panel Icons

You don't need to build shortcuts or toolbars with all the Control Panel options. That's because Windows itself already has a few shortcuts to the more popular icons built in. Here is a list of some popular icons and the alternative ways to get there:

Administrative Tools

Administrative Tools This item can also be displayed on the Start panel, either as a link to the main Administrative Tools folder or as a menu. I prefer menu, as discussed in Chapter 6.

Date and Time

Date and Time Right-click on the date or time in the Notification Area, then choose Adjust Date/Time from the pop-up menu.

Display

Display Right-click the Desktop and choose Properties from the pop-up menu.

Folder Options

Folder Options In any folder, choose Tools ➤ Folder Options.

Internet Options

Internet Options In Internet Explorer, choose Tools ➤ Internet Options.

Network Connections

Network Connections Right-click on the My Network Places icon on the Desktop, then choose Properties from the pop-up menu.

Printers and Faxes

Printers and Faxes This item can be placed directly on the Start panel; refer to Chapter 6.

Sounds and Audio Devices

Sounds and Audio Devices Right-click the Volume control in the Notification Area and choose "Adjust Audio Properties" from the pop-up menu. (You may have to click the Show button to see the Volume control thing in the Notification Area.)

System

System Right-click the My Computer icon on the Desktop and choose Properties from the pop-up menu. Or, even quicker: Win+Break.

Taskbar and Start Menu

Taskbar and Start Menu Right-click the Taskbar and choose Properties from the pop-up menu. If you right-click the Start button and choose Properties from the pop-up menu, then you're automatically switched to the Start Menu tab in this dialog box.

User Accounts

User Accounts Click the user account picture at the top of the Start panel, then in the window that appears, click the Home button.

KEYBOARD MASTER

Summoning the System Dialog Box

Win+Break

This is the quickest way to summon the System dialog box. The break key can be found in the upper right part of your keyboard; it shares the Pause key.

Any Geeky, Keyboard Way to Get to a Control Panel Icon?

Despite how cute or friendly the computer mouse is, it's your keyboard that rules the computer-input universe. If you love to type, then you can use the *power of your keyboard* to quickly get into some Control Panel areas, but you must be precise with what you type.

All typing must take place in the Address bar; you cannot use the Run dialog box to access specific icons in the Control Panel:

1. Open the My Documents icon on the Desktop.

Or it can be any folder window; what you're after is the Address bar.

2. Press F4.

This activates the Address bar.

3. Type `Control Panel\Display`.

And there is the Display Properties dialog box.

Like folders, the Control Panel has a certain hierarchy. The "parent" is always the Control Panel itself. The "children" are all the Control Panel icons. You can open any icon by typing its name after Control Panel and a backslash. The problem is knowing what the names are. Windows can tell you, but to take advantage of the keyboard, you must memorize the names (or at least type them correctly).

To see the Control Panel's icon names you have to view the icons in the List view:

4. Close the Display Properties dialog box.

You're now back at the Control Panel window.

5. Choose View ➢ List

Now the icons are all listed with their names. It's those names that you type after Control Panel and a backslash to display the various dialog boxes.

For example, if you want to see the Phone and Modem Options icon, you type:

`Control Panel\Phone and Modem Options`

Press Enter and you're there.

Of course, once you get the name right, the Address drop-down list keeps a record of that name. You can easily recall recently typed names using the drop-down list and your keyboard's Down arrow key.

How About a Single Key Shortcut to Get to the Control Panel?

There is no single keyboard shortcut programmed to get to the Control Panel, though it would have made sense. For example, I'd love to see Win+C mapped to bring up the Control Panel, but there's no way to do that. Alas.

However, any shortcut icon in Windows can be assigned a Ctrl+Alt key combination. If you've created a Control Panel shortcut icon, then you can easily assign it a Ctrl+Alt key combination. Here's how:

1. Right-click the Control Panel shortcut icon.

It can be anywhere; on the Quick Launch bar, on the Desktop, or in a folder. Just right-click it to bring up its pop-up menu.

2. Choose Properties.

The Control Panel Properties/Shortcut dialog box appears, as shown in Figure 11.6.

3. Ensure that the Shortcut key box is selected.

Click the mouse in that box if you're not sure.

4. Type C.

The shortcut Ctrl+Alt+C appears in the box.

That's going to be the new shortcut to display the Control Panel.

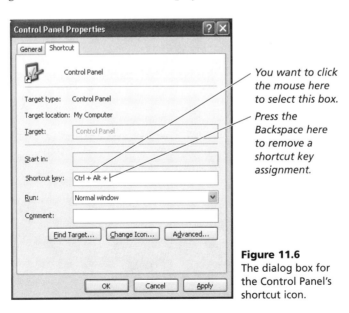

You want to click the mouse here to select this box.

Press the Backspace here to remove a shortcut key assignment.

Figure 11.6
The dialog box for the Control Panel's shortcut icon.

5. Click OK.

Now try out the new shortcut key:

6. Press Ctrl+Alt+C

And there's the Control Panel's window.

Windows lets you assign Ctrl+Alt key combinations to any shortcut icon. However, Windows *does not* warn you should the key combination you've chosen already be in use by some other shortcut icon. And there's no way to list all the shortcut keys that you've assigned.

I've chosen Ctrl+Alt+C on my computer because C = Control Panel. If you're already using Ctrl+Alt+C for something else on your computer, then you can choose another key command. Keep in mind that not all computers will have this shortcut. So when you go to fix Earl's computer and press Ctrl+Alt+C, don't be surprised if nothing happens. (Then you can show Earl this trick and he'll think that you're the Ultimate Computer God!)

 Ctrl+Alt shortcut keys are assigned to one shortcut icon at a time. Don't be surprised if you open another Control Panel shortcut icon and discover that it has no shortcut key. Also, don't be surprised if you remove that one shortcut icon and the keyboard shortcut goes away.

PART 2

All the Intermediate-Level, Good Stuff about Disks, Files, and Stuff Like That

12

The Complete Summary of File Manipulation Commands, 90% of Which You Didn't Know

I'm shocked at how many ways there are to copy a file in Windows. It's ridiculous! Copying a file is a basic operating system activity. Good old cryptic operating systems, like DOS and Unix, let you copy files using plain text commands. So in DOS you had the COPY command and in UNIX—being the more cryptic and time saving of the two—you had the CP command. But there was only one command! Not like Windows where there are numerous mousy and keyboardy ways to copy a file.

Copying a file is basic, kindergarten Windows stuff. So are moving files, renaming files, and deleting files. I assume that you come to this book with your own private arsenal of copying, moving, renaming and deleting techniques. So the purpose of this chapter is to show you a few variations on those copying, moving, renaming, and deleting themes, plus some copying tips and tricks you may not have been aware of.

Mousy Variations and Keyboardy Tricks:

- Copying a file, all the variations
- Copying a file by type
- Gathering files from across a hard drive
- Renaming rules and regulations
- Renaming a group of files
- Foraging and flushing the Recycle Bin
- Marking a file read-only
- Password-protecting files and folders

10,000 Ridiculous Ways to Copy a File: Use the Right One for You

Yes, one can even find order in the ridiculous. Overall, there are three ways to copy any file: with the mouse by itself, with the keyboard alone, or by using any of the several copying commands available after an icon has been selected. The following sections summarize each of these for you—mostly to get this stuff out of the way before I show you some things you may not have thought of. (And who knows, maybe you're unfamiliar with one of these copying methods and would prefer it to what you're using now!)

You Must Know This: File-Copying Terminology

Whenever you copy a file you're making a duplicate. The original stays where it is and the copy is an exact byte-for-byte copy of the original. The location of the original file is referred to as the source. The place to which you're copying the file is the destination, or sometimes the target.

Do You Know All Three Ways to Use the Mouse to Copy a File?

When you use the mouse to copy a file, you drag the file's icon from the source folder to the destination. That's easy to know; dragging and dropping icons is a basic function in Windows.

There are two limitations to copying a file with the mouse. First, you must have the source and target folders visible to do it. That way, you can drag from the source window to the target window, as illustrated in Figure 12.1.

If you can't manage both the source and target on the screen at once, then you can click the Folders button to display the Folders list. Then you can drag the icon to the target folder on the Folders list. (Drag the icon up or down in the Folders list to scroll the list of folders.)

The second limitation is that when you use the mouse, Windows only *copies* files when you are moving between disk drives. If you drag from somewhere on the C drive to somewhere else on C, the source file will actually move. So you can drag to copy from C to A or from C to D, but not from two folders on drive C. To force a copy when moving within a drive, you must press and hold the Ctrl key while dragging the file. This is known as a Ctrl+drag (control-drag). As you press Ctrl, the plus sign appears by the mouse pointer, indicating that you're copying a file and not merely moving it.

Finally, you can right-click and drag the icon with the right mouse button. When you release the mouse button, a pop-up menu appears. From that menu, choose Copy Here, and the file is copied; no need to press the Ctrl key.

So that makes three ways: Drag only, Ctrl+drag, and Right-click+drag.

Source window

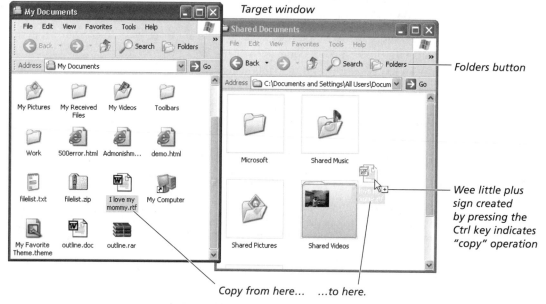

Target window

Folders button

Wee little plus sign created by pressing the Ctrl key indicates "copy" operation

Copy from here...   ...to here.

Figure 12.1 Copying a file from here to there.

KEYBOARD MASTER

Turning the Folders List On or Off

Alt+V, E, O

To turn the Folders List on or off you must access the View ➤ Explorer Bar ➤ Folders command. Using your keyboard, that works like this.

Yes, You Can Even Use the Keyboard to Copy Files

The only pure way to use the keyboard to copy files is to open a Command Prompt (DOS) window and type-type-type away! But that's just too weird for this book. (Actually, if you ever find a book on using the Command Prompt in Windows, snatch it up quickly! Such information is rarely documented and would be a treasure to have.)

The biggest obstacle to using the keyboard is that you must select the file to copy. This can be done: press the Home key to select the uppermost left icon in a folder window. Then, you can use the arrow keys to move around and select whichever file. (Also see the sidebar, "You Must Know This: Selecting Files," for more keyboard-selection tips, awkward as they are.)

 If the file part of the folder window isn't "active," then press the Tab key until it is.

Once the file is selected, press Ctrl+C to copy it. Then switch to whichever window is the target, and press Ctrl+V to paste the file, which completes the Copy operation.

Yes, I know this is obtuse. But the fact is that Windows just isn't geared toward keyboard file copying. On the positive side, however, these are the same keyboard commands used to copy and paste stuff in most (if not all) applications.

You Must Know This: Selecting Files

The easiest way to select files is by using the mouse. You can select files individually by clicking on their icons. To select a group of files you can drag the mouse over the files, or pluck them off one by one by holding the Ctrl key down as you click.

If you need to select all the files in a folder, choose Edit ➤ Select All or use the Ctrl+A keyboard shortcut.

To select all but a few files, first select those few files, then choose Edit ➤ Invert Selection. (Alt+E, I).

If files are shown in the List or Details view, you can click on the first file in a group, then Shift+Click on the last file to select everything in-between.

You can use the keyboard to select individual icons; the arrow keys choose which icon is selected.

To select more than one icon using the keyboard, hold the Shift key as you use the arrow keys to move around in the folder window.

To select a group of individual files with the keyboard, hold down the Ctrl key as you use the arrow keys to highlight various icons. Press the Spacebar once to select an icon, then continue to move about using the Ctrl key in combination with the arrow keys.

The Various Rest of the Ways (Four of Them) to Copy a File

After selecting a file's icon, or a group of icons, then the file is ripe for copying using any of these commands:

- Choose Edit ➤ Copy (then use Edit ➤ Paste in the target folder).

- Choose Edit ➤ Copy to Folder, and then use the Copy Items dialog box to select the target folder.

- Choose "Copy This File" from the list of File and Folder Tasks in the folder window's task pane.

- Right-click the file and choose Copy from the pop-up menu. (Then you'll have to paste it using one of the many paste commands.)

These are all good methods for copying a file, and I admit that I have no preference. As a keyboard person, however, I tend to use Ctrl+C to copy the files first, then Ctrl+V to paste them.

Anyway to Make a Copy of a File in the Same Folder?

I don't think it's right to say that you make a copy of a file in the same folder. No, it's a *duplicate*. But Windows just isn't a clever enough of an operating system to have a Duplicate command. So you have to cheat:

1. Right-drag the icon down just a hair in the folder.

Use the mouse's right button to drag.

2. Release the mouse button.

A pop-up window appears.

3. Choose Copy here from the menu.

The duplicate is given the name "Copy of..." followed by the file's original name. That's because no two files in a folder can share the same name. (Supposedly when that happens, it creates some sort of paradox and your screen would implode into a parallel universe.)

You can change the name of the selected icon by pressing the F2 key and then editing away. But remember the file must have its own unique name.

How Can I Copy This File to Drive A?

Though this does count as a file-copying operation, the best way to copy a file to drive A (or any removable disk) is to right-click the file and choose Send To ➢ 3 1/2 Floppy (A:) from the pop-up menu. Ditto for any other removable disks that may appear in the Send To list. In fact if you have a CD-RW or CD-R disk ready for writing, then you can also choose that disk drive from the Send To submenu.

If you're trying to use the Send To list with a group of selected files, then it's best to choose it from the menu: choose File ➢ Send To and then choose your destination from the menu.

The Best Way to Copy a Bunch of Files of a Specific Type

Suppose you need to copy all the image files from a folder to a Zip disk, so that li'l Janine down in Production can send them off to the printers. But, lo, the folder contains 459 files! How can you be sure you'll get all the image files?

1. Choose View ➢ Details.

The files are listed in Detail view, which displays them in columns as shown in Figure 12.2.

2. Click the Type heading.

This sorts all the files in the list by their type.

3. Scroll down and find the first file of the type you're looking for.

Whatever type it is—graphics file, document, whatever. (Note that there are different types of graphics files.)

4. Click the first file in the list, the first one in the group you're copying.

5. Shift-click the last item in the list. This selects all the files between, which are now ready for copying.

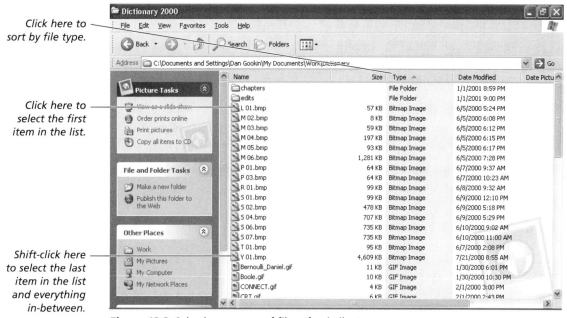

Click here to sort by file type.

Click here to select the first item in the list.

Shift-click here to select the last item in the list and everything in-between.

Figure 12.2 Selecting a group of files of a similar type

Any Way to "Gather" Files Across a Disk for Copying?

Just as Windows is missing a Duplicate file command it's also missing a Gather command. Well, come to think of it, no computer operating system on this planet has a Gather command. I must be remembering something from a past life on a planet where the computer operating systems actually had useful commands. But I digress...

Alas there is no perfect way to gather files from several folders for one mass copy. You must do it one folder at a time. The only exception is if you're copying files with similar names or of similar types. In that case you can use the Search command to help locate the files and then copy them from the Search Results window.

For example, suppose you were clever and named all the files that belong to a certain project in the same manner. These files, no matter what they're type or which folder they live in, all start with FPB, which stands for Financial Planning Booklet. To gather them all up for copying to a CD-R and sending to the printer, you would do the following:

1. Press Win+F, the keyboard shortcut for the Search command.

Or you can click the Search button (or press Ctrl+F) in any folder window.

There is no need to go on the Internet for this operation; if Windows wants you to connect to the Internet, tell it no. (Microsoft doesn't need to know what you're searching for.)

2. Click "Documents" in the task pane.

3. Enter the common part of the documents' names.

So if everything starts with FPB, type FPB* into the text box. The asterisk is a wildcard that can be replaced with anything else in the filename.

If the files are similar in any other manner, such as their creation date, size, type, or what have you, then click the "Use Advanced Search Options" link to give the Search command more information.

4. Click the Search button.

Soon a list of matching files appears in the Search Results window. You can peruse the list to ensure that all the files you need have been gathered. If so, great.

It helps to view the found files in the Details view; Choose View ➤ Details from the menu or press Alt+V, D.

5. Press Ctrl+A to select all the files.

If some of the files don't belong, go through the list and Ctrl+click to deselect the errant ones.

6. Copy your files.

Actually, you'll probably use the File ➤ Send To command if you're copying them to a removable disk drive.

(Also see Chapter 15 for information on using a CD-R or CD-RW drive; these drives must be prepared for use before you begin your copying operation.)

10,000 Similarly Ridiculous Ways to Move a File

Moving a file is just like copying, though it's really a cut-and-paste operation instead of copy-and-paste. Many of the tips and techniques covered in the previous sections also apply to moving files. But here are the specific moving file instructions, most of which you already know:

Select the file and choose Edit ➤ Cut or Ctrl+X, which flags the file as ready for moving. The file is only moved when you use the Paste command in the target folder, either Edit ➤ Paste or Ctrl+V.

Choose Edit ➤ Move to Folder to use the Move items dialog box for moving the file(s).

Choose "Move This File" or "Move the Selected Items" from the folder's task pane to move things.

Drag a file between two folders to move it.

If you need to move a file between two disk drives, then press the Shift key as you're dragging the mouse. Shift undoes the automatic Copy operation that normally takes place when you drag files between two disk drives.

 Use the right mouse button to drag one or more files between two folders. Then, when you release the mouse button, choose "Move Here" from the pop-up menu.

One big difference between copying and moving files is that you cannot use the Send To submenu to move a file. Send To is generally a copy operation only. So if you need to move a file to Drive A, use a cut-and-paste operation instead of Send To.

Stuff You Must Know About Renaming Files

I suppose there should really be only one file-renaming rule: The name of the file should make sense. Ever take a look in the `Windows\System32` folder? Do any of those file names make sense? How about the long filenames that are basically a jumble of numbers between two curly brackets?

`{E636D69D-3D67-4C0B-9656-D84DF55A68B3}`

What's up with that? I thought computers were supposed to be easy to use. What's the point of making something deliberately cryptic? I feel like I'm on the outside of an inside joke. But I digress...again.

The Most Important Thing About Renaming Files

I suppose the most important thing to remember about renaming files is the F2 key. Despite "F2" having no logical relationship to "renaming a file," it's a handy key to know.

The Official File Naming Rules (If You Really Care to Read Them)

First the, "this makes sense" rules:

 All files must have a name.

 No two files in a single folder can share the same name.

If you try to violate either of these rules, then angry armed monkeys will parachute into your office or computer den and open fire with sticky grape syrup guns. Or Windows may just refuse to let you complete the operation.

So the moral of the story: If you cannot rename the file, then you've probably violated one of the above rules.

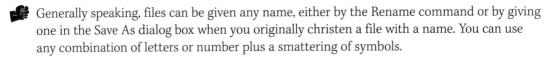

Here are some more rules:

 Generally speaking, files can be given any name, either by the Rename command or by giving one in the Save As dialog box when you originally christen a file with a name. You can use any combination of letters or number plus a smattering of symbols.

Contrary to popular myth, you can start a file's name with a number or symbol.

Do not use any of these characters, which are used for special purposes in a filename:

" * / : ? \ | < >

Short and to the point is the best length for a filename, but if you want to get technical, Windows will let you use up to 200+ characters for a file's name. Golly.

If you want a filename always to sort at the beginning of the list alphabetically, then give it a name starting with an underline underscore character (_).

The Most Horrible File Renaming Sin of All Eternity

Never, ever rename a folder that contains a program. Specifically, never rename any folder, file, or program in the Windows folders or in the Program Files folders. (If you do, then pray that System Restore still works, so that you can get your computer back.)

Can I Rename a Group of Files?

Believe it or not, but it's possible to rename a group of files in Windows XP. This is something previous versions of Windows wouldn't allow; you could only rename one file at a time. Now you can rename a group of files, which can be handy. Windows lets you rename the first file in the group, then it gives that same name—plus an incremental number—to each of the other files in the group.

For example, you name the first file Tiffany and then the remaining files selected are given names Tiffany (1), Tiffany (2), on up through Tiffany (330), or however many files you selected.

Here's how to do the renaming files as a group trick:

1. Select more than one file.

   Obviously this trick works only if more than one file is selected for renaming.

2. Press F2, the powerful keyboard Rename command.

   You'll notice that all the files stay selected, but the first file in the list is open for renaming. That's okay.

3. Rename the first file; press Enter when you're done.

   And the rest of the files in the list snap into place, each one given the first one's name, followed by parenthesis and a number.

You can rename files and folders in this manner, giving them all sequential names. And if you screw up, Windows lets you undo the renaming for each file; just keep pressing Ctrl+Z (or choose Edit ➤ Undo) until all the renaming is undone. But you must be quick! Windows can only undo a rename operation *immediately* after you use the Rename command.

Why Can't I Rename a File's Extension?

A file's extension is the very last part of the filename, typically a dot followed by one to four letters (usually three letters). Windows uses the extension to determine the file type. For example, all files ending in `.txt` are assumed to be plain text files and the Notepad program is used to open them.

When you rename a file's extension, what you're doing is really changing the file's type—which is an improper thing to do and Windows will display a warning dialog box if you try (see Figure 12.3).

The best way around this problem is not to display the extensions at all:

1. Choose Tools ➤ Folder Options from the menu. The Folder Options dialog box appears.

2. Click the View tab.

3. Put a check mark by "Hide Extensions for Known File Types" from the scrolling list.

4. Click OK.

Now Windows won't display the filename extension and won't let you edit it when you rename a file.

Always click No in this dialog box.

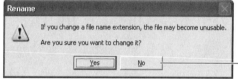

Figure 12.3 Don't rename a file's extension!

There are instances where you might want to have Windows display the extensions. For example, I do a lot of web page publishing, so I really need to know the exact filename extensions. In my case, I show the extensions and I'm just careful not to change them when I edit a file's name.

Changing a file's extension does not change the file's basic nature. Even though changing a TXT file to a GIF file may fool Windows into thinking that the file is now a GIF graphics image, the file itself has not changed.

What Is a "DOS-Safe" Filename?

Older computers that run the DOS operating system or even earlier versions of Windows do not support long filenames. Even Windows 95 through Windows Me might not support long filenames over a network. So to be safe, each file really has two names: the shorter DOS-safe filename and the longer name that Windows displays on the screen.

The shorter, DOS-safe name can only be up to 8 characters long, letters and numbers only. Those eight characters are followed by the optional period (dot) and a three-letter extension, but that's all!

So suppose you have the file:

March 2002 Financial Statements

To make that filename DOS safe you have to squeeze it down into 8 characters, something like this:

0303FS

Ugh! See the insanity DOS users had to put up with for years?

There is no point in bothering with DOS-safe names unless you have to. For example, say you're sharing a file on a network with a another computer. In that case, it's best to name the file using only eight (or fewer) characters. Anything longer, and the other user might only see the first part of the filename. Using the example above, the they might see MARCH2~1 or something equally hideous.

Yeah, you could just say "Hey! It's *your* fault not mine!" Nothing wrong with that, because it's true!

What's the Point of the Recycle Bin?

The Recycle Bin exists to lessen your pain.

In the olden days, Windows would utterly obliterate any file you wanted to delete. After all, you said you wanted to delete the file. How was Windows to know that you would frivolously change your mind and want it back? Sheesh. Some users...

Silly Recycle Bin Stuff You Already Know

To rescue any file from the Recycle Bin, follow these steps:

1. Open the Recycle Bin icon on the Desktop.

2. Select the item(s) you want to restore or un-delete.

3. Choose "Restore this Item" (or "Restore the Selected Items") from the Recycle Bin Tasks pane. And your files are recovered. Simple. Logical. Works every time.

How Can I Find Something I Deleted Yesterday?

Open the Recycle Bin and choose View ➤ Arrange Icons by ➤ Date Deleted.

Lordy! The Recycle Bin Is Just A-Brimmin' with Stuff

If you're certain that there's nothing in the Recycle Bin worth recovering, then you can empty it, flushing all the contents and revoking any chance at getting something back.

Right-click the Recycle Bin icon on the Desktop and choose "Empty Recycle Bin" from the pop-up menu. *Ka-choooo*! It's all gone.

There's no need to empty the Recycle Bin on a regular basis. Windows will, over time, yank out older stuff from the Recycle Bin to help keep its size down. If you are concerned with the Recycle Bin's size, however, you can make it a monthly habit to empty the thing out.

Life Would Sure Be Easier If the Computer Didn't Ask Me to Confirm My File Deletions

The Delete Confirmation dialog box just slows things down. To disable that warning message, do this:

1. Right-click on the Recycle Bin icon on the Desktop.

2. Choose Properties from the pop-up menu.

The Recycle Bin Properties menu appears, as shown in Figure 12.4.

3. Remove the check mark in the box next to "Display Delete Confirmation Dialog."

4. Click OK.

You're free! You're free! You're free!

Remember that these settings affect only your own account on the computer. If another, more timid person uses the same computer then they will still see the Delete Confirmation dialog box.

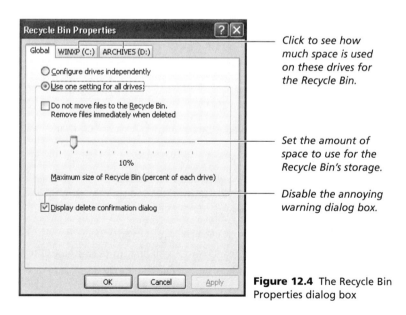

Figure 12.4 The Recycle Bin Properties dialog box

Any Way to Bypass the Recycle Bin and Just Zap a File Straight to Everlasting Hell?

To really delete a file, or group of files, select them and then press the Shift+Delete key combination. That destroys the file with no possibility of recovery.

Now it's true that some utilities can still rescue files deleted with Shift+Delete. In fact, the government routinely pulls such "deleted" files off the Bad Guys' computers. So if security is important to you, then you should use a utility such as Norton WipeInfo to fully erase information from your hard drive.

 WipeInfo is part of the Norton Utilities, which you can purchase online or at any fine software store.

Protecting Files from Death, Destruction, or Mere Accidental Erasure

Obviously your files are important to you. It's your stuff! You created it! And Windows XP tries its best to protect your stuff from accidental tampering or erasure by any of a large and growing group of potential nimrods. Even beyond the account security (and you do have a password-protected account, right?) there are many things you can do to protect your files and folders from any accidental mischief, as the following sections describe.

How Can I Prevent Even a Doof Such as Myself from Modifying a File?

First, don't ever use the computer. But beyond that, you can always lock up a file by slapping a Read-Only attribute on it:

1. Right-click the file you want to protect.

2. Choose Properties from the pop-up menu.

3. In the bottom of the Properties dialog box, click to put a check mark next to "Read Only."

4. Click OK.

> The file is now protected with read-only status. That means that you can open the file, you can view or print its contents, but you cannot change the file or delete it. If you make the attempt, a warning dialog box appears.

Files copied from CDs typically inherit the Read-Only attribute from the CD. (All files on a CD are Read-Only, which is the nature of the CD.) So if you encounter a Read-Only file and wish to change it back to a readable/writable file, then repeat the above steps but *remove* the check mark by "Read Only."

 It's easy to spot Read-Only files: view the Details panel in the folder task pane. If a file is read-only, you'll see "Attributes: Read-Only" displayed.

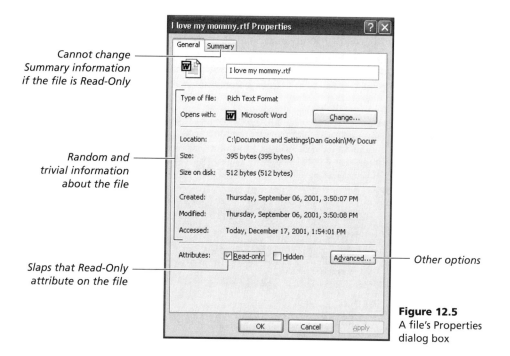

Cannot change
Summary information
if the file is Read-Only

Random and
trivial information
about the file

Slaps that Read-Only
attribute on the file

Other options

Figure 12.5
A file's Properties
dialog box

Can a File Be Password Protected?

No, not really.

Microsoft Office documents can be password protected. In Word, for example, follow these steps:

1. Choose File ➤ Save As to save the document.

2. Click the Tools button in a Save As dialog box.

3. Pick the proper Tools menu item for your version of Word:

Choose General Options in Word 2000.

Choose Security Options in Word 2002.

4. Enter a password in the appropriate place(s) in the dialog box.

Note that there are two passwords: one to open and one to modify. Also you can set Read-Only and other security options in this dialog box as well. Figure 12.6 shows the Security dialog box for Word 2002 (from Office XP).

5. Click OK.

6. Continue saving the file.

Now the file will be protected with a password, preventing unauthorized persons from messing with it.

Other applications in Microsoft Office have similar security tools. Financial packages, such as Quicken, QuickBooks, and Microsoft Money also have password protection for their data files.

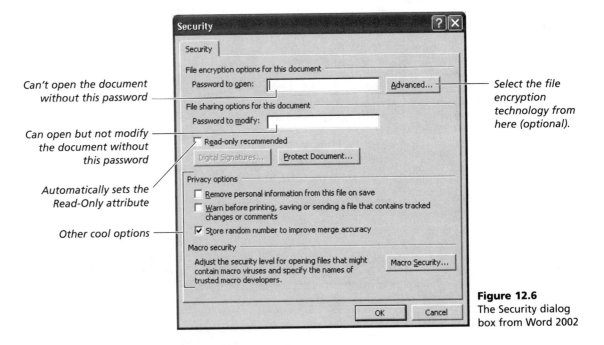

Can't open the document without this password

Can open but not modify the document without this password

Automatically sets the Read-Only attribute

Other cool options

Select the file encryption technology from here (optional).

Figure 12.6
The Security dialog box from Word 2002

What About Encrypting a File?

Windows XP Professional will let you encrypt a file. This is not the same as password-protecting the file. No, an encrypted file is simply rendered unreadable to any account that doesn't have access to it. So if you encrypt one of your favorite recipes, only your account (or anyone using your account) can access the file. If anyone else tries, then they'll see an "Access Denied" dialog box displayed.

Here's how to encrypt a file:

1. Right-click the file you want to encrypt.

2. Choose Properties from the pop-up menu.

3. In the General tab, click the Advanced button.

The Advanced Attributes dialog box appears, as shown in Figure 12.7.

4. Put a check mark by "Encrypt Contents to Secure Data."

This item is available only if you have an NTFS file system and if you're using Windows XP Professional.

NTFS stands for the NT File System, a type of hard drive formatting designed for Windows NT. It's a more efficient way of storing files on a hard drive than the older Windows format was, which was called the FAT system. NTFS is good. FAT is bad. Especially those polyunsaturated FATs.

5. Click OK, then OK again to close both dialog boxes.

Back in the file's folder window you'll see the file displayed, but with green text in its description. Similarly, in the Details area of the task pane, you'll see that the file's Attributes read "Attributes: Encrypted."

Now for the weird, unexpected part: encrypting a file merely denies access to the file by anyone other than yourself. So if another account on your computer tries to open the file, they'll see an "Access Denied" dialog box. That's it. There's no password, and as far as your account is concerned, the file opens just like any other.

 It's possible to allow specific accounts access to your encrypted file: In the file's Advanced Attributes dialog box (Figure 12.7), click the Details button. That displays a dialog box where you can specify which accounts have access to the file. Just click the Add button and follow along with the steps to add another user.

The final insult to this trick is that there's no point in encrypting a file in a password-protected folder. That's because no one is allowed access to the password-protected folder in the first place, which means encrypting files there is pretty redundant.

Figure 12.7 Encrypt that file!

Can You Explain Why Password Protecting a Folder in Windows XP Is Just So Weird?

Password-protecting a folder is not possible in Windows XP. Restricting access *is* possible, which is like password-protecting a folder, but not really the same thing. Ugh. This can be confusing, so why not take a moment to chew the cud of Windows XP system security?

First: Password-Protect Your Windows Account

Sure, Windows will let you password-protect folders even if your account doesn't have a password. But when you do that, Windows laughs at you behind your back; that's because password protecting a folder only works when your account has a password.

The moral of the story: Get your account a password if you don't already have one. See Chapter 1.

Second: Ensure That Your Computer's Hard Drive Is NTFS

Password-protecting a folder only happens if your hard drive is formatted in the NTFS style. Here's how to check for which system your hard drive uses:

1. Open the My Computer window.

2. Click to choose Drive C, or whichever drive you want to password-protect folders on.

3. Examine the Details part of the folder's task panel.

    It should say "File System: NTFS" over there. If so, the drive is able to handle password-protected folders.

4. Close the My Computer window.

If you have a FAT or FAT32 type of hard drive (shown in Step 3), then you must convert it over to NTFS before you can password protect folders. See Chapter 13 for instructions.

Third: Understand What Password Protecting a Folder Is Not

In my little world, when I think of password-protecting a folder, I imagine applying a secret keyword to that folder. So in the future, when I would go to open that folder, a Password dialog box would pop up and ask for the password. I'd type it in, and the folder would open. That's what I think of when I see "password-protected." Alas, that's not what Windows gives you.

Fourth: Know How Password-Protecting a Folder Works in Windows

In the world of Windows, password-protecting a folder simply means that you can get into that folder only if you can login and enter the proper password for that folder's owner.

For example, suppose you log into my computer as "Dan Gookin" and type in my password ("none"). By doing that, you're given access to all my password-protected folders: you can open them, view their contents, open files and so on.

Now suppose you log into my computer as "Daquita Parks" and type in her password. Now you try to access any of Dan Gookin's protected folders and all you see are empty folders. Yes, you can open the password-protected folders, but you don't see squat.

No, only by logging into an account using the proper password do you get access to password-protected folders.

Because of this scheme, it's best to password-protect your account's main folder, which is located in the Documents and Settings folder. That way all the subfolders for your account will be protected automatically—protected from other snooping users on the same computer.

Fifth: That Sounds Really Dumb

It may be a dumb way to password-protect folders (mostly because how you and I use passwords in other computer applications is different), but it is secure. With a password-protected account and folders, no one can see your stuff in Windows XP. That's pretty secure.

Sixth: The Summary

Got it? Probably not, which means two things: I need to write a bullet list summary and Microsoft will probably change this password scheme for the next release of Windows. No problem on either account:

- You can only password-protect a folder if your Windows XP account has a password attached and if your hard drive is NTFS formatted.

- Password protected folders can only be read by your account; so you must log in and use your password to get into the folders

- Other users on the same computer can access your password-protected folders, but when they open them all they'll see is an empty folder.

- Password protection for a folder applies to that single folder and then all subfolders. Therefore, it's best just to protect your account's main folder and not apply protection to individual folders.

Of course, you might say, "But, Dan! I'm may be the only confused one here, so let me see if I understand this. You add a password to a folder, but then you are never asked for that password again as long as you're properly logged into the account for which the folder exists? Is that right?"

Yes, that is right.

Seventh: Going through the Motions of Password-Protecting a Folder

Chances are that Windows has already password-protected your account's folders. Even so, here are the steps you would take to protect a folder (or to ensure that the folders are already protected). Follow merrily along:

1. Open the My Documents icon on the Desktop.

Why not password protect the My Received Files folder? Some of those raunchy Internet jokes you keep could be embarrassing if found by the spouse!

2. Right-click the folder you want to password-protect.

Such as the My Received Files folder.

3. Choose "Sharing and Security" from the pop-up menu.

The folder's Properties dialog box is displayed, as shown in Figure 12.8. If you're using a password-protected account on a computer with an NTFS hard drive, then you'll probably find the "Make this Folder Private" item checked, but disabled. That's because a folder higher up in the tree is already protected, and this folder has inherited that protection. This is a good thing.

If the item is disabled and un-checked, then you have a FAT-type of hard drive, which doesn't support password protection. Oh well.

Now somewhere in the parental chain of folders, up who-knows-where, is the main folder that's being password protected. You can climb up the parental folder tree to find that folder, but there is an easier way:

4. Click the "Another Folder" link in the bottom of the Sharing tab.

The Properties dialog box you now see should be for your account's main folder (under the Documents and Settings folder on Drive C). That's the folder that has password protection. And so, by the rules of inheritance, all its subfolders have the same protection.

What does this mean? It means that by protecting your account's main folder, you restrict access to all your private folders to only those who know your account's password. If anyone else tries to view the folder's contents, they'll see only empty folder windows. That's pretty much it to password-protecting a folder.

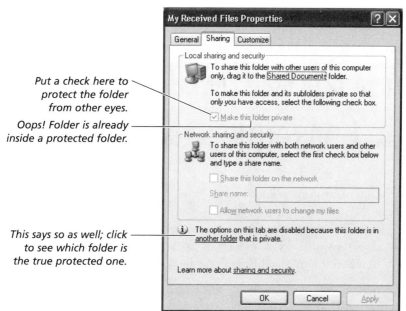

Put a check here to protect the folder from other eyes.

Oops! Folder is already inside a protected folder.

This says so as well; click to see which folder is the true protected one.

Figure 12.8
Checking a folder's password protection

I'm Not Giving Up! Surely There Has to Be a Way to Add Password-Protection to Files and Folders in Windows!

Of course there is yet another way to add password protection to files and folders in Windows. (And don't call me "Shirley.") You can password protect anything by shoving it into a compressed folder, then slapping a password on that folder. That doubly protects the file by first restricting access to only those who know the password and second by encrypting the file's data.

There are advantages and disadvantages to compressing files for security's sake. Chapter 14 holds all the methods, secrets, and details.

13

Bow to Drive C or Suffer the Perilous Consequences

You really, really, really need to know your C drive. Not intimately, of course. Most of the so-called Power Users of days gone by have given up on understanding all the junk on Drive C. I'm told that there's no single person at Microsoft who has a full grip on the whole entity we call Windows. So apparently there's no need to know all of Drive C, even at the highest echelon of the digital priesthood.

So the question really is, if you're going to bow to Drive C, how *deep* do you go? Do you perform a British butler bow, which is one of those formal "I respect you but say nasty things about you behind your backs" types of bows? Or is it one of those samurai bows where you never break eye contact all the way down; "I don't trust you one inch you maniacal balding banshee with a pigtail and a three foot straight razor."

There are only a few things you need to be comfortable with when you explore the bowels of your computer's Drive C. A working knowledge is all that's necessary to help get out of tight spots and become more of a whiz around the office when it comes to maniacal disk drives.

Necessary Knowledge and Maniacal Mayhem:

 Perusing goodness and excitement on Drive C

Understanding the various important folders

Converting from FAT to NTFS

Reformatting Drive C (or not)

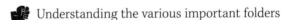 Using your D (and E and F) drive

Taking advantage of pathnames

176

If Drive C Is So Important, Why Don't They Call It Drive A?

Oh, be picky! Drive C is important because it's your computer's hard drive—the main place inside your computer for storing information. Files. Programs. It's all put on Drive C.

Drive A, for historical reasons, is the first floppy drive in your computer. B is the missing second floppy drive. C is next. (See the sidebar, "COCKTAIL PARTY TRIVIA, Part III," for the trivial details.)

I find it odd that most computer users, whether new or old, generally accept that the hard drive is "C" and not "A" or some other letter. It doesn't seem to concern anyone that the naming system is so nutty. I suppose they feel that so much is screwy with computers that there's no reason to ask.

What If Windows XP Is Not on Drive C?

If you have a computer with multiple operating systems, then Windows XP may not be on Drive C. For example, I upgraded a Windows 2000 system in my office with Windows XP Professional. Now Windows 2000 sits on Drive C and Windows XP is on Drive D. (Uninstalling Windows 2000 is like pulling a fat summer tick out of a frantic, fleeing Chihuahua.) So every time I read something about Drive C–this or Drive C–that, I have to remember that everything to do with Windows XP is on Drive D, not C.

The trick I use to ensure that I remember which drive is which is to attach a drive label to the Windows XP drive; I name that drive "WINXP" and the other drive "WIN2K" for Windows 2000. Here is how to name a drive:

1. Open the My Computer folder.

My Computer is the folder that contains all your disk drives; see Chapter 10.

2. Right-click the drive whose label you want to change.

It doesn't have to be Drive D; you can give a label to any disk drive (but not CDs or DVDs that are read-only). For example, you can change the label on a floppy disk or ZIP disk.

3. Choose Properties from the pop-up menu.

4. Enter a name (or "label") for the disk in the text box on the top of the General tab.

(Go back and see Figure 10.4 for this item's location.)

If there is already text in there, you can erase or edit it. Your new label replaces the existing label. In fact, if your computer manufacturer saw fit to naming your disk drive after its own company (e.g., IBM or Micron or Compaq), then feel free to rename your disk drive to something more personal. Death to the corporate scum!

Oh, and there are naming rules: If you have NTFS disk, then you can give it a name up to 32 characters long. If you have a FAT disk, you're stuck with only 11 characters. (See "What benefits do I get from converting to NTFS?" later in this chapter for more information on NTFS and FAT.)

5. Click OK.

And your disk has a new name, as shown in the My Computer window.

The drive name is merely a label used by the operating system. It has no impact on the drive or the files, and it's only used for display. Internally, the operating system always refers to the drive by its letter, not the label. But you, as a human, will note the label, which hopefully lets you remember which of your drives is which.

NERD'S CORNER

Cocktail Party Trivia, Part III

JOHN: *Drive C doesn't make sense to me. It's the most important drive in my computer, yet it's given a C! Are disk drives graded on "the curve?"*

EVERYONE: *Ha-ha.*

PHIL: *Actually, no, John. You see, when the IBM PC was developed, it came standard with one or two floppy disk drives only.*

MARY: *Indeed. I hear that hard drives back then were horrendously expensive.*

PHIL: *You're correct, Mary. So IBM elected to name the first floppy drive A and the second B. This was how they were named for the then popular CP/M operating system, so absolutely no thought whatsoever went into this decision.*

JOHN: *Then came the hard drive.*

PHIL: *Yes, John. The first hard drive was given letter C, the next available drive letter. And it's been that way ever since.*

JOHN: *So why isn't the CD-ROM drive always named D?*

PHIL: *Excellent question, John. Because CD-ROM drives didn't become standard equipment on a PC until the late-1990s. Before then, users would add extra hard drives to their PCs, which were given priority in the drive letter-naming scheme. So the CD-ROM drive is given the first available letter after the last possible hard drive.*

MARY: *This whole scheme doesn't really make any sense! I need another drink. (Exits.)*

PHIL: *Well, everyone, while Mary is boozing it up to mask her mental inadequacies, you should all know that other operating systems don't bother with naming disk drives at all! For example, in Unix-type operating systems, there is only one "file system" with only one root directory. Disk drives are "mounted" in that file system, so that they appear as subdirectories.*

JOHN: *Wow, that's clever.*

PHIL: *Yes, but that's Unix. We all have Windows. So we can only dream...*

(Pause.)

EVERYONE: *Ha-ha!*

Gawking at Drive C

Drive C is where you'll find all the vital files for your computer. It helps to be briefly acquainted with that drive, especially the main folder on the drive, the root folder:

1. Open the My Computer icon the Desktop.

Providing that you didn't just open this folder from the previous section's lesson.

2. Open Drive C.

What you're looking at now is the root folder—the top-most grandparent-iest folder on Drive C. What you see might look something like Figure 13.1.

(Keep this window open for a few more sections as you peruse the file folder folders on Drive C.)

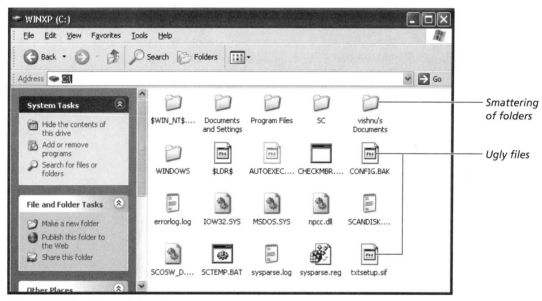

Figure 13.1 Looking at Drive C

I Want to Clean the Root Folder. Anything I Can Delete?

Heavens no!

Generally speaking, only the computer itself uses the root folder. There should never by any of your personal files there, and therefore nothing for you to delete.

Windows XP itself sets up only three folders in the root, which is all it needs:

Documents and Settings where all the personal configuration information is kept, as well as the various My Documents folders

Program Files for all applications

Windows for the operating system

Figure 13.2 shows the root folder of my Windows XP Professional system where only these three folders exist; that's all the necessary for Windows XP to boot. (Compare that with Figure 13.1, which is a former Windows Me system upgraded to Windows XP Home.)

Now even though Windows needs only three folders, don't interpret this as a reason to go plowing through the root folder and deleting non-required files and folders like you're pulling weeds! Don't delete any folder you didn't create yourself. Just be aware of what is Windows and what your computer manufacturer or dealer may have installed—or what might be left over from a Windows XP upgrade of an older computer. But don't randomly delete things!

In Figure 13.1 you see a typical Windows XP Home setup. This image is from a system I upgraded from Windows Me, so there are some leftovers from that system. For example, you see a folder called Vishnu's Documents. "Vishnu" was the name of the old Windows Me computer, and the Vishnu's Documents folder contains the original contents of the Windows Me computer's C:\My Documents folder. You may find a similar folder on your computer, should you have upgraded to Windows XP from a previous version of Windows.

Also, there are super secret folders and files that Windows uses, which are normally hidden from view. You can display these files by using the Folder Options/View dialog box, but there is no need to do so.

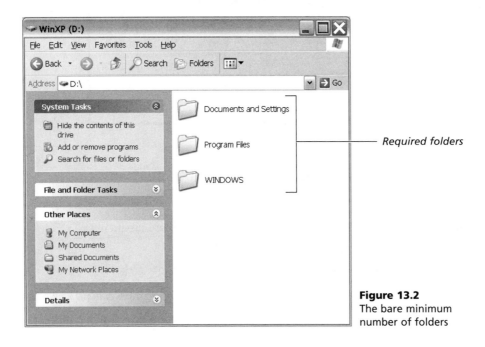

Figure 13.2
The bare minimum number of folders

Do I Need to Know Anything About the Windows Folder?

Yes. The Windows folder is important and you may be asked to visit that folder by tech support or to accomplish some task. Be careful! You need to know these things about the Windows folder:

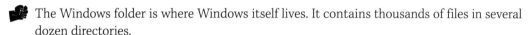 The Windows folder is where Windows itself lives. It contains thousands of files in several dozen directories.

Some of the folders and files in the Windows folder are actually organized, which I find amazing. For example, the Fonts folder in the Windows folder is where your computer's fonts are kept. Other folders hold various interesting or unique things.

One important folder in the Windows folder is SYSTEM32. This is where many support files—the infamous DLLs!—are kept.

Avoid the temptation to run programs you may find in the Windows folder; anything worth running there can be found in the All Programs menu, usually in the Accessories ➤ System Tools submenu.

Do not move, rename, or delete anything you find in the Windows folder.

 Trampling through the Windows folder and deleting files and stuff is usually the only real reason you would ever need to reinstall Windows. Even then, you should try to do a System Restore first.

Anything Worth Noting About the Program Files Folder?

A most interesting folder to dive into is the Program Files folder. That's where every program file on your computer should have been installed. When you open the Program Files folder, you'll see folders for just about everything on your computer. There's the Adobe folder, the Microsoft Office folder, the Norton Utilities folder, and other names you'll recognize (which will differ from PC to PC).

As with the other main folders, there's really nothing here to fuss over, no secrets. All the programs have their own commands on the All Programs menu. In fact, the only time you might venture into this folder is *after* removing a program, in order to delete any left over files. (And then, delete only the files that the uninstall utility says you can.)

I suppose that the most important point of the Program Files folder is to use it. Mind the programs you install. Double-check to ensure that they're smart enough to install themselves into the Program Files folder and not elsewhere.

For example, I just installed Quicken on my Windows XP computer and noted that it wanted to put itself right in the root folder. No way! So I used the Setup dialog box to redirect Quicken's installation program to stick itself in the Program Files folder.

Remember that you never delete anything from the Program Files folder. Always use the uninstall command to remove programs. There is even a link in the System Tasks pane (to the left of the file window) called "Add Or Remove Programs." Use that to uninstall stuff; never just delete files.

How Does the Documents and Settings Folder Fit into the Picture?

The Documents and Settings folder contains individual information and files from each of your computer's accounts. But there's no need to mess with it; whenever you log in, Windows creates the proper links to the items in that folder you need. For example, no matter who uses the computer, the "My Documents" folder represents the personal contents of that user's My Documents folder. (Clever thing, this Windows XP.)

Open the Documents and Settings folder. In there you'll find several subfolders. There will be a general All Users folder, plus a folder for each account on the system: your account, Guest, and any other accounts you've created.

There is also an invisible folder for the Default User. Windows uses this folder when you create a new account. Don't mess with it. (Though it's okay to mess with the All Users folder, as described elsewhere in this book.)

Note that the Default User account is where you'll find the Shared documents folder. In actuality, the Default User's "My Documents" folder is really the Shared Documents folder, which all accounts on the computer can use for saving common files or files you want to share on the network or with each other. It's up-for-grabs time all the time in the Shared Documents folder.

 Some systems have an Owner or Administrator account for the main computer operator. It's established so that Windows has an account ready to use when you first install or setup your computer.

Where Did These Other Folders in the Root Come From?

Any other folders in the root directory came from a number of potential places:

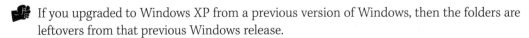 If you upgraded to Windows XP from a previous version of Windows, then the folders are leftovers from that previous Windows release.

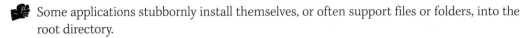 Some applications stubbornly install themselves, or often support files or folders, into the root directory.

The manufacturer may be using folders in the root directory for programs and utilities that come with your computer, programs that they stupidly installed in the root instead of in the Program Files folder. Stupid manufacturers, stupid.

This is no sin. Just don't delete or try to move the folders elsewhere. Yes, like a blindfolded man walking through a room full of cacti, it may be painful but eventually you'll learn to live with it.

What Do I Need to Know About FAT and NTFS?

All you need to know about FAT and NTFS is that NFTS is the better choice. That's it.

No Really, What is FAT?

Fat is the ester of glycerol combined with either one, two, or three fatty acids. Though it has many negative connotations, when handled by a master it can make food taste great.

Or is that the right kind of fat?

Oh! Computer FAT. The disk FAT. The redundantly named FAT table. That thing! Oh, well, that's something else entirely…

FAT is an acronym for File Access Table. It's the method the operating system uses to store files on the hard drive. The technical specifics of that system are boring to the point of nausea. Suffice it to say, it's an older system, one developed for DOS and modified over the years to work with large-capacity hard drives.

The FAT32 system was the last version of the FAT developed.

The only thing truly weird about the FAT is that it's often called the "FAT table," which is repetitive: File Access Table table.

What is NTFS?

It's the Windows NT File System, the type of disk storage system you desire.

Most new Windows XP computers and Windows 2000 or Windows NT computers you upgrade already use NTFS.

Hey! My Older Windows Disk Doesn't Recognize That NTFS Disk!

Yup, older operating systems (DOS and Windows) will not "see" an NTFS disk in your file system. So if you've partitioned your hard drive in some manner to share both Windows XP and another operating system, don't be surprised when that older operating system won't see the NTFS disk.

The same goes for booting from a floppy disk: if you boot from a DOS floppy disk, then you cannot access files on an NTFS drive.

Now if you really need to access the NTFS drive, for example, to reformat it for use with DOS (and Windows XP can work on FAT disk drives, but not without losing some features), you can do so. However, you cannot use any DOS tools to reformat the drive. Instead, you need a third-party disk partition or FDISK-equivalent program. I use System Commander (www.v-com.com) on my computer to handle this chore (when needed).

How Do I Know Whether I Have NTFS or the Stupid FAT System?

The My Computer window will tell you. Refer to the section "How About Password Protecting An Entire Folder?" in Chapter 12 for the specifics.

What Benefits Do I Get from Converting to NTFS?

If you have an older FAT hard drive you can convert it to the more useful NTFS file system. The benefits you receive are:

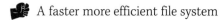 A faster more efficient file system

The ability to password protect your folders

A longer volume name

More leg room in coach

Free ice cream with your meal on Sundays

Boasting rights

 Converting to the NTFS system does not delete any files from your hard drive.

Converting your older FAT hard drive to NTFS is no big deal. Just be aware that it's a one-way ticket; you cannot convert back. Also, some older disk utilities will not work on NTFS. Plus, you cannot boot your computer with a DOS floppy disk and access information on the NTFS disk. Okay. That's enough restrictions.

The NTFS conversion must be done from a Command Prompt window:

1. From the Start panel choose All Programs ➢ Accessories ➢ Command Prompt.

A DOS window appears.

Now if you want to know what's going on, you can type HELP CONVERT and press Enter. This displays the options for the command, though none of it makes any sense to me.

First, before you get started, you need to know the volume label (name) of your disk drive:

2. Type VOL and press Enter.

You'll see the volume label displayed, as in:

```
Volume in Drive C is TOOLOUD
Volume Serial Number is 4052-3A77
```

Above, the volume label is TOOLOUD. Keeping that in mind (and on the screen), continue with the command to convert Drive C to NTFS:

3. Type: `CONVERT C: /FS:NTFS`

Check your typing. There is no period at the end of the command.

4. Press Enter.

If Drive C is already NTFS, the program will tell you so. Otherwise you see:

```
The type of the file system is FAT32
Enter current volume label for Drive C:
```

5. Type the volume label for Drive C.

You should see this from the previous `VOL` command. Type that information in. If the volume "has no label" then just press the Enter key.

Most likely next you'll see:

```
Convert cannot run because the volume is in use by another process.
Convert may be run if this volume is dismounted first.
Would you like to dismount this volume?
```

6. Type `N`.

No, you don't want to do that now. No point in upsetting the apple cart. But don't despair! The program next asks:

```
Would you like to schedule it to be converted the next time the system restarts?
```

7. Type `Y`.

8. Type `EXIT` to quit the Command Prompt window.

Now, the next time your computer starts, the conversion from FAT to NTFS will take place automagically. It only takes a few minutes, then you'll be up with the new hard drive in no time.

Though it probably goes without saying, but cannot go without mentioning, don't turn off or reset your computer while the conversion is taking place. That would be a Bad Thing.

Do I Ever Need to Reformat Drive C and Reinstall Windows?

Never. It is completely unnecessary to ever have to reinstall Windows or to reformat your hard drive. Most of the problems you experience with your computer can be fixed using tools and techniques provided with Windows.

The only time you really need to reinstall Windows is if major chunks of your file system, specifically the Windows folder, have been damaged or erased. In that case, it is necessary to reinstall Windows to rebuild its file system.

I Heard That Reformatting Hard Drives Was Routine

It's not! It has become so because lousy tech support people all across the land resort to the drastic option of reformatting a hard drive when they're feeble troubleshooting skills fall short.

Reformatting a hard drive is *not* routine!

It was never intended to be routine. Computers are designed to be used as-is until the hardware fails. It is not in the design of the beast to have its hard drive reformatted. There is no logical nor necessary reason ever to do so.

Doesn't Reformatting the Hard Drive Speed Things up and Clean Things Out?

Yes, reformatting your hard drive does speed things up because you've effectively defragmented the entire drive. Any good disk defragmenter, such as Norton's, can do just as good a job and without have to reformat the entire hard drive.

No, reformatting doesn't clean anything up. Computers are designed to carry useless files and as long as those files are merely taking up space, they don't do anything any harm. Besides, if the useless files did have the ability to wreck havoc, then Windows XP has ample tools to remove those files without having to resort to a complete reformat.

My Tech Support Says the Only Way to Fix This Program Is to Reformat

Look at the clock. I'll bet you've spent more than 15 minutes with the tech support guy or gal. That's their time limit. After that, they have to get rid of you, so they usually tell you to reformat just to dump the call and keep up with their quota. There is no reason to reformat a hard drive. All problems, save for disaster to the file system, can be fixed using the tools available in Windows. Get yourself another tech support person or a supervisor.

You Must Know This: When You Really, *Really* Need to Reformat

There is only one instance where reformatting the hard drive and reinstalling Windows is absolutely necessary; if for some reason there are files missing from the Windows or Windows\System32 folders, then you'll have to reinstall Windows. For example, lets imagine some doofus (or kid) randomly deletes great swaths of files from those folders. If so, the only way to recover is to reinstall Windows.

Reformatting the hard drive is an even more rare occurrence. The only time it's really necessary is if the hard drive has become corrupted somehow, either after a virus attack or if somehow the disk itself is physically damaged. The only time I've reformatted a hard drive was when I was uninstalling Windows 2000. I had to reformat to replace the NTFS file system with the older FAT file system for some or another reason—not a normal occurrence.

What's the Point of Hard Drive D (E, F, G, etc.)?

Any extra drives you have beyond Drive C are just bonus storage places for your computer. There are no rules or regulations about these drives. You can create whatever folders you like on drive D, E, or F or whatever; you can store files there, archives, music files, whatever you want. It's all up to you.

The most important thing about having those drives is to remember to use them!

You Must Know This: The Last Drive Letter

Under Windows, you can have drive letters all the way up to Z. Most of those letters are reserved for use with networked disk drives. For example, someone else on the network shares his or her hard drive. You can "map" that drive to, say, drive "W" on your computer.

You can also reassign drive letters for removable drives in your system, such as Zip drives or CD-ROM drives. Doing this is explained in Chapter 26.

Note that Windows understands that it can have up to Z disk drives; there are no options to switch or settings to make in order to allow that many disk drive letters.

How Come I Have Drive D and Not Just a Larger Drive C?

There are two ways you can get a D drive (or any extra hard drive) on your computer. The first is to add a second physical hard drive. Two hard drives mean you have a C, the original hard drive, and D, the new hard drive.

The second way you get more hard drives is to *partition* a single physical hard drive into several *logical* hard drives. So the 40GB hard drive in your computer becomes a 20GB Drive C and a 20GB drive D. That's perfectly fine as well. (Typically the dealer makes these partitioning decisions. Honestly I don't know why they do that; I can't see any logical reason to partition a drive, so you'll have to ask whoever partitioned what their reason was.)

If you have a single hard drive that's been partitioned into several logical hard drives, then you can unpartition the drive and just have a single, large Drive C. This is only possibly using third-party disk partitioning utilities. They will let you destroy the old logical disks D (and E and F and so on) and combine all the space onto the original Drive C.

Refer to programs such as System Commander and Partition Magic for more information. Ensure that these programs are fully Windows XP–compatible before you buy them.

How Can I Use Drive D?

I've had many Drive Ds in my years using a PC. The first Drive D was used exclusively for programming; I put all my programming tools on Drive D, as well as the programs I'd create.

Most recently, I tend to use Drive D for games. Games take up a ton of disk space, so I have a folder in Drive D's root called `Games`, and I install all my games into that folder

Drive D can also be used for long-term storage of files that typically occupy a lot of space on Drive C. Files such as graphic images, fonts, downloaded web pages, MP3 files, and so on can all easily be stored on Drive D. Just remember to keep everything organized by using folders.

Can I Change Drive Letter Names?

Yes: changing disk drive letters is covered in Chapter 26, which concentrates on disk management (a technical part of computer administration).

However, you cannot change the drive letter of a boot disk or any disk that has Windows on it (either XP or an older version of Windows). Now this is officially according to Microsoft. However I've discovered that there are certain boot and partition utilities on the market that can render certain disk drives "invisible" and let you assign new letters to the drives that remain.

For example, I use System Commander on my Windows XP Home computer, and it has successfully fooled Windows XP into believing that its hard drive partition is really Drive C (when it's really drive E or something). Use these utilities at your own peril, however!

Driving Around the Disk: Understanding "Pathnames" Can Really Save Your Butt

A pathname is merely a written way of saying where a file or folder is on your hard drive. It's technical, and I suppose Microsoft would rather have us do without pathnames, but they still exist; witness the Address bar any time you select an icon or folder—ding!— there's a pathname.

It's important to know about pathnames for two reasons. First, despite its graphic nature, occasionally Windows requires you to type in a pathname or make note of a pathname.

Second, knowing how to type a pathname to get somewhere is a great shortcut!

Witness That Pathname in the Address Bar

The Address bar is one common place a pathname rears its ugly head:

1. Open the My Documents icon on the Desktop.

2. Open the My Pictures folder.

And the pathname to the My Pictures folder appears in the Address bar, as shown in Figure 13.3. That specifies the exact location—the pathname—of the My Pictures folder on your hard drive.

The way you read this pathname is from left to right, as shown here:

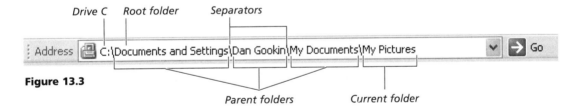

Figure 13.3

Or to phrase it another way:

To get to the My Pictures folder: Open Drive C, the Documents and Settings folder, Dan Gookin folder, My Documents folder. And there you are.

189

But My Address Bar Doesn't Display Pathnames!

Windows is configured to show the full pathname in the Address bar—unless you or someone else have told it not to. Here's how to regain that setting:

1. In any folder window, choose Tools➤ Folder Options.

2. In the Folder Options dialog box, click the View tab.

3. Ensure that there is a check mark by "Display the Full Path in the Address Bar" in the scrolling list.

4. Click OK.

Can You Visit a Pathname Place?

Suppose some manual somewhere tells you to find the SHELL32.DLL file located in the Windows\System32 folder. Can you do it?

Here's how I would do it:

1. Open the My Computer window.

2. Open Drive C.

Or whichever drive contains the Windows folder.

3. Open the Windows folder.

4. Open the System32 folder.

5. Look for the SHELL32.DLL file.

Wow! Lots of files in that folder! It will take some time to scroll down to the SHELL32.DLL file, but—dagnabbit—there it is!

Of course, now that you know what a pathname is and how it relates to the Address bar, there is a quicker way to get to the file:

6. Close the SYSTEM32 window on your screen.

7. Press Win+R to bring up the Run dialog box.

8. Type: C:\windows\system32

That's the pathname of the folder you want to open.

9. Click OK.

And the folder appears on the screen.

You can also type the pathname directly into the Address bar. However, don't type the name of the file unless you want Windows to attempt to run or open that file.

For example, there is a file named EULA.TXT in the C:\Windows\System32 folder. The file is the text copy of the Microsoft End User License Agreement you didn't read when you initially installed Windows XP on your computer. Here's how you would "run" that file:

NERD'S CORNER

EULA

Say Yoo-lah. That's how they pronounce it at Microsoft.

10. Close the window.

11. Press Win+R.

12. Type: C:\windows\system32\eula.txt

13. Click OK.

And there is Notepad with the copy of the EULA in it.

(You could have also typed the command into a window's Address bar and gotten the same results.)

14. Close Notepad.

Some places in Windows don't have pathnames. Specifically:

 My Network Places

My Documents

Desktop

My Computer

To get to these places, simply type their proper names into the Address bar. (Alas, you cannot use the Run dialog box to open these folders; only the Address bar.)

KEYBOARD MASTER

Accessing the Address Bar

F4

This focuses the keyboard's attention on the Address bar, where you can type in a pathname to open a folder, run a program or open a document.

14
Archiving Techniques
to Save Your Butt

Archiving is nothing more than storing stuff on your computer. Well, it's more like *intelligently* storing stuff on your computer. Unlike merely saving something to disk, archiving is the art of storing stuff you want to keep around for a while. And it makes you sound more important if you say, "Let me check my correspondence archives for that letter." Better yet, say "missive" or "dispatch" instead of "letter." And if you really want to impress them, call it an "epistle." Who cares if it's merely a note to the UPS man to stop leaving the parcels where the dog can pee on them, it's an *epistle* and, by gum, it's archived!

In addition to the basic file tools for storing and organizing your stuff, the best archiving tool Windows has to offer is file compression—either in the form of the blue compressed file or folder or the Compressed Folder, which is merely a gussied-up ZIP file. This chapter explains all that's important about ZIP, zat, and the other zing, plus all the necessary ups and downs of archiving your stuff.

ZIP, Zat, and the Other Zings:

 Understanding archiving

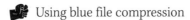 Using blue file compression

 Knowing when to use blue file compression and when to create a compressed folder

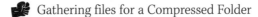 Compressing a file

Gathering files for a Compressed Folder

Using Compressed Folder alternatives

Another aspect't of archiving is backing up, or creating a secondary copy of your computer's information on a CD for safe-keeping. This is covered in Chapter 15.

Why Archive?

You archive for one of two reasons. First you archive because you have the space. You have a Drive D, or a CD-R, or just a really roomy hard drive. Take advantage of that space and store your stuff.

Second, you archive because you *lack* the space. This is where archiving is done on removable disks or where you take advantage of compression techniques that let you store more junk in less space.

How you archive is up to you. There are no rules. You can organize stuff by project, client, year, or however you see fit. Remember, the more organized you are, the easier it will be to find things when you need them. Also, the easier it will be to store new stuff when the time comes for that.

What the Heck Is a Blue Compressed Folder?

One of the many attributes you can slap on a file in Windows XP is "compressed," which is where Windows stores that particular file—or an entire folder or branch of folders and files—in a compressed state on the disk. This is *not* the same as a Compressed Folder (also known as a ZIP file), which has its own icon and its own set of limitations.

I call them blue compressed folders (or files) because when they're compressed, Windows shows them in a folder window using blue text instead of black. That's your clue that the file or folder is compressed. Beyond that, the blue compressed file or folder acts and works just like any other file or folder in Windows. The only real difference is that it's compressed and therefore takes up less space on the hard drive—ideal for archiving purposes.

NERD'S CORNER

Compressed Folder versus Compressed Folder

Yeah, I hate that there are two types of compressed folder in Windows, both of which are generally referred to as a "compressed folder." That's why I refer to the ZIP-file type of Compressed folder as a "Compressed folder" and the other type, the compressed folder attribute, as a "blue compressed folder."

Ack! Oh, bother. At least it isn't as crazy as the expanded and extended memory standards of a decade ago.

My Grandmother's Hair Is Blue, Did Bill Gates Have Anything to Do with That?

Probably not. Have your grandmother tell her hairdresser to use less bluing in her rinse.

How Do I Blue Compress Things?

To blue compress a file or folder, follow these steps:

1. Right-click the file or folder you want to blue compress.

2. Choose Properties from the pop-up menu.

3. In the General tab, click the Advanced button.

   Blue file compression is actually a file attribute. Clicking the Advanced button displays the Advanced Attributes dialog box, as shown in Figure 14.1.

Click to compress the file. Remove to decompress the file.

Compressed files cannot be encrypted.

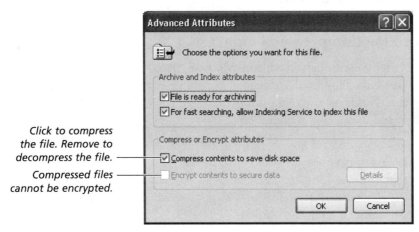

Figure 14.1
Blue compression happens here.

4. Put a check mark by "Compress Contents to Save Disk Space."

5. Click OK, then OK again to close both dialog boxes.

   If you're blue compressing a folder, the you're asked whether or not you want the compressed attribute to apply to the folder only or to all subfolders as well. Make your choice, then click OK.

The file or folder is now flagged as compressed by the blue text that describes the file, or you can see that it's compressed by viewing the file's Details in the folder's task pane.

 Technically, the blue compressed file uses the old DriveSpace technology to save on disk space. Files are compressed and decompressed as they're accessed.

Whenever a blue compressed folder or file is accessed, Windows automatically decompresses it, which adds time to the operation but still the compressed file takes up less disk space.

Why Would I Want to Decompress a Blue Compressed Folder or File?

There really is no reason to decompress a blue compressed file or folder. Windows handles the decompression for you whenever you open the file. And if you copy or move the file to a removable disk, then the file is decompressed automatically to allow other computers to read it.

If you do want to decompress a file or folder, and remove its blue compression attribute, then repeat the steps in the previous section but *remove* the check mark by "Compress Contents to Save Disk Space." That's it.

 I don't compress any file on my main hard drive. I only compress my archives on Drive D. That's because blue compression ads a wee bit of overhead to the time it takes to open or save a file. For the stuff I work on every day, I'd rather not have that happen. But for the files in the archives, it's not a big issue because I don't wade through the archives every day.

So If Archiving Is Merely Saving My Old Stuff, and I Have the Room, Do I Need to Bother with Blue Compression?

By all means, if you have the room on your hard drive, or if you buy a second hard drive, then use it for storage. Keep your files uncompressed. While the files do occupy more room that way, getting at them is a tad faster than when they are compressed.

Also note that some files are compressed already, and so saving them in a blue compressed state doesn't save you any disk space and may actually cost you time. For example, GIF, JPG, MP3, MPEG, and TIFF files are all stored in pre-compressed formats. You cannot save any disk space by blue compressing these files. So if you're creating an MP3 music archive, just keep it uncompressed.

Likewise, do not attempt to use compression on CD-R disks. It's best to keep the files there as "raw" as possible, so that they can be read by other computers as well as future operating systems that may not recognize Windows compression.

You Must Know This: Can You E-Mail a Folder?

You can attach any file to any e-mail message. It's basic, cinchy e-mail stuff. And if you're sending multiple files, why not then zip them all up into a Compressed Folder and e-mail them that way. Saves time and hassle.

But can you e-mail a folder? No! You can't!

The main reason you can't e-mail a folder is that folders really don't exist. A folder is merely a database on the hard drive that lists files and other folders (or databases). The folder itself isn't an actual object. For example, while a folder in a filing cabinet might contain several documents, a folder in your computer is merely a list of the documents it supposedly contains. The documents themselves are stored elsewhere.

Compressed Folders, on the other hand, are really files—ZIP files, which like any file can be attached to an e-mail message and sent.

What About Blue Compressing a Whole Disk?

Apparently this isn't possible, though I wouldn't recommend it anyway. Instead of blue compressing an entire disk, merely blue compress folders on that disk. That way you can be selective about which archives get compressed.

For example, blue compress folders that would contain documents because they compress easily and save lots of disk space.

Do not blue compress folders containing JPG or TIFF graphics files, as they don't compress well. Ditto for MP3 music files. In fact, the only graphics file format worth blue compressing is Windows own BMP or Bitmap Image Format, which compresses nicely and saves lots of space.

Welcome to the Land of Compressed Folders

A compressed folder is Windows way of representing a ZIP file on your computer. These are special file archives, more of the traditional archives that were originally used to send files back and forth on the Internet. Older versions of Windows required third-party utilities to manage and work with Compressed Folders, but Windows XP lets you integrate them right into the folder system, so working with them is easy, though they do have a few limitations.

ZIP or Zip: What's the Difference?

A ZIP file and a Zip disk are two different animals. The ZIP file is basically a Compressed Folder; all Compressed Folders use the `.zip` file extension, which is how Windows recognizes them as Compressed Folders and not some other type of file.

The Zip disk is a storage device developed by Iomega. It has nothing to do with ZIP files, unless you create or copy ZIP files to a Zip disk. In this book, as well as other things you may read, ZIP (all caps) refers to the file format, whereas Zip (initial cap) refers to the Zip drive.

I Just Downloaded a Compressed Folder. Now What?

First, ensure that you've saved the Compressed Folder in a logical place. Everything I download from the Internet or save as an e-mail attachment goes into my Downloads folder right there in the My Documents folder. I generally store—nay, *archive*—all the stuff I get there.

Second, you'll need a spot to decompress the files. Generally this depends on the type of content. For example, if an editor is sending back a batch of author review chapters, then I'll need to decompress the files to that special folder. Otherwise, I explode the files into a temporary or Junk folder and, from there, copy them off to wherever I see fit.

Third, I follow these steps:

1. Right-click on the Compressed Folder.

2. Choose Extract All from the pop-up menu.

    Note that the Send To submenu applies only to the Compressed Folder here—not its contents!

    The Extraction Wizard begins. Oh, joy! A wizard.

3. Click the Next button.

    Unlike other endless wizards, the Extract Wizard gets right down to business, as shown in Figure 14.2. Normally, it suggests a folder to extract to, which is merely a new folder given the same name as the Compressed Folder.

    So if you're extracting files from `12-31AR.ZIP` the Wizard suggests creating a folder named 12-31AR and putting the files into there. If that sounds grand, then all you need to do is move on to Step 4, and you're in business. Otherwise, you use the Browse button to find a folder for extracting the files (see Figure 14.3).

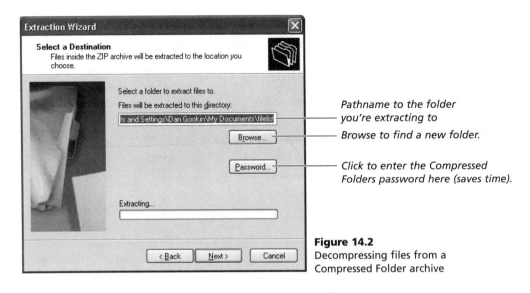

Pathname to the folder
you're extracting to

Browse to find a new folder.

Click to enter the Compressed
Folders password here (saves time).

Figure 14.2
Decompressing files from a
Compressed Folder archive

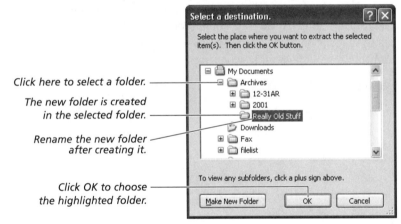

Click here to select a folder.

The new folder is created
in the selected folder.

Rename the new folder
after creating it.

Click OK to choose
the highlighted folder.

Figure 14.3
Finding a new folder
for your files

If you use the Browse button, the Select a Destination dialog box appears. Keep in mind that this dialog box only selects a folder into which the files in the Compress Folder archive will be extracted. If you want to create a new folder, use the Make New Folder button. Click OK after selecting the folder.

4. Click the Next button.

That's it! You're done. Unless the archive is password-protected, in which case a Password Needed dialog box appears where you must enter the password(s).

Because you most likely want to visit the folders you just extracted:

5. Ensure that there is a check mark by "Show Extracted Files."

6. Click the Finish button.

And the folder window opens, where you'll find your extracted files.

If what you downloaded was a program you're about to install, then locate the SETUP or INSTALL program in the folder. Run that program to install your software. And install the software to its own folder, preferably in the Program Files folder on Drive C. When you're done installing, you can delete all the extracted files if you like; there is still a copy of those files stored in the original Compressed Folder archive you downloaded. The duplicates are no longer necessary.

Sometimes the Compressed Folders Are Program Files. Is That Right?

There is a special type of Compressed Folder that appears as a program file or "executable." This must be created using a special ZIP file utility. It converts the normal ZIP file (or Compressed Folder) into what's called a *self-extracting archive*. That way, the files can be extracted even on a computer that doesn't have a ZIP file utility or the Compressed Folders tool. So Earl with his old Windows 95 computer can run the ZIP/Program file, which automatically extracts and optionally even runs a Setup program to get him all ready to go.

When you download a self-extracting archive in Windows XP, it appears just like other program files. There's no need to bother opening it as a Compressed Folder; just run the program and the files extract automatically.

Alas, there is no way to make a Compressed Folder self-extracting in Windows. But if you have WinZip you can convert any ZIP file into a self-extracting EXE file: Use the Actions ➢ Make .Exe File menu command. Or you can right-click on any WinZip file icon and choose Create Self-Extractor (EXE) from the pop-up menu. (These commands may change with future releases of WinZip.)

I Need to Collect and Compress Files for Sending. Tell Me How!

There are two ways to create and build an archive in a Compressed Folder. If you're just putting one file into a Compressed Folder, then follow these steps:

1. Locate the file you want to compress.

2. Right-click the file and choose Send To ➢ Compressed Folder from the pop-up menu.

And there, in the same folder, you'll find a new Compressed Folder given the same name as the original file. The Compressed Folder is ready to be copied to a removable disk or e-mailed or whatever.

And, yes, it's okay to delete the Compressed Folder after you're done using it; you still have a copy of the original file on your hard drive.

If you need to stick more than one file into a Compressed Folder, then it's better to create the Compressed Folder first, then copy files into it:

1. Open the folder in which you want to create the new Compressed Folder.

   For example, if I'm uploading something to the Internet, I'll put it in the My Documents\Put folder, which is where I put all the stuff that's to be sent to the Internet (and then deleted).

2. Choose File ➤ New ➤ Compressed Folder from the menu.

   And there it, ready for renaming.

3. Type in the folder's new name.

   If you've elected to have Windows show the file extensions, then you must rename the Compressed Folder with a `.zip` extension.

4. Open the new Compressed Folder.

   Now you're ready to start adding stuff.

5. Minimize the Compressed Folder window.

   The best way to add things to the Compressed Folder is to copy and paste them. You can't use the Move to folder or Copy to folder commands, as the Compressed Folder is not a "real" folder.

6. Open the folder that contains the file(s) you want to add to the Compressed Folder.

7. Select the file(s).

8. Press Ctrl+C to copy.

    It's possible to copy folders and paste them into a Compressed Folder. This is the only way to get a folder into a Compressed Folder; you cannot create a subfolder inside of a Compressed Folder.

9. Restore the Compressed Folder's window.

10. Press Ctrl+V to paste in the file(s)

     You can also open both the Compressed Folders window as well as the source folder (from which you're copying) and then use the Taskbar's pop-up menu to arrange both windows vertically. Then you can drag and drop folders between the windows.

11. Repeat steps 6 through 10 for all the files you need to add to the Compressed Folder.

    After copying all the files, then the Compressed Folder is ready to be sent, or saved to a floppy disk, or whatever.

KEYBOARD MASTER

Quickly Summoning a Compressed Folder

Alt+F, W, C

This quickly slaps down a compressed folder, providing that another item in the New sub-menu does not begin with C. So be careful!

How Do I Password Protect a File Inside a Compressed Folder?

You cannot add a password to individual files inside a Compressed Folder, but you can password-protect the entire folder: Open the Compressed Folder and choose File ➤ Add a Password. The Add Password dialog box appears (Figure 14.4), which I assume you're pretty adept at filling out.

 Don't forget that password!

Now here's the weird thing: The password *does not* prevent you from opening the Compressed Folder. You can open it and look around, even opening subfolders inside the Compressed Folder. But you cannot open or extract any file from the Compressed Folder unless you know the Password.

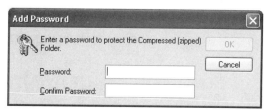

Figure 14.4 Slapping a password on a Compressed Folder

If this scares you, then you can remove the password: Open the Compressed Folder and choose File ➤ Remove Password.

I Forgot My Compressed Folder Password!

You're screwed.

I Can't Use Word to Open Documents in My Compressed Folders!

Yes, because Compressed Folders are not really folders! They're special ZIP file archives that don't really exist other than as a bunch of zeros and ones. The computer can read Compressed Folders and display them on the screen just like a real folder, but you cannot browse to the folder using a Browse or Open dialog box.

 Technically, when you try to open a Compressed Folder using an Open dialog box, the program assumes that you're trying to load a ZIP document, not open a folder.

Note that it is possible to open a compressed folder and double-click a document there to open and edit that document. However, many applications open the document "read-only," meaning that you cannot save it back to disk, specifically back to the compressed folder. To avoid that, use the File ➤ Save As command instead to save it elsewhere on the hard drive.

Any Advantage to Keeping WinZip as Opposed to Using Windows' Own Compressed Folders?

WinZip offers a much better interface, more logical commands, and more flexibility over using Compressed Folders. Figure 14.5 shows the WinZip 8.0 interface, which I find much more friendly and open to suggestions than using the Compressed Folder setup that Windows gives.

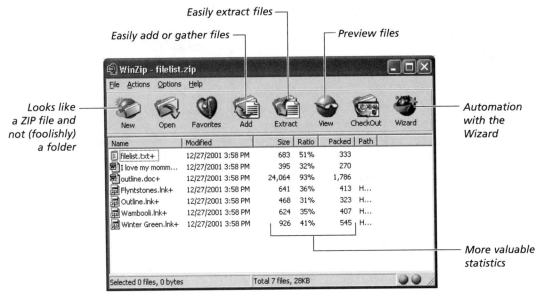

Figure 14.5 WinZip in action

But is it worth the cost? Definitely! First, it costs nothing to download a free evaluation copy from www.winzip.com/. Second, a "real" copy is yours for only $29 US. If you're into Compressed Folders, then you'll sing, "Bless you, WinZip" every day that you use this program.

 I am in no way associated with WinZip, other than I have purchased, used, and can recommend use of their fine product.

If you're really heavily into archiving and want an even better solution than WinZip, I can also recommend WinRAR from RarSoft (www.rarsoft.com/). It's like WinZip on steroids, supporting a higher level of compression, better compatibility across the board with various file compression programs, plus a more inventive interface and feedback than WinZip offers. While I'm not a full

WinRAR convert, I can recommend the product and know many fellow computer nerds who sing its praises daily.

An evaluation copy of WinRAR can be downloaded free, or you can purchase it online for $35 US.

 Both WinZip and WinRAR add special commands to an icon's pop-up Shortcut menu as well as the Send To submenu. You can use those commands to easily extract or add files to an archive.

What If I Have WinZip but Want to Continue to Use the Compressed Folders?

You can use both Compressed Folders and WinZip, and even WinRAR as well, if you like. Although a ZIP archive file may display one icon or another, you can right-click the file and choose the Open With command to display all the programs capable of opening that file.

In Figure 14.6, for example, you see that the file can be opened with WinZip, the Compressed Folders that Windows uses, or even WinRAR. So whichever program you want to use can instantly be chosen, no matter which program "owns" the file's icon.

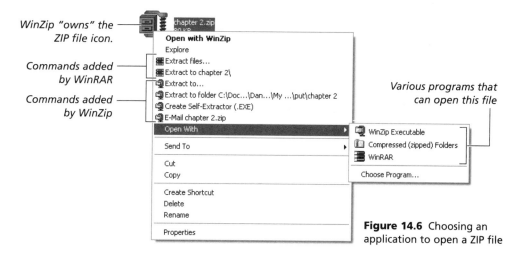

Figure 14.6 Choosing an application to open a ZIP file

It Seems Like Compressed Folders Are a Bother with Blue Compression Around

Indeed, why bother with the manual overhead of a Compressed Folder when Windows can compress files and folders on-the-fly? But Compressed Folders still do have a place. While it may be inefficient to store your archives in a Compressed Folder, they still do come in handy for sending things via e-mail or on the Internet.

So if you're going to be transmitting files to another computer, then archiving them in a Compressed Folder has several advantages:

- Many files can be compressed into one folder so that everything can be sent at once.

- The files in the Compressed Folder are, well, *compressed*, so the files take less time to send and receive.

- The Compressed Folder is really a ZIP file, which is the most common file archive format on the PC.

None of this can be done with blue compression. Also, you need to know how to use Compressed Folders because many of the files you receive on the Internet will be stored in that file format.

What Are the Pros and Cons of a Compressed Folder versus a Blue Compressed Folder?

Table 14.1 lists the pros and cons of this type of compression verses using a Compressed folder for archiving. My bottom-line advice, however, is this: If you're archiving files on a hard drive and want to save on space, blue-compress the entire archive. Do not, however, blue compress files on a removable disk, as that compression format may not be readable by all computers.

Table 14.1 *Differences between Compressed Folders and Blue Compressed Files*

COMPRESSION TECHNIQUE	PROS	CONS
Blue Compressed Files/Folders	Files are still accessible by Windows and can be manipulated using all the file commands	Compressing and decompressing is done as the file is accessed, which slows disk access somewhat Compressed files lose their attribute when the file is copied or moved. Cannot e-mail a blue compressed folder (just as you cannot e-mail any folder, only the contents of that folder).
Compressed Folders	It's really a file, which can be sent to other computers or e-mailed. Allows password-protection for each Compressed Folder.	Other computers must also use Compressed Folders or a ZIP file utility to access the files. Cannot open or access files in a Compressed folder; files must be removed from the folder to be made useful.

Only use Compressed Folders (or Zip files) when sending files over the Internet. If possible, try to avoid using them on your hard drive or for archiving, unless you're taking advantage of their password security.

NERD'S CORNER

Cocktail Party Trivia, Part IV

JOHN: *Compression sure has come a long way since the early days of the ZIP file!*

MARY: *You mean the ARC file, John!*

EVERYONE: *Ha-ha.*

PHIL: *No, actually you mean the LIB file.*

EVERYONE: *Huh?*

PHIL: *One of the original archiving programs on the PC was called LIB, which stood for library. All LIB let you do was combine several smaller files into a single larger file. That way you could send all the files by modem without losing any of the pieces.*

JOHN: *Were the files compressed?*

PHIL: *No, John. Compression was first added by the PKARC utility, which not only combined many files into one ARChive...*

MARY: *Clever!*

PHIL: *(Continuing)...but used compression so that the files took up less space. Then came the PKPAK utility, and then eventually the ZIP utility. Each one offered greater levels of compacting the files.*

JOHN: *And a Compressed Folder is merely Windows own way of displaying ZIP files.*

PHIL: *Exactly. Before Compressed Folders were integrated into Windows, you had to buy a third-party program, such as WinZip, to manage your ZiP files.*

MARY: *PKARC, PKPAK, ZIP, what's next?*

JOHN: *RAR! (Everyone is silent.) Oh, no, don't be frightened. That's just the name of the newest, hip disk compression program.*

PHIL: *That's right, John, the RAR file compression program offers even better compression than ZIP, but has a ways to go before it supplants ZIP's wide-spread use and popularity.*

15

All the Necessary Information About Burning a Data CD-R or CD-RW Disk

Creating your own CDs on the computer is so common that it's difficult to think back to when such a task was pure fiction. I remember in the 1980s hearing that there were only two sites in the world where a CD could be made. Now you can drive down any street in America and chances are there's a computer in one of the houses with a CD-R drive and possibly some teenager (of any age) creating his own music CD. It's become so common not a second thought is given—unless you're in the music industry in which case you freak out that your copyrighted stuff is getting ripped off. But that's another story.

You can use any computer with a CD-R, CD-RW or DVD-RAM drive to create your own CDs. While you can make music CDs, the subject of this chapter is using your CD-R drive for "burning" data CDs. It's actually quite easy to do (easier than it was when these doohickeys first appeared), plus it's beneficial for security as well as archiving. So this chapter covers all that good and easy stuff in addition to the useful things you may not know about creating and using your own data CD-R and CD-RW disks.

The Easy, Good, and Useful Stuff:

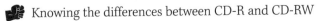 Knowing the differences between CD-R and CD-RW

Buying the proper disk

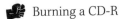 Burning a CD-R

 Working with a CD-R disk

Using a CD-RW disk

Backing up your stuff to a CD-R or CD-RW disk

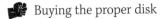

This chapter does not cover DVD-R, DVD-RW, DVD-ROM or DVD+RW drives, mostly because the author doesn't have such a drive, but also because there are no built-in Windows tools for creating DVD disks.

How Can I Tell If My Computer Can Burn a CD?

Not all computers are sold with CD-R or CD-RW drives. While the CD-ROM drive or DVD drive is pretty standard PC hardware, CD-R/CD-RW drives are still special-order items. So there's no point in trying to burn a CD unless you're certain that you have the proper hardware. How to tell? Look at the drive! The drive will be labeled either as "CD-R," "CD-RW," or "Recordable" or "Re-writable" or possibly some combination of these.

There are rare instances when the drive may not have any uniquely identifying label on it. For example, I have an external FireWire drive that I know is a CD-R/CD-RW drive, and yet you can't tell that by looking at the drive. (Stupid drive.)

Any Other, Sure-Fire Way to Tell If I Have a CD-R Drive?

Perhaps you have one of those very black IBM computers, like I do! And the console is so glossy you can't read the front of the CD-ROM drive to see if it's a CD-R or not. In that case, it's best to use the science of software!

1. Open the My Computer icon on the Desktop.

Look at your removable disks!

CD-RW Drive (G:)

Windows can be smart enough to recognize a CD-RW Drive, so it might say so right there on the screen. (Of course, I could point out that Windows is *not* recognizing my DVD drive, but that's not the subject here.)

Even if your CD-RW drive isn't labeled as such, some further poking can confirm that Windows just isn't being stubborn:

2. Right-click the CD-RW drive icon.

3. Choose Properties from the pop-up menu.

4. Click the Recording tab.

Is there a Recording tab? If so, great! You've hit the mother lode. It's a CD-R/CD-RW that you have! Yee-ha! Figure 15.1 explains what you're looking at.

If you don't see a Recording tab, then you most definitely don't have a CD-R drive. Complain to the dealer if you thought you were owed one. (Or it could be hardware trouble.)

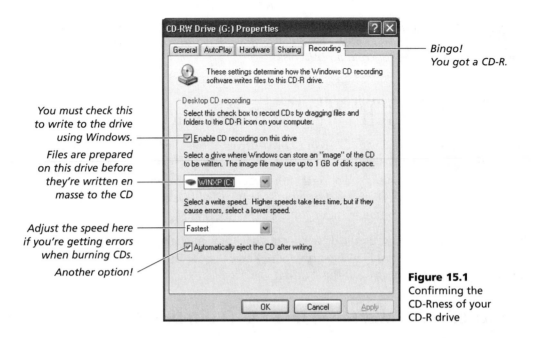

You must check this to write to the drive using Windows.

Files are prepared on this drive before they're written en masse to the CD

Adjust the speed here if you're getting errors when burning CDs.

Another option!

Bingo! You got a CD-R.

Figure 15.1
Confirming the CD-Rness of your CD-R drive

You must enable CD recording on the drive for Windows to be able to access the drive and record files to a CD-R or CD-RW disk. If the "Enable CD Recording on This Drive" item isn't checked, check it now.

5. Click OK.

6. You can close the My Computer window as well.

What's the Difference between CD-R and CD-RW?

As far as the hardware is concerned, nearly all CD-R drives sold today are also CD-RW drives; the hardware can handle both types of disk. Only older computers may have a CD-R only drive, and it is my experience that such a computer would probably not be Windows XP–compatible anyway, so it's neither here nor there.

Bottom line: CD-R disks are cheaper, but they can only be written to and never erased. After the disk is full, you cannot reformat it and use it again. It's done!

CD-RW disks work just like CD-R disks, but they can be reformatted and used over again. It's not exactly like using a floppy disk, but it's close, which makes CD-RW disks ideal for back up.

Oh, well, you can use CD-R disks for backup as well, but you can't reuse them; once they're full, that's it! (Traditional backups were done to removable data cassettes, which were reused over and over. CD-RWs can operate in a similar manner, which is why more people use them for backing up.)

Also, CD-R disks are cheaper than CD-RW, but with recent price drops the differences aren't that much.

Buy your CD-R disks in bulk! I typically buy a spool of disks (no jewel cases), about 50 for $25-$30. CD-RW disks also come in bulk, as do CD-R music disks. And if you really need the jewel cases, you can buy them separately.

Is There a Difference in Which CD-R Disk I Buy?

Not any more. Some disks are labeled as Music CDs and others are labeled for data. I've used both and haven't noticed any difference between them, though it kind of makes sense to buy the Music CD-Rs if you plan on creating musical CDs (supposedly they're more compatible with CD players). Otherwise, I've not had any trouble with any CD-R disk.

Do note the capacity on the CD-R disk. The standard CD-R stores up to 700MB of junk. Some high capacity CD-Rs are available that supposedly store up to 850MB.

Bad CD-R disks do happen. If a disk can't burn, then you can try setting the speed to something lower for the next one (see Figure 15.1). And do throw away the bum disk; no sense in keeping it.

How About Burning Music CDs?

Creating your own music CDs is also possible using your CD-R drive. In fact, that's the number one use of the drive on most computers.

In Windows, the best way to create a musical CD is by using the Windows Media Player program, which is covered in Chapter 20.

The "Let's Create a Data CD-R" Tutorial

After determining that you have a CD-R drive and obtaining a CD-R disk, you're ready to start writing to the drive. That's as easy as sticking the CD-R into the drive; Windows takes care of the rest. Follow these steps:

1. Stick a CD-R disk into the CD-R drive.

Don't mess with CD-RW disks yet; that comes later in this chapter.

Windows recognizes the CD-R disk immediately (providing that you've enabled the drive for writing as described earlier in this chapter). You'll see one of the What-the-Heck-Do-I-Do-with-This-Disk dialog boxes displayed, as shown in Figure 15.2.

2. Click OK.

A folder window for your CD-R drive opens. The CD-R drive is now ready for copying files.

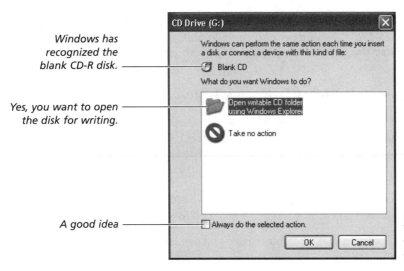

Windows has recognized the blank CD-R disk.

Yes, you want to open the disk for writing.

A good idea

Figure 15.2
Windows supposes that you want to write to a CD-R disk.

3. Select files to be copied the CD-R drive.

Various techniques for this are covered in the sections that follow. Note that you are merely selecting files to be copied, even though you're using common file copying commands. (More on this in the section, "What Are Some Interesting and Various Ways to Copy Files to the CD-R?")

As you copy files, Windows tells you that those files are waiting to be put on the CD-R, using an annoying pop-up bubble shown in Figure 15.3.

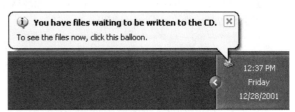

Figure 15.3 The annoying Notification Area CD-R pop-up bubble

The annoying pop-up window serves as an important reminder: the silly secret here is that the files aren't actually written to the CD-R disk. They're stored in another location on the hard drive (specified in the drive's Properties dialog box, Figure 15.1). You must tell Windows to write the files to the CD-R disk before you eject the disk. Otherwise nothing is written.

4. Open the CD-R drive's window.

There you see the files and folder waiting to be copied, as shown in Figure 15.4. The files appear ghostly because they haven't really been written yet; they're just sitting in a holding bin, awaiting the time you direct Windows to burn the CD.

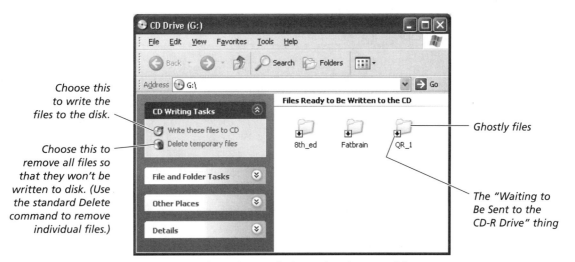

Choose this to write the files to the disk.

Choose this to remove all files so that they won't be written to disk. (Use the standard Delete command to remove individual files.)

Ghostly files

The "Waiting to Be Sent to the CD-R Drive" thing

Figure 15.4 Files waiting to be burned to the CD-R disk

5. Choose "Write These Files to CD" from the task pane.

Oh no! It's Wizard Time. In this case, it's the CD Writing Wizard, which has you follow the necessary steps of finishing (or not) the CD-writing operation.

6. Give the CD a name.

Technically, this is a *volume label*, which is just the disk's name that will appear in the My Computer window. Otherwise the name isn't used for much.

Windows suggests naming the CD-R after today's date—a good idea if you're creating a backup disk.

7. Click the Next button.

Windows writes the files to the CD, which takes some time. The time depends on the writing speed of your CD-R drive and the amount of junk you're writing. But be aware that it may take quite a bit of time.

When writing is done, the disk is ejected. It's done!

8. Click the Finish button.

And now do like everyone else does: stick the CD-R back into the drive to assure that all the files are there.

NERD'S CORNER

Where the Files Waiting for the CD-R Are Really Kept

Windows doesn't write any files to the CD-R disk until you tell it to, or until the disk is ejected, or however it works. But that's not my point here! The point is that until the files are written to disk, Windows stores them in a secret location. There they sit and wait until you're ready to burn the CD-ROM.

The secret location is found in your account's main folder in the C:\Documents and Settings folder. In your account's folder open the Local Settings\Application Data\Microsoft\CD Burning folder to see where the files sit and wait to be burned to the CD-R.

What Kind of Data Best Goes on a CD-R?

CD-Rs are best used for storage or archiving of vital files or stuff you want to keep. That implies data files or the stuff you create. For example, I have a set of CDs that contains everything I've ever written. I have another batch of CDs that contain all graphics files and images. Another set contains audio files. Still another one has a bunch of fonts and shareware programs. Then there are disks full of old e-mail. You get the idea.

Because CD-Rs are relatively indestructible, I keep anything on them I want to keep but don't necessarily want to junk up my hard drive with. Yet by having that information on a CD-R, I can get access to it simply by inserting the disk.

Here are some things you should never put on a CD-R:

Do not install programs to the CD-R. Programs must be run from the hard drive. (I suggest installing programs onto Zip disks if you need to have a program installed on a removable disk, but even then you better have a darn good reason!)

Do not save your current stuff to the CD-R disk. Only archive older stuff that you don't plan on changing.

Do not download to a CD-R disk. Download to the hard drive. If you've collected downloads over the years, then archive them to the CD-R drive, which is great. But do not download directly to the CD-R drive.

What Are Some Interesting and Various Ways to Copy Files to the CD-R?

There really aren't any interesting techniques for copying files to a CD-R, other than the standard file-copying techniques used by Windows.

My favorite trick for gathering files unto the CD-R is to folder-hunt and then use the File ➤ Send To ➤ CD-RW drive command. But really, any file copying command works: Copy and Paste, Copy to Folder, Ctrl+C and Ctrl+V.

If you plan on moving files (as opposed to copying them), then I recommend that you first copy the files, then burn the CD. Only then should you delete the originals—after ensuring that everything went according to plan.

How Can I Tell How Much Data I'm Writing to the CD-R?

Alas, in Windows it's tough to tell how much data you're writing to the CD-R disk ahead of time. Some third-party CD burning programs give you exact file sizes, including estimated time to burn the CD and other fun graphics and statistics. But in Windows you have to guess—or use the dreaded DOS prompt to get the answer. This is not the most painless thing in the world:

1. Have a bunch of files already selected and ready to be burned to the CD-R.

Follow the instructions presented earlier in this chapter.

2. Open a Command Prompt window.

From the Start panel, choose All Programs ➤ Accessories ➤ Command Prompt.

The Command Prompt window opens in the C:\Documents and Settings*your account* folder, which is good because it means there's less for you to type here.

3. Type CD "LOCAL SETTINGS" and press Enter.

If you're successful, you'll notice that the prompt changes to reflect your new folder. If you're not successful, try again and mind your typing!

4. Type CD "APPLICATION DATA" and press Enter.

5. Type CD MICROSOFT and press Enter.

6. Type CD "CD BURNING" and press Enter.

Finally, you've arrived at the proper folder, the one where Windows is keeping the temporary files you plan on burning to the CD-R. Using the DIR command is the only way in Windows to determine the bulk of bytes to be written:

7. Type DIR /S and press Enter.

A lot of crap scrolls up the screen, but what you're looking for is the last bit of text displayed, which looks something like this:

```
Total Files Listed:
        133 File(s)   21,799,112 bytes
         20 Dir(s)    5,646,595,072 bytes free
```

The first number of bytes (21,799,122) is the amount of stuff you're writing to the CD-R drive. In this case, it's roughly 21MB.

 If the value is higher than 700,000,000, then all that stuff may not fit on a single CD-R disk.

Yes, this is an ugly and awkward way to find out how many bytes are to be written to the drive. I wish there was a better way, but using Windows alone, there isn't.

8. Type EXIT and press Enter to close the Command Prompt window.

I Tried to Use the "Delete Temporary Files" Task and It Removed All the Files from the CD-R

Yes, choosing "Delete Temporary Files" from the CD-R drive's task pane (Figure 15.4) removes *all* of the files waiting to be burned. You cannot selectively remove files unless you highlight a file in the folder, then delete it as you would any file in any folder.

Can I Write More Files to the CD-R after It's Been Burned and Ejected?

Certainly. Just reinsert the disk and add more files to it. As long as there is room, Windows continues to add files to the disk.

If you open the CD-R disk, you'll see the files waiting to be added as well as the files currently on the disk in the folder window (Figure 15.5). Windows lets you continue to add files to disk until the disk is full.

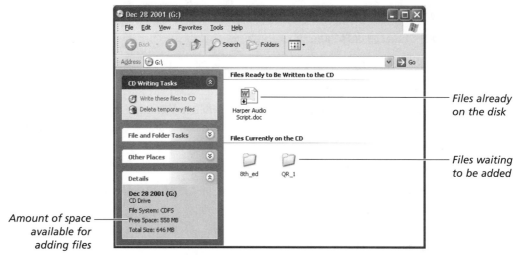

Figure 15.5 Adding more files to an already-burned CD-R

I Heard That Erasing Files on a CD-R Wastes Disk Space, Is That True?

Yes. That's because the file isn't really deleted from the CD-R disk, it's merely covered up. So when you delete a file on a CD-R you're just telling the computer to ignore the part of the disk used by that file; the disk space can never be recovered.

My advice: Only write to the CD-R files you plan on keeping. If you're deleting files from a CD-R, then you probably aren't thinking the process through well enough.

I Ejected a Disk without Burning the Files!

When you tell the computer to spit out a partially written CD-R, Windows displays a CD Writing Wizard warning dialog box, as shown in Figure 15.6.

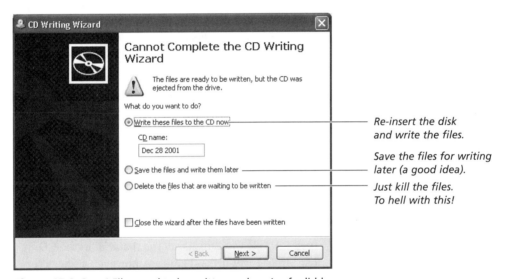

Figure 15.6 Oops! Files need to be written and you've foolishly ejected the disk!

Depending on why I ejected the disk I'll choose either the first or second option. Yes, it's possible to have the files sit and wait for the disk to be reinserted and written later. No problems with that. (They stay in a secret location on the disk until you're ready to start writing.)

Is There Any Way to "Final Burn" the CD-R?

Using Windows CD-R burning software, the CD-R disk is always open to adding files until the disk gets full. For example, you can take a partially burned CD-R out of one computer, stick it into another computer with a CD-R drive, and add even more files. That's the way it works in Windows.

Most Windows XP computers will be able to read any CD-R created by Windows XP. Older computers, and older versions of Windows, however, may have trouble reading the disks.

With some other CD-R burning software, such a technique is referred to as leaving the CD-R disk "open." There is a "final burn" option that prevents new data from being added to the disk. Windows lacks this feature.

So I assume that if it's a final burn you're after, then you'll have to get other CD-R burning software which supports that feature. The most popular software is available from Roxio. It's called Easy CD Creator. Visit Roxio on the web at `www.roxio.com`.

I've Heard That Other Computers Can't Read from a CD-R That Hasn't Been Final Burned

This might be true: older CD-ROM drives on older computers may not be able to read from a Windows XP CD-R disk. Unfortunately, there's no way around that in Windows XP.

Other CD-R burning software may provide options for burning compatible CDs. Again, refer to your favorite software store for details on these programs, such as the Roxio Easy CD Creator.

Why Bother with a CD-RW Disk?

CD-RW disks work just like CD-R disks. They're almost identical, save that you can utterly erase a CD-RW and then use it over again. For that reason, many people consider them a valid and necessary backup media.

Beyond that difference, CD-RW disks work just like CD-R disks; all the material in the CD-R tutorial (earlier in this chapter) also applies to CD-RW disks. There are, however, a few differences, which the following sections demonstrate.

What Is Different between a CD-RW Disk and a CD-R Disk?

The disks themselves are difficult to tell apart. Some of the nicer CD-RW disks have "CD-RW" written on them. But some of the low-end, buy-em-by-the-dozen disks are as blank and plain as a CD-R. Windows, however, can tell the difference.

How Does Windows Know the Difference between a CD-R and CD-RW?

Even if you can't tell the difference between the two disks, Windows gives you a few clues:

First, the CD-RW disk is recognized and flagged as such in the My Computer window. Figure 15.7 shows a CD-RW disk in the CD-RW drive. (A CD-R disk would have "CD-R" displayed, not "CD-RW".)

Second, it takes longer to write to a CD-RW drive than a CD-R, so if you notice that the going is going slowly, then it's probably a CD-RW disk you're using instead of a CD-R. (Eh, but that's kinda hard to tell by "feel.")

Third, a CD-RW can be erased, so an option appears in the CD Writing Tasks pane titled "Erase this CD-RW." Choosing that command removes all files from the disk and prepares you to start over.

Figure 15.7 A CD-RW disk is detected and ready for writing.

How Would I Back Up My Stuff Using a CD-R or CD-RW?

The easiest way to back up your stuff is simply to create a CD with copies of all the files in the My Documents folder and in all its subfolders. Even on my oldest computer, that's only about 430MB of files, so I just stick in a new CD-R and drag the folder over to that drive—in a few minutes I have a safety copy of everything. Simple.

Even if you have more than 650MB of stuff in the My Documents folder, then you can probably find other subfolders that can be backed up individually. For example, the Web Pages folder in My Documents (where I keep my raw web page information) holds about 250MB of stuff alone, so it's possible to back up that specific folder "branch" to a CD-R, then backup everything else to another CD-R.

 No matter what the course or strategy, ensure that you always have a recent backup copy of your stuff handy.

Of course, the best backup is a full copy of the hard drive, which isn't possible using a single CD-R. For that job it's best to use a dedicated tape backup system (though some software will let you copy a backup across several CD-R disks).

 *Though I haven't used it myself, if you're curious about a CD-RW backup program, check out Retrospect Express from Dantz Development (*www.dantz.com*).*

Doesn't Windows XP Come with Back Up Software?

Windows XP Home does not have any backup software. Boo! But it makes sense. I've been writing about backing up your data since 1987. No one does it. At least most home users don't. Many are curious about it. Many wish that they backed up, especially after losing all their data. But...eh?

Windows XP Professional, on the other hand, does come with backup software. Specifically, you can run the Backup Wizard to select those files you want to back up and where you want to back them up to. For example, you can elect to back up all your personal files to a CD-RW disk. It's very easy; if you can work a Windows Wizard, then you can back up your stuff.

 At most large organizations, backup is handled across the network by some form of network back up. For individuals, you must make a concentrated effort to maintain and keep up with your back ups.

To run the Backup Wizard in Windows XP Professional, pop-up the Start panel and choose All Programs ➤ Accessories ➤ System Tools ➤ Back up. The Backup Wizard starts and guides you through the steps required to back up your stuff. (See Figure 15.8.)

The most important step is to choose the backup place, which should be your CD-R or CD-RW drive. The second most important step is to back up often; schedule back up using the task scheduler or just keep in mind that you should back up at least once a week or more often if you really, really love your data.

 While Windows XP Home lacks backup software, that doesn't mean you should neglect the task of backing up. As an alternative, I recommend GoBack from Roxio (the CD-R/RW people) or Norton Ghost, if you're fond of the Norton Utilities. In fact, even for Windows XP Pro, these are great software programs to have.

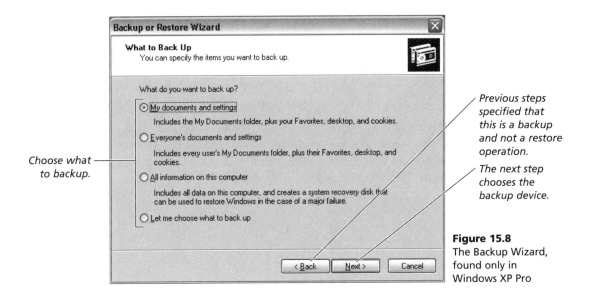

Choose what to backup.

Previous steps specified that this is a backup and not a restore operation.

The next step chooses the backup device.

Figure 15.8
The Backup Wizard, found only in Windows XP Pro

How Often Should I Use a CD-R or CD-RW to Make a Copy of My Documents?

Use the CD-R drive to make a CD copy of the My Documents folder every month or so. You can use a CD-R disk on a daily basis to copy over all the projects your currently working. For example, at the end of the day today I could copy over the folder containing this book's files. That would give me a daily backup I could use in case something happens to this book's files between today and tomorrow.

If the folder is too large to copy to a single CD-R, then copy over individual folders to several CD-Rs. For example, the My Pictures or My Music folders can go to separate CD-R (or RW) disks, then the rest of the files could be copied to a third disk.

And if you think all this is a hassle, then consider getting backup software to handle the chore for you.

How Long Should I Keep My Backup CDs?

I keep my backup CDs for at least three months. After that I just toss them, or if they're CD-RW disks I erase them and use them over again.

Keep your backup CDs in a safe place. I use a fire safe for mine. So I know that no matter what happens I will have a safety copy of my stuff.

How Do I Use a Backup Disk?

Say that something horrible happens to your hard drive and all your files are gone! Windows has some recovery tools, such as System Restore, which gets you back most of the Windows settings. But if you're missing your documents, then you need to pull them from the safety of the backup CD; just stick the CD back in the drive and copy over the files you need.

Now a "real" backup program is more sophisticated. When you use a true backup program, you can use it to select which files to restore from the backup. The backup software can even rebuild your computer as it sat on a specific date—fancy stuff. But again that can only be done with backup software, which Windows XP Pro has and Windows XP Home lacks.

PART 3

Nifty Audio and Graphics Information That No One Shares

What You Need to Know About Graphics to Survive

The best thing to know about computer graphics is that it's easy to make graphics look good and have absolutely no artistic ability whatsoever. Talent helps, of course. It's nice to have some sense of art to draw anything. But for the basic shapes or stickmen-drawing crowd, the PC has some wonderful tools and programs available to help even those with two right hands and no thumbs produce some good-looking graphics.

Of course, this chapter isn't about learning to draw or paint, or stylizing, or using texture, or learning how to properly dapple paint with a mouse. This chapter is about the many graphical mysteries, solutions, and secrets hidden right there in Windows.

Graphical Secrets and Solutions Revealed:

- Using Windows programs to work with graphics
- Grabbing images from a scanner or digital camera
- Previewing and viewing images in Windows
- Choosing which program opens a graphic image
- Understanding graphics file formats
- Using Windows programs to convert graphics file formats

Windows is an Operating System. What's Graphics Got to Do with It?

At its core, Windows is an operating system. It's designed to rule over your PC's hardware, provide a proper and safe playpen for your applications, and present an interface for you (the human) to control everything. At least that's the textbook definition.

The ugly reality is that in addition to being an operating system, Windows is also about ten thousand other programs. Originally these tag-along programs were called *applets*, meaning "tiny applications." But they've grown to encompass any little program or utility once made by a third party but now fully absorbed into the Microsoft hegemony. Like the Borg in *Star Trek*, Windows is a collective of interesting programs that have been assimilated from weaker companies.

Included in the Borg-Windows collective is a smattering of graphics programs, some of which are useful and most of which can freely be deleted from your hard drive to make room for the more useful stuff.

Can I Use Windows to Create Graphics Images?

Certainly. The number one tool for this is the Paint program, which you can run by choosing All Programs ➢ Accessories ➢ Paint from the Start panel.

Paint (shown in Figure 16.1) is an all-purpose graphics creation program. It has a smattering of simple tools that let just about anyone create simple images or illustrations. Compared to other graphical programs, however, Paint is rather weak. It has few effects and the assortment of tools is lacking.

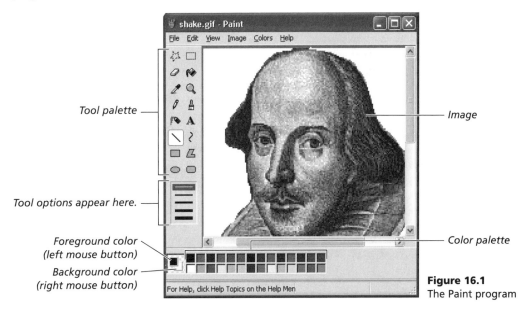

Tool palette

Tool options appear here.

Foreground color
(left mouse button)

Background color
(right mouse button)

Image

Color palette

Figure 16.1
The Paint program

223

Paint's true power is that it can open and save in a variety of graphics file formats (covered later in this chapter). So as a graphic conversion tool, it's pretty handy. But as your computer's sole graphics creation tool, it's rather weak.

If you upgraded your Windows XP computer, then you may have a copy of the old Windows Imaging program.

NERD'S CORNER

The Origins of Paint

The Paint program has been with Windows since the beginning. And even before that! Back in the days of DOS, Microsoft bundled the original Paint program with the first Microsoft mouse.

Designed for the IBM PC (and "compatibles"), the Microsoft Mouse came with a number of interesting programs, one of which was called PC Paintbrush (by ZSoft). That gave you something interesting and fun to do with your mouse (though with the ancient printers of the time it took an eternity to get a hard copy of the image).

Above is a screenshot image of PC Paintbrush from my archives. You can see the similarities to Paint right away.

Incidentally, PC Paintbrush saved its files in the PCX format, which was at one time the most common PC graphics file format available. It's still used in many graphics programs (and by some computer book publishers).

Can the Image Preview Program Edit Images?

The Windows Picture and Fax Viewer program, also known as Image Preview, is not a graphics creation program. As such, it cannot edit images, merely preview or print them. You can rotate the image, zoom in or out, and you can preview the image. But that's about it. Figure 16.2 shows this program in action (if you want to call it action).

Tools

Shrink-to-fit button

Zoom buttons

Rotate image buttons

Print

Open image in an editing application

Figure 16.2
The Image Preview program

KEYBOARD MASTER

Useful Keys in Image Preview

Here are some handy keys to know when you're using the Image Preview program

Ctrl+E
Edit the image (open it in Paint or Microsoft Photo Editor).

F11
Start a slide show.

Left arrow key
Previous image

Right arrow key
Next image

Ctrl+A
See the image actual size

+
Zoom in

-
Zoom out

(You can also zoom using the wheel button on your wheel mouse; roll forward to zoom in, roll back to zoom out.)

What Can I Do with the Microsoft Photo Editor?

The Microsoft Photo Editor would have been a killer application ten years ago. Now it merely fills in the gap for people who have scanners or digital cameras and don't have any other software to use for working on those images. (Most digital cameras and scanners do come with software, often better stuff than the Microsoft Photo Editor.)

 The Microsoft Photo Editor is available only on Windows XP Home systems; it does not come with Windows XP Professional. I don't know why. Seems like it should be the other way around, but it's not.

The biggest irk I have with Photo Editor is that on all my Windows XP computers, I cannot find it on the Start panel's All Programs menu. It just isn't there! The name of the program is PHOTOED, but for some reason the Run dialog box refuses to start the program as well. So there's two (of the zillion) ways to start a program that don't really work with Photo Editor.

 You can visit Photo Editor in its folder: C:\Program Files\Common Files\Microsoft Shared\PhotoEd\. Once there, consider creating a shortcut icon to the Microsoft Photo Editor, one that you can paste on to the All Programs menu.

Perhaps the simplest way to start Photo Editor is to attempt to open a TIFF, JPG, or GIF image. Unfortunately, this may also open some other graphic program, such as Image Preview. (Ugh.) So...after all this, the only consistent way I've found to open Photo Editor is to right-click on an image's file icon and choose Open With ➢ Microsoft Photo Editor from the pop-up menu.

 ## You Must Know This: Graphics File Formats Supported by Photo Editor

The latter part of this chapter goes into detail on what these formats mean and how they're best used. For now, know that you can save an image in Photo Editor using any of the following common graphics file formats:

 BMP   JPEG   PNG

GIF   PCX   TIFF

Figure 16.3 shows a typical Photo Editor window. The best places to look for image-editing tools are the Image, Effects, and Tools menus. If you're used to other image-editing programs, however, you'll be rather underwhelmed. So let me sum it up by saying the few positive things you can do with Photo Editor:

- Photo Editor will let you get at your scanner or digital camera via the Scan button or File ➤ Scan Image command.

- You can resize your image using the Image ➤ Resize command.

- You can crop the image by using the selection tool and then Image ➤ Crop command.

- You can save the image in another graphics file format by using the File ➤ Save As command, then using the "Save as Type" drop-down list.

These are about the most useful commands in Photo Editor. You can try messing with some of the commands in the Effects menu, but they're not nearly as nice as those in third-party photo editing applications.

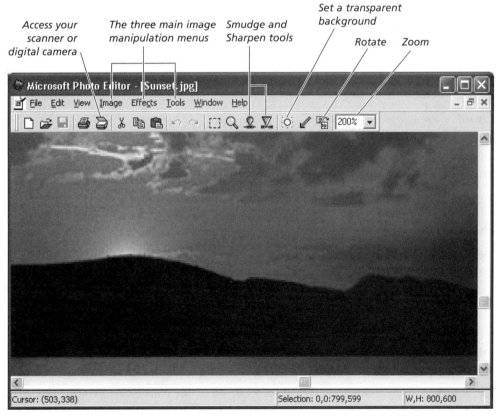

Figure 16.3 Everything that's anything inside the Microsoft Photo Editor

Where Can I Get a Decent Image-Editing Program if None Come with Windows?

Generally speaking, scanners or digital cameras come with photo-editing software. So when you purchase either, you get a fairly decent set of software tools for capturing, editing, and working with digital images. It's those programs that you should use and not the feeble line up Windows offers.

If your scanner or digital camera didn't come with any software, then I recommend Adobe's Photoshop Elements, which is an easy-to-use and powerful tool for editing photographs and images. Another program that's also highly recommended is Paint Shop Pro from JASC (www.jasc.com). Both Photoshop Elements and Paint Shop Pro can get you started and looking good, without having the pay the hefty prices for the "professional" graphics applications, such as Photoshop.

Which Windows Programs Let Me Get at My Scanner or Digital Camera?

Assuming that your scanner or digital camera is properly installed, you can use any of the following Windows programs to acquire an image:

- *Paint* Choose File ➤ From Scanner or Camera

- *Photo Editor* Choose File ➤ Scan Image

- *Word* Choose Insert ➤ Picture ➤ From Scanner or Camera

- *Excel* Choose Insert ➤ Picture ➤ From Scanner or Camera

That's a short list, but remember that the best program for acquiring images and editing them probably came with the digital camera or scanner.

Why Does Windows Have a Zillion Ways to View an Image?

It's not that Windows has a zillion ways to view an image, it's just that Windows doesn't have a consistent or logical way to view an image. Let me run down the gamut; follow along as I illustrate the seven ways that you can view or preview an image in Windows. Mind you: this is not all of them! Heaven's no!

First, the easiest way to view an image in a folder window is to choose View ➤ Thumbnails from the menu. This displays all the files in the folder in Thumbnail view, with image files appearing as tiny previews of the images themselves.

Second, there's Image Preview, or the Windows Picture and Fax Viewer: Double-click to open just about any image and the Image Preview window pops into view.

Third, there's the slideshow: In folders that Windows has identified as holding graphics files, you can click the "View As a Slide Show" link in the Picture Tasks pane. That runs the Image Preview program in Slide Show mode. You can sit back and watch as each image in the folder is displayed one after the other. Ho-hum.

I suppose the real question about the slide show is, "How does Windows know that the folder contains mostly graphics?" The answer is that Windows doesn't; it's just assuming that the folder contains graphics files based on hidden information. Here's how to change that:

1. Locate the folder you want to customize.

Don't open the folder; open its parent folder.

2. Right-click on the folder's icon.

3. Choose Properties from the pop-up menu.

4. Click the Customize tab.

Ah! This is where you tell Windows how to display the files in the folder by explaining what type of files will live in that folder. Figure 16.4 shows what's important here.

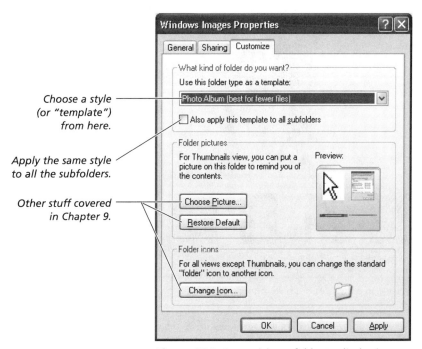

Choose a style (or "template") from here.

Apply the same style to all the subfolders.

Other stuff covered in Chapter 9.

Figure 16.4 Customizing a folder to display images

5. Choose "Photo Album (best for fewer files)" or "Pictures (best for many files)" from the list.

The difference is subtle; if the folder actually does have fewer files (say, less than 20), then choosing Photo Album automatically opens the folder in Filmstrip view. Otherwise you get the Thumbnail view with either option.

 Choosing either option, Photo Album or Pictures, is what clues Windows into the fact that you have a folder full of pictures. When you do that, then the Picture Tasks panel appears on the folder's task pane, and you're allowed access to the Filmstrip view for that folder.

6. Put a check mark by "Also Apply This Template to All Subfolders" if you want the entire folder branch to carry the same characteristics.

7. Click OK to lock in the new settings.

Fourth, there's the Filmstrip. This option appears only if the folder has been customized to display pictures (as described above). When you choose View ➢ Filmstrip from the menu, you get a quasi-slide show/thumbnail view of the files in the folder, as shown in Figure 16.5.

Figure 16.5 The Filmstrip view in a pictures or photo album folder

Fifth, you can preview a whole lotta images as a screen saver:

1. Right-click the Desktop.

2. Choose Properties from the pop-up menu.

3. Click the Screen Saver tab.

4. From the Screen Saver drop-down list, choose "My Pictures Slideshow" as your screen saver.

Windows then uses random images chosen from the My Pictures folder (as well as its sub-folders) for your screen saver. But there's more:

5. Click the Settings button.

A very handy dialog box appears, described in Figure 16.6.

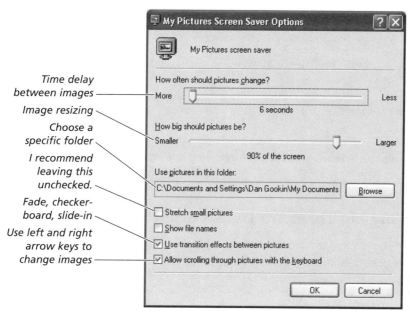

Time delay between images — Time delay between images

Image resizing

Choose a specific folder

I recommend leaving this unchecked.

Fade, checkerboard, slide-in

Use left and right arrow keys to change images

Figure 16.6
Options and stuff for the My Pictures Screen Saver

6. Make any changes settings in the dialog box.

For example, suppose you set up one specific folder to contain images you want for your screen saver. If so, then copy images into that folder then specific that folder in this dialog box by using the Browse button.

 If you do create a special Screen Savers folder for the My Pictures Slideshow screen saver, then remember to put real images in there and not shortcuts; the screen saver cannot display shortcuts to images elsewhere on the hard drive.

7. Click OK to close the various dialog boxes.

And enjoy your fifth way to preview images in Windows. On to the next:

Sixth, you can instantly slap any image down as your Desktop wallpaper: right-click the image and choose "Set as Desktop Background" from the pop-up menu. Minimize your windows (Win+M) and you'll see the image right there behind all your icons on the Desktop. (Use the Display Properties dialog box to switch the image back to "None" if you need to.)

Finally, you can slap an image down on a folder if you like. This is done the folder's Properties dialog box ➤ Customize tab. (Figure 16.4). Click the Choose Picture button and you can slap down any image on the folder icon, which shows up in Thumbnails view only.

KEYBOARD MASTER

Selecting Special Graphics File Views

Alt+V, H
Displays your graphics files in the Thumbnail view.

Alt+V, P
Displays your graphics in the Filmstrip view.

Alt+V, S
Sends you back to Tiles view when you tire of previewing the images.

Filmstrip View Is Nifty, but There Are Times I Really Don't Want It

If you would rather not have a folder open up with thumbnails or Filmstrip view, then you merely need to tell Windows *not* to treat it like a graphics folder and just display the files in a generic manner. Here's how:

1. Right-click on the folder's icon.

That's right, you must be in the folder's *parent* folder; you cannot make these changes when the folder is open. (Press the Backspace key to go up to the parent folder.)

2. Choose Properties from the pop-up menu.

3. Click the Customize tab.

(Refer to Figure 16.4.)

4. Choose "Documents (for any file type)" from the list.

This tells Windows not to treat the folder in any special manner.

5. Click OK.

Now when you open the folder, the files are displayed as icons, or tiles, or even thumbnails, but the graphics options are no longer available.

Any Way I Can Get an Image to Open in My Program Instead of the Dorky Image Preview?

To temporarily open an image in another graphics application, follow these steps:

1. Right-click on the file's icon.

2. Choose Open With from the pop-up menu.

Don't choose anything from the submenu yet. Instead, peruse Figure 16.7.

A selection of other graphics programs should appear in the list. For example, if you choose a Windows Bitmap (Paint) file, you'll see two items in the menu, as shown in Figure 16.7. One of those is the silly Image Preview program (officially known as "Windows Picture and Fax Viewer") and the other is the program that created the file.

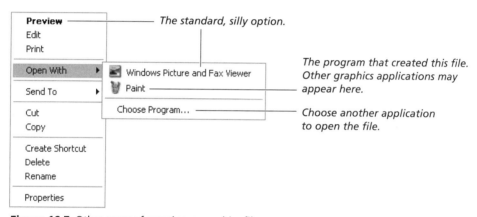

Figure 16.7 Other ways of opening a graphics file

3. Choose the program you want to open the file.

And the file is opened.

Now all this may seem like an awkward set of steps to wade through just to get a graphics file to open in the program that created it. And it is! I mean, if I click on a Paint document then—well, *dernit!*—I want Paint to open that file! To make this happen, you must reassociate a graphics file type with a specific program. Here's how:

1. Right-click on the file's icon.

2. Choose Open With ➤ Choose Program from the pop-up menu.

Yes, you choose this even though the program you want is listed in the submenu. What you need to do is make that association permanent.

The Open With dialog box appears, as shown in Figure 16.8.

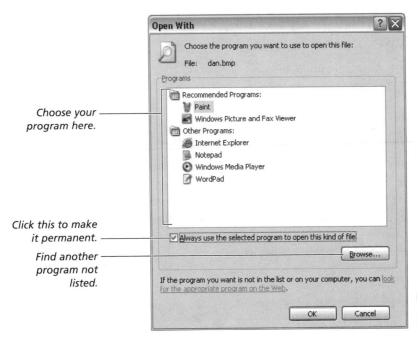

Choose your program here.

Click this to make it permanent.

Find another program not listed.

Figure 16.8 Choose a permanent program to open this document with.

3. Choose your program from the list.

   Chances are that it will be listed right up top. If not, use the Browse button to hunt for the program.

4. Put a check mark by "Always Use the Selected Program to Open This Kind of File."

   Doing this step is the important one.

5. Click OK.

   Your file opens in the selected program. But more importantly, now when you double-click files of that type of open them, they will open in the program you just selected—not Image Preview or something else. And if you still want to use another program, then just right-click and take advantage of the Open With submenu.

Where Is That Nifty Tool That Lets Me Print Images in a Folder?

The nifty tool is the Photo Printing Wizard. It appears in any folder set up to display graphics (see the section "Why Does Windows Have a Zillion Ways to Preview an Image?" on customizing a folder). If so, then there is an item in the Picture Tasks panel called "Print Pictures." Click that item to start the Photo Printing Wizard.

I don't really see any reason to walk through the Wizard with you; it's pretty self-explanatory—and actually a fun little Wizard to work with. The only thing to remember is how to find it, which is to click the Print Pictures link in the Picture Tasks pane in a picture folder window.

The Crazy World of Graphics File Formats

There is so much to this crazy world of graphics that entire books are written on the subject. Crazy books. Books for graphics artists and books for programmers— folks who would never share a table during lunch in real life.

This book touches graphics as far as Windows is concerned, which is more of a grab than a touch; even though it's supposedly only an operating system, there are lots and lots of things going on inside Windows that have to deal with graphics.

The last, possibly craziest, thing you need to know about graphics is the alphabet soup world of graphics file formats. You would think, logically, that there would be only one graphics file format. But there isn't. There are about half a dozen popular file formats and then about six dozen other possible formats, plus hundreds of proprietary formats for each graphics application that ever existed. It's a mess, but not a huge mess. Nothing that the next several sections won't help clear up for you.

Which Format Is Best for Saving an Image?

When you save an image, you're usually given the option of a file format to save the image in. Choosing one type or another depends on where the image is going; whether you're sending it via e-mail, or copying to a disk to send to a digital photography studio, or you're just saving it to work on it again later.

Overall, the best format for saving an image is the *native* format—the format the application that created the image uses.

For example, the best format for saving images created in the Paint program is the Windows Bitmap (BMP) format. The best format for saving images created in Adobe Photoshop is the Photoshop (PSD) format. And on and on: if the application that created the image has its own format, save the image in that format first. That's the best format.

The reason to bother with other formats is basically transportability. Saving in a non-native format is necessary when the image must be shared with another application.

Which Format Is Best for Sharing Images between Applications?

If you're creating or editing an image to be used in another application, then save that image in the TIFF (or TIF) file format. This is the Tagged Image File Format, which is commonly read by most major applications.

For example, if you're creating an image in some painting program and want to save that image for use in a Word or Excel document, save the image as a TIFF.

TIFF images are also the most common graphics file format for sharing graphics images between various image-editing applications.

Which Is the Best Format for E-Mailing Photographs?

JPEG is the best graphics format for e-mailing images. See Chapter 18 for the full details.

When Is the GIF Format Necessary?

GIF is another common Internet file format, similar to JPEG in that the file sizes are small and, well, it's popular. GIF is better suited for line art and other non-photographic images. However GIF is limited in the number of colors it can display. As such, it's not as popular as JPEG and, in fact, isn't fully supported by all major graphics applications.

I would say that there is no real reason to use the GIF format unless either the JPEG formatted version of the image appears kind of fuzzy or you are specifically directed to save the image in the GIF format. (Well, and GIF images can be animated, which is nifty. You need special software to animate them, as you might guess.)

What's the Point of the PNG Format?

The PNG ("ping") file format is designed to replace both the JPEG and GIF file formats for use on the Internet. Unlike the other two formats, PNG is completely in the public domain, meaning that there are no fees or usage restrictions applied to those images. (The application developers pay the fees, not you the user.)

PNG is also more advanced technically than either JPEG or GIF, and it shares the best features of both.

As more and more applications accept the PNG format, you'll eventually see it replace JPEG and GIF. In fact, future editions of this book may merely list JPEG and GIF in a sidebar on the way graphics files used to be formatted.

What's This Art File Format?

AOL users have a special, proprietary graphics image format called ART. It's a compressed graphics file format, similar to JPEG, but one that can only be read by the AOL software.

If you're using AOL, then please do not use the ART file format for saving images to disk or for e-mailing images to non-AOL users. In fact, avoid the ART file format altogether: to turn the ART option off, go to "Web Preferences" and uncheck the "Use Compressed Images" option. The world will thank you.

Why Bother with the Windows Bitmap File Format?

There is only one place that the Windows Bitmap (BMP) file format is used, and that's in Windows itself! While you can e-mail BMP images, the files are huge and the results on the receiving end aren't always spectacular. It's much better to convert the BMP image into a JPEG for e-mailing.

Note that it's not really necessary to convert BMP images into TIFFs for photo editing; most programs that can read TIFF files can also read the BMP file format.

The only true place where BMP images find a home is as Desktop wallpaper in Windows. Even then, however, Windows XP is equally adept at displaying GIF, JPEG, and PNG images on the Desktop as it is BMP images.

How Do I Convert an Image from One Graphics File Format to Another?

The best program I've seen for this is called GraphicConverter from Lemke Software in Germany. Alas, it only works on the Macintosh. But you're not stuck out of luck in Windows. The best way to convert an image is to open it in an image editing program then use File ➤ Save As to save it in another format.

For example, to convert a BMP image into a GIF in Paint, follow these steps:

1. Open the BMP image.

2. Choose File ➤ Save As.

   The Save As dialog box appears.

3. Use the "Save As Type" drop-down list in the Save As dialog box to choose the file format you want, as shown in Figure 16.9.

   In this case, you'd choose GIF.

4. Continue saving the file.

   Give the file a name and choose a location, then click the Save button to save it.

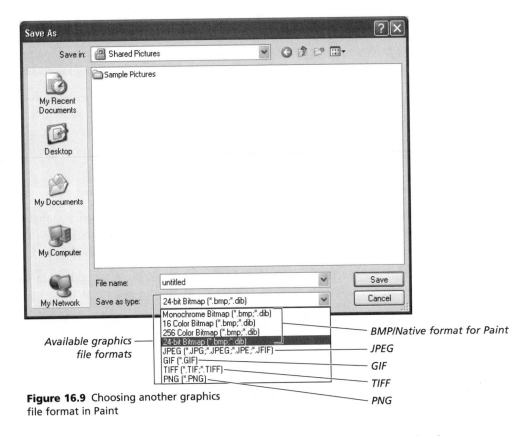

Figure 16.9 Choosing another graphics file format in Paint

This type of conversion can also be done in the Photo Editor program. For example, if you want to convert a TIFF image into a JPEG in Photo Editor:

1. Open the TIFF image in Photo Editor.

2. Choose File ➢ Save As from the menu.

3. Use the "Save As Type" drop-down list to choose the proper file format.

   Furthermore, you can use the More>> button to display additional options for the file conversion—a trick that the Paint program doesn't offer.

4. Continue saving the file.

   Give the file a name, choose a location, then click the Save button to save the graphics image in the new file format.

 The Paint Shop Pro utility, mentioned earlier in this chapter, is also a good tool to use for converting images from one file format to another. (www.jasc.com)

Why Would I Want to Convert Any Other Format into a Windows Bitmap?

The only use for the Windows bitmap format is for wallpaper on the Desktop, but even then Windows XP can handle GIF, JPEG, and PNG images on the Desktop as well. So there isn't any real reason to bother with Windows Bitmap graphics, unless it's just a file or doodle you create in Paint, in which case you'd be saving that file in Paint's native (BMP) file format.

What Can I Do with a PPS (PowerPoint Slideshow) File When I Don't Have PowerPoint?

The PPS file is not a graphics file format. It's actually a document created by the Microsoft Office PowerPoint program, which builds graphics images into slideshows. You've probably seen these: They lower the lights, they turn up the heater, you can lean back just so far in you chair, then a sonorous, monotone voice lulls you to sleep while a PowerPoint slide show is projected on the far wall. Now, thanks to PPS files, you can relive the same experience right there on your PC!

Seriously, if you ever receive a PPS file, such as an e-mail attachment or a download from a website, then you need to use PowerPoint itself, or the PowerPoint Viewer, to display the file on your PC.

If you don't have PowerPoint, then you can download a free PowerPoint viewer from the Microsoft website: visit www.microsoft.com and search for Microsoft Office, then PowerPoint, then for the viewer file. Note that it's a hefty download, several megabytes. But it's the only way you can see the PPS files on your computer.

Image-Scanning, Digital Camera, and Photo-Editing Tips

The best way to work your scanner or digital camera is by using the program that came with your hardware. For a scanner, typically there are two programs: a scanning capture program that operates the scanner itself, then a photo editor, where the scanned image ends up for editing, saving, printing and so on. Digital cameras typically have a program that reads images from the camera and saves them to disk or dumps them into a companion photo-editing program.

Oh, and there are options for sending images directly to a special printer and on and on. But the real burning question on your mind should be: What has all this to do with Windows XP?

The answer, as you might be getting used to by now, is *nothing whatsoever!* Windows is an operating system, a mere host to the scanner or digital camera that makes all those digital images happen. There are areas or spheres of influence where the digital image world and the Windows word do rub elbows, but they aren't really central to your graphical operations. So to clear up any fuzzy images or missing pixels, I've concocted this chapter to explain those rare boundaries where Windows XP and your scanner or digital camera do cross paths.

Images Rendered Clearly and Pixels Found:

- Going to where Windows and Digital Images Meet
- Using the feeble image-editing programs included with Windows
- Cropping and resizing images
- Rendering images less fuzzy
- Working with a scanner or digital camera
- Storing your images properly
- Choosing a format for the image

Digital Images and Windows XP

Windows is *not* a scanning program, neither is it a program that reads pictures from your digital camera and copies them into a folder on the disk. Don't be disappointed! This is a good thing; as long as Microsoft doesn't assume that digital imaging is part of the operating system, other companies will produce ample applications and there will be variety, competition, and innovation. Indeed, a good thing.

While several of Windows programs will let you access your scanner or digital camera (see Chapter 16), and there is a Scanners and Cameras icon in the Control Panel, that's as close as Windows comes to your digital imaging hardware.

The ugly truth is that, to Windows, your scanner or digital camera are like city and country cousins. They're related, but they do different jobs in different places. I've been using scanners for years and rarely, if ever, has Windows been needed or wanted in any scanning operation—even with all the new scanning features.

Do I Need to Use the Scanners and Cameras Icon in the Control Panel?

No, you don't. While it may seem like this is the place to go to install your scanner or digital camera, I recommend instead following the advice about installation given in your scanner or camera's manual.

For example, some scanners recommend that you install their software first, then hook up the scanner. Other scanners have you set up the hardware first, then install the software. Either way, you're better off than you would be if you used the Scanner and Camera Wizard in the Control Panel's Scanners and Cameras icon.

Once installed, your scanner or camera will show up in the Scanners and Cameras window. From there you can access some of the scanner or camera's hardware properties, but you still cannot really scan or capture any images from this window.

 The scanner or digital camera only shows up in the Scanners and Cameras window if it is installed and switched on.

Why Do I Need a Scanning Program?

The scanning program is what operates the scanner. It's how you tell the scanner that you're ready to scan an image, designate the image's resolution, set other control options, and so forth. The scanning program controls the scanner and transfers the image into a photo-editing program for further manipulation. Most scanning programs can also be run independently, saving the images directly to disk as JPEG or TIFF files.

What throws most people is that scanning is a two-step operation. The first involves using the scanning program; the second involves image editing.

For example, if you use the Microsoft Photo Editor program, you click the Scanner button and your scanning program runs. That's the program that controls the scanner and captures the image. When that's done, control is returned to Photo Editor where you can edit, save, and print the image.

How Do I Get the Images from the Camera to the Computer?

This is accomplished either by using software that came with the camera or by taking the "digital film" out of the camera and inserting it into the computer where the images can be accessed directly.

In the case of a software connection, a program typically comes with the camera that controls the PC-to-camera connection. You then use this program to beam or transfer the images from the camera into the computer, or to select which images you want copied over. The program can either be run by itself, or it's accessed through a File ➢ Acquire or File ➢ Twain command.

For accessing the images directly, the digital film (usually a floppy disk or some type of memory card or stick) can be inserted into a disk drive or special reader, which then grabs the images and displays them for copying, or you can use the Windows Explorer program to copy over the images.

Again, all of this is handled by the software that comes with the camera; Windows has no native method of grabbing images from a digital camera (or scanner).

Why Do I Need an Image-Editing Program?

Flatly, because the photo-editing programs offered by Windows are weak and feeble. Everyone say that aloud: *They are weak and feeble.* Thank you.

The scanning program really only operates the scanner. The program or method for getting digital images from your camera into the computer does only that. To really work with the image, you need image-editing or photo-editing software.

Now your scanning program probably lets you save an image directly to disk. And there are digital cameras that hook up directly to a special printer and let you print off a "roll" of film. But you can't really do anything with the images, such as resize, crop, or save them in any special formats unless you do so in some sort of image editing program.

Digital Image Editing Tips and Stuff

Yeah, I know, this is a Windows book. But Windows doesn't really have anything to do with digital imaging or tweaking the stuff you scan or photos you click. So, just because I happen to be in a very good mood today, I'm offering the following sections to assist you with basic digital image editing. Where applicable, I do use the Microsoft Photo Editor program, which comes with Windows XP Home. (Sorry XP Pro users!)

At What Resolution Should I Scan the Image?

Generally speaking, it depends on whether or not you want to edit the image. If you're just scanning an image to e-mail or use as Desktop wallpaper, then 100 dpi (dots per inch) is a great resolution to use. If you want to edit or enlarge the image, choosing 200 or higher is best. And for scanning negatives or slides, very high resolutions of 1200 to 2400 dpi are a must.

What Resolution Should I Use for Taking Digital Pictures?

If the image is for the Web or e-mail, then consider snapping it at the lowest resolution your digital camera supports, which will be something like 800x600. (If there are any resolutions lower than that, then don't use it; it's too low!)

If you're planning on enlarging an image or editing or doing special effects, then click at a higher resolution. The only way to know if you're using too high or too low of a resolution is to try snapping the pictures at different resolutions and see what works best for you. (I find my camera's highest resolution, which is like 1600x1200, to be more than I've ever really needed.)

Why Crop?

Cropping is the art of trimming an image, cutting away the excess. Here's how it's typically done:

1. Select the portion of the image you want to keep.

Figure 17.1 shows how I've used the selection tool in Photo Editor to pick a rectangular region of the image.

2. Choose the crop command.

In Photo Editor, it's Image ➤ Crop, then press Enter in the Crop dialog box. (Photo Editor's Crop dialog box is very complex, but if you have an area of the image selected, just press Enter or click OK in the dialog box to crop the image.)

And there is your cropped image.

Cropping is necessary to remove parts of the image you don't want, to improve the way the image is framed, or to increase the focus on a specific item in the image.

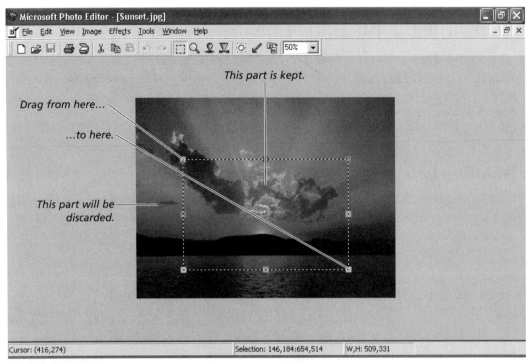

Figure 17.1 Selecting a chunk of an image for cropping

 I know some photographic purists who believe that cropping is "cheating" and that you should only crop in the camera. Well...they're full of it!

How Can I Resize the Image?

There is a difference between the size of the image on the screen and how it prints. It all has to do with the complex relationship between the number of pixels on the screen and the image's dots-per-inch (dpi) resolution—complex stuff that you probably don't want to numb your brain over.

The bottom line in resizing image is to look for the Resizing command. In Photo Editor, it's Image ➤ Resize, which displays a Resize dialog box that lets you change the image's dimension. Figure 17.2 explains all.

Two important things about resizing an image:

First, if you want the image to look right, then ensure that you resize both the width and height equally or proportionally. In Figure 17.2, *do not* click the "Allow Distortion" check box. Otherwise the image will stretch and skew and look weird when you resize it.

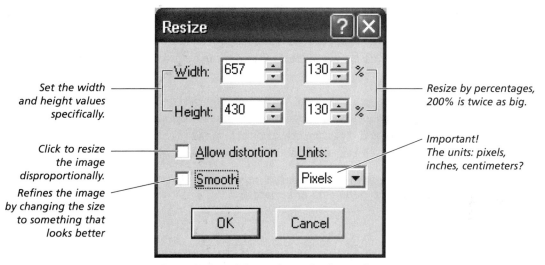

Set the width and height values specifically.

Resize by percentages, 200% is twice as big.

Click to resize the image disproportionally.

Refines the image by changing the size to something that looks better

Important! The units: pixels, inches, centimeters?

Figure 17.2 Resizing an image in Photo Editor

 If you want to resize the image to a specific size—say the resolution of your screen—but it won't exactly fit, then err on the side of excess; make the image larger than necessary, then crop it to fit.

Second, use the proper measurements. If you're sending an e-mail image, then you probably want to resize it (grow or shrink) so that it's about 300 to 400 pixels across, which is a good size on any PC monitor. However, if you're resizing to print something, choose the inches measurement so that you'll have a good idea how large the image will print.

It always surprises me how an image looks one size on the monitor but will print another size on the printer. *Always* double-check the picture's size in inches before you print. If you want it larger or smaller, then resize it.

 If Photo Editor won't let you resize an image large enough because of some stupid pixel limitation, then change the image's resolution: Choose File ➢ Properties and type a value such as 300 into the Resolution box. Click OK.

Can You Help My Images from Looking Less Fuzzy?

If you enlarge an image too much, or crop and enlarge a small part of an image, then the result may be too fuzzy. In that case, the only real thing you can do is to rescan or reclick the image at a higher resolution.

What you're running into with fuzziness is a lack of information in the image. Enlarging too few pixels to fill a larger area looks, well, gross. If you scanned the image at 100 dpi and it's too fuzzy, then rescan it at 300 dpi and try again; if you took the image at a lower resolution in your digital camera, then retake it at a higher resolution.

 It does take longer to scan images at higher resolutions, not to mention that higher-resolution images gobble up disk space.

Why Do I Get an Image That's So Big on the Screen?

Again, this has to do with resolution. The monitor has a resolution of about 96 dpi (actually "pixels per inch"). If you scan an image at 300 dpi and then display it on the screen, it will look about four times bigger than it really is.

The solution is to use your photo-editing program's Zoom command to zoom "out" and see the whole image on the screen at once.

Can My Scanner Eat Film Negatives and Give Me Real Pictures?

Certainly, providing that your scanner has a transparency adapter. That's because negatives and transparencies require backlighting—not reflected light—to be scanned. Also, the scanner has to be able to handle the higher resolutions required to read negatives and transparencies (though typically any scanner with a negative or transparency adapter is capable).

I Need to Just Print the Photos in My Camera!

If you're lucky, then your camera connects directly to a photo printer and—one button-push later—the images are spewing out of your printer like crisp bills from an ATM. If you're not so lucky, then you have to get the images out of your camera and into the computer.

Once the pictures are inside the computer, you have a number of options for printing the images. If your camera has an image transfer program that beams (downloads) the pictures from the camera to the computer, then check to see if there is a printing option. Note that you won't be able to crop or fix any photos, but you can just print them all.

The worst option is to use your photo-editing software to print the images. While that does work, most photo-editing programs really aren't geared toward printing a batch of images at a time, making the process cumbersome and time-consuming.

The final option, and the one I find hard to believe is the really the best, is to use the "Print Pictures" link in the Picture Tasks panel of a folder window (specifically, a folder window set up to display graphics). Clicking that item runs the Photo Printing Wizard (covered in Chapter 16). That's really the best way to print scads of pictures without having to mess with the details in a photo-editing program.

I Need to Get This Image as My Wallpaper

Making your own wallpaper is really what life is all about. Well, not specifically, but it can be fun and it always surprises others who don't know the "trick" that it's something *you* can do.

First, the easiest way to make any image (that was previously saved to disk) become your wallpaper is to right-click that image and choose "Set As Desktop Background" from the pop-up menu. Ah...but that's too easy! Also, it usually involves stretching or shrinking the image to make it fit perfectly. There is a better way.

First, discover your screen resolution:

1. Right-click the Desktop.

2. Choose Properties from the pop-up menu.

3. Click the Settings tab.

4. Observe the Screen resolution item in the lower left corner.

On my screen it says, "800 by 600 Pixels," which is what the publisher's Production Department has me set my monitor to when I'm writing a book. (Otherwise I use 1024x768.)

5. Remember that value!

Now, massage the image you want to use as wallpaper. It can be any image either already on disk or one that you scan or snap and save to disk. I'll assume that it's already saved to disk.

6. Open the image in your image-editing program, or Microsoft Photo·Editor.

I'll be using Photo Editor for this example.

7. Resize the image—as best you can—to match your screen resolution.

Here's where you need to get tricky. Be sure to constrain the image as you resize; change the horizontal and vertical aspects of the image equally. Start by resizing the horizontal edge (width) of the image.

In Photo Editor:

a. Choose Image ➤ Resize.

b. Set the measuring Units to Pixels.

c. Ensure that "Allow Distortion" is not checked.

d. Enter the width of your screen into the Width box.

If you're lucky, the vertical edge (height) will be the same as your monitor. Chances are, however, that you'll be unlucky and it will be greater than or less than your monitor.

If the vertical edge is larger than you monitor, okay. Otherwise, you'll have to resize again and set the horizontal size (width) to something larger.

 The idea is to resize the image to approximately the same size as your monitor. If you're going to err, make the image larger than the monitor.

8. Crop the image to exactly the size of your monitor.

   This is where things can get tricky in some programs. If you're blessed, then you can crop and see the dimensions of the new image displayed.

   In Photo Editor:

   a. Choose Image ➤ Crop.

      The Crop dialog box appears, as shown in Figure 17.3.

   b. Ensure that "Pixels" is chosen as the Unit of measure.

   c. Make sure that the values in the Left and Right boxes add up to your screen width—minus one!

   d. Make sure that the values in the Top and Bottom boxes add up to your screen height—minus one!

 The value has to be "minus one" in Photo Editor because it counts zero as the first value. So a screen width of 1024 pixels would crop from 0 to 1023; the height of 768 crops from 0 to 767.

   e. Click OK.

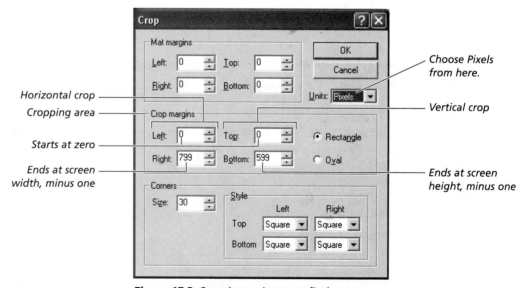

Figure 17.3 Cropping an image to fit the screen

Now the image should be perfectly resized to fix on your monitor. Only one more thing to do:

9. Save the image as a Windows Bitmap (BMP).

In Photo Editor, the File ➢ Save As command summons the Save As dialog box, from which you can use the Save As Type drop-down list to choose Windows Bitmap (BMP).

With some graphics programs, you may have to use a File ➢ Export command to save in the BMP format.

Save the file in the main My Pictures folder.

10. Select the new file as your Desktop.

Instructions for this can be found in Chapter 4.

Where Do I Keep My Images?

You should keep your images in the My Pictures folder, located right there inside the My Documents folder. This is the spot where most smart software will first attempt to place your images. For example, the Paint program (which, I'll admit, isn't a smart program) attempts to save everything in the My Pictures folder first, which is also where it first goes to look for any images you want to open and edit from within Paint itself.

You Must Know This: Organize Your Images!

Don't just let all the images pile up in the My Pictures folder! Organize! Use your folder creation skills to build subfolders and organize your images!

How you organize things depends on what type of images you collect. You can create folders for images in certain categories, based on events, projects, subject matter, and so on.

One strategy I use is to store images by date. That's how I keep "raw" images, which I then copy out to other folders that are more specific or relevant.

But no matter which organizational strategy you choose, be organized!

I Try to Store My Images in the My Pictures Folder, but My Scanning/Digital Camera Program Won't Let Me

If your graphics software insists upon storing the images in its own secret location—and you just can't seem to change that location— then I can only tell you one thing: You have a stupid program. Get something else.

Is There Anything Wrong with Storing Images on the Desktop?

Not wrong, just sloppy. Rather than store images on the Desktop directly —which can be handy— just store shortcut icons to the images instead.

When Is It Necessary to Use a CD-R for Storing Images?

Using a CD-R for your images is a great storage strategy, one you should consider using right away if you have CD-R and scanner.

First, always scan and save your documents to the hard drive. This is what the hard drive is for; do not save directly to the CD-R drive. Then, when you have all the images you're certain you want to keep—even if only temporarily—burn them to the CD-R. Refer to Chapter 15 for the details.

Remember to label the CD-R so you know which images it contains.

 Using a CD-R to store images is a great way to keep the hard drive from becoming too crowded. Ditto for Zip disk and other hard drives on your computer: Use the storage space you have.

Which Graphics File Format Is the Best to Use?

The graphics file format you save your scanned images in depends on where the image is going.

If you're going to be editing the image, then save files in your photo-editing program's native format: for Photoshop, use Photoshop (PSD); for Corel Draw use Corel Draw (CDR). If there is no native format, as with Microsoft Photo Editor, then use TIFF.

If the image is going to be shared between other graphics programs or pasted into applications such as Word, then save the image as a TIFF.

For the Internet, the best format is JPEG. If the image is mostly line art, such as a drawing, signature, button, or other graphic, then use the GIF format.

Also see Chapter 16 for more information on the graphics file formats.

Which JPEG File Saving Option Is Best?

JPEG is a compressed file format. The image is compressed to save disk space and you can select how much compression to use when you save the file. The more compression you choose, the smaller the image file size; the less compression you use, the larger the file.

The JPEG compression options are typically numbered 1 through 10, with 1 being the highest compression (smallest file size, but worst image) and 10 being the lowest compression (larger file size, but great image). However, in Photo Editor, the compression options are listed from 1 to 100 for some reason (see Figure 17.4).

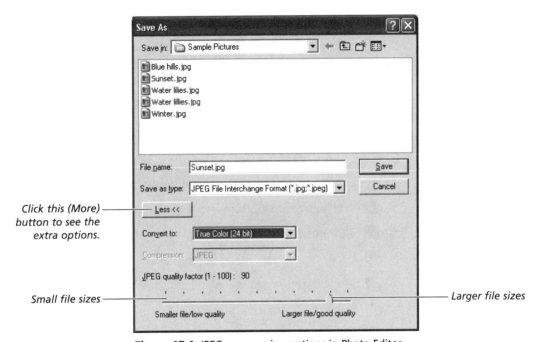

Figure 17.4 JPEG compression options in Photo Editor

In my travels, I avoid using levels 1 through 3 because the image, though small, looks crummy (fuzzy and tacky and bad). There seems to be no visible difference in quality between levels 8 and up. I generally use levels 6 or 7 depending on how fat I want the file. For general purposes, level 6 is great.

18
Graphics and the Internet

When you think of graphics and the Internet, you really mean graphics and the World Wide Web. The Web was the first, best solution for viewing both text and graphical information on the Internet; it's the main reason the Internet is so popular. Put another way, the Internet had been around for a dozen or so years before the Web provided an easy way to access and view information. Graphics have a big pull.

Of course this chapter doesn't just cover the Web. Another place where graphics and the Internet meet is in your e-mail program. You can both send and receive graphic images via e-mail, which is now so much in demand that it's a major selling point of many computers (though even computers in the 1980s could receive e-mail graphics). Anyway, the subject here involves untangling the graphics from the Web and your e-mail.

Mysteries unknotted and images brought into focus:

 Grabbing an image from a web page

Turning off the Image Toolbar

Choosing a format for saving the image

E-mailing an image in the proper format

Sending BMP or TIFF images

Forwarding an image

Dealing with odd image formats and other problems

 This chapter assumes that you're using Internet Explorer as your web browser and Outlook Express as your e-mail program.

How Can I Get an Image from a Web Page into My Computer?

Images on Web pages are easy to steal...uh, I mean borrow for personal use. You see, there is this thing called a *copyright*. And just about 100 percent of the images you see on the Web are copyrighted. That means that their use is restricted to those who have specific permission to use them on the Web.

For example, I once owned a Hummer—one of those massive jeep-like vehicles very popular with Arnold Schwarzenegger after the Gulf War. So I took pictures of my Hummer and put them on my web page. Then, a few months later, someone e-mails me to say that some Hummer dealer in the southwest has stolen my pictures and put them on his website—a naughty no-no if there ever was one; the dealer did not have permission to use my photos.

Now there is an exception to this rule: you can download an image for your *personal use*. So you can find copyrighted images of your favorite supermodel or hunky soap opera star and download them to your hearts content. You can store them on your hard drive. You can look at them dreamily and let them distract you from your work. But you cannot print up a T-shirt with the image and sell it, or package a "Johnny Hunkster CD Photo Disk" collection for sale on eBay.

The Simple Way to Steal an Image

The Internet Explorer web browser really knows when you want to copy an image from a web page, or at least it seems that way. Whenever you point the mouse at an image on a web page, a tiny pop-up toolbar appears; it's the Image Toolbar, as shown in Figure 18.1. You have four options: Save, Print, E-mail or Open the My Pictures Folder.

So, if you want to copy the image to your hard drive, point the mouse until that pop-up toolbar appears, then click the Save button. A Save Picture dialog box appears, which you can use to save the picture. Easy.

Save button
Print button (displays Print dialog box)
E-mail button
Open the My Pictures folder button

Figure 18.1 A Web image with the image toolbar

Anyway to Turn off That Annoying Image Toolbar?

Yes, the Image Toolbar may, in fact, be more of a pain than a useful tool. You can shut it off if you find it obscures your view of a web page or if it just plain annoys you. (And you can still save pictures to disk, as covered in the next section.)

To shut off the Image Toolbar:

1. Choose Tools ➢ Internet Options from the Internet Explorer menu bar.

2. Click the Advanced tab in the Internet Options dialog box.

3. Scroll down to the Multimedia part of the list.

4. Remove the check mark by "Enable Image Toolbar (requires reset)".

And there you have it, though you may need to restart Windows for the change to take effect.

And, of course, you can always reactivate that annoying toolbar by repeating the above steps to put a check mark by "Enable Image Toolbar (requires reset)."

Using the Pop-up Menu to Steal an Image

Another way to save an image from a web page is to right-click on that image. When you do, a pop-up menu appears, as shown in Figure 18.2. The menu contains several areas because it deals with the entire web page as well as the graphic you right-clicked on. The important stuff is highlighted in the figure.

Choose "Save Picture As" from the pop-up menu to get the Save Picture dialog box, from which you can save the image.

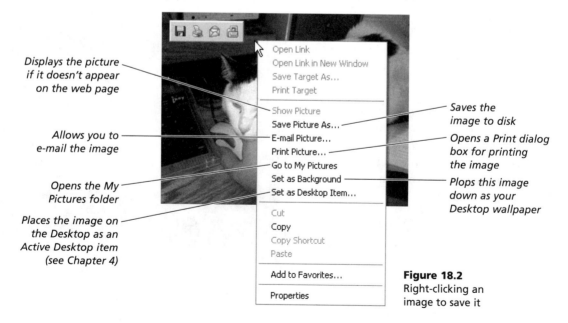

Displays the picture if it doesn't appear on the web page

Allows you to e-mail the image

Opens the My Pictures folder

Places the image on the Desktop as an Active Desktop item (see Chapter 4)

Saves the image to disk

Opens a Print dialog box for printing the image

Plops this image down as your Desktop wallpaper

Figure 18.2
Right-clicking an image to save it

In Which Exciting Formats Can I Save the Image?

When you use the Save Picture dialog box, you can choose a folder for the file, a new name, or a particular file format. Figure 18.3 illustrates what you can do and how you can use the dialog box.

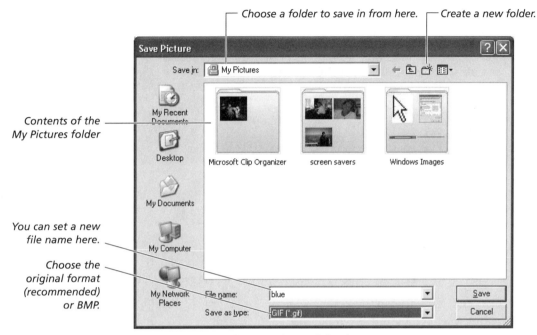

Figure 18.3 Using the Save Picture dialog box.

The folder pre-selected by Windows is the My Pictures folder. So if you need to save in a specific folder, you can browse there by using the controls in the dialog box. Or you can create a new folder.

The file's name is the same name as the original file you grabbed from the web page. In some cases the name may be rather strange. For example, newspapers and other large organizations may assign index numbers to their images. So that picture of the President and his wife may be titled PSN10293881_artfile_0ATTF9.JPG. Ugh. You can change that to another filename by using the "File name" text box in the Save Picture dialog box.

Finally, the file's format is listed in the "Save As Type" part of the dialog box. It will be the same type as the original file image: JPEG or GIF or PNG. Plus Windows offers you the option of saving the image as a BMP (Windows Bitmap). My advice is to always save in the image's original format; use an image-editing program to change a graphic file's type if you desire later on, as discussed in Chapter 16.

 For more PNG information, visit the following web page:
www.wambooli.com/help/imaging/PNG/.

You Must Know This: Web Graphics File Formats

There are three common file formats used on the Web: JPEG, GIF, and PNG. Of the three, JPEG is the most common. It's a more-or-less "free" image format, so it's widely supported and very popular.

The GIF format is licensed. Because of this, web browser developers must pay a fee (to CompuServe or AOL/Time Warner) to display GIF files. Because of this limitation, GIF files aren't as popular as JPEGs, though there are an abundance of them on the Web. (I remember my first web browser didn't display GIF images at all.)

PNG is the format of the future. It's entirely in the public domain so there are no licensing restrictions, and it's a better format than either JPEG or GIF. The problem is that PNG isn't widely supported. Yet.

The Images and E-Mail Cocktail

Another spot where you'll find images and the Internet crossing is with your e-mail. Sending an e-mail attachment is a snap, and the most popular attachment is the graphic image, typically a picture of the kids or of some family event being e-mailed to all the far-flung relatives and relations.

But, dernit, folks need to learn how to e-mail images properly! I remember fussing and futzing over my wife's computer one day because it would hang up in the middle of the *four-megabyte* e-mail file attachment download. We had no idea what the attachment was, only that the computer would conk out before the full breadth of the 4MB file could be received.

Eventually, after much time, agony, and fist pounding, we got the file. It was a TIFF image. An image of a cat. Just a stupid cat sitting there, looking at the camera. A 4MB TIFF of a god-forsaken cat. Oh, yeah. It was worth it. Really.

So my purpose in guiding you through the following sections is to ensure that first you're never the sender of the 4MB Cat TIFF image and second that you never have to suffer through receiving a 4MB Cat TIFF image.

NERD'S CORNER

Cocktail Party Trivia, Part V

JOHN: I'll bet I know something you don't, Phil.

PHIL: Okay, John.

JOHN: You could always e-mail graphic images. Ha! (Swigs his gin.)

PHIL: Well…you got me there, John. (A beat.) But it really depends on the e-mail program, you know. For example, today's Internet e-mail was based on the original e-mail developed for use by the military in the 1960s. It could send only text.

MARY: Then I'm glad they improved it so we can send file attachments, such as graphics, sound, photos of our cats, and other files. That must be an American invention, because we're just so smart.

(Laughter.)

JOHN. Mary's right.

PHIL: No, actually, Mary isn't correct. E-mail really hasn't been improved. The e-mail you send today is just text, plain text, nothing more. Even if you attach an image file, it's still plain text.

JOHN: But how can that be?

PHIL: When you attach a file to an e-mail message, it's converted into text and just stuck on to the end of the message. You don't see this because your e-mail program…

JOHN: Outlook Express!

PHIL: … or whatever, converts the file into text for sending. Then the e-mail program on the other end converts that text back into a file for saving on the computer.

MARY: That explains why sometimes I attach a large file and my e-mail program reports the file size to be even larger when I send it.

PHIL: Correct. The process of converting a file into text makes the file larger. So that 4MB TIFF image may balloon up to 5MB or more when it's converted into text. It's inefficient, true, but it's the way things work now.

(Long pause.)

JOHN: How about those 49'ers? Woo-hoo!

Which Is the Best Graphics File Format for E-Mailing an Image?

If you're sending an image, ensure that it was saved to disk as a JPEG file. (The filename extension can be either .jpg or .jpeg.) Photographs compress best into the JPEG format, because the files will be small and take less time to send than other file formats.

As far as the image size goes, a good rule to follow is about 300 to 400 pixels wide, which looks good on any monitor. That isn't a hard-and-fast rule; merely a guide. Remember that there are people out there who have monitors that show only 640 pixels across. If you size your image so that it looks good on your 1600x1200 monitor, then it may be way too huge on a monitor with a smaller resolution. Be mindful of that. (The folks with the smaller resolutions can only see part of the larger image, which is a pain.)

To save an image as a JPEG, use the File ➤ Save As or File ➤ Export command in your image-editing program. Choose JPEG as the file type.

To resize an image, use the image editing program's resize command. Ensure that you're measuring the image's size in pixels, and then enter a new horizontal dimension for the image.

What about Sending a GIF Image?

GIF images are also a good choice for sending photographs as e-mail attachments. However, GIFs don't render photographs as well as the JPEG file format does. GIF is much better for artwork or drawn images. Many people find this confusing, which is why I simply say to send the images as JPEGs and not bother with GIFs.

 Eventually the PNG or "ping" format will take over and replace both the JPEG and GIF file formats. However, at this time, not many Internet programs are PNG-compatible. When they are, in a few years, then this JPEG versus GIF argument will be moot.

Which Are the Worst Formats for a Graphics File Attachment?

Try not to send a TIFF or BMP file as a graphics file attachment; those files are just too large and often incompatible with many PCs. Also don't try to send images saved in an application's native format, such as PSD (Photoshop) images for the same reasons. JPEG was developed to be a common bridge between computers for graphics images, so use that format unless you really have to send in another format.

But What If I Need to Send a BMP or TIFF Image?

If you must, then you must. However, if you must send a BMP image, then compress it first: copy it into a Compressed Folder and send that Compressed Folder instead. The BMP graphics file format compresses very well, so a 120K BMP image will fit nicely into a 24K Compressed Folder (or ZIP file). Send the image that way instead of just attaching that bulky BMP file.

TIFF images, on the other hand, do not compress at all. If you're directed to e-mail a TIFF image, then you're stuck sending a huge file. Generally speaking that's okay; if they want a TIFF then they'll understand that it will take some time to send. But don't send a TIFF to anyone who didn't specifically request it.

 Again, remember that you can convert TIFF and BMP images into JPEGs for easy sending. See Chapter 16 for more information.

I Want to E-Mail an Image from a Web Page

If you're already saved the image to disk, then you merely need to attach its file to your e-mail message. However, there's a way to instantly send an image you see on a web page. Here's how:

1. Right-click on the image you want to e-mail.

A pop-up menu appears; go back to Figure 18.2 to see it.

2. Choose "E-mail Picture" from the pop-up menu.

A dialog box appears asking if you want to modify the image's size before you send. Figure 18.4 displays the details.

3. Resize the image, if necessary.

Figure 18.4 shows you the details. It's only necessary to resize if the original image is quite large. Remember not everyone may have the same monitor resolution as you do. If you suspect the image might be too large, then use the dialog box to resize it. Otherwise, choose "Keep the Original Sizes" and click OK.

A new message window appears, titled "Emailing" followed by the name of the image you're sending.

4. Fill in the To field.

Type the address of the person to whom you're sending the message. Or optionally use your Address Book—everything works like Outlook Express or just about any other e-mail program.

Note that the subject is already filled in for you—it's an image you're e-mailing.

Also note that the image is already firmly attached.

Keep this option in mind if the image is quite large.

Okay for smaller images or images you want to keep the same size

Clicking the "Show more options" item displays the rest of the this information

Specific options for resizing the image

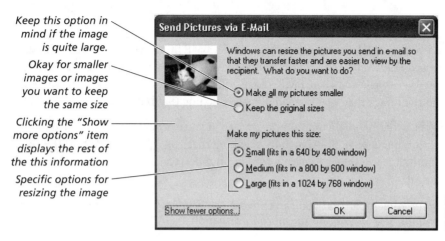

Figure 18.4
Resizing a web page image for e-mailing

5. Write some contents.

Ha! I'll bet you never thought that picture of your drunken, nude tirade in the Mexican restaurant would ever make the Stupid Idiots on the Internet web page! Ha!

6. Click the Send button to send it off.

And you're done.

 To cancel the message, just close the window before you send.

I Want to Resend an Image E-Mailed to Me

If you've just received an image attachment and would like to pass it along, merely forward the message. In Outlook Express, click the Forward button. This creates a new message with the Subject ("Fw" for Forwarded), Attachment, and contents all done for you. (You can re-edit the contents if you like.) All you need to do is fill in the To field; type the name of the person you want to send the image to, as shown in Figure 18.5.

If your e-mail program doesn't automatically include the attachment (the Attach field is blank), then you must save the attachment to disk from the first message, then create a new message and attach the same file.

Enter the recipient(s) here.

Optionally enter CC people here.

Forwarded subject

Attachment included automatically (nifty!)

Original message quoted (which you can edit)

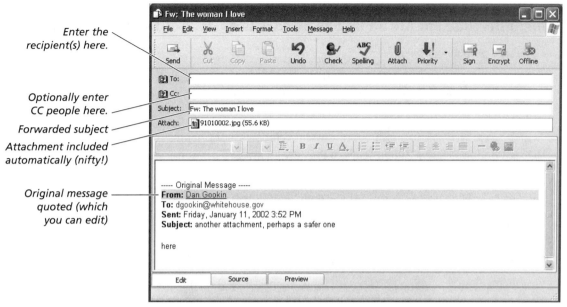

Figure 18.5 Forwarding an e-mail with attachment

KEYBOARD MASTER

Useful Keys to Know in Outlook Express

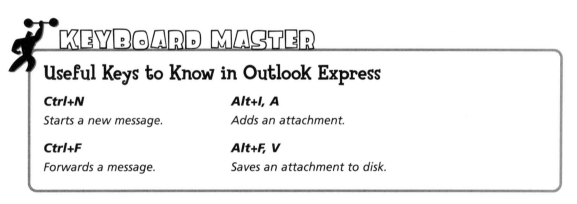

Ctrl+N

Starts a new message.

Ctrl+F

Forwards a message.

Alt+I, A

Adds an attachment.

Alt+F, V

Saves an attachment to disk.

Cousin Bertha Sent Me a File She Swears Is a GIF, but I Can't Open It

Then it's probably not a GIF.

One of the problems with Windows is that it's possible to rename a file to something-dot-GIF, which doesn't really change the file type at all. If you attempt to open the file and it will not open, then it's not a GIF.

GIF files are viewable in a number of ways in Windows (see Chapter 16, the section titled "Why Does Windows Have a Zillion Ways to Preview an Image?"). If none of those ways works, then it's not a GIF file.

In any case, whenever someone sends you a file that you cannot open, then reply to the e-mail and tell them so.

I'm Sending E-Mail Image Attachments That Can't Be Opened by Others

As long as you're sending JPEG or GIF attachments, they should be accessible by anyone who's on the Internet. Remember, these are the graphics formats used by the Web. So if your pals can view images on Web pages, then they can view any GIF or JPEG graphic you send. There are, unfortunately, exceptions.

There are some versions or implementations of AOL that will not display graphic images in a message or allow e-mail attachments. This has to do with the AOL user's account; some are configured to accept graphic files as attachments, some are not. Bottom line: It's an AOL problem.

The second most common incident of people not being able to receive attachments comes with web-based e-mail programs. Some of these, as well as other proprietary e-mail applications (like AOL), cannot receive e-mail attachments at all. Again, this is not your problem; tell the recipient to sign up with a local ISP so that they can use Internet e-mail just like the rest of the human race.

 AOL users: do not use the ART file format when sending images as attachments. Refer to Chapter 16 for more information on the ART file format.

I Can't Open My Attachments Because Windows Believes Them to Be Unsafe

Whether attachments are safe or unsafe, Windows really doesn't know. So it guesses. And it basically guesses that all attachments are unsafe, even JPEG, GIF, or any other type of image.

Now it hasn't fully been proven, but as far as I know there is no way to contract a virus by viewing or saving an image e-mail attachment. This may change in the future, but if you try to save an image attachment and Outlook Express claims that it's unsafe to do so, then you merely need to reverse a few options:

1. Choose Tools ➤ Options.

2. Click the Security tab.

3. Remove the check mark by "Do Not Allow Attachment to Be Saved or Opened That Could Potentially Be a Virus."

4. Click OK.

You're almost done, but you need to restart Outlook Express for the change to take effect.

5. Quit Outlook Express.

6. Start Outlook Express.

Now you can save the attachments.

Of course, a larger question looms, and that's whether or not your system is now vulnerable to an e-mail virus. There are two things you can do: first, get anti-virus software that will scan your e-mail. I recommend the Norton AntiVirus. Second, use another e-mail program, such as Eudora, which isn't as susceptible to viruses as Outlook Express. Visit www.eudora.com for more information.

19

The Wee Graphics:
What You Don't Know About Icons

I believe this to be the first computer book about Windows that devotes an entire chapter to the subject of icons. You'd be lucky in any other computer book to even get a section on icons. Maybe a sidebar, or perhaps a paragraph, "Oh, yeah, and you can create your own icons. Such fun!" and that would be it. What a gyp! Take that book back and demand something with substance. Something for an intermediate Windows user, such as yourself. Something like, like, like this chapter!

Valued Icon Information for the Intermediate Windows User:

- Changing the look for a shortcut icon
- Locating icon files in Windows
- Creating your own icon (kinda) with Paint

Why Do I Want to Change a File's Icon?

You don't want to change a file's icon! You can't. Most icons are fixed on their files. There are several types:

First, there are program files, which have their own icon associated with them. The program file itself contains an icon *resource*, which is a little picture or stash of pictures the program uses as its own icon.

Second, there are data files that carry an icon based on their file type. For example, your Microsoft Word documents have a Word icon they use. That's what identifies them with Word.

There are also "unknown" files that use the generic I-don't-know-what-type-of-file-this-is icon in Windows. Best to leave those files alone.

There is, however, a type of icon you can change, which is what this chapter is all about. It's the shortcut icon. Those you can blessedly change at your heart's desire, often to the amazement of your friends and frustrations of your enemies.

Shortcut icons are identified as such by the little swoopy arrows in their lower left corners.

Slapping Down a New Icon on a Shortcut

You can change the icon applied to any shortcut in Windows. It's cinchy, and it works no matter what type of file the shortcut represents. I did this on one of my computers for my car mileage log. It's just an Excel file and I have a shortcut to that file on the Desktop. But the shortcut file has an icon of a tiny car on it instead of the Excel icon. Those who have seen this think that it's pretty neat, and really anyone can do it:

1. Right-click the shortcut icon.

2. Choose Properties from the pop-up menu.

The shortcut icon's Properties dialog box appears (Figure 19.1). This dialog box deals with the shortcut itself, not the original file at all.

To see the original file, click the Find Target button in the shortcut icon's dialog box. That displays the folder window in which the original file is located.

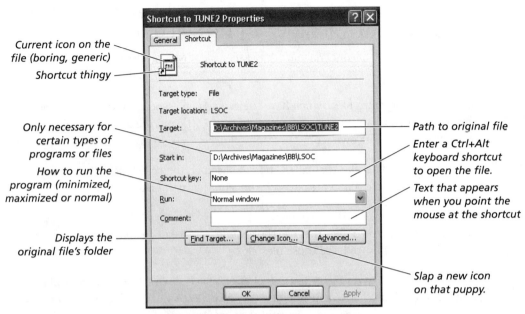

Current icon on the file (boring, generic)

Shortcut thingy

Only necessary for certain types of programs or files

How to run the program (minimized, maximized or normal)

Displays the original file's folder

Path to original file

Enter a Ctrl+Alt keyboard shortcut to open the file.

Text that appears when you point the mouse at the shortcut

Slap a new icon on that puppy.

Figure 19.1 The Properties dialog box for a shortcut icon

3. Click the Change Icon button.

The Change Icon dialog box appears, listing scads of interesting icons you can slap down on the file. Figure 19.2 shows what's up.

4. Pluck out a new icon for the file.

Click to choose the icon you want; or use the Browse button to search for more icon files. Don't forget that you can scroll to the right to see more icon files.

5. Click OK to close the Change Icon dialog box.

6. Click OK to close the shortcut file's Properties box.

And the new icon beautifully adorns the shortcut icon.

Of course, this is just simple stuff. There is more you can do with icons and shortcut files. But this does show you the basic operation of how things are done.

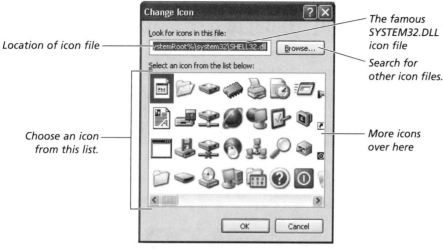

Figure 19.2 Choosing a new icon for the file

I Remember Using This Huge Icon File Windows Has, but Forget Where Windows Hides It

Obviously one of the areas that could use some improvement is the stash of new icons. In the previous section, you visited the SYSTEM32.DLL icon file, which is where Windows keeps most of its icons. This is not, fortunately, the limit. There are many other files you can browse to and pick up interesting icons for your shortcut files. Here's the short list:

In the C:\Windows\SYSTEM32 folder you can find the following icon files:

```
SHELL32.DLL
URL.DLL
MORICONS.DLL
```

That last one, MORICONS.DLL, actually contains some gems from Windows 3.1—which should bring back some memories if you've been using Windows for a decade or so.

You might also consider browsing to the C:\WINDOWS folder and opening the EXPLORER.EXE file for even more icons to peek at.

Finally, there's the Themes folder, which is where Windows gets icons for any of the Desktop display themes you may choose: C:\Program Files\Plus!\Themes. The files there are mostly individual icon files (ending in .ico), and they may not be present on some Windows computers.

Giving a Folder a New Icon

One thing folders share in common with shortcut files is that you can change their icons. This is covered in Chapter 3.

How Can I Make and Use My Own Icon?

Making your own icon is entirely possible in Windows. You just use the Paint program to create an image of a specific size, save it to disk as an icon file, then use it. It works! But it doesn't work well.

First you need to create an icon file. That's a Paint file (BMP) that's given the ICO filename extension, which identifies it as an icon file. This works for creating simple icons:

1. Start Paint.

2. Press Ctrl+E to display the Attributes dialog box.

You need to set the canvas size to 48x48 pixels, as shown in Figure 19.3.

Enter 48 for the Width.

Enter 48 for the Height.

Set measurements to Pixels.

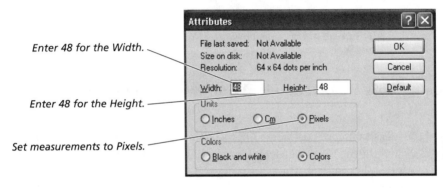

Figure 19.3
Setting up a Paint image as an icon

3. Choose Pixels as the Units.

4. Enter 48 for the image Width.

5. Enter 48 for the image Height.

6. Click OK.

Now Paint is set up for you to create your own icon.

7. Use the Paint tools to make something beautiful.

 It's best to make your icon fill the entire 48-by-48 square. Paint is not really an icon-creation program, so any icon you create will appear as a full square, not "cropped" like other icons.

For my sample icon, I filled the canvas with blue and then drew a red dot in the middle of the blue. Stunning.

8. Save the icon file: Choose File ➤ Save As.

The Save As dialog box appears, showcasing the My Pictures folder.

9. Create an Icons folder in the My Picture folder (if one doesn't already exist).

Remember: Organize! Click the New Folder button in the Save As dialog box to create the Icons folder inside the My Pictures folder.

10. Open the Icons folder to save your icon file there.

11. Type the icon's name into the File name box, being sure to add .ico at the end of the name.

For example, type `Dumptruck.ico` into the File name box; `.ico` must be added to the end of the filename to specify this as an icon file.

12. Click the Save button.

And the icon file is saved.

13. Quit Paint.

The second step is to apply the icon, either to a shortcut, a folder, or one of the common Desktop icons in Windows. The steps for this are found at the start of this chapter.

The only disappointment you'll have is that the icon file doesn't really behave like you think an icon would. Don't be surprised if the icon is all black! Or perhaps only one or two of the colors show up; that's the limitation of using Paint as an icon creation tool.

There are other icon tools available on the Internet, most of which do a fair job of creating icons. One such example is the IconCool program, available as shareware from `www.iconcool.com/main.htm`, shown in Figure 19.4. Programs such as IconCool are geared toward creating icons, so they come with plenty of helpful tools and utilities to make the icons look good—much better than Paint can accomplish.

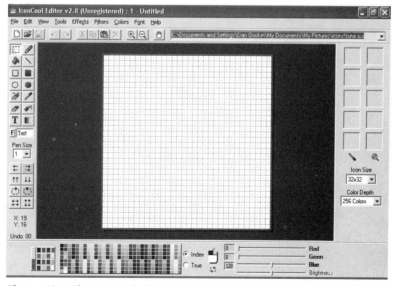

Figure 19.4 The IconCool editor, obviously much more advanced than Paint

20

For All Issues Audio, we Worship at the Temple of Windows Media Player

The Windows Media Player is your central location for all things audio and video in Windows. It's an involved and thorough program, but not one that's difficult to figure out. In fact, most of the time the Media Player works automatically; you stick in a music CD or DVD, and the Media Player takes over and plays the music or shows the movie. There's really nothing more to it.

Now I could bore you with complete documentation of the Windows Media Player (which I'll just call "Media Player" from now on), but I won't. Instead, I've pulled out what I feel are some of the most useful parts and presented them in a clear, logical, and useful manner in this chapter solely for your benefit. Such a deal!

Useful Parts Clearly and Logically Documented:

- Using the Media Player
- Selecting tracks from a CD
- Building a Playlist
- Adding WAV files to a Playlist
- Creating a music CD
- Listening to music on the Internet

Hello, I'm Windows Media Player and You Better Like Me or You'll Never Hear Anything Again

The Media Player is where you go when you want to hear more than an error message beep. Any time you can imagine any sound coming from Windows, it's most likely the Media Player that's responsible. It's a heavy task, one that Media Player handles in a complex yet uncomplicated manner.

(Of course, some programs, such as games, are responsible for their own sounds. So I suppose Media Player isn't the total Master of the Audio Universe I'm making it out to be—but it's close!)

Media Player Stuff You Should Already Know

The question isn't really how to start the Media player, but rather where you can go and *not* find a Media Player icon: It's on the Start Menu, Quick Launch bar, there's a shortcut icon on the Desktop, and I'm sure it's on the All Programs menu somewhere.

After starting Media Player, you'll see it's "skin" displayed on the screen. Figure 20.1 has the walkabout for you.

 I'm assuming that you're using the Media Player with the Default Media Player skin, as shown in Figure 20.1. If you are using another skin, then you won't be able to find the controls as listed in the text or figures.

In its basic mode of operation, the Media Player runs whenever you stick a music CD (or movie DVD) into your computer's CD (or DVD) drive. It plays. Ta-da!

The Media Player also appears if you elect to open (or "play") any sound files on the computer, or if you attempt to open a sound file on the Internet.

 KEYBOARD MASTER

Media Player Accelerators

Ctrl+M
Displays the Menu bar:

Ctrl+1
Displays the Media Player in "Full" mode

Ctrl+2
Displays the Media player in "Skin" mode

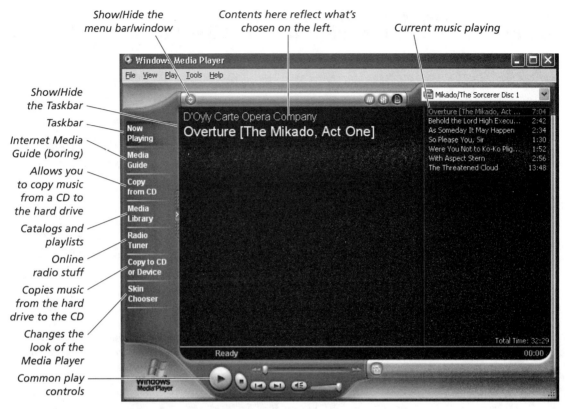

Show/Hide the menu bar/window

Contents here reflect what's chosen on the left.

Current music playing

Show/Hide the Taskbar

Taskbar

Internet Media Guide (boring)

Allows you to copy music from a CD to the hard drive

Catalogs and playlists

Online radio stuff

Copies music from the hard drive to the CD

Changes the look of the Media Player

Common play controls

Figure 20.1 The Media player on the screen

I Want to Insert a Music CD and Have Media Player Not Automatically Play It

Easy: when you first insert the disk, choose "Take no action" from the Audio CD dialog box, as shown in Figure 20.2. If you also put a check mark by "Always Do the Selected Action," then music CDs will never play automatically. You can still access the music via the Media Player, but the disk will mercifully remain silent after insertion.

If you don't have a music CD handy, or you've made this change and you want to change it back, then you can do so quite easily:

1. Open the My Computer icon.

2. Right-click your CD-ROM drive.

3. Choose Properties from the pop-up list.

4. Click the AutoPlay tab.

The CD Properties/AutoPlay dialog box is the spot where you can tell Windows exactly what to do depending on what type of disk is inserted, as shown in Figure 20.3. In this case, you're dealing specifically with a Music disk:

5. Choose "Music CD" from the drop-down list.

6. Click to choose "Select an Action to Perform."

7. Choose "Play Audio CD Using Windows Media Player" from the list.

Or if you'd rather never hear the disk play, choose "Take No Action."

8. Click OK.

And you can close the My Computer window as well.

Now Windows will do whatever you want when a music CD is inserted.

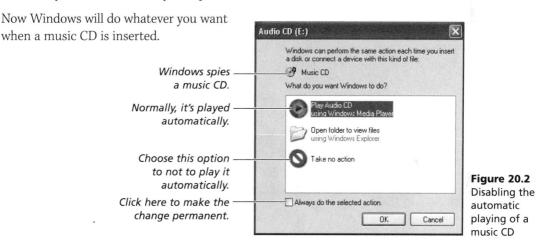

Windows spies a music CD.

Normally, it's played automatically.

Choose this option to not to play it automatically.

Click here to make the change permanent.

Figure 20.2
Disabling the automatic playing of a music CD

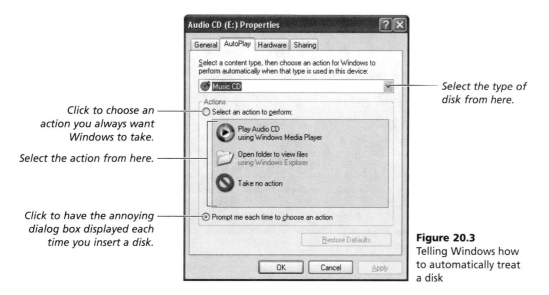

Click to choose an action you always want Windows to take.

Select the action from here.

Click to have the annoying dialog box displayed each time you insert a disk.

Select the type of disk from here.

Figure 20.3
Telling Windows how to automatically treat a disk

My Music CD Has Only Three Worthy Tracks and the Rest Is Junk

You can be selective in how you play music from a CD. It's easy:

1. Stick the CD in the drive and conjure up Media Player to belt out its tunes.

   Figure 20.4 shows Media Player in action spewing out a CD's music.

2. Ctrl-click the mouse to select the tracks you don't want to hear.

   Press the Ctrl key and click to select a bunch of tracks to disable.

3. Right-click on the tracks you don't want to hear.

4. Choose "Disable Selected Tracks" from the pop-up menu.

   And Media Player dutifully skips over those tracks.

 This trick works only once; if you remove the CD and then re-insert it later, Media Player will forget which tracks stink and which to play. To make Media Player remember, you should create a Playlist for the CD, as described later in this chapter.

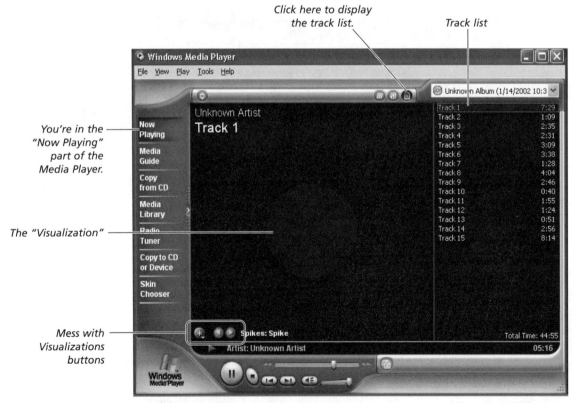

Figure 20.4 Playing a music CD

KEYBOARD MASTER

Shortcut Keys for Playing the Media Player

Ctrl+P

Pauses or plays the CD. (This is an exception to the normal Ctrl+P keyboard shortcut, which displays the Print dialog box just about everywhere else in Windows.)

Ctrl+S

Stops the playback. (Again, this is an exception to the norm, Ctrl+S is generally the Save command's keyboard shortcut.)

Ctrl+E

Ejects the CD.

F8

The all-important and vital mute button.

F9

Nudges the volume down a bit.

F10

Nudges the volume up a bit.

How Can I Copy a Chunk of Songs from a CD?

One of the most versatile aspects of Media Player is that it lets you copy the music tracks from a CD, save and catalog them on disk, then arrange them in "Playlists," which you can customize to contain your own favorite songs. It's a multi-step process:

First, you copy the music from your smattering of CDs.

Second, you build the Playlist.

Third, you play the Playlist.

Playlists are covered in the next section. For now, you can take the following steps to copy some or all of the audio tracks from your favorite CD to the Media Player's Media Library:

1. Start Media Player, if it's not started already.

2. Insert a music CD.

The music will start playing. Tra-la.

3. Click to select "Copy from CD" on the left side of the Media Player.

The tracks on the CD are listed in the Media Player, ready for you to select those you want copied to the hard drive, as shown in Figure 20.5.

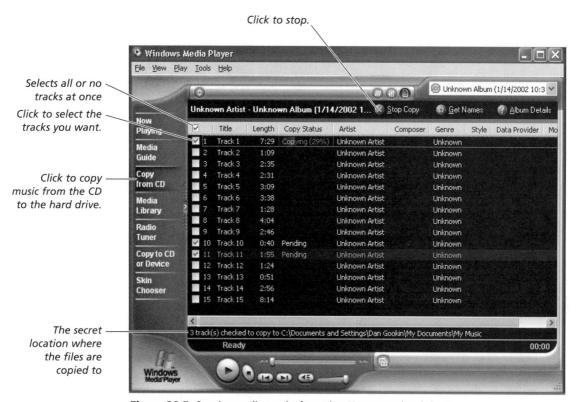

Figure 20.5 Copying audio tracks from the CD to your hard drive

4. Remove the checkmarks by the tracks you do not want to copy.

So if you only want tracks 1, 10, and 11, remove all but those check marks. Otherwise there's no problem with copying all the tracks—providing that you have room on the hard drive.

 Yes, you probably do have room on your hard drive for copying over a ton of music from your CD collection. However doing this a lot will fill up disk space fast. Of course, one way to save disk space is to copy over only those tracks you really enjoy and not the entire disk.

5. Click the Copy Music button.

Wait. This takes some time, depending on the speed of your CD-ROM.

Eventually all the files are copied.

Oh No! Media Player Wanders Out to the Internet!

As you copy the files, Media Player may attempt to access the Internet to get information about the CD, the individual tracks, the artist, and other useful stuff, which is displayed in the Media Player window. If this information cannot be obtained, then the fields describing the CD and its tracks are filled with "Unknown."

You can manually change "Unknown Artist," "Unknown Album," and so on by right-clicking them in the Media Player and choosing Edit from the pop-up menu. It's tedious, but if the CD isn't recognized or you cannot connect to the Internet, then it's the best you can do.

6. Remove the CD from the drive.

Now you could copy more songs from more CDs if you like, especially if you're starting a collection. To do so, simply repeat Steps 2 through 6 and go crazy! But when you're done, you'll need to check out where Media Player has placed your audio tracks. That location is the Media Library; for each CD you copy from, Media Player creates a new album entry in the Media Library. (And the albums may have strange names that you'll want to edit.)

7. Click the Media Library button.

It's located on the Media Player's Taskbar.

8. Ensure that the Audio portion of the Media Library "tree" is open, and that the "Album" part is open as well.

The CD you just copied from is listed in the Audio\Album part of the Media Library. In Figure 20.6, the album I just copied is listed as "Unknown" (the online database couldn't find any information about it), as are all the tracks I copied from the CD (shown on the right).

Now you can play these songs just as easily from your hard drive as you did from the CD: Just open an album, choose a track and click the Play button. The entire album plays one song after another. Because it's all digital, you get the same quality music from the hard drive as you do on the CD.

You'll notice that in addition to album name, artist, and track names, the Internet database also catalogs your songs by genre, such as Rock, Classical, Blues, Jazz and so on. If you click the Genre category in the Audio Media Library, you can listen to various tracks from various albums based on their music type. Say hello to an evening of show tunes!

Figure 20.6 The songs you copied from the CD

How Come I Can't Play a Real Audio File in Media Player?

Windows Media Player and the Real Audio program are archenemies—like Batman and the Joker. They don't get along. To please a Real Audio file you need to download (or pay for) the Real Audio Player. I recommend this only if you *really* need to hear Real Audio files.

I'm not a big fan of Real Audio. The player works okay, but it tends to take over your computer. After installing the latest version, I noticed Real Audio icons and menu items *all over the place*, which I find annoying. And then, even though I paid for my copy, I was barraged with urgent notices to upgrade and get the latest version, which I find offensive. So, no, I'm not a Real Audio fan. I don't recommend Real Audio Player.

Fortunately most places that have Real Audio sound files available also offer them in a Windows Media Player format as well. If so, choose Windows Media Player.

Understanding the Playlist Concept Can Save Your Butt in Media Player

I've found that the easiest way to maintain my sanity while working with the Media Player is to take advantage of the Playlist concept.

A *playlist* is merely a collection of audio files. They can be tracks from a CD, WAV files, or anything really, but they're all stored in a handy container called a playlist. I create playlists based on my listening moods, each with tracks from different CDs or other sources, but all neatly organized and personalized. Yup, the playlist can really help you get more from Media Player than just using it to play CDs like a CD player.

Dinking with a Playlist

Playlists are accessed from the Media Library. They appear in the scrolling list on the left side of the window, along with the Audio, Video, Radio Tuner Presets, and Deleted Items parts of the Media Library, as shown in Figure 20.7.

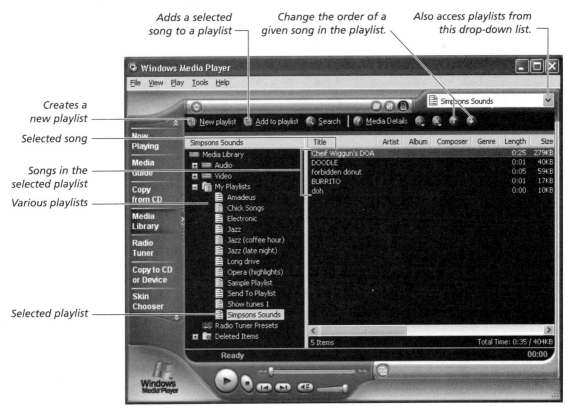

Figure 20.7 Fun things to notice in the Playlist area

279

The songs are copied from various Audio sources into a Playlist, which is covered in the sections that follow. Once there, the songs play one after the other whenever you open a playlist to hear some tunes.

To rearrange the order of songs in a playlist, select the song you want to move, then use the Up or Down buttons to change its order.

Deleting a song is accomplished by right-clicking it and choosing "Delete from Playlist" from the pop-up menu. Note that this does not remove the song from the Library; it's only zapped from the playlist.

Playlists are fun to use and add variety to your music. I highly suggest that you indulge in creating them. The following sections have various suggestions for using and working with playlists.

How Do I Create My Own Playlist?

A Playlist is merely a collection of audio files from other parts of the Media Library, such as any tracks you've copied from a CD to the hard drive. So after copying over a few CDs (or a few select tracks), you're ready to build a custom Playlist. Here's how:

1. Click the New Playlist button.

   Refer to Figure 20.7 for its location.

2. Type a name for the playlist in the New Playlist dialog box.

   Name the playlist after the types of tunes you wish you place into it. Say afternoon work songs, or chick tunes, or late night Jazz. My favorite playlist is the one I created for long-distance driving. I called it "Long Drive." It's a compilation of fast-moving, heavy back-beat, gravel-pounding, hard pumping...well, you get the idea.

3. Click OK to create your playlist.

   You'll see your playlist appear in the Media Library scrolling list/tree thing. It's toward the bottom, under the My Playlists heading.

4. Click to select your playlist.

   Because this is a new playlist, the right side of the window says, "No items added yet." Obviously the next step is to peruse your songs in the Media Library for those you want to add to the playlist:

5. Select your music from the Media Library.

   For example, The Door's "L.A. Woman" is a great driving song. So I click on "Doors" under Artist in the Media Library.

6. Click to select the track you want to copy.

   Or Ctrl+click to select several songs at once.

7. Click the Add to Playlist button (at the top of the Media Player window).

If the button is "disabled," then you probably clicked too long on the song title, selecting it for editing; just click again.

 You can also right-click on a song and choose "Add to Playlist" from the pop-up menu, then use the Playlists dialog box to choose a playlist.

8. Add the song to a playlist by choosing it from the Add to Playlist drop-down menu. (See Figure 20.8.)

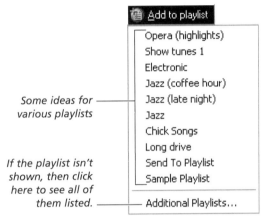

Some ideas for various playlists

If the playlist isn't shown, then click here to see all of them listed.

Figure 20.8
Adding music to a playlist

You can continue adding music to your playlist by repeating the steps over and over. I don't know if there is any upper limit on the number of tracks (or play time) allowed in a playlist; if there is a limit, I've not yet reached it.

After creating the playlist, you're ready to play and listen to it. You can do that by choosing it from the Media Library scrolling list, or from the drop-down list in the upper right corner of the Media Player's window. Click the Play button and…listen.

 KEYBOARD MASTER

Adding Tracks to a Playlist

Alt+A
After selecting the track, use this key combination to add it to a playlist:

Can Media Player Add WAV Files to a Playlist?

WAV files are the traditional sound file format used by Windows. The startup sound, shutdown, error beeps and such—just about anything you would find in the Sounds icon in the Control Panel—are WAV files. Even sounds you would record yourself, these are all WAV files. And, yes, you can add them to a Playlist if you like. In Media Player, follow these steps:

1. Press F3.

F3 is the Search command key, which opens up the Search for Media Files dialog box, as shown in Figure 20.9.

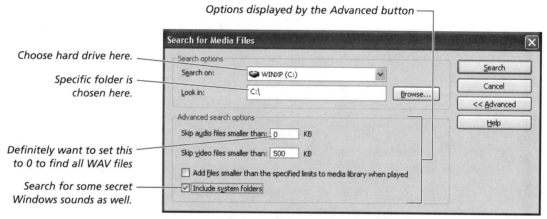

Figure 20.9 Searching for WAV files on the hard drive

2. Click the Advanced button in the Search for Media Files dialog box.

3. Enter 0 into the "Skip Audio Files Smaller Than KB" text box.

You want to ensure that you'll catch all the WAV files. For example, I have an "Audio" folder that contains dozens of WAV files that are quite small. Burps and such.

3. Put a check mark by "Include System Folders."

It would be nice to have a catalog of all the various Windows bleeps and snorts as well, don't you think?

4. Click the Search button.

And Windows goes a-hunting. Sit and watch in amazement as (hopefully) the Media Player finds oodles of audio files.

What Media Player May Find

When Media Player looks for audio files it looks for all types of audio files. The final list will include some of the following:

MIDI files *These are music files, but not of recorded music. The MIDI files play your computer's internal synthesizer, which generates the music. Because of this, MIDI files are very small. Also, because of this, MIDI music cannot be copied onto a music CD; the music must be recorded first.*

WAV files *These are sound files used by Windows and also found on the Internet. They can easily be copied and played from a music CD using Media Player.*

MP3 files *These are special compressed audio files found mostly on the Internet. They're like WAV files in that you can play them in Media Player and record them to a CD, but they're very compressed and take up less disk space than WAV files.*

Other Audio file formats *There is an entire spectrum of audio file formats, from AIFF to AU and beyond, most of which are specific to certain computers or applications. Media Player can play the most popular of these.*

5. Click the Close button.

6. Click the Close button again.

Now all your audio files have been found and are listed in the Media Player. They're not organized, which I suppose is the reason for wanting to put them into a playlist in the first place.

7. Click the Media Library button on Media Player's Taskbar.

8. Open the Audio\All Audio branch of the Media Player's scrolling list.

Give it a second...soon you'll see a huge scrolling list of all the audio media files on your computer, including all the WAV files you just picked up. Haphazard, right?

The more audio files you have, the longer it takes to open All Audio.

9. Scroll the list of audio files over to the right, until you can see the "Type" heading.

10. Click the Type heading.

This sorts all the audio files by their type, so all the WAV files will be together, as will all the MIDI, AU, MP3 and other files.

11. Scroll over a little further to the right until you can see the "Filename" heading.

12. Click the Filename heading.

The files are now sorted by Filename (and location) first, then type. That organizes them somewhat better than the way Media Player lists them.

With all that out of the way, now you're ready to create your playlists and stick your WAV files into them. For example, you can create a Simpsons playlist for Simpsons sounds or audio bites; a Star Wars playlist; one for Jim Carrey quips; and so on.

13. Click the New Playlist button.

14. Give your playlist a name.

And the playlist is created and placed into the My Playlists list.

15. Now return to the All Audio portion of the Media List and choose the sound files you want to add to your playlist.

Click to select a sound file. Ctrl+click to select multiple sounds files.

16. After selecting a bunch (or all) of the sound files, click the Add to Playlist button.

17. Choose your playlist from the drop-down menu.

If your playlist isn't shown, then choose Additional Playlists from the drop-down menu. This displays the Playlists dialog box, from which you can choose your playlist, then click OK.

And, lo, your sound files are copied into the playlist for endless hours of acoustic amusement.

How Does the My Music Folder Fit into All of This?

The My Music folder is the main folder Media Player uses to store and organize the files in its Media Library. It also uses the Shared Music folder, which is common to all accounts on the computer.

If you like, you can continue to use My Music as you would any folder on the hard drive. However, I recommend using the Media Player as the sole place where you store and organize the music and audio files you mess with on your computer.

I Want to Make a Music CD!

Oh, yeah! The fun part about Media Player is that you can make music CDs using all the musical files you've stored on the hard drive. It's cinchy:

1. Start Media Player if it's not started already.

2. Stick a CD-R (or CD-RW) disk into the drive.

Refer to Chapter 15 for more information about these types of disks and burning data CDs.

If Windows prompts you about what to do with the disk, then choose the option that enables the disk for writing.

3. Choose a playlist you want to copy in the Media Library.

This step is kind of optional, though I find it works best if you create playlists of songs you want to copy first, then copy the playlist to the CD.

4. Click the Copy to CD or Device button.

And you get the screen where you copy the songs to CD, as shown in Figure 20.10.

5. Click to select the songs you want to copy.

Only the songs with check marks by them are copied to the CD.

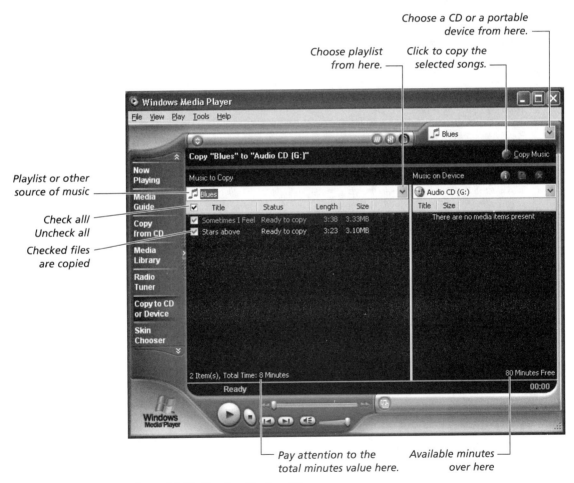

Choose a CD or a portable device from here.

Choose playlist from here.

Click to copy the selected songs.

Playlist or other source of music

Check all/ Uncheck all

Checked files are copied

Pay attention to the total minutes value here.

Available minutes over here

Figure 20.10 Copying files to a CD

Do not try to copy more music than will fit on the CD. These disks can hold about 80 minutes of music on average. Pay attention to the time value shown below your Playlist as you select songs to burn on the CD (see Figure 20.10).

6. Click the Copy Music button.

Media Player first converts your audio files to a proper CD format, then it copies them over to the disk. The amount of time this takes depends on the speed of your CD-R drive.

When the operation is complete, the music CD automatically ejects from the drive. And there you have your music CD. Easy.

You Must Know This: Copyright Information

Is it illegal to burn your own CDs? I suppose the battalion of lawyers working for the Music Industry would insist so. Alas, burning CDs is what most teenagers spend their afternoons doing.

The copyright issue is messy and all tangled up. But it sort of boils down to this: If you buy a CD, you own the rights to listen to the music on that CD. (You don't own the rights to the music itself.) You can, for personal purposes, create a compilation of music from various CDs that you own. The idea here is that you have paid for the rights to listen to the music and are merely listening to it in your own collection—just as if you were swapping CDs in and out of the CD player.

You cannot, however, burn a CD and sell or even give it to a friend. That is making an illegal copy of the music and giving it away without paying the artist what they're due. Even creating your own Christmas collection or theme compilation and giving it away is illegal. Now this may not stop you, but I feel it's pretty clear-cut on what's fair to the artist who created the work.

Can I Use a CD-RW Instead of a CD-R for Music?

CD-RWs can hold music just as they hold data. Here are the differences between using a CD-RW and CD-R:

 CD-RW disks cost more than CD-Rs.

 CD-RW disks can be erased and used again. (This must be done in the CD-RW drive's window; choose "Erase this CD-RW" in the CD Writing Tasks pane.)

 CD-RW music disks can be played only in CD-RW drives. Now there may be some CD drives that can read a CD-RW disk, but not all of them.

My advice? Stick with CD-Rs for music.

How Can I Add Music to a Cd-R I've Already Made?

When a CD-R is burned, it's burned. It's done. It's finished. It's over. Unlike data CD-Rs, which you can continue to insert into a CD-R drive and write and write to until the disk is full, once a CD-R disk is burned it's complete; no further information can be written to the disk.

This is why it's so very important that you line up a Playlist or album complete with all the songs you want when you burn a music CD. Don't think you can do a second pass with another album or Playlist. When the disk is burned, it's ejected and done.

Windows Can't Copy My WAV Files Because They're Not 16-Bit 44Hz. How Do I Convert Them?

It's easy to update a WAV file to the required 16-bit 44Hz sampling rate required for that sound file to be written to a CD. In fact it's so easy that you think the stupid Media Player would just do it automatically for you. But no. It forces you to take all these extra steps:

1. Locate the original WAV file.

This is perhaps the most difficult step. If you don't know where the WAV file lives, then Media Player can tell you, though it can't open the folder for you:

a. Right-click the WAV file.
b. Choose Properties from the pop-up menu.
c. In the Properties/General dialog box, locate the Location item, which gives the full pathname to the file.
d. Drag to select that pathname with the mouse.

Select only the pathname, up to the last backslash—not the last part, the filename itself. So if the pathname is:
`C:\My Documents\Audio\Homer - Doh.wav`

Select only: `C:\My Documents\Audio\`
(Also refer to Figure 20.12.)

e. Press Ctrl+C to copy the pathname.
f. Click OK to close the Properties dialog box.
g. Open the My Documents icon on the Desktop.
h. Press F4 to activate the Address bar.
i. Press Ctrl+V to paste in the pathname you copied.

Now you can locate the file in the proper folder.

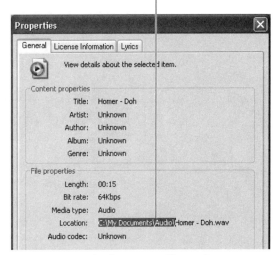

Select only this part of the pathname.

Figure 20.11 Selecting a WAV file's pathname

2. Right-click the WAV file.

3. Choose Open With from the pop-up menu.

   If you're lucky, you can choose Open With ➤ Sound Recorder, which means you've probably been through these steps (or similar steps) already. If so, choose Sound Recorder and skip merrily on up to Step 5.

4. Locate the Sound Recorder program listed in the Open With dialog box.

   And if it isn't listed there—which is likely—then you'll have to follow these ridiculous sub-steps:

 Please keep in mind throughout this ordeal that Media Player could—if it were a nice program—convert the WAV files for you as it copied them to the CD. Keep that in mind.

   a. Click the Browse button.
   b. Browse to Drive C.
   c. Browse to the Windows\System32 folder.
   d. Scroll over to find and select the `SNDREC32.EXE` program.
      Nice of them to hide it down here.
   e. Click the Open button.
      Now that you've rescued the Sound Recorder from oblivion...you're returned to the Open With dialog box, with "Sound Recorder Accessory" selected. Whew.

5. Click OK.

   And, finally, your sound opens in the Sound Recorder application, a kind of primitive Media Player, as shown in Figure 20.12. (You can use this program to record your own sounds, providing your PC has a microphone attached.)

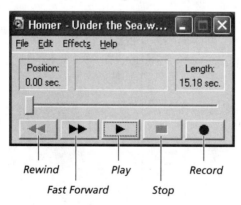

Figure 20.12
The Sound Recorder program

Cocktail Party Trivia (Aside)

PHIL: *Actually, the Sound Recorder has been with us since Windows/386, which is a long, long time ago.*

MARY: *Back to the party....*

6. Choose File ➢ Properties from the menu.

7. In the Properties dialog box, click the Convert Now button.

The Sound Selection dialog box appears.

8. From the Attributes drop-down list choose "44.100kHz, 16-Bit Mono."

Or if you know the sound to be in stereo, choose "44.100kHz, 16-Bit Stereo." (The stereo option uses more bits and creates a larger sound file, which isn't necessary if the sound isn't in stereo, which most WAV sounds aren't.)

9. Click OK.

10. Click OK to close the Properties dialog box.

11. Choose File ➢ Save to save the sound file.

12. Close the Sound Recorder.

Now you can record that WAV file to the CD.

13. Reward yourself with a nice, sweet treat for going through so many annoying steps!

Media Player and the Internet

Finally, there's sound on the Internet, which is something I admit that I'm not crazy about. It's probably because I have a slow (typical modem) Internet connection and not one of those blazing fast cable modems or DSL or whatever T1 nonsense. If I did, then it probably wouldn't bother me to download megabytes of MP3 files or swap audio files with my buddies or listen to "streaming radio" on the Internet. For me, all that is pure luxury, so I'm going to write about it with a snotty and condescending attitude. After all, if *you* have a fancy, schmancy high-bandwidth modem, then you probably know about all this stuff already. What's my point in boring you?

I'd repeat my copyright admonition (from earlier in this chapter), but if you ignored it before there's no point in repeating it here. Or, to put it another way, musicians need to make a living too. Every time you illegally copy their music, you're depriving them of a living. So if you like their music, pay for it.

I Want to Save the Song That I Found on the Internet but Media Player Insists on Just Playing It Instead

Some songs on the Internet are play-only. Media Player recognizes this and if you're not provided with any opportunity to download or save the song for keeps, then it just can't be done.

That is, it just can't be done using Media Player. There are tools out there that will let you download and save just about any music or audio you hear on the Internet. Visit any shareware website, such as `www.filemine.com/`, to locate Internet music utilities that will help you grab those songs that Media Player seems to hide from you. (I'm not real big on this activity, so I have nothing to recommend or avoid.)

Are the MP3 Files That Play from the Internet Saved on My Computer?

Some media files, yes, can be saved on the hard drive. Others, the "streaming" type, cannot be saved (mostly for copyright reasons). But you can still play the streaming music, you just can't save it to disk.

To find out if you're lucky enough to keep a file, such as an MP3 file playing in the Media Player, choose File ➤ Save As from the menu. Now if the command is dimmed, then you cannot save it to disk. Otherwise, use the Save As dialog box to save your music to disk.

The music you save appears in the Media Player's Media Library, usually under the Artist's name. If that's confusing, then remember that you can place individual tunes from separate artists into a Playlist, which makes them handier to organize and listen to.

Can I Add Music on the Internet to the Media Library?

You can add any music on the Internet to the Media Library, even music that you can save to disk. Just choose File ➤ Add to Media Library ➤ Add Currently Playing Track. This sticks that track's location on the Internet into the Media Library, typically under the Artist's name.

To hear the track, click to select and play it as you normally would, however Media Player will promptly march out to the Internet and begin playing the song. If your Internet connection isn't automatic (or constant), then you'll have to manually dial up in order to hear the song.

Is That All There Is to the Media Player and the Internet?

No, there are lots of things you can do on the Internet with Media Player, including clicking the Media button in Internet Explorer to see the (Microsoft-approved) content of the Media Bar. But like I said at the start of this chapter, the Media Player is a vast thing, one that certainly deserves its own book—much more than the hefty chapter I've written here.

PART 4

There's More Internet Out There Than You Know

21

Connecting to the Internet (or Not, as the Case May Be)

Internet stuff is one of the basic parts of using a computer. Well, *now* it is. The Internet wasn't always part of a computer or, more specifically, an operating system. But thanks to much drum-banging and trumpet-ringing, the Internet is presently a whole and happy part of the Windows experience—so much so that you most likely know all the basics, the ins and outs, and other essential Internet information. After all, it ain't that hard.

So rather than bore you with a slew of Internet basics and points and clicks, I'm gearing the subject of this chapter toward some basic issues regarding connection and disconnecting with the Internet. This subject is glossed over in many beginner books (including those that I've written), or explained in a manner that assures you that it works properly all the time. So rather than concentrate on what works, I present what often doesn't work when you try to connect to the Internet.

Internet Promises and Connections Broken:

- Disconnecting from the Internet on-purpose and on-accident
- Using two Internet connections
- Telling Windows which connection to use
- Sharing a connection
- Bothering with a firewall

 The main thrust of this chapter is with telephone modem connections to the Internet. I do not cover any broadband or high-speed connections here (Cable, DSL, T1), mostly because I don't have one!

Click! You're Offline. Again.

Our modern phone system is something of a miracle when you think about it. After all, compare your computer keyboard and the touch pad on a telephone. Regardless of how many bonus buttons your phone may have (Redial, Flash, Mute, and so on), the core operation of the device is done through a 12-button keypad. There is no Enter key. And the * and # keys are seldom used when making a connection. You punch in a number and that number rings. And if you get the wrong number, chances are that you misdialed or didn't know the proper number in the first place. Think about that: the telephone is a stubbornly accurate device.

Now take your computer. (Take it to the dump!) There are 104 keys on the keyboard including *two* Enter keys. Connecting to the Internet may be as easy as dialing a phone, but to do so on a computer requires so much work and takes place in so many different spots in Windows it's no wonder we're all not crazy and spending time alone in front of the devices into the wee hours of the morning and never leaving our chairs and...oh. Never mind.

Let me sum up:

The phone system was never designed to deal with data. Old Alexander Graham Bell built an analog system for the human voice. And that works quite well, thank you. So, in a way, we should consider it a miracle to be able to use a computer over the phone system at all. We should be thankful! But we're not. And there's nothing wrong with that.

Why Does My Connection Randomly Drop?

Here are the reasons why your Internet phone connection may randomly drop—and what you can do about it:

There Is Noise on the Line!

Nothing you can do about this. The noise can be the result of radio interference, trees, squirrels (I'm serious), sunspots, and so on. The result of the noise is that it interferes with the *carrier signal*, which leads either your modem or the ISP's modem to believe the line has been dropped.

Call Waiting!

If you have call waiting, then the "beep" signal you hear when someone else is calling you will cause the line to be dropped. Refer to your phone book for information on which numbers to dial to temporarily disable call waiting. Then follow these steps:

1. Open the Phone and Modem Options icon in the Control Panel.

   The Phone and Modem Options dialog box appears.

2. Click the Dialing Rules tab (if necessary).

   You'll see a list of dialing locations. If you have a desktop computer, then there's only one location, the "New Location." Otherwise, for a laptop computer you can enter multiple locations so that the laptop's modem knows how to dial out of your uncle's house in Pocatello, the Hilton in Sophia, Bulgaria, or the Motel 6 in Walla Walla, Washington.

3. Click the Edit button.

The Edit Location dialog box appears with a slew of rules for dialing the phone, dialing long distance (area codes) and other wonderful stuff. What a great place to play, as shown in Figure 21.1. (And you can see how creating different locations for a laptop would be beneficial.)

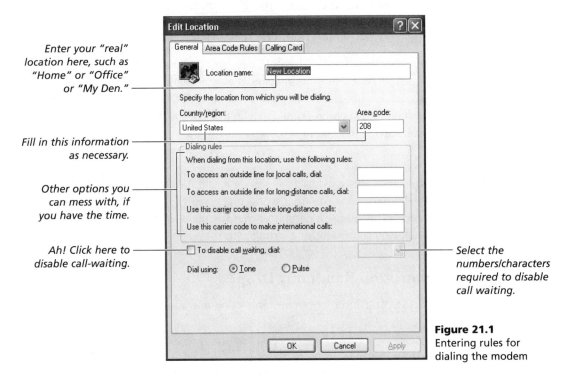

Enter your "real" location here, such as "Home" or "Office" or "My Den."

Fill in this information as necessary.

Other options you can mess with, if you have the time.

Ah! Click here to disable call-waiting.

Select the numbers/characters required to disable call waiting.

Figure 21.1
Entering rules for dialing the modem

4. Click to put a check mark by "To Disable Call Waiting, Dial."

5. Choose the proper numbers/characters from the drop-down list.

6. Click OK to close the Edit Location dialog box.

7. Click OK to close the Phone and Modem Options dialog box.

The changes you made ensure that call waiting will not interfere with your Internet connection for the duration of the phone call. It does not permanently disable call waiting.

NERD'S CORNER

Cocktail Party Trivia, Part VI

JOHN: I hear they're coming out with a new 75 baud modem.

PHIL: (Spits up his drink.)

JOHN: Surprised you, huh?

PHIL: (Wiping the drink from his shirt.) Where did you read that, John?

JOHN: I just made it up.

PHIL: Oh, I see.

JOHN: Is it possible?

PHIL: Certainly, it's possible but improbable.

MARY: I hate it when you use those Einstein words... (Gulps her gin & tonic.)

PHIL: Modem speed is measured in BPS, or Bits Per Second, and not baud, which is a term from the old teletype days. While a 300 BPS modem did run at 300 baud, faster modems do not maintain that same ratio. So we in the know use BPS. And a 75 "baud" modem would be slower than the original 300 BPS modems used with computers in the late 1970s.

JOHN: Oh.

PHIL: When they were first designed, the phone company figured that the fastest data could travel through the phone lines was about 1200BPS. Newer technology made 2400BPS possible, and the phone company believed that to be the fastest data would ever flow over the phone lines.

JOHN: But they were wrong.

PHIL: Of course. Eventually modems would compress the data being sent and decompress received data, allowing speeds of first 9600 BPS and then 14,400BPS. Further compression and newer technologies allowed faster speeds of 28,800BPS and eventually the 56,700BPS speed we have today, which all experts agree is as fast as the equipment can handle.

JOHN: Well, that may be all the phone lines can handle, but I sure could use another scotch.

EVERYONE: Ha-ha!

Bad Wiring

Bad wiring happens either inside of your house or between your house and the phone company's office. If you suspect the wiring outside of your house, then you can call the phone company and have them run a check on the line for you. If anything is wrong, they'll fix it.

If the program happens *between* your modem and the phone company's connection on the outside of the building, however, then it's *your* problem and you'll have to hire an electrician to help you fix it.

The Modem Gets Too Hot

This happens more frequently than you would believe. For some reason, the PC's case gets too hot. If so, then some of the hardware, such as the modem, stops working properly.

The first step is to figure out why the modem is getting too hot. Be sure that your PC has adequate room in front and behind for proper ventilation. Check to ensure that the internal fan (on the power supply) is still working; some cooling fans do fail, which means the computer gets hot and, lo, the modem stops working.

Second, work to ensure that the modem is cooled. Move things away from your PC's vents. Or, if the fan is busted, then replace the power supply or buy a supplemental fan.

Your ISP Is Getting Nasty

Some ISPs limit the amount of time you have online. This may not even be an advertised policy, but after a given time (say 90 minutes), they may drop you simply to cycle the line and get someone else online. I've not heard of that happening from any ISP, but many ISP users have suspected it for a long time.

How Come I Can Never Connect Faster Than *Blah-Blah* BPS?

Most modems in today's PCs are of the 56Kbps variety. That means that, under optimal conditions, in secret government laboratories, tested by people wearing protective eye coverings and white lab coats, the modem can actually communicate at over 56,000 bits per second. Wow.

Now take the modem out of the lab.

Under the very, *very* best of conditions, the fastest a 56Kbps modem can spew out data is at 50,000K. That's it. No more. (They never tell you that, you know.)

Typically, your 56K modem runs at anywhere from 36K to 49K, depending on the line conditions and other random technical factors.

The phone company really determines all this. If you live in a neighborhood where good equipment was installed and your house is fairly new, then 50K should be standard most of the time. (The speed will fluctuate, however, given line conditions.)

But the phone company doesn't always have to be so nice. There's a rural community 8 miles east of me where the fastest modem connection available is only 14Kbps. That's because the phone company maintains older equipment there. Nothing illegal about that; the phone company doesn't guarantee any connection speed to the Internet, only that your phone works.

Even worse, there is a new neighborhood in town where our (cheap ass) phone company (whom I won't name, but it starts with a "V" and rhymes with *horizon*) installed older, used equipment instead of the latest stuff. So even though it is a new development, the people in those homes can only connect to the Internet at 14.4Kbps. Bummer.

 To check your connection speed, after you are connected, double-click on the wee modem guy in the Notification Area. That displays a Status dialog box, similar to the one shown in Figure 21.2, where you can see the true connection speed. Click the Close button to rid yourself of this dialog box.

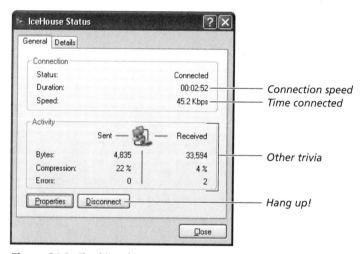

Figure 21.2 Checking the connection speed

> *Avoid those so-called "Internet Accelerators!" They're a scam. Hocus-pocus. Your Internet connection is a hardware thing and software cannot make it go faster. Also, some of the so-called Internet Accelerators are simply masqueraded advertisements and impossible to uninstall. Beware!*

Why Does the Internet Disconnect after 15 Minutes?

It Could Disconnect Because of a Lack of Activity or It Could Be Any of the Reasons Given above in the Section, "Why Does My Connection Randomly Drop?"

If you find the 15-minute rule to be consistent, then check with your ISP to see if anything is up. You might also adjust or disable the automatic disconnect feature, as covered in the next section. (Change the value to something high so that if you're playing an online game or some other activity, the computer doesn't think that you're "done" and hang up on you.)

How Can I Get the Internet to Disconnect after 15 Minutes?

You can add a timeout to your Internet connection so that the line automatically drops after any given interval of inactivity. This can be handy; one day I came back to my office late at night to discover that my Internet connection was still active after 14 HOURS. That wasn't what I wanted. So I switched on an automatic disconnect as follows:

1. Open the Internet Options icon in the Control Panel.

2. Click the Connections tab.

3. If necessary, select your ISP from the list.

4. Click the Settings button.

Your Internet connection (or ISP's) Settings dialog box appears.

5. Click the Advanced button.

The Advanced Dial-Up dialog box appears, as shown in Figure 21.3.

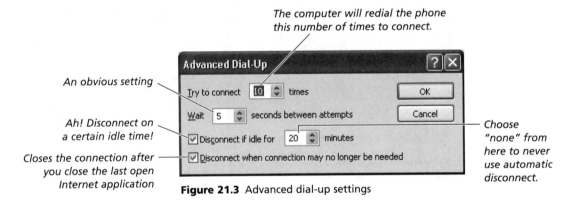

Figure 21.3 Advanced dial-up settings

6. Click to put a check mark by "Disconnect If Idle for…Minutes."

7. Enter an idle time in the Minutes box.

You know: 15 minutes, 20 minutes. I have a computer that automatically checks e-mail. It's set to disconnect after only 3 minutes of idle time.

Or if you want to stay online forever, don't check this item!

8. Click OK.

And now your time-out is set. Or is it? There is another time-out value in another dialog box, and I'm not sure how it affects things, but it's worth checking anyway.

Back in the Internet connection (or ISP's) Settings dialog box:

9. Click the Properties button.

10. Click the Options tab.

And you have yet another dialog box that offers a hanging-up option. Confusing? You bet! See Figure 21.4.

11. Set the disconnect time in the "Idle Time before Hanging Up" drop-down list.

I suppose using the same time as you selected in Step 7 would be appropriate. Or if you never want the connection to drop, choose "never."

12. Click OK, and so on, until all the dialog boxes are closed.

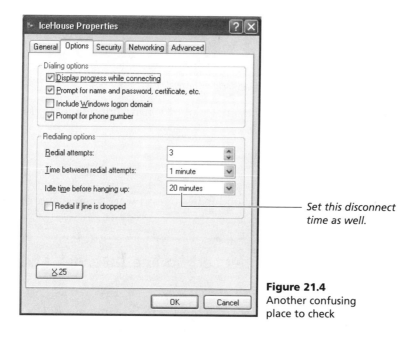

Set this disconnect time as well.

Figure 21.4
Another confusing place to check

Why Won't the Internet Connection Drop after I Close the Internet Explorer Window?

This is a tricky one. Sometimes this seems to work; you open a bunch of Internet Explorer windows and perhaps Outlook Express. Then, when you're done, you close all the windows and an Auto-Disconnect dialog box appears. Wonderful! The computer has read your mind!

But sometimes it seems like Auto-Disconnect doesn't happen. That could be for a number of reasons.

First, if you originally connected to the Internet by opening the Internet connection directly, then you have to close it just as directly. Automatic disconnect works only when you open an Internet application (such as Internet Explorer), which forces the computer to connect to the Internet, then you close that application.

Second, the computer could be downloading an automatic Windows Update. If so, then it still believes the Internet connection to be "busy," so you'll have to manually disconnect: Double-click on the modem guy in the Notification Area and click the Disconnect button in the Status dialog box (Figure 21.2).

Third, you may not have the Auto-Disconnect option on:

1. Open the Control Panel's Internet Options icon.

2. Click the Connections tab.

3. Choose your ISP from the list.

4. Click the Settings button.

5. Click the Advanced button.

   You see the Advanced Dial-Up dialog box (Figure 21.3).

6. Ensure that there is a check mark by "Disconnect When Connection May No Longer Be Needed."

7. Click OK to close all the various dialog boxes.

   And pray that this works, because:

Fourth, sometimes the Auto-Disconnect option just doesn't work. I can't figure out why. Ugh.

Something Else Is Connected to the Internet and Doing Something?

It's true. There are many programs that may connect to the Internet without you knowing it. Or they may sit idly by and wait until you connect so that they can work stealthily in the background. True, some of these could be nasty programs. But many parts of Windows, such as Automatic Updates, may work in the background as well.

The way to tell whether or not some stealth program is operating behind your back is to observe the Status dialog box, shown in Figure 21.2; double-click on the "connect" icon in the Notification Area. If you see the number of bytes received increasing, then something is going on in the background.

The problem with knowing what something is going on in the background is that you can't really pinpoint what the heck it is. And even if you knew what it was, it's even harder to try and stop it.

By the way, it's okay to disconnect from the Internet despite whatever is going on in the background. Such programs deserve to be disconnected. Rude bastards.

How Can I Prevent the Internet Connection from Dialing Up Automatically?

If you have a high-speed Internet connection, then it's on all the time and the Internet is always ready. I suppose Windows wants us regular modem people to feel the same way, so anytime any brief request for the Internet is made, up pops the "Connecting To..." dialog box, often to much panic and distress. But you can turn that off, which is done in the Network Connections window:

1. Open the My Network Places icon on the Desktop.

2. Click the "View Network Connections" link in the Network Tasks pane.

3. Choose Advanced ➤ Dial-Up Options from the menu.

The Dial-Up Preferences dialog box appears.

4. Put a check mark by "Always Ask Me before Autodialing."

5. Click OK.

6. Close the Network Connections window.

Hopefully this should work. However, it *is* Windows, and one never knows.

What's the Point of Having Two Internet Connections?

There's nothing new or unusual with having two ISPs. In fact, before the Internet really took over, I had several accounts I'd swing through to pick up my e-mail: MCI Mail, CompuServe, Prodigy, and the "real" Internet. Having separate mailboxes was handy, and some of the online services had features others lacked.

Today, having a second ISP gives you a second e-mail box (perhaps a private or secret one?) plus another avenue to the Internet should your main ISP get busy or die. With the relatively inexpensive costs of most ISPs, having two or three is really quite common. And, fortunately, Windows manages all those connections quite well.

Where Does Windows Bury the Internet Connection Information?

If you want to view multiple Internet connections, or if you need to add a second connection, then you must visit the Internet Options icon in the Control Panel. Click on the Connections tab to see which connections you have, as shown in Figure 21.5.

Note that AOL shows up in the scrolling list of connections. Also, if you have any direct connections to another computer or a broadband (high-speed) Internet connection, it would be listed there as well.

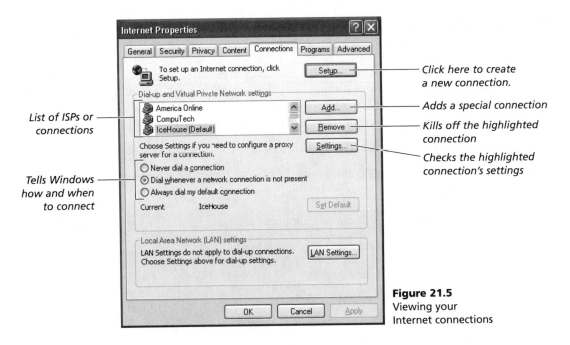

List of ISPs or connections

Tells Windows how and when to connect

Click here to create a new connection.

Adds a special connection

Kills off the highlighted connection

Checks the highlighted connection's settings

Figure 21.5
Viewing your Internet connections

Unless you specify that Windows dial the "default" connection (the third option in Figure 21.5), you'll see a window appear whenever you connect to the Internet, allowing you to indicate which connection to use, as shown in Figure 21.6.

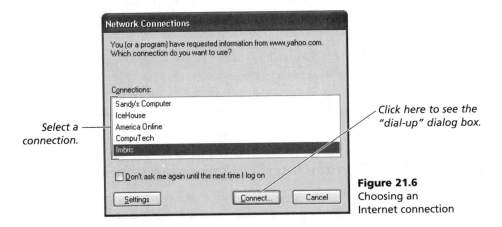

Select a connection.

Click here to see the "dial-up" dialog box.

Figure 21.6
Choosing an Internet connection

How Do I Add a Second Connection?

To add a second ISP to your list, click the Setup button in the Internet Properties/Connections dialog box. This runs the Internet Connection Wizard, which sets up a new ISP for you.

 If you're adding AOL—and I really wish you wouldn't (I'm not an AOL fan)—then use AOL's installation disk instead of the Internet Connection Wizard.

If you're adding a special connection, click the Add button in the Internet Properties dialog box. The types of special connections are listed in the New Connection Wizard dialog box, as shown in Figure 21.7. Choose one of the type you're adding, then work through the Wizard (you know the drill…).

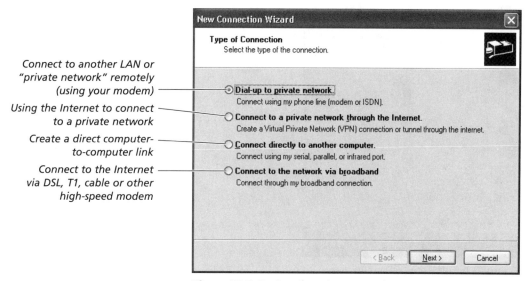

Figure 21.7 Options for other types of Internet connections

Can I Tell Windows to Use a Certain Connection as My Main One?

To make a connection the "default," or the one that Windows chooses to use whenever you connect to the Internet, select that ISP or connection in the Internet Properties/Connections dialog box (Figure 21.5). Then click the Set Default button. That entry will then have the text "(Default)" appear after it, indicating that it's the one Windows should use.

If you don't choose a default (and, Lordy, I loathe that word), then whenever you go to connect to the Internet, you're offered a menu of connection options, as shown in Figure 21.6. Choose one, then click the Connect button.

What's the Handiest Way to Choose an ISP When I Specifically Want to Connect to One or the Other?

My favorite way to pick a connection when I have multiple connections is to setup and use the Connect To link on the Start panel, as shown in Figure 21.8. Connect To lists a submenu of all my Internet connections, so I can quickly choose one without having to fumble around with other options or digging through various network windows.

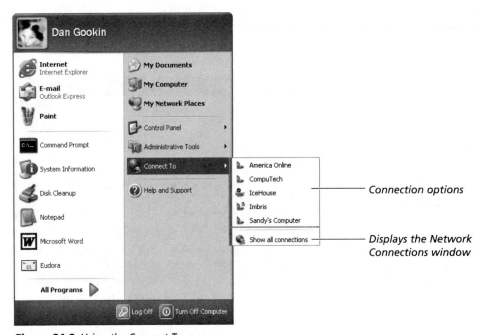

Figure 21.8 Using the Connect To menu

To set up the Start panel to display the Connect To submenu, follow these steps:

1. Right-click the Start button.

2. Choose Properties from the pop-up menu.

The Taskbar and Start Menu Properties/Start Menu dialog box appears.

3. Click the Customize button.

4. Click the Advanced tab.

5. Scroll through the list until you find the Network Connections area.

6. Choose "Display as Connect to Menu."

7. Click OK, then OK again to set everything up.

Now you're Start panel boasts the handy Connect To menu.

Did You Know That You Could Connect to the Internet through Another Computer's Modem?

My feeling is that modems should be given their own phone line. Especially if you use the computer a lot, sharing a single phone line with a modem and say, a teenager, just doesn't work. This is something everyone pretty much knows; the phone company is often called out to install additional phone lines for modems. And teenagers.

If you have more than one computer in the home or office, then the question arises should you get even more phone lines? Or say you're one of the lucky few who has a high-speed Internet connection, such as a DSL, or T1, or cable modem. Now everyone could fight over that single computer, duking it out like sugared-up 7-year-olds skirmishing over a burst piñata. Or you can be sensible and share your high-speed Internet connection with everyone else in the house.

It's called Internet Connection Sharing, and it allows several computers on a network to use a single computer as their Internet "host" (of sorts). It can be configured between Windows XP and any other Windows computer (though not Windows 95), and you don't even need a high-speed Internet connection; Internet Connection Sharing works with plain old modems as well as super-fast I-paid-too-much-for-this high-bandwidth connections.

 Obviously sharing a connection is possible only if your computers are on some type of local area network.

How Do I Configure This Computer to Share Its Internet Connection?

I believe the computer with the fastest modem should be the one to share. Hey! It's only fair. Don't squirm. Don't struggle. Just heed these steps:

1. Open the Network Connections window.

If you've configured your Start panel to have the Connect To submenu, then choose Connect To ➤ Show All Connections. (Refer to the section "What's the Handiest Way to Choose an ISP When I Specifically Want to Connect to One or the Other?" earlier in this chapter, and see Figure 21.8.)

Otherwise:

a. Open the My Network Places icon on the Desktop.
b. Click the "View Network Connections" link in the Network Tasks pane.

The Network Connection window is shown in Figure 21.9.

2. Right-click the Internet connection you want to share.

3. Choose Properties from the pop-up menu.

The Internet connection's Properties dialog box appears.

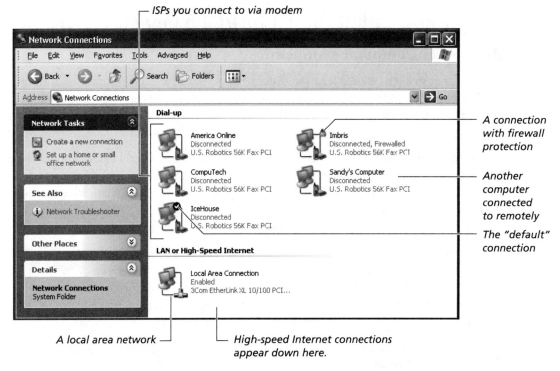

ISPs you connect to via modem

A connection with firewall protection

Another computer connected to remotely

The "default" connection

A local area network

High-speed Internet connections appear down here.

Figure 21.9 Where Windows hides your Internet connections (a second place)

4. Click the Advanced tab.

This is where you can share this Internet connection, as shown in Figure 21.10.

5. Click to put a check mark by "Allow Other Network Users to Connect through This Computer's Internet Connection."

If you receive a warning here that the connection's password is not available ("saved") to all users, then follow these steps to fix things:

a. Click Cancel to close the connection's Properties dialog box.

b. Double-click to open the connection's icon in the Network Connections window.
A Connect dialog box appears, which is where you enter your user name and password for that ISP.

c. Click to select the option "Anyone Who Uses This Computer."

d. Click Cancel. Your change will be saved despite your clicking the Cancel button.

e. Right-click the connection's icon (again).

f. Choose Properties from the pop-up menu.

g. Click the Advanced tab.

And continue by repeating Step 5 (above).

Activates firewall protection (covered elsewhere in this chapter)

A check mark here enables Internet Connection Sharing.

Forces this computer to connect to the Internet even when it's offline (good for when this is a modem connection and not high-speed)

Allows the other users to disconnect this computer from the Internet (okay to check)

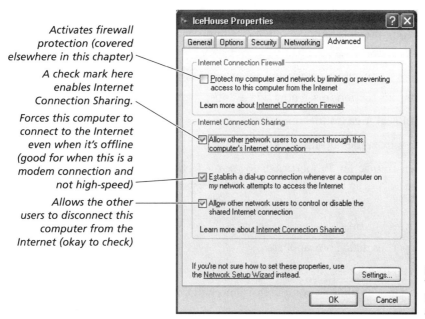

Figure 21.10
The Internet connection's Properties dialog box ➤ Advanced tab

6. Click OK.

The next warning you receive applies to other computers on the Network. Internet Connection Sharing requires that the other computers be configured to use TCP/IP over the local network—which is probably the case already. However, if you've been assigning specific IP addresses to each computer, you'll have to change over to server-assigned IP addresses. This is covered in the next section.

(Click Yes to close the Network Connections dialog box, if necessary.)

Sharing your own computer's Internet connection doesn't affect its operation as far as you can tell. The only difference you might see is if you have a plain old modem connection. In that case, you may notice the modem dialing into the Internet at seemingly odd times. Don't panic! It's just someone else on the network using your Internet connection.

 And you can disable Internet Connection Sharing by merely unchecking the check box in Step 5 above.

How Can I Access the Internet from Another Computer?

So your snotty partner has finally condescended into sharing his or her speedy Internet connection. Goody. Here's how to set up your poor or perhaps even modem-less computer to use that connection over your local area network. There are two things to do, but in Windows XP when you've done the first, the second is accomplished automagically.

307

First, you must ensure that your TCP/IP settings are set up so that the server—the Internet Connection Sharing computer—is handing out your computer's IP address. Sounds confusing, but it's easy to fix:

1. Open the Network Connections window.

(Refer to the previous section to see how this is done; also see Figure 21.9.)

2. Right-click your Local Area Connection.

3. Choose Properties from the pop-up menu.

4. In the Local Area Connection Properties dialog box ➢ General panel, locate and select the Internet Protocol (TCP/IP) item in the scrolling list.

5. Click the Properties button.

The TCP/IP Properties dialog box appears.

6. Choose "Obtain an IP Address Automatically."

The Internet Connection Sharing computer will now supply this value whenever you restart you computer.

7. Click OK.

8. Click the Close button.

If you're lucky, say you're using another Windows XP computer, then at this stage the computer may actually fetch the connection information from the host (the Internet Connection Sharing computer), and you're set. You can confirm this by seeing the shared connection appear in the Network Connections window, as shown in Figure 21.11.

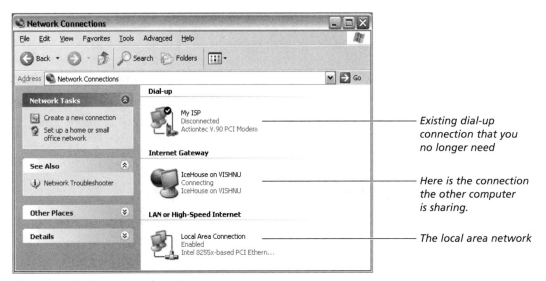

Figure 21.11 The shared connection appears.

Now if your computer is not a Windows XP system, then you'll need to configure it manually. Windows 98 and Windows Me computer can also use the Internet Connection Sharing. (And I think Windows 2000 computers can too, though I've not tested it.) This is handled at the bottom of the Internet Options/Connections dialog box; refer to a Windows 98 or Windows Me book for more information. (I don't have to document *everything* here!)

What's the Point of the Firewall?

A computer or Internet firewall is, like its real-life counterpart, a safety device. A firewall (in the real world) is a wall designed not to burn or to burn at a slow rate, which helps prevent the spread of a fire. In the electronic world, a firewall is either protective hardware or software designed to keep unwanted elements from wandering around where they are not wanted.

Windows XP offers some limited firewall protection, which is set in the Internet connection's Properties dialog box ➤ Advanced tab (see Figure 21.10). Click to put a check mark by "Protect My Computer and Network by Limiting or Preventing Access to This Computer from the Internet." Click OK and you're set.

There are other, third-party firewalls available that offer better and more customized protection than Windows XP does. I recommend the Norton Internet Security or Norton Personal Firewall program. You can also inquire with your ISP about hardware firewall protection, which is important if you have a high-speed connection.

I'm ambivalent about the firewall. Had I a high-speed connection, I would probably get Norton's firewall solution or perhaps a hardware firewall in a router (or other Internet hardware).

If you have any troubles on the Internet, such as being unable to receive e-mail attachments or download files, then blame the firewall; merely removing the check mark disables it.

22 Beating Internet Explorer into Submission

I used to try and limit myself to only three hours on the Internet a day. Then, as the Internet grew duller—or my passion over it diminished—I found myself limited to an hour a day. Now I'm down to about 10 minutes of web surfing a day. I do a lot more e-mail than I used to, but the Web has either lost its wonder, or the information there just isn't as fun and unique as it used to be. Or maybe it's that I finally got a grip on Internet Explorer and don't have to waste as much time as I used to, screeching and sliding all over the information superhighway.

Internet Explorer is not a bad or evil program. It's very flexible. Like many things that Microsoft produces, it's obviously the product of a committee as opposed to being the inspired genius of a single madman. And therein lies the problem: there are just so many useful knobs and buttons to push that it's hard to make a decision on which way to go. So I've drawn up this hefty chapter in an attempt to beat Internet Explorer into submission—show you where all the useful junk lies buried, which options to ignore, and which useful gadgets to fully employ. That should help make your web browsing experience more fruitful and possibly less time-consuming.

Junk Revealed, Options Presented, and Gadgets Engaged:

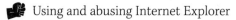 Using and abusing Internet Explorer

Dealing with "cookies"

Toiling over certain annoying settings

Understanding and organizing your favorites

Studying history

Saving a web page to disk

Don't Be Dumb and Ignore These Useful Tools

There are a few things "they" gloss over in some other books on Internet Explorer, useful things that apparently they just don't have the time to explain. Rather than assume you know these things—which I feel are all basic—I though I'd list 'em here for your review or edification (or both).

Yes, You Can Move the Toolbars

Internet Explorer has five toolbar like–things, four of which you can move. Everything is shown in Figure 22.1. The items you can move are the Menu bar (which you probably *don't* want to move), the Standard Buttons bar, the Address bar, and the Links bar. The Status bar always appears at the bottom of the window.

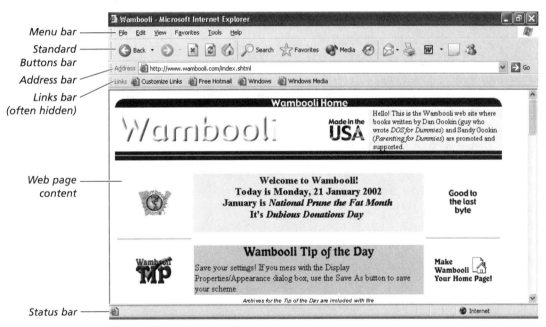

Figure 22.1 Internet Explorer

The secret to moving the toolbars is the dimple area to the toolbar's left. You point the mouse at that thing, then drag the mouse to move the toolbar. Consider the dimple area to be the toolbar's handle.

The only toolbar you'll most likely have to move is the Links toolbar, which appears to the right of the Address toolbar on most new Windows XP computers. Just drag that toolbar down a notch to situate it beneath the Address toolbar.

You can drag toolbars up, down, left, or right, placing them on separate lines or all on the same line. But you probably don't want to. So here's the first secret in this chapter: Once you have the toolbar's positioned as you like them, choose View ➢ Toolbars ➢ Lock the Toolbars. This prevents the toolbars from being moved, which you can see by the absence of their dimple areas.

When you get all the toolbars to where you want them, lock them in place!

Do I Really Need All the Toolbars?

Internet Explorer lets you show or hide any of the toolbars you want. The secret is in the View ➢ Toolbars submenu. Use that menu to choose which toolbars you want to see or hide. Everything is optional, and most everything has a keyboard equivalent, so if you're adept at the keyboard you can almost do without the toolbars at all.

KEYBOARD MASTER

Keyboard Shortcuts for Common Internet Explorer Activities

Ctrl+O
Opens a web page/Lets you type in a new address.

Alt+←
Go back (view the previous web page)

Alt+→
Go forward

Esc
Stop!

F5
Refresh the current page

Alt+Home
Go to the Home page

Also: Use the arrow keys to scroll up or down, Home key to move to the start of the page, and End key to move to the end of a page.

I Don't Want Any Toolbars, Just Give Me a Full Screen Web Page!

The brilliant F11 key is used to switch Internet Explorer between full screen (no menus, no toolbars, no nothing) mode and normal junky mode. After pressing F11 you see a screen full of nothing but web page (not even the Taskbar), with only a small, token toolbar on top, as shown in Figure 22.2. (You can even remove that single toolbar by right-clicking its dimple area and choosing Auto-Hide from the pop-up menu; move the mouse back to the top of the screen to see the toolbar again.)

To get back to normal mode, press F11 again.

Right-click here and choose "Auto-Hide" from the shortcut menu. ⌐
⌐ Essential buttons and stuff
Closes Internet Explorer ⌐

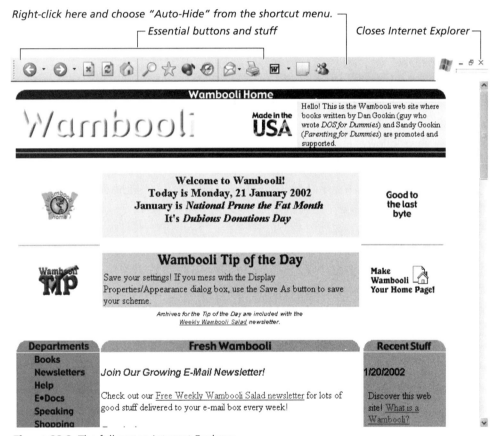

Figure 22.2 The full-screen Internet Explorer

If you have an IntelliMouse, you can use the wheel button to scroll the page, up or down. Also, the left inside button on the wheel mouse is mapped to the "Back" command in Internet Explorer. It's a handy thing to use, providing you have an IntelliMouse.

Unraveling Internet Explorer Mysteries

Despite the Web being almost old hand to anyone with a computer, it surprises me how many mysteries there are about it. And not just the Web, but also Internet Explorer. For example, I'm appalled at how many people never bother to change their home page. And despite all the news, there is still a concern out there over *cookies* on the Internet. The following sections will help you unravel these mysteries—and more—as they specifically apply to Internet Explorer.

Home Page? Home Page? I Don't Need No Stinkin' Home Page!

The home page is merely the first page you see when you start Internet Explorer (IE). So if you find yourself always wandering to a specific page on the Internet when you first start browsing the web, why not make that page your home page?

 Sample home pages are search engines, such as Google, or all-in-one portals like Yahoo News sites, such as cnn.com, *also make fine home pages.*

To set the home page, follow these steps in Internet Explorer:

1. Visit the page you want to make your home page.

It's much easier to do this first than mess with remembering the address and manually typing it in later.

2. Choose Tools ➤ Internet Options.

This summons the Internet Options dialog box, which you can also get to from the Control Panel. The Internet Options/General dialog box is shown in Figure 22.3. The top part of the dialog box deals with setting up a home page.

3. Click the Use Current button.

Or if you'd rather start with a blank slate, click the Use Blank button.

Remember: It's *your* home page.

4. Click OK.

And the Home page is set.

 The home page will appear next time you connect to the Internet. You can also instantly get to your home page when you click the Home button in IE.

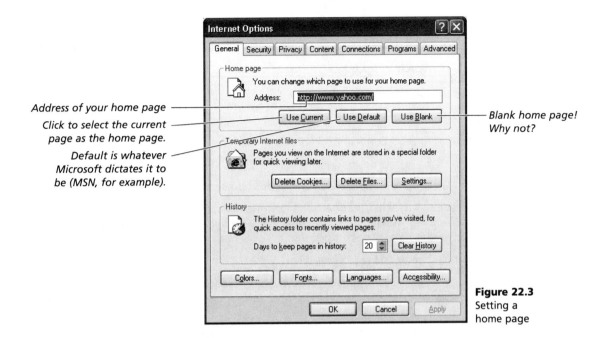

Address of your home page

Click to select the current page as the home page.

Default is whatever Microsoft dictates it to be (MSN, for example).

Blank home page! Why not?

Figure 22.3
Setting a home page

What the Hell Is a Cookie?

A cookie is a bad name given to a useful thing. They first appeared with the Netscape Navigator web browser, so you can blame someone at Netscape for calling them "cookies" and not "info tags" or something far more descriptive and far less cute. Anyway, a cookie is merely information that a web page saves on your computer.

For example, you go to visit Amazon.com and it saves a cookie on your computer that identifies who you are. So when you return to Amazon, it boasts, "Hello, Phyllis! Nice to see you again. I have some suggestions for you about some totally awesome computer books written by Dan Gookin." Or perhaps the cookie saves your shoe size from a fashion web page, or it remembers whether or not you're registered for the Wall Street Journal web page (www.wsj.com).

NERD'S CORNER

Just a Few Lines on Cookies

JOHN: I thought cookies were bad.

MARY: Yes, don't cookies contain viruses?

JOHN: Only when you drop them on a moldy towel! Ha-ha!

EVERYONE: Ha-ha!

JOHN: But seriously, can cookies compromise your computer's security?

PHIL: Oh, relax everyone. A cookie is harmless. It's beneficial in that a web page that uses cookies can remember who you are. When you come back, the web page acknowledges you, or your previous visit, or something else it deems worthy.

JOHN: But doesn't it have to access your hard drive?

PHIL: Yes, but the web page is allowed to access only its own cookies; it cannot even see cookies saved by other web pages or even other information on the hard drive. No, folks, cookies are harmless.

MARY: That's what you say! Try eating a dozen or so and then putting on this dress.

JOHN: Yeah...

Where Does Windows Hide the Cookies?

Just like Mom used to, Windows hides cookies on your hard drive. These are tiny text files that contain the information various web pages have saved to your hard drive. Each account in Windows XP has its own special cookie folder. Here's how to see yours:

1. Right-click on the Start button

2. Choose Open from the pop-up menu.

This opens the Start menu folder, which you don't need, but it makes it easy to get to the Cookies folder.

3. Click the Up button to get to your account's main folder.

And there you'll find the Cookies folder.

4. Open the Cookies folder.

It's full of tiny text files, each of which starts with your name followed by the @ (at sign) and then a web page address, such as:

```
dan gookin@amazon.com
```

You can even open the cookie to view its contents, though this isn't much help:

5. Open one of the cookie files.

   Yuck. Garbage. The information is coded, though an expert can read it. It really depends on the web page, so some will write cryptic information and others may just write plain text.

   For example, if you've ever been to my home page, www.wambooli.com, then it's written a cookie to your hard drive. The cookie merely states that you've seen the annoying pop-up window on my web page (the one advertising my free weekly newsletter). The cookie does a good thing: it disables the pop-up window for the next seven days. It says "Yes, you've viewed the pop-up window." After that, the cookie deletes itself and you see the annoying pop-up window again, then the whole process starts over.

6. Close the Notepad window you used to view the cookie content.

7. Close the Cookies window as well.

 Do not delete files in the Cookies folder directly. There is a better way to rid yourself of the cookies, covered in the next section.

Do I Need Cookies?

Certainly. But if they make you nervous you can turn them off and delete them all from your hard drive.

 Remember that many of the websites you've been to will forget who you are when you delete or disable cookies. You may have to reregister at some of them. On my Wambooli web page, you'll once again see the annoying pop-up window displayed. And so it goes.

Here's how to delete your cookies, if they truly bug you:

1. Choose Tools ➤ Internet Options from Internet Explorer's menu.

2. In the General tab (see Figure 22.3), click the Delete Cookies button.

   An "Attention" dialog box appears.

3. Click the OK button to delete your computer's stash of cookies.

 Cookies also have expiration dates attached to them. Supposedly they could live forever, but most cookies are designed to die within a certain amount of time after they've been saved on your hard drive.

   After deleting the cookies, you can configure IE to never accept another cookie again.

4. Click the Privacy tab.

5. Click the Advanced button.

   The Advanced Privacy Settings dialog box appears, as shown in Figure 22.4. Here is where you can control your computer's cookie consumption.

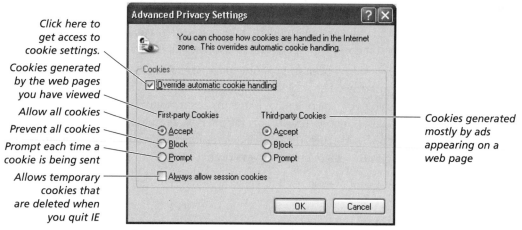

Click here to get access to cookie settings.

Cookies generated by the web pages you have viewed

Allow all cookies

Prevent all cookies

Prompt each time a cookie is being sent

Allows temporary cookies that are deleted when you quit IE

Cookies generated mostly by ads appearing on a web page

Figure 22.4 Allowing or preventing cookies

6. Make adjustments in the Advanced Privacy Settings dialog box.

Use Figure 22.4 as your guide. For myself, I typically leave this dialog box alone, allowing all cookies.

 The "Prompt" option sounds useful, but it's a real pain in the head. I tried it once, and you would be surprised how many cookies some web pages send you; it took longer to allow or deny the cookies than to read the web page.

7. Click OK, and OK again to get back to work.

What Is the Content Advisor and Why Do I Care?

The Content Advisor is Internet Explorer's way of trying to filter obscene or questionable material you might see on the Internet. It's activated from the Internet Options dialog box ➤ Content tab, as shown in Figure 22.5.

I do not recommend using the Content Advisor. The best reason I can give is that other things out there just work better. If you really want to be "safe" on the Internet or prevent your kids from wandering into places unknown or startling, then use common programs such as CyberSitter or NetNanny. These tools work better and are easier to configure and not as nasty as IE's Content Advisor.

Visit www.cybersitter.com or www.netnanny.com.

 By the way, I think the Content Advisor is nasty because if you set the password and forget it, no power on earth can recover the settings for you. In fact, the only way to recover is to create a new account and start using it in Windows XP; a forgotten Content Advisor password cannot be recovered. You've been warned!

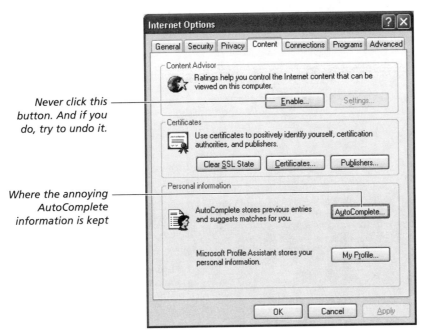

Never click this button. And if you do, try to undo it.

Where the annoying AutoComplete information is kept

Figure 22.5
The stirring Content tab

AutoComplete Drives Me Nuts, Can I Turn It Off?

AutoComplete is that Internet Explorer tool that finishes typing certain websites for you. So you type in `www.ama` and all the sudden `www.amazon.com` pops up. Just press the Enter key and you're on your way. Figure 22.6 shows how this works. So, in a way, AutoComplete is a real boon to saving typing molecules.

Partially typed address

Possible matches (press down arrow key, then Enter to select)

Figure 22.6 AutoComplete in action

If this bugs you, for example, you have some sites that attempt to auto-complete that embarrass you, then you can turn off AutoComplete:

1. Choose Tools ➢ Internet Options.

2. Click the Content tab.

Refer to Figure 22.5.

3. Click the AutoComplete button.

You see the AutoComplete dialog box, as shown in Figure 22.7

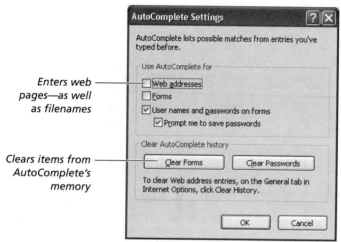

Enters web pages—as well as filenames

Clears items from AutoComplete's memory

Figure 22.7
Various AutoComplete settings

4. Remove all necessary check marks from the AutoComplete dialog box.

Oh, just uncheck them all, though the most offensive one I find is the "Web Addresses." (Note that this also affects AutoComplete for other text boxes in Windows where you would type in a filename.)

5. Optionally click the Clear Forms or Clear Passwords buttons if you want to wipe out AutoComplete's memory for those items.

6. Click OK.

Removing this option does not remove any previously typed web pages from the Address drop-down list. To do that, you must clear the history:

7. Click the General tab.

8. Click the Clear History button.

9. Click the Yes button in the confirmation dialog box.

And the history list is cleared as well. (Be sure to read more about History later in this chapter.)

10. Click OK to close the Internet Options dialog box.

What's the Point of the Temporary Internet Files?

Occasionally one of my readers will stumble onto the temporary Internet files folder. They will marvel at the sheer bulk of files in there and ask about deleting them. But then they also want to know why the files are there, and they become obsessed over them and end up never leaving the computer, constantly deleting temporary Internet files in a mad cyclical frenzy that only painkillers can stop.

Temporary Internet files, also known as the web *cache*, is the location where Internet Explorer saves all the junk you see on the web pages you visit. Every little picture, graphic, ad, or any other visual element is saved to disk. After all, it has to be saved somewhere so that you can see the silly web page. But then, the items saved to disk have an advantage, too; when you revisit the web page, it takes less time to load because most of the images are already saved (i.e., *cached*) on your disk. So the temporary Internet files are a good thing, even if they do occupy a huge chunk of hard disk real estate.

Long story. Ugh.

Every account on your computer has its own private temporary Internet file folder. Its location is in the Documents and Settings folder, your account, and then: Local Settings\Temporary Internet Files. And it's a massive folder! My account's folder shows 1,818 "objects" for about 12MB of junk.

Obviously, some people fret over that junk. I don't see why: most Windows XP systems have roomy hard drives. 12MB is nothing! Nothing! But yet, they may want the cache deleted, perhaps for security reasons or maybe just 'cause. Whatever. Follow these steps to remove the temporary Internet files:

1. Go to the General tab in the Internet Options dialog box.

Refer to Figure 22.3.

2. Click the Delete Files button.

A dialog box questions your actions, but also asks if you want to also delete all offline content, which is a good idea.

3. Put a check mark by "Delete All Offline Content."

4. Click OK.

And the temporary Internet files are gone. (It may take a while.)

 It will take longer to load graphic-intensive web pages the next time you revisit them on the Internet.

And while you're at it:

5. Click that Settings button.

A dialog box appears where you can adjust how Windows keeps track of temporary files on your hard drive. It's pretty obvious how it works, so I won't bore you with any details or provide an image here. In fact, most of the settings don't need to be messed with, but at least you now know where these settings are made should you want to fiddle with them in the future.

6. Click OK to close the Settings dialog box.

7. Click OK to close the Internet Options dialog box.

Using Favorites without Letting Your Bookmarks Run Away on You

Windows has two tools to help you return to the web places you've been before: The History list of everywhere you've been, and Favorites, which I still stubbornly refer to as "Bookmarks" despite that being a Netscape term. Whatever they are, there are ways to use them properly and effectively so that, unlike Hansel and Gretel, you never get lost as you wander through the World Wide Web.

NERD'S CORNER

Cocktail Party Trivia, Part VII

JOHN: Oh! (Slapping his thigh.) Isn't that silly that Microsoft chose to make up their own term, "Favorites," as opposed to using "Bookmarks"—just because their biggest rival used that term! Ha-ha!

PHIL: Oh, yes, John. Microsoft is silly. But "Favorites" was also used by another Internet company to mean bookmarks.

JOHN: Really?

PHIL: Yes, at the same time Netscape was calling them "Bookmarks," AOL was referring to them as "Favorites" or "Favorite Places."

JOHN: So Microsoft just "borrowed" the term from AOL?

PHIL: More or less. But what's really funny is that AOL eventually bought Netscape. So the company that used "Favorites" bought the company that used "Bookmarks." Isn't that weird?

JOHN: No. In fact, it's a let-down Phil. I think you're losing your grip.

MARY: Yes, Phil. John is looking more and more attractive in my eyes all the time.

JOHN: That's the gin talking.

Why Bother with Favorites When There's the History List?

The Favorites list is more of a personal thing than the History. The History list is merely a record of where you've been for the past several days, every website and every page on those sites, all carefully logged and available for scrutiny or revisiting. Despite its detail, it is a temporary thing; eventually items in the History list lapse. (History is good for three weeks, typically.)

The Favorites list, on the other hand, is something you create directly and permanently. Adding an item to the Favorites list keeps it there until you remove it. That way you can make note of those places you visit most often on the Internet or those places you feel you may want to visit again. In fact, a carefully maintained Favorites list is one of the most efficient ways to browse the Internet, as the following sections demonstrate.

(The History list is covered later in this chapter.)

I Really Don't Need the Favorites Menu on the Start Menu

The Favorites menu is used primarily as an Internet Explorer device. Its original purpose was to keep track of web places you grew fond of. However, in Microsoft's never-ending battle to weld the web browser to the operating system, Favorites also appears all over Windows.

For example, in the Help and Support Center there is a Favorites button and a separate list kept of your favorite places in the help system. Older versions of Windows also kept files and folders as "Favorites," so you could easily browse to a favorite folder on the hard drive. (That particular feature was dropped from Windows XP.)

One place outside of IE where you may find the Favorites list is on the Start panel. I suppose that's okay if you want to start your Internet day by choosing a favorite site from that list; IE would then dutifully connect to the Internet and bring up that page. On the other hand, a Favorites list on the Start panel is kinda junky, so here's how to remove it:

1. Right-click on the Start button.

2. Choose Properties from the pop-up menu.

3. Click the Customize button.

4. Click the Advanced tab.

5. Remove the check mark by "Favorites Menu."

If there isn't a check mark there, then you're just hunky-dory.

6. Click OK.

And the Favorites menu is gone, gone, gone from the Start panel.

Why Do I Have to Scroll Endlessly through the Favorites Menu?

The reason the Favorites menu grows so long is that you haven't taken the time to organize it. No, you just have a list of "best places" all added one after the other without so much as a thought to organization. And if you've been reading this book for any time now, you *know* that I'm a stickler for organization. (Yes, I love organization, but I'm not too terribly fond of authority.)

To begin to organize your favorites in Internet Explorer, choose Favorites ➤ Organize Favorites. This opens the handy Organize Favorites dialog box, as shown in Figure 22.8. This is where you'll spend the next several sections modifying and customizing your list of favorites.

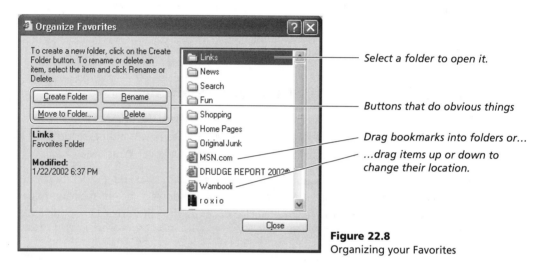

Figure 22.8
Organizing your Favorites

KEYBOARD MASTER

Quick shortcuts for the Organize Favorites dialog box

These are the keyboard equivalents for the four buttons used in the Organize Favorites dialog box:

Alt+C
Creates a folder.

Alt+M
Moves a bookmark to a folder.

Alt+R
Lets you rename a bookmark.

F2
Another rename command (commonly used in a folder window).

Alt+D
Deletes a bookmark.

Delete
Of course, you can always use this to delete instead.

Do I Really Need All of the "Suggestions" That Appear on IE's Favorites List?

No. Windows comes with a list of its own favorites for you, mostly Microsoft-related sites such as MSN. There is no point in keeping these entries if you don't plan on using them; feel free to delete: Click to highlight them in the Organize Favorites dialog box and click the Delete button.

 There is no "Undo" command in the Organize Favorites dialog box. Be careful what you delete!

If the Menu Is Too Wide, Then Rename Your Bookmarks!

One of the frustrating things about the Favorites menu is that occasionally it gets way too wide. That's because you saved a web page bookmark and the web page itself suffers from a very long name, such as "Old and Exciting DOS Programs You Can Still Run in Windows XP." That one bookmark will make the Favorites menu as wide as all that text—which is gross. The solution? Edit the name:

1. Choose Tools ➤ Organize Favorites.

2. Select the long name in the Organize Favorites dialog box.

3. Press the F2 key.

4. Type in a shorter name.

For example, you can change "Shopping at the #1 Computer store, DataBlech!" to just read "DataBlech." You can use the cursor keys to edit the name. Be creative.

5. Press Enter to lock in the new name.

Organize Bookmarks of Similar Web Pages into Custom Folders

When I first started surfing the net, I spent most of my time perusing various Doomsday websites. I was thrilled by it all—especially the anti-Doomsday sites that make fun of the Doomsday sites. (Sadly, after Y2K few of these sites are still online.) So as my Favorites list grew longer and longer, I decided to put them all into a special Doomsday folder.

You can create lots of interesting folders to help you organize your Favorites. The folders appear on the Favorites menu as submenus—similar to the concept of the All Programs menu on the Start panel. (See Chapter 6.) Here's how to create and use a new folder:

1. Open the Organize Favorites dialog box.

Choose Tools ➤ Organize Favorites from IE's menu bar.

2. Click the Create Folder button.

The new folder appears in the Organize Favorites dialog box, named "New Folder."

3. Rename the new folder to represent a category of bookmarks.

Examples: News, Shopping, Fun, Financial, Travel, Search, and so on. Create folders for your hobbies and sports interests, should you have any. I have a folder where I keep friends' and associates' home pages. There's even a folder into which I saved all the original nonsense that appeared on the Favorites menu. I call that folder "Original Nonsense."

After creating the folder, use it! You must manually copy items into the folder:

4. Select a bookmark to move into the folder.

5. Click the Move to Folder button.

A special Browse for Folder dialog box appears, as shown in Figure 22.9.

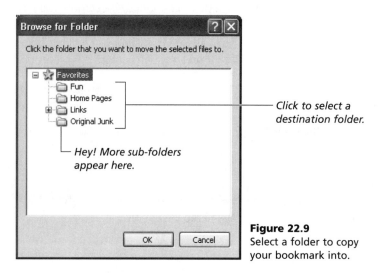

Click to select a destination folder.

Figure 22.9
Select a folder to copy your bookmark into.

6. Click OK to move the folder.

And the link is moved—you're on the road to Organization City.

 You can also drag bookmarks into folders, though because of the relatively small size of the Organize Favorites dialog box, I recommend using the Move to Folder button instead.

NERD'S CORNER

Where the Favorites *really* dwell

The Favorites menu, like many other things in Windows, is really a collection of shortcut icons and folders stored elsewhere on the hard drive. As you might suspect (being used to Windows XP so far), each account has its own Favorites folder, which is kept under the account's name in the Documents and Settings folder.

⭐ Favorites   *There's no need to wander off into the special Favorites folder; it's much easier to deal with Favorites by using the Organize Favorites dialog box, as described in this chapter. So it's just a nerdy thing that I thought I would point out—like the Cookies folder earlier in this chapter or the History folder, which you'll read about in a few pages.*

How Can I Add a Bookmark Directly into a Folder?

If you're using the Ctrl+D keyboard shortcut to "drop" a bookmark, then Internet Explorer places that bookmark right at the end of the Favorites list—not very conducive to your organizational strategy. I'll agree that Ctrl+D is handy, and I often use it. But then I have to go back and edit the Favorites list and move things round—which is a bother.

A better solution, especially if you want to add a bookmark to a specific Folder in Favorites, is to do this:

1. Choose Favorites ➤ Add to Favorites.

2. Click the Create In button to make the dialog box appear as in Figure 22.10.

Here you can do two useful things at once: You can rename the bookmark, for example, shorten it so as to keep the Favorites menu narrow, and you can select a specific folder to bury the bookmark in, as shown in Figure 22.10.

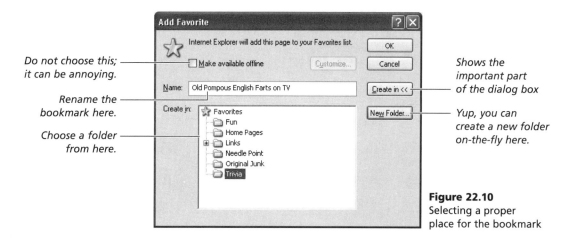

Do not choose this; it can be annoying.

Rename the bookmark here.

Choose a folder from here.

Shows the important part of the dialog box

Yup, you can create a new folder on-the-fly here.

Figure 22.10
Selecting a proper place for the bookmark

327

3. Optionally type a new shorter name for the bookmark (or edit the existing bookmark).

4. Select a folder to save the bookmark in.

5. Click OK.

   And the bookmark is saved.

Obviously if you just want to save the bookmark on the Favorites list and find a place for it later, just use Ctrl+D instead of the Add Favorite dialog box.

KEYBOARD MASTER

Adding to a Specific Favorites Folder

Alt+A, A

Rather than use Ctrl+D to add a bookmark, use this key combination to add the bookmark to a specific Favorites folder.

Why Are All My New Folders at the Bottom of the Menu?

The Favorites menu is a first-come, first-served deal. When you add anything to it, such as a bookmark via Ctrl+D or a new folder, that item is placed at the bottom of the list in the Organize Favorites dialog box, which means it also appears at the end of the Favorites menu. Want to fix that? Then drag things around!

To change the order of a folder (or submenu) in the Favorites menu, just drag it up or down in the Organize Favorites dialog box. When you do, an "insertion bar" appears in the list, showing where the menu or item will then be placed.

Be careful when you do this! It's also possible to drag and drop bookmarks or even menus into other menus.

What's the Point of the Links Bar?

I love the Links bar, which is actually represented by the Links folder in the Favorites list. Every bookmark you stick on the Links folder becomes a button on the Links bar, and every subfolder you stick in the Links folder becomes a menu on the Links bar. In fact, on my computer (the one I really use, not my test computer), the Links bar is what I use 99 percent of the time when I want to visit a favorite Internet locality.

Figure 22.11 shows one way the Links bar can be setup. You can see how I've organized it by category, each of which is a drop-down menu. Then various bookmarks exist on the menus. All-in-all-it's a quite handy thing to have.

 To ensure that the Links bar is visible, choose View ➢ Toolbars ➢ Links from the menu.

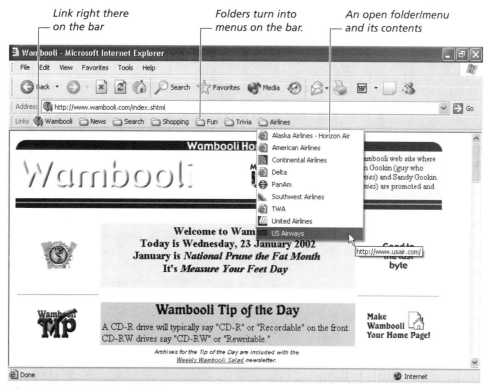

Figure 22.11 Using the Links bar

I Visited This Web Site Yesterday...

People are of two minds about the History list. Some people love it, finding it a handy way to dig through previously visited websites to find some hidden or neglected jewel. And other people, why they mind the History list quite a bit, finding it a nosy intrusion on their privacy.

Of course, with Windows XP's security, you should not fear that anyone will snoop through your History list. No one will ever know where you've been or why you would find 19th Century women's undergarments so tempting—providing that your account is wrapped up tightly with a password.

 You access the History list in Internet Explorer by clicking the History button. This displays the History panel on the left side of Internet Explorer's window, shown in Figure 22.12. You can refer to the figure for the interesting things to do there; this is all basic Windows stuff.

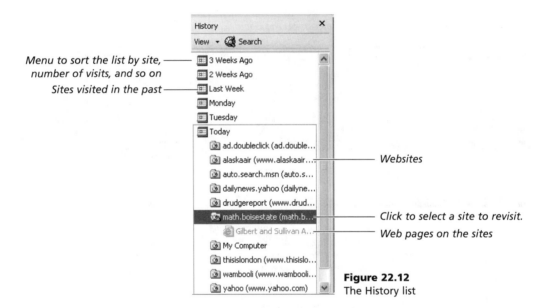

Menu to sort the list by site, number of visits, and so on

Sites visited in the past

Websites

Click to select a site to revisit.

Web pages on the sites

Figure 22.12
The History list

Summoning the History List

Ctrl+H
Displays (or hides) the History list in Internet Explorer.

Removing Unwanted Things from History

One of the most surprising things about the History list is how it so remembers *everything*. I'm not simply referring to any naughty sites you may have wandered into, but also advertising sites.

For example, in Figure 22.12 you see a link to `ad.doubleclick`, which is one of those odious advertising networks on the web. I didn't go to DoubleClick's web page, but its website did send an ad to one of the pages I visited. Ugh. How obnoxious. Like I really care what Brittney Spears looks like naked.

To remove a specific item from the history, right-click on it. Choose Delete from the pop-up menu, and it's gone.

You can also delete entire weeks and days by right-clicking on the day or week heading in the list, then choosing Delete from the pop-up menu.

Or, if you find you're doing this too often, you can dispense with the History all together, which is covered in the next section.

NERD'S CORNER

Hidden History

History

No, this isn't a History Channel special, though it could be. (And I really do love the History Channel.) Like Cookies and Favorites, the History list is kept in your account's secret folder in the Documents and Settings folder on the hard drive. Beneath your account's folder is the Local Settings folder, and within that folder you'll find the famous History folder. It even has its own special folder icon, as shown here.

As with the other secret folders uncovered elsewhere in this chapter, there's really nothing you can do with the History folder. All the settings, options, and deletions happen elsewhere, as described in the text. So now you know.

I Don't Like History!

I can't blame you for disliking the History. To me, it's snoopy. And although my account is password protected, I'm just uncomfortable with the notion that my every movement on the Internet is being tracked. It makes me paranoid, like that little old lady neighbor and her stupid binoculars. And she's always on the phone. Egads! It gives me the creeps.

In Internet Explorer, choose Tools ➤ Internet Options. This displays the Internet Options/General dialog box, which was shown way back in Figure 22.3.

To delete everything from the History list, click the Clear History button. Windows wants to know if you're sure. Sure, you're sure. Click the Yes button. The History is gone. (Even the history in the Address drop-down list is vanished. Amazing!)

To utterly disable the History thing from going on, enter 0 as the number of "Days to Keep Pages in History." That effectively does away with History tracking.

There. So much for the 17th Century...

Should I Bother with the Search Button in IE?

I've never used the Search button in Internet Explorer. Never bothered to. Just did it now to see what it would do so that maybe I could find something interesting to write about it. I couldn't.

Look. If you need to search on the Internet, go visit Google at www.google.com. It's the best there is currently. There are others, and I would list them here, but if you type Search Engines and have Google search for that, it will cough up more than I could list here—and it will list *current* search engines that will still be around in a few years when this book is an *old classic*.

But the Search button in IE? Fugheddaboutit.

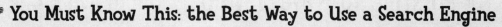

You Must Know This: the Best Way to Use a Search Engine

The best way to search using a search engine like Google is to use two or three key words relating to the subject. Don't junk up the search with a lot of proper English. For example:

I would like to know the lyrics to the Brady Bunch theme song.

Bad. Bad. Bad. Instead try:

Lyrics Brady Bunch Theme

You don't need to type "song" because it would be implied by "Theme." Also, there will probably be more matches for "Brady Bunch" than the other words, so why not list it first:

Brady Bunch Lyrics Theme

Above, the search engine will look for four key words: Brady, Bunch, Lyrics, and Theme. But Brady Bunch always goes together, so you can put that in double quotes, so that the search engine treats it as one word:

"Brady Bunch" Lyrics Theme

I would even go so far as to say that "Theme" is optional here. So the final result—from "I would like to know the lyrics to the Brady Bunch theme song"—is at last:

"Brady Bunch" Lyrics

That should get you what you want to know.

Apply a similar logic to other searches you do. Here's a fancy bullet-list summary:

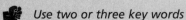 *Use two or three key words*

Avoid unimportant words or English phrasing; be blunt!

Group things together with double quotes, otherwise the search engine will match the words individually.

If the search engine yields a lot of results, check for a "Refine" option. That allows you to add more words to the search—or search within the results—to further narrow down the results.

Remember that the information you get on the Internet is not guaranteed to be accurate. Internet sources should not be cited. If you really need to do research, go to the library.

Is It Possible to Save a Web Page to Disk?

Certainly you can save a web page to disk. Internet Explorer sports a lovely File ➤ Save As command, which you can use to save or archive any web page to disk. Simple. Easy. Silly.

But there's one problem: there are just too many weird file formats to choose from for saving a simple web page to disk. It's not like a word processor, where you can choose between Plain Text, Word 2000, WordPerfect, RTF, and other common file formats. When you save a web page you're given a drop-down menu of odd and unusual choices, all of which look and sound similar with no true distinctions.

Which web page file format is best? I don't know! It depends on what you need in the file you're saving. Here's my summary of the "Save As Type" drop-down list from IE's Save As dialog box:

Web Page, complete (*.htm, *.html) This saves the web page to disk along with all the images from that web page. If the web page you're saving contains images that you want to save as well (so you can see the whole thing offline), then choose this option.

The Web Page, Complete option saves the web page in two places. First, there's an HTML (or web page) document on disk. Second, the images, sounds, and other "external" parts of the web page are saved in a special folder. Both the HTML document and folder have the same name (though the folder ends with _files).

So, for example, if you go to www.wambooli.com and save it to disk as Wambooli, you'll end up with two new things on the hard drive: a file called Wambooli.htm, which is the HTML web page document, plus a folder named Wambooli_files, which contains all the graphics, sounds, and other web-nonsense.

Wambooli.mht

Web Archive, single file (*.mht) This is the one I have a tough time figuring out. The best way I can put it is that the MHT file format is basically an e-mail message; so the Web page ends up looking like an e-mail message that you saved to disk. All the relevant information in the web page is saved along with the web page, so that you can e-mail this file to someone else and they see the full web page.

Web Page, HTML only (*.htm, *.html) This format, like it says, just saves the web page to disk. Web pages are basically text, though mixed in with the text are special formatting commands, commonly known as HTML. So what you get is a junky-looking text file—should you view it using Notepad or WordPad. But if you open the file up using IE or some other HTML-friendly program (FrontPage, Word, Excel, or whatever), then you see the web page as it's supposed to look— but without any graphics files. In their place, you'll see the "missing image" icon.

Text File (*.txt) This format merely saves all the text from the web page. The text isn't formatted (because the HTML codes are stripped out), but you do get all of the text, which is easier than selecting and copying text from a web page.

Yes, You Can Save Only Text from a Web Page!

There are two ways to yank text from a web page. The first is to save the Web page to disk as a text file. (See the previous section.) The second, more crude way, is to select text on the Web page and copy it by pressing Ctrl+C. Then you can paste that text into any application that accepts text, by using the Ctrl+V paste command.

Some programs will accept text pasted from the Web page in the same text format as the Web page. Other programs may merely interpret the text as plain old, boring, unformatted text.

Which Should I E-Mail, the Web Page or Merely Its Address?

I'm always in favor of e-mailing the address. I say so for many reasons: First, the address is very small, maybe a line of text. Second, it takes no time to send a wee bit of text. And third, an address is very compatible with any e-mail program.

Sending a Web page address by e-mail is as easy as choosing File ➢ Send ➢ Link by E-mail from IE's menu.

If you must send the entire web page, then you can choose File ➢ Send ➢ Page by E-mail, which sends the whole dang doodle page. Or you can save the page to disk as a web archive, which you can then e-mail. Either way, the recipient gets an exact copy of the Web page, which displays properly in Outlook or Outlook Express.

The Web pages you send may not look good, or may not even show up, in non-Microsoft e-mail programs. Consider that when you go off and send a page to someone.

335

23

Confronting Your
Basic E-Mail Frustrations

I'm pleased that e-mail is so easy, so basic, so simple that most computer users can pick up on it in a jiffy. Honestly, the biggest problem beginners ever have with e-mail is not having anything to write about. (And before that, it was not having anyone else they knew who could receive e-mail.) But today, it seems that just about everyone can figure out the subtleties of "To" and "Subject," and the more esoteric aspects of "Cc" and even "Bcc." And it's satisfying to note that most beginners can actually dream up contents more worthy than, "Hey, isn't e-mail neat? I just love the computer!" Oh, bother....

So instead of singing you the song of e-mail basics, this chapter is a dance around esoteric e-mail edges. It covers some of the more frustrating aspects of e-mail, such as inbox management, fighting spam, and the intricacy of forwarding e-mail—and any little irk or quirk that can wiggle under your fingernails as you churn out missives long and necessary. It's all demystified, and de-muddled here for your electronic epistle-writing pleasure.

Mysteries Demystified and Muddles De-Muddled:

 Managing your e-mail and your e-mail folders

Creating new folders

Using Message Rules to organize your e-mail

Deleting and un-deleting your mail

Ridding yourself of unwanted e-mail (spam)

Working with file attachments

Understanding the Bcc field

Sending unformatted e-mail

Forwarding e-mail without driving your friends nuts

This chapter dwells on using Outlook Express as your e-mail program. Outlook Express (OE) is included with each version of Windows. It is not the same thing as Outlook, which is part of the Microsoft Office suite of programs.

This chapter does not cover using AOL, Hotmail, Juno, or any other non-standard or web-based e-mail program (such as Yahoo Mail). While these alternatives may also have similar features, that's just too much information to document here.

Managing Your E-Mail versus Living a Life of E-Sin and E-Sloppiness

Ever own a horse? Been around horses? How about a barnyard? Pig pen? That country stuff reminds me of e-mail. The similarities are close enough to be scary: if you don't take care of the barnyard, you'll soon be hip deep in "it." And if you don't manage your e-mail, you'll soon be hip-deep in it, too. And thus was born the concept of the e-mail box.

In the old days, there were only the basic mailboxes, similar to the basic mailboxes that come with OE:

 Inbox

 Outbox

 Deleted Items (called "Trash" in other e-mail programs)

Today there are as many folders as you can dream up. OE itself comes with two additional folders straight out of the barn:

 Sent Items

 Drafts

The Sent Items folder is comparable to the Outbox in other e-mail programs; those programs use the Outbox to store both pending outgoing e-mail as well as e-mail that has already been sent—similar to the way the Inbox stores both read and unread incoming e-mail.

The Drafts folder is used to hold e-mail that has been composed but not queued up for sending. These pending messages are saved until you edit or simply send them, which is covered elsewhere in this chapter.

Of course, this is not the limit on the number of mailboxes you can have in OE. As with organizing your files, it pays to create new folders for your e-mail and to organize your e-mail into those folders.

Where Did My E-Mail Folders Go!

The typical OE screen is divided into four areas: Folders, Contacts, folder contents, and message contents, as shown in Figure 23.1. Note that the contents on the right side of the window reflect the contents of the folder that is chosen from the Folders list on the left side. (Or, if you bother with "news," then it displays the messages and message contents from a newsgroup, but I'm not covering "news" in this book.)

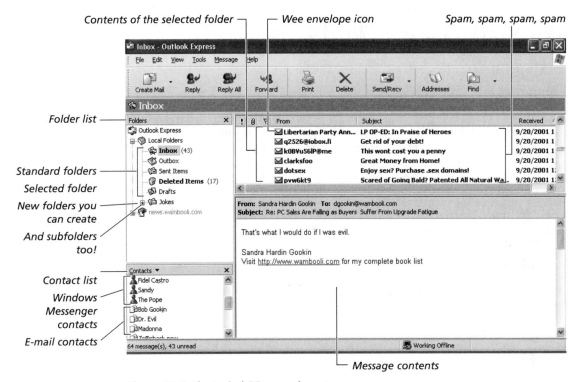

Figure 23.1 The typical OE screen layout

To change the view of any or all of this stuff, you need to use the Window Layout Properties dialog box; choose View ➤ Layout from the menu. Then use the dialog box, as covered in Figure 23.2, to display or hide various parts of Outlook Express.

KEYBOARD MASTER

Go Directly to Your Inbox

Ctrl+I
Displays the Inbox folder in OE.

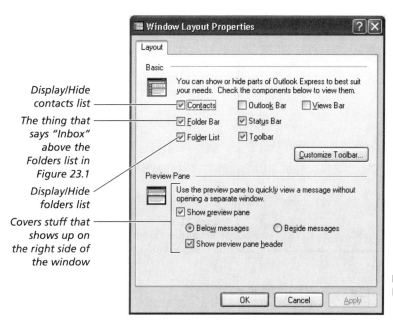

Display/Hide contacts list ⎯⎯⎯⎯

The thing that says "Inbox" above the Folders list in Figure 23.1

Display/Hide folders list

Covers stuff that shows up on the right side of the window ⎯⎯⎯

Figure 23.2 Showing or hiding various parts of OE

My Inbox Must Be Three Stories Tall, How Can I Better Organize My Messages?

The easiest way to organize your incoming e-mail is to create new folders—and subfolders—into which you can copy and save your e-mail. For example, I have and use the following folders:

Business   Online Orders

Internet   Personal

Then I have subfolders in each of them for various other categories. For example, my Personal folder has the following subfolders:

Family   Jokes

Friends   Puzzles

Fan Mail   Theater

Hate Mail

 Generally speaking, after I read a message, I move it from the Inbox into the proper folder or subfolder. I can do that by dragging the message by its wee envelope icon or by choosing Edit ➢ Move to Folder and then selecting the appropriate folder from the Move dialog box.

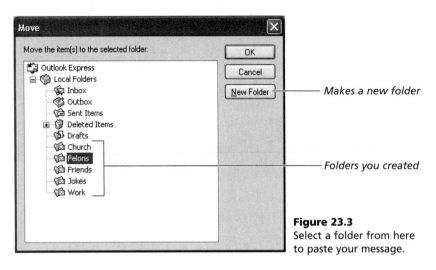

Figure 23.3
Select a folder from here
to paste your message.

KEYBOARD MASTER

Moving a Message into a Folder

After reading a message, stick it into the proper folder with this keyboard shortcut:

Ctrl+Shift+V

This displays the Move dialog box. It helps to think of it as a "Super Paste" command; the Paste keyboard equivalent is Ctrl+V, so Ctrl+Shift+V is like pasting the message into another folder.

(Note: You can only use this command when viewing the e-mail folder; when you display messages individually, use Alt+F, M which activates the File ➢Move to Folder command from the menu.)

How Can I Make a New Folder (or Two)?

New e-mail folders are as easy to create as new folders in Windows Explorer. Follow these steps:

1. Right-click on the parent folder in the Folders list.

For example, if you want to create a new main-level folder, right-click on Local Folders (the top level).

If you want to create a subfolder named Filthy inside the Jokes folder, then right-click on the Jokes folder.

2. Choose New Folder from the pop-up menu.

A Create Folder dialog box appears. Ignore what it says, because I've already given you the proper set-up instructions.

3. Type the name for the new folder.

4. Click OK.

And the folder is created right where you want it.

 You can rename any folder you created by selecting it and pressing the F2 key.

Is There Any More Efficient Way to Get E-Mail from the Inbox into a Specific Folder?

The best way to get your e-mail into a specific folder is to drag it over, or use the Edit ➤ Move to Folder command (Ctrl+Shift+V). That's what I do. You can, however, configure OE so that it automatically deposits e-mail into specific folders based on "message rules."

The advantage to using Message Rules is that it organizes your e-mail as each message arrives. The downside is that you may forget this and neglect to read some messages.

 *Mailboxes that contain unread messages appear in **bold text**. That's your clue that a new message has arrived and is awaiting your eyeballs' inspection.*

How Can a Message Rule Help Me File Away My E-Mail?

A Message Rule is OE's way of filtering messages based on their content or the contents of the To, From, or Subject lines. When an e-mail message matches certain criteria, such as the message is "From" one "Joe Shakespeare," you can direct OE to automatically perform some action on the message: move it to a folder, delete it, forward it, and so on. Message rules are one of the more powerful aspects of Outlook Express.

For example, suppose you have an online brokerage account at E*Trade. And every time E*Trade sends you a missive, you manually file it off into your E*Trade folder. You can create a message rule for this so that the message is moved automatically. Here's how:

1. Locate a message in your Inbox from which you wish to create the rule.

It must be a typical message, such as one of the automatic replies that E*Trade sends out, or a message from a specific person or with a consistent subject line or some tell-tale give-away in the message body itself. The key is being *consistent*; the rule doesn't work unless the messages are consistent.

2. Choose Message ➤ Create Rule from Message.

The New Mail Rule dialog box appears, as shown in Figure 23.4. Refer to the figure for an overview of how the dialog box works.

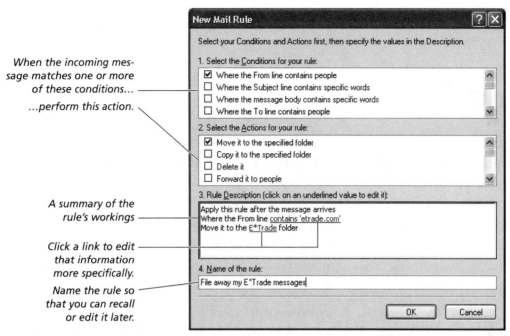

When the incoming message matches one or more of these conditions... ...perform this action.

A summary of the rule's workings

Click a link to edit that information more specifically.

Name the rule so that you can recall or edit it later.

Figure 23.4 How the New Mail Rule dialog box works

3. Choose a condition for your rule.

In the case of the E*Trade missive, the From field will always contain `etrade.com`. That's good enough to match all the messages you need. In this case, ensure that the check mark is by "Where the From Line Contains People." No other item in the list should be checked.

If the message can be flagged better by Subject, then choose "Where the Subject Line Contains Specific Words" instead.

The more specific you can get with identifying the message, the better the rule will behave.

4. Modify the condition.

As you click to put a check mark by a condition in Area 1 of the dialog box, the condition's description appears in Area 3 (see Figure 23.4). The key part of the condition is underlined—a link. It's usually good to click that link to refine what the rule looks for.

For example, the E*Trade filter says: "Where the From line contains myrecords@etrade.com."

However, E*Trade also sends out messages from `customerservice@etrade.com`, and you want *all* E*Trade conversations going into the E*Trade mailbox. Some editing is required.

5. Click the "contains" part of the rule description from Area 3 in the dialog box.

A special refining dialog box appears, as shown in Figure 23.5. This is where you can get much more specific.

6. Refine the condition.

For example, in Figure 23.5, I would do the following:

a. Type `etrade.com` in the top text box.
b. Click the Add button.
c. Select "`myrecords@etrade.com`" from the list.
d. Click the Remove button.
e. Click OK.

This effectively refines what the rule is looking for down to just "`etrade.com`."

Figure 23.5 Refining the condition

7. Click OK to return to the New Message Rule dialog box.

Now that you've identified the message, you need to tell OE what to do with it:

8. Tell OE what to do with the message by using Area 2 of the dialog box.

In this case you want to move the message to the E*Trade mailbox folder, so you would put a check mark by "Move It to the Specified Folder." The following text is added to Area 3, the Rule Description: "Move it to the specified folder."

Again, more modification needs to take place; OE needs to know which "specific" folder.

 Some of the actions you can take don't require any further definition. For example, if you choose "Delete It" from the list in Area 2, then the message rule deletes the e-mail; no further action or choices are required.

9. Refine your action.

In this case, you need to tell OE which folder to move the message to. You'll notice on the screen that is doesn't really say which specific folder the message is to be moved to. Time to be specific. Follow these steps:

a. Click on "specified" in Area 3, the Rule Description.
b. Choose the folder from the Move dialog box.
c. Click OK.

And now the rule has been modified to say: "Move it to the <u>E*Trade</u> folder."

 Any time you see underlined text in Area 3, the Rule Description, you can click that text to refine or modify the selection.

10. Recite the contents of Area 3, the Rule Description.

It should read like a sentence, like a command, as shown in Figure 23.4: "Where the From line contains 'etrade.com' move it to the E*Trade folder." Makes sense.

11. Name the rule.

You give it a name so that you can identify the rule later, should you need to modify or remove it. In this case, I've called it, "File Away My E*Trade Messages."

12. Click OK.

Outlook Express congratulates you on making up a rule.

13. Click OK again.

The rule will be put to the test the next time you pick up e-mail.

This chapter contains more rule examples in the section that covers spam. Filtering spam is one of the best things you can do with a message rule—or several dozen of them, as spammers are quite clever.

Remember that there are powerful commands available to a message rule. You can be as clever or specific as you like. However I recommend creating a simple rule at first and seeing how it works. Then explore the New Mail Rule dialog box (Figure 23.4) in more detail as you understand things more clearly.

NERD'S CORNER

Cocktail Party Trivia, aside

JOHN: Those rules certainly can be powerful.

PHIL: I fear that's one of the reasons they're neglected. It takes time to set up the rules and, as one would expect, Outlook Express doesn't exactly present the message rules in a manner that's easy for most people to comprehend.

MARY: That's probably because there are too many men working at Microsoft.

Where Are the Rules Hidden?

To review any or all of your message rules, choose Tools ➤ Message Rules ➤ Mail. This displays a dialog box full of all your e-mail message rules in the order OE filters them, as shown in Figure 23.6.

If you need to quickly change a rule, just select it from the list and use the bottom part of the dialog box to make minor modifications. To add further descriptions or actions to the rule, however, you'll need to select it and click the Modify button.

To delete a rule, highlight its name and click the Delete button.

Note that it's possible to turn a rule off without deleting it: simply remove the check mark next to the rule you want to disable. That way you won't have to completely re-create a rule should you change your mind again in the future.

Specific rules for USENET newsgroups

Remove a checkmark to disable, but not delete a rule

Change the priority of the message rules

The infamous blocked senders list

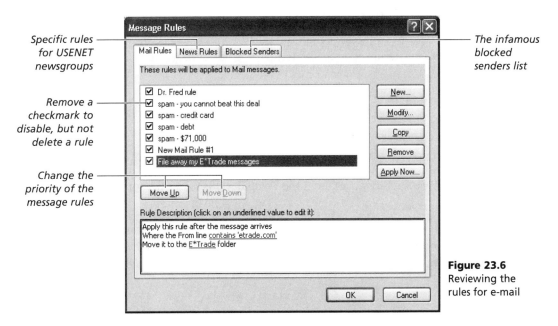

Figure 23.6
Reviewing the rules for e-mail

Any Way to Undelete a Message?

Deleted messages end up in the Deleted Items folder. They stay there until you empty the folder, which can happen automatically or manually, depending on how you have OE set up.

Note that e-mail messages transferred from the Inbox via a message rule will appear "unread" in the Deleted Items folder. Don't let that bug you.

To undelete a message, open the Deleted Items folder and click to select the message you want recovered. Then choose Edit ➢ Move to Folder (or Ctrl+Shift+V) to move that file to another folder.

How Can I Automatically Empty the Deleted Items Folder?

To automatically dump everything from the Deleted Items folder, follow these steps:

1. Choose Tools ➢ Options.

The Options dialog box appears.

2. Click the Maintenance tab.

3. Put a check mark by "Empty Messages from the 'Deleted Items' Folder on Exit."

4. Click OK.

Now when OE quits, it automatically removes all the messages from your Deleted Items folder.

Or if you don't like the automatic deletion, then repeat these steps to remove the check mark.

How Do I Manually Remove Messages from the Deleted Items Folder?

To permanently remove any message from the Deleted Items folder, select the message and punch the Delete button on your keyboard. A warning dialog box appears; click the Yes button and the message is gone!

To delete the whole swath of messages, choose Edit ➢ Empty 'Deleted Items' Folder. Thwoop! They're all gone.

Any Way to Un-Delete a Message I Removed from the Deleted Items Folder?

Alas, no: once a message is removed from the Deleted Items folder, it's gone for good.

The reason for this is that your e-mail folders are not really folders on disk at all; each mailbox is actually a text file on disk, with the messages stored in the text file like one long letter. When you remove a single message, you're deleting a chunk of text from the middle of a file. Windows cannot recover that missing chunk of text. The moral: Be careful what you delete from the Deleted items folder!

My Message Is Stuck in the Drafts Folder Limbo

The Drafts folder is used to store composed yet un-sent e-mail. So, say you're writing a message and you elect *not* to send it: you close the New Message window and OE pops up to say, "Do You Want to Save Changes to This Message?" You click Yes. The message is gone, but it's not sent. It's not in the Outbox. Hmmm....

Yes, it's in the Drafts folder. A Saved Message dialog box appears to confirm this, but many people simply click OK and don't pay any attention.

To recover the message, open the Drafts folder and then open the message. Optionally edit the message, but this time instead of closing the message window, click the Send button. The message is then sent off on its merry way, never to dawdle in the Drafts folder again.

How Can I Back up My E-Mail Folders and Their Contents?

Backing up is one of the best things you can do for your computer, and backing up your e-mail is vital. The problem with Outlook Express, however, is that it's very nasty about where it hides your e-mail messages and their files and folders on your hard drive. Extremely nasty, in fact—almost to the point where one would suppose Microsoft would prefer you *did not* back up your e-mail stuff. But don't let that stop you!

First, if you're going to back up, you know to back up the My Documents folder and all its contents. But a better approach, especially if you want to get everything on your computer, is instead to back up your account's folder in the Documents and Settings folder on Drive C (or whichever drive is the main Windows XP hard drive).

Documents and Settings is what really holds all your personal stuff, and it's much easier to say, "Back up your account information from Documents and Settings" than to hunt down individual files all over the whole stinkin' hard drive. But I digress.

Second, if you need to get specific, for whatever reasons, the folders Outlook Express uses can be found by browsing to the following location:

1. Open the Documents and Settings folder.

It helps to display the Folders panel in the Windows Explorer window; click the Folders button to display the Folders panel.

2. Open your account's folder.

3. Open the Local Settings folder.

4. Open the Application Data folder.

(And just to confuse you here, notice that there are many folders in your account with the names "Local Settings" and "Application Data.")

5. Open the Identities folder.

There should be only one identity listed, which is a combination of letters and numbers enclosed in curly brackets. See—this is being made difficult on purpose!

 The only way there will be more that one identity is if you have set up a separate e-mail identity in Outlook Express. If so, then more than one will be listed, each identity having its own set of folders in OE.

6. Open the identity folder—the long number thing.

7. Open the Microsoft folder.

8. Open the Outlook Express folder.

And there—finally!—you see various files representing the folders in OE. The names will be similar, but not identical. The folder contents are slightly cryptic, but mostly text. Don't mess with 'em!

Obviously here is the point where you could copy or backup your e-mail folders specifically, should you need to do so.

Fighting Spam

Onward e-mail soldiers
Off to fight more spam....
With message rules and tools
All spam we will slam!

No, you don't have to put up with spam in your e-mail. Spam—unwanted, junk, or mass anonymous e-mail—is the bane of Internet life. In a typical day, you'll get a general mixture of spam messages in with your regular load of e-mail. And they tell me it's going to be getting worse as e-mail grows more common and more and more devices become Internet-aware. (In a few years, text spam message on cell phones will be all the rage.)

Oh, I could go on and on about spam, and I often do in my free weekly newsletter. But unlike the weather, there is something you can do about spam. Using OE's message rules and Block Sender command, you can effectively filter out most of the e-mail not directly intended for you. It's actually quite fun to built up a repertoire of message rules and observe how they operate, dumping received spam directly into the Deleted Items folder. It's...satisfying.

 Unwanted e-mail is referred to as "spam." The Hormel Company makes a meat product called SPAM (or Spam), which stands for "spiced ham."

From Whence Cometh Thy Spam?

It's entirely possible to have an e-mail address and be on the Internet and never receive any spam. I know! I've done it! I have a backup account with a very good ISP that filters out all the spam. Plus I'm very guarded with the account. I don't do any of the following things with that account, things that often lead to your e-mail address being added to a spam list:

- *I do not post messages to USENET newsgroups.*
- *I do not participate in IRC or any online chat.*
- *I do not send or reply to e-mail greeting cards.*
- *I do not post this e-mail address on a web page or provide a link from a web page to this e-mail address.*
- *I do not use this particular e-mail address for online shopping.*
- *I do not use this particular e-mail address to sign up for any services, mailing lists, or free offers.*
- *I've encouraged my friends not to use this particular e-mail address to (thank-you-no) sign me up for joke-a-day e-mail messages or forward my name along to seven of their friends so that Bill Gates will send them a free ticket to Disney World.*

As long as you can keep your address private, and ensure that no one else abuses it, you can have a fairly spam-free time in e-mail. But the second you slip up and let your e-mail address leak out there, it's all over.

I Really Don't Want Any More Messages from "Lovekitten@yahoo.com"

Spammers realize that you open and read all your e-mail. The subject matter is often innocent, "Hey!" or "I'm thinking of you," but the names are typically the same. You can take advantage of that in OE by using the Blocked Senders to list to permanently remove any e-mail from a specific individual.

The Blocked Senders is like a specific message rule: When the From line contains this specific e-mail address (or person), delete the message, no questions asked.

To add a pest to the Blocked Senders list, highlight their message in the Inbox and choose Message ➤ Block Sender. A dialog box tells you what's going to happen. At this point the sender is on the list, but the dialog box is asking if you want to clean up all the messages in your Inbox that are from this particular nasty person. Click Yes to do so.

The nifty thing about blocking someone is that you'll never see any trace of a message from them, not even in the Deleted Items folder. Yippee!

How Can I Remove Uncle Cedric from the Block Senders List?

Oh, accidents do happen. In your zeal to block e-mail from certain spammers, you may have accidentally included a friend or relative. You can easily remove them from the nasty blocked senders list:

1. Choose Tools ➤ Message Rules ➤ Blocked Senders List.

The Message Rules/Blocked Senders dialog box appears, listing the names of your forbidden senders.

2. Locate and highlight the name you want to unblock in the list.

3. Click the Remove button.

And they're off the list.

Peace can once again reign in the family.

You can temporarily remove an address from the list by simply un-checking it. Mail will flow from that person again, but if you realize the errors of your ways, you can stick them back on the list simply by restoring the check mark.

How Can a Filter Help Me Kill off All Those "Free Viagra" Messages?

Fortunately, the spammers send common messages over and over. There's a pattern. For example, I know of no one who would personally send me an e-mail with the word "mortgage" in the subject. Ditto for "Viagra" (unless it was a joke). The word "Free" is also a clue that I have a spam and not a legitimate message.

Not all spam is easy to spot, but enough of it fits the pattern that you can create a small armada of Mail Rules to effectively filter out most of the unwanted e-mail from your Inbox.

For example, I've been getting a lot of spam recently with the subject "Custom Software Services." Here's how to design a Mail Rule in OE that automatically deletes such messages as they're received:

1. Click to select an offending message in your Inbox.

Ensure it's one of the messages with a typical, spam subject. Here are some of the subjects (or keywords in the subject) that I routinely filter:

Credit card Loan Debt Lose weight Free Prescription Hair loss Porn Hardcore Snoring Herbal Viagra Internet spy XXX

2. Choose Message ➤ Create Rule From Message.

The New Mail Rule dialog box appears, similar to Figure 23.4.

3. Un-check "Where the From Line Contains People."

You want OE to look for key words in the Subject line, not the From line.

4. Check "Where the Subject Line Contains Specific Words."

5. In Area 2, choose "Delete It from Server" as the Action.

This way it won't even be downloaded to your Inbox; the mail will be removed from your ISP's server and you'll never see it.

6. Click "Contains Specific Words" in Area 3, the Rule Description.

You need to hone the words that the Rule will look for in the Subject line. Spammer's aren't dumb, and they do alter their subject lines subtly. So you need to edit out all but the key words.

7. Use the dialog box to specify only those key words you want the Rule to search for.

In this case, type the key words you want the Rule to filter. (Refer to the list above for inspiration.) Click the Add button to add your key words to the list. Figure 23.7 shows an example.

 Use meaty words! Avoid smaller words like "the" and "of" and "and." Use those red-hot words that utterly flag this as a spam message.

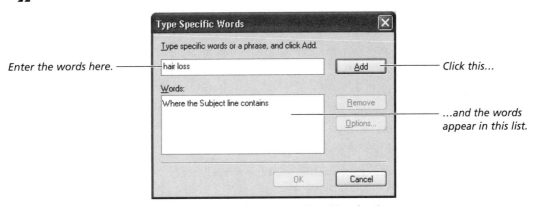

Enter the words here. ——————

Click this...

...and the words appear in this list.

Figure 23.7 Creating key words to filter for the Mail Rule

8. Click OK.

9. Confirm the Rule, as listed in part three of the dialog box, the Description:

For example:

```
Where the Subject line contains 'hair loss'
Delete it from the server
```

10. Type a name for the rule.

In my example here, I would write `spam - hair loss filter`. I start all my anti-spam filters with the word "spam" so I can easily spot them in the scrolling list, as shown in Figure 23.6.

11. Click OK, then OK again to get rid of the final dialog box.

And the Rule is created and ready to filter away at your incoming messages.

Tips and Suggestions for Composing, Replying, Sending, and Forwarding Your E-mail

The daily soap opera of your e-mail has its high and low points. I would say my low point is when I get *yet another* message forwarded to me (and several dozen other people), five or six quoted layers deep with copies of everyone else the message has been forwarded to (hundreds of people in all), about the old Internet hoax that the government is going to be levying a tax on all e-mail. Ugh. That's a low point.

Before forwarding any e-mail message, check to ensure that you're not spreading an electronic rumor or Internet hoax: the website www.truthorfiction.com/ *is an excellent source for what's true, what isn't, and why it should or shouldn't be forwarded to anyone.*

The following sections will help you avoid low points and, hopefully, generate a few high points in your e-mail travels.

I'm Trying to Send an Attachment but I Can't Find It!

You can attach any file on your hard drive to any e-mail message. The secret, as with any file on disk, is knowing where you saved the file. This is why I'm a big fan of organization. In fact, at one time I used to have an Upload folder into which I put files I wanted to send to others or attach to an e-mail message. No matter, you must remember *where* you saved the file in order to attach it.

If you cannot find the file, then use the Search button in any folder window, or press Win+F to bring up a Search Results window. Then use that window to locate your file.

If you just created the file, then use the Advanced search options to locate files created in the past day or so.

Remember that scanned images or digital pictures must be transferred into the computer and saved to disk before you can send them. (I just get that question a lot via e-mail; people are so excited that the scanner worked they forget to save the image to disk.)

What's the Best Strategy for Sending Several Attachments to the Same Person?

You can attach almost an unlimited number of files to a single e-mail message. Most e-mail programs accurately interpret this and decode the attachments properly, so it isn't a problem.

Even so, if you do plan on sending more than one attachment, consider copying all your attachments into a Compressed Folder (or ZIP file). Then send that Compressed Folder as the single attachment instead of messing with the multiple files.

> ### You Must Know This: When *not* to send a file by e-mail
>
> *I've sent some really huge e-mail attachments in my day. But the largest file I send is usually 2MB. That's a pretty hefty size for an e-mail attachment anyway. In fact, I've discovered that many Internet e-mail programs might not be able to handle a file 2MB in size or larger. When that happens, the e-mail "bounces" and I get an "undeliverable mail" message from my ISP's e-mail server.*
>
> *The sad fact is that often there is a limit to the size of a file you can send. When you reach that limit, your alternative is to go through the regular mail. For example, rather than send 5MB of video images through the e-mail to a pen pal in Australia (Hi, John!), I just burned a CD-R with the video files and mailed it.*

Why Does Outlook Express Split My Attachments?

There is an obscure option in OE that splits long messages. For example, this option would take an e-mail message with a 400KB attachment and shred it into four separate messages, each 100KB in size. I don't know why this option exists, but some e-mail programs must have some sort of limitation on the maximum file size they can accept.

The problem is that splitting a long message makes the attachment incompatible with other e-mail programs (including older versions of OE). So my advice is to turn the message-splitting option off. Here's how:

1. Choose Tools ➤ Accounts.

   An Internet Accounts/Mail dialog box appears, listing any e-mail accounts you have set up. (Remember that you can have more than one.)

2. Choose your account from the list.

3. Click the Properties button.

   A Properties dialog box for your e-mail account appears.

4. Click the Advanced tab.

5. Remove the check mark by "Break apart messages larger than __ KB."

This disables message splitting.

6. Click OK.

If you ever notice that some messages you receive are split (you get a "Part 1/4" and then "Part 2/4" and so on), then suggest to the sender that they follow these steps above to prevent OE from splitting their messages.

Or better still—recommend that they buy this book and rise to the same level of computer user-ness that you've attained!

I Can't Open This Attachment!

If you can't open an attachment, then don't try. Don't attempt to use the Open With dialog box, do not attempt to associate the attachment with any other program or application on your computer. If you cannot open the attachment, then you cannot open it. The computer is actually quite smart about these things.

The best thing to do if you receive a weird attachment is to respond to the sender and ask them what the heck it was. Be polite. Say, "What the hell did you send me!?" Then hope that they know what they did and can resend the file to you in a format your computer can read, such as the JPEG graphics file format.

 One common file format that people mistakenly send is the PPS or PowerPoint Slideshow. This is a media presentation document created by the PowerPoint program from Microsoft Office. You can obtain a PowerPoint Slideshow viewer from the Microsoft website: visit www.microsoft.com/ *and browse to the Office section, then the Downloads for Office section. (I don't have a specific address for it.)*

What Is the Bcc Field?

The Bcc field is for Blind Carbon Copies. It's a way to send e-mail to someone and *not* have their name appear in the To or Cc fields. There are two ways Bcc is commonly used:

First, if you want someone to receive a copy of an e-mail epistle, yet you don't want anyone else to know that you've sent them a copy. The Bcc field is "swallowed" by the Internet e-mail program; copies of the e-mail are sent to the people on the Bcc field, but no record appears when anyone reads the message.

 When you receive an e-mail message and you notice that your name is not on the To or Cc field, then you can safely assume that your name was instead put on the Bcc field. (This is how most spam is sent out.)

Second, people who forward jokes or funnies in the e-mail usually put their entire list of friends and cohorts in the Bcc field. That way you don't get one of those huge e-mail messages with a mile-long header every time you get yet another funny cow joke via e-mail.

I Can't See the Bcc Field in the New Message Window?

The BCC field is normally turned off in OE. To display it, choose View ➤ All Headers from the New Message window. This displays the Bcc field right below the Cc field.

You add people to the BCC list just as you do the To or Cc fields. Everyone, no matter which field they're listed in, receives the message. But the people in the Bcc field do not appear in the header of the message everyone receives.

This Unix Nerd Tells Me Not to Send My E-Mail in HTML Format. Is He Being a Jerk?

E-mail is all basically plain text. You can prove this to yourself in a rather dramatic way:

1. Select a colorful, formatted e-mail message in your Inbox.

It doesn't have to be your Inbox, any e-mail folder will do. Just sift around until you locate a colorful, formatted e-mail message, fancy fonts, all that jazz.

2. Choose File ➤ Properties.

3. Click the Details tab.

4. Click the Message Source button.

A window appears, such as the one shown in Figure 23.8, that lists the message in its raw text form. The message its actually formatted like a web page, using HTML commands— which are plain text—to format the message and include images, fancy fonts, and other formatting. But at its core, the message is plain text, as you can see in Figure 23.8.

5. Close the Message Source window.

6. Click OK to close the dialog box.

I point this out for a very important reason: not all e-mail programs see your e-mail the way you do. If the other person has Outlook Express, or their e-mail program can understand how Microsoft formats an e-mail message, then they see things just as you do. Otherwise, the e-mail message they see looks *exactly* like what you see in Figure 23.8.

Figure 23.8 At its core, all e-mail is plain text.

As you're composing a new message, click the Source tab at the bottom of the New Message window. This shows you how your e-mail message really looks—raw codes and all.

To be considerate, and to ensure that your e-mail is readable by everyone, often it's necessary *not* to format it. Instead, you can opt to use plain text only in your e-mail. In the New Message window, choose Format ≻ Plain Text. You may see a warning dialog box, telling you that you'll lose any formatting already in the message. It's okay; Click OK.

Now you can proceed to type the message, but without any formatting. Sure, it may be dull, but it's very compatible.

How Can I Forward a Message without Getting Line Upon Line of Headers, Forwarded Names, and Duplicates of the Same Message?

Easy: Edit the message.

As you go to forward a message, the message you're forwarding appears in the contents part of the message window. Just click the mouse down there and edit away, removing whichever parts of the message you don't want. For example, if you see row upon row of these > things in the forwarded message, just go and edit them out. (Alas there is no Search and Replace command for OE; you have to search and replace manually.)

The > symbol is used in many e-mail programs to "quote" the original message. As e-mail gets forwarded and re-forwarded, the column of > symbols grow like moss on a tree during a wet spring. Alas, in OE you just have to trim them out manually.

Another trick you might attempt is to place your gang of people on the Bcc line of the message instead of the To or Cc line. In fact, whenever I forward a message to a group of people, I fill in the fields like this:

To: (myself)
Cc: (blank)
Bcc: (Everyone else goes here)
Subject: Fw: Yet another forwarded joke!

By putting myself in the To field, I copy the message to myself. But when the message arrives to all my online pals, all they see is "To: Dan Gookin" and "From: Dan Gookin" and they're not bothered with any other obnoxious e-mail headers.

 This discussion folds nicely into managing your e-mail address book, which is covered in the next chapter.

24

Just Enough Address Book to Make Your Life Easier

I'm not a big Address Book fan. I use it, sure. It's handy for keeping the names of frequent e-mail contacts, creating groups, and other convenient things. But I don't do *everything* there is to do in the Address Book. That's because I believe there is a limit to what the Address Book can do, and if you exceed that limit then you're merely wasting your time. Or, to put it another way, as a general-purpose personal information manager, the Address Book stinks.

This chapter touches briefly upon the Address Book in Outlook Express, which I'll call "OE" from now on to save typing molecules. My basic philosophy with the Address Book is to ignore it. Beyond that, there are some insights and guidelines offered in this meager chapter that will help you to become an above average Address Book user. I hope.

Gifts Given and Sacrifices Offered:

- Getting away with as little of the Address Book as possible
- Putting names and information in to the Address Book
- Modifying Address Book entries
- Using groups to send out gang e-mails
- Exporting Address Book information
- Playing vCard games

 Outlook Express is the e-mail program that ships with Windows XP, both Home and Professional releases. It is not the same program as Outlook, which is similar but sold separately or bundled with Microsoft Office. The commands listed in this chapter are specific to Outlook Express, not Outlook.

Knowing How Much of the Address Book to Use
Without Wasting the Rest of Your Life

All e-mail programs need an address book. That's where the e-mail addresses of people you commonly write to are kept. Names of the humans go along with the e-mail addresses, so that you know the difference between `bobc`, `bobg`, `bobt` and `bobz`. It's really a very simple thing.

So when you create a new e-mail in OE, you type `bobc` in the To field and OE looks up in the Address Book for `bobc` and automatically puts his true e-mail address in there. Nifty. Handy. A boon to e-mail users everywhere. This much you know.

You should also know about e-mail nicknames. This is a handy way to save complex e-mail addresses using handier shortcuts. For example, some AOL addresses are bizarre and may only resemble your friend's name at a distance of 50 meters. In that case, you create a nickname, such as `pal`, and you can use that instead of memorizing the jumble of letters assigned to users at some Internet services.

There. That's it. That's all the Address Book you really need to know.

The Rest?

The rest of the Address Book?

Yes. There's more. A lot more. A whole heapin' pile of mile-high worms and guts and smelly stuff that you really, really don't want to get into unless you have the time.

I Have the Time

I suppose the fascination of having a name and e-mail address just wasn't enough for the programmers at Microsoft. They figured, "Hey! As long as we're having them enter the name and e-mail address, why not have them enter their real street address!"

And someone else chimed in, "Yeah, and their phone number!"

And the new girl added, "All their phone numbers!"

And so you have the monstrosity that exists today as the Outlook Express Address Book. Figure 24.1 lists the nonsense for my wife's entry into the Address Book. "Egads," say I.

As you can see from Figure 24.1, I fill in only the basic information. The rest I feel is a waste of time—especially because other programs can do it better (such as the Palm Desktop, which I can use with my PalmPilot), and—the main reason—the Outlook Express Address Book is rude and won't talk to other programs. But more on that later in this chapter. (Oh, it's a page-turner—trust me.)

Blood type entries in here ⎯

Put where they hide their
guns and jewelry here. ⎯

Pet's names; IQ score; location
⎯ of secret moles go here.

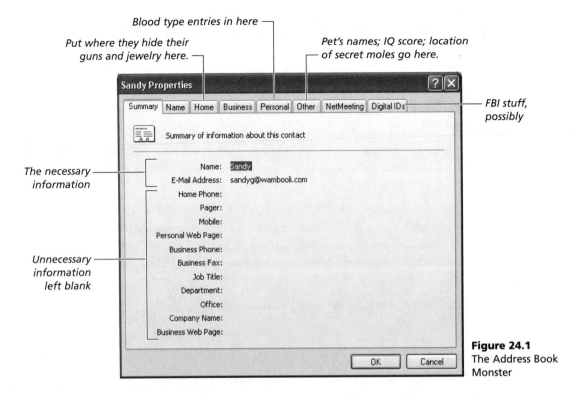

The necessary
information

Unnecessary
information
left blank

FBI stuff,
possibly

Figure 24.1
The Address Book
Monster

Summoning the Address Book

Before diving too far in the murky muck, here is the basic command you need to know in order to summon the Address Book in OE: Tools ➤ Address Book. That brings up the Address Book window, as shown in Figure 24.2.

 You can also summon the Address Book by clicking on the Address Book icon located next to the To, Cc, or Bcc fields in a New Message window. Though in that case, you get a special window where you can easily slide names into the To, Cc, and Bcc fields, as shown in Figure 24.3.

 **KEYBOARD MASTER**

Conjuring up the Address Book

Ctrl+Shift+B
Summons the Address Book window from anywhere in OE. Hint: Think "B" as in "Book," Address Book.

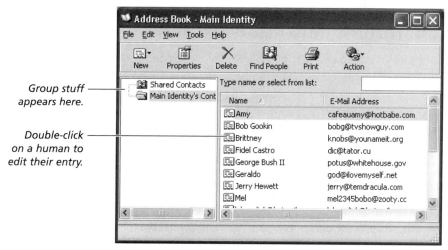

Group stuff appears here.

Double-click on a human to edit their entry.

Figure 24.2 The Address Book itself

Select a person from the list.

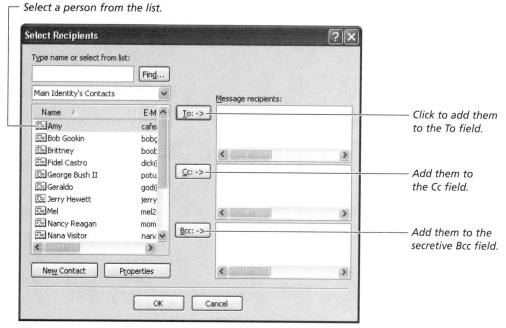

Click to add them to the To field.

Add them to the Cc field.

Add them to the secretive Bcc field.

Figure 24.3 Adding contacts to your New Message

Getting Those Names into the Address Book

Suppose you just have a lot of time on your hands. Say you're retired and your golf day was ruined by the weather or by dumb old Irwin's pacemaker acting funny. (Damn him and his fatty foods!) Anyway, you have a few extra hours of your remaining life left and, well, nothing's on TV (is it ever?) so you decide to randomly go through your Outlook Express Address Book and fill in the names of everyone you've ever met plus the 43 Presidents of the United States.

My opinion: That's a waste of time! Why bother anyway, when you can automatically add people to your Address Book?

 While the techniques in the following sections do add people to your Address Book, it merely saves their names and e-mail addresses (and sometimes just the e-mail addresses). To fill in the rest of the information you need to open the Address Book and futz around filling things in—if you have the time.

How Can I Just Automatically Add Folks I Correspond with to My Address Book?

It's a computer, right? It's supposed to make things easy. Sometimes it does. For example, to get names into your e-mail address book there are a number of interesting, handy and quite useful tools.

I know, I know—I was shocked too when I discovered these. But you can get used to being pleasantly surprised by some aspects of Windows.

In Outlook Express, follow these steps to configure the program to automatically add the names of people you correspond with to the Address Book:

1. Choose Tools ➤ Options.

2. Click the Send tab.

3. Ensure that there is a check mark by "Automatically Put People I Reply to in My Address Book."

 Only people you reply to are added to the Address Book. This doesn't include all the spam messages you get or those people you never write back to.

4. Click OK.

I'd Rather Just Individually Add People

To be picky about things you can add people one at a time to your address book. And this technique works even if you don't reply to the message.

If you're previewing the message, choose Tools ➢ Add Sender to Address Book.

If you're reading the message in its own window, choose Tools ➢ Add to Address Book ➢ Sender. Unlike the previous example, which is easy and obvious, this one also throws an Address Book entry (Properties window) for that person in your face. Just click OK.

I Need to Add People Manually Because They Never Send Me E-Mail

You can always fill in the Address Book by summoning its window and choosing File ➢ New Contact from the menu. This displays an utterly blank window, which you can then fill in with the important information about your e-mail contact. Figure 24.4 shows you what's important; ignore everything else.

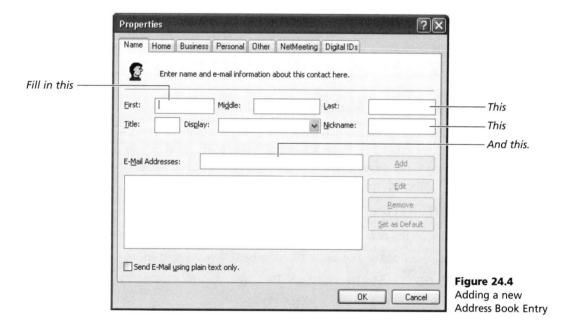

Figure 24.4
Adding a new
Address Book Entry

 Filling in the Nickname is perhaps the most important chore. For nicknames, I generally use the person's first name or, for a common name, first name plus an initial. True nicknames, such as Oogie, Pookums, and Schnookie are also acceptable.

KEYBOARD MASTER

Creating a New Address Book Entry

Ctrl+N

In the Address Book window, use this to create a new entry.

Updating Someone's E-Mail Address

I receive messages almost daily from people who are changing their e-mail address. It seems that they waffle between AOL, Hotmail, and Yahoo, but that could just be my impression.

When people change their e-mail address you need to update the Address Book. This can be quite cinchy: Just re-add the new address to the Address Book using one of the easy methods covered earlier in this chapter. Then, open the Address Book and you'll notice two entries for that person. Delete the old one. Simple.

Or, if you have the time and can type with a certain degree of accuracy, then you can manually edit their Address Book entry. But—jeez!—with some of those AOL account names, can you trust yourself to type them accurately?

What About People with Multiple E-Mail Addresses?

It's possible to store multiple e-mail addresses for a single person in the Address Book. For example, suppose you already have an entry for me (dgookin@wambooli.com) in your Address Book. But then I give you my super secret address, which is dan@gookin.com. Here's how you can add both addresses to the same Address Book entry:

1. Open the Address Book.

2. Double-click on the name of the person you want to update.

Or you can click once on the name, then choose File ➤ Properties.

Or you can right-click on the name and then choose Properties.

However you do it, a Properties dialog box appears.

3. Click on the Name tab.

You'll see a screen similar to Figure 24.4, but filled in. Note the E-Mail Address box in the middle of the window.

5. Enter their new or alternate e-mail address in to the E-Mail Addresses box.

6. Click the Add button.

The new e-mail address is placed in the list at the bottom of the window.

You can choose which address to use by highlighting it and clicking the Set as Default button. Only one e-mail address may be selected as the default address.

 Default is a horrid term that the computer industry often uses when it means "the option chosen for you when you haven't yet chosen anything else."

The disappointing thing here is that OE only lets you keep one Address Book entry, and therefore one nickname, for each address. If you want to have multiple nicknames for multiple e-mail addresses with a single person, then you need to create multiple Address Book entries—a pain.

Killing off Someone from the Address Book

 Easy enough: Open the Address Book and click to select the entry you want to remove. Click the big Delete button. They're gone.

Printing Addresses

Printing your Address list is rather simple. I've been surprised that I've actually had to print mine out a few times for maintenance and upkeep. Sometimes seeing things printed on paper is easier for me to manage than scrolling up and down lists.

There's really only one decision to make when printing addresses. Well, two actually, both of which are covered in Figure 24.5. The first decision is whether to print one or more "selected" entries. The second decision is whether to print the information in Memo, Business Card, or Phone List mode. Here's the scoop:

Memo The more informative of the options, this lists the person's name and e-mail address

Business Card Very similar to the memo option, but takes up less paper when you are printing your whole list.

Phone List This looks like a phone book listing. It prints the names categorized alphabetically.

Choose the option you want depending on whatever information you're after. So if you just want a printed list as a backup, use Business Card. For printing up a phone list, to take on the road for example, then choose Phone List.

 I'm sure it goes without saying, but the Phone List will be rather bleak unless you bother to enter phone numbers for the folks in your Address Book. Ditto for the Memo option; if you haven't filled in all that silly information then don't expect it to magically appear when printed.

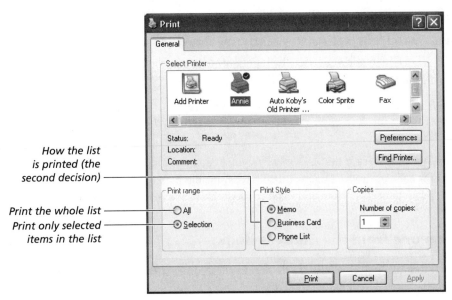

How the list is printed (the second decision)

Print the whole list

Print only selected items in the list

Figure 24.5
Printing decisions

I Know There's a Better Way to Send Everyone in My Family an E-Mail. What Is It?

Oh. Look. It's another gang e-mail—a funny from Aunt Dottie or more political ranting from Uncle Bob. You can tell it's a gang e-mail because the message looks like this:

From: UncleBob@bob.net

Date: Saturday October 3, 2003

To: Alex Andrea Anthony Brittle Brook Carol Chris Dan Darin Donna George Gwen Janessa Jason Jesse Jillian Jordan Judi Julliana Karen Keenan Kirk Lana Linda Margie Matt Melanie Michael Mike Molly Pam Sandy Shannon Susan Tina Vince Yara

Subject: Re: Redneck Humor

That's a mild example. I've seen To *and* Cc fields that fill two or three screens. Obnoxious! Please don't be one of those people!

How Not to Be "One of Those People:" Create a Group

Groups are a great thing when you want to send a message to a buncha people but don't want to flood their screens with endless lists of names on the To or Cc fields. This is an easy, sane, and recommended thing to do:

1. Open the Address Book.

2. Choose New ➢ New Group.

The Group's Properties dialog box appears.

3. Give the group a name.

For example, my wife has a big list named "Theater," which she uses for updating folks on events surrounding our community theater. I have a list called "Family" that contains all the e-mail addresses of people in my immediate family. Be just as descriptive with your group's name.

 Create a group called "All" that contains everyone in your Address Book. That way you can write everyone at once simply by specifying the All group name.

4. Click the Select Members button.

Use the Select Group Members window to slide contact names over into the group. Press the Ctrl key so that you can click the mouse to select multiple contacts.

 To select all the contacts, or just a large swath of them, click to select the first contact in the list, then press the Shift key and click to select the last contact in the list.

5. Click the Select button to add the selected contacts to your group.

6. Repeat Steps 4 and 5 as necessary to build the list.

7. When you're done adding people, click the OK button.

8. Click the OK button in the group's Properties window.

The group is now created and listed on the left side of the Address Book window.

Adding New Names to Your Group

Unlike adding names to the Address Book, you must specifically add new contacts to your groups. Start by adding the new name to your Address Book just as you would add anyone. Then you need to add them to the group:

1. Double-click the group name on the left side of the Address Book window.

2. Click the Select Members button.

3. Add the user, just as you added contacts when you first created the group.

4. Click OK.

5. Click OK to close the group's window.

You Must Know This: Group Limits

I haven't found any official documentation that says there's a size limit to the number of people you can add to an e-mail group. However, from personal experience I can tell you that once your group reaches about 133 contacts, Outlook Express stops. It's too much for that puppy to handle! So, I limit my groups to 100 members and if I need to, I'll create another group.

The Super Secret, Best Way to Use a Group

To use a group, specify its name as a nickname when you create a new message. So, for example, to send a message to everyone telling them that you've amazingly lost 5 pounds, type All into the To field of the message. OE automatically expands the group's name into the names of everyone in the group, sending your message off on its merry way.

The best place to stick the group name is in the Bcc field. Put your own name in the To field. That way, everyone getting the message doesn't see everyone else listed, which makes things all neat and spiffy.

Can I Get the List of Names out of the Address Book and into Some Other Program?

Yes, you can export your Address Book information to other programs. Providing.... (and this is the sucky part)...that those other programs understand the Outlook Express Address Book format. I'll leave it up to you to carry out the proper chants and rituals to make that happen. Here is the best advice I can offer:

Use the Windows Address Book (WAB) file format for attempting to import Address Book information between Windows (specifically Microsoft) applications. For everything else, use the delimited text file format (CSV).

I Need to Make a Backup Copy of My Address Book for My Copy of OE on a Laptop. What Do I Do?

Because you need a copy of the Address Book for another Windows program, in this case another copy of OE, you use the WAB file format: Choose File ➤ Export ➤ Address Book (WAB) from the Address Book's menu. This summons a common Save As dialog box, which you can then use to save the Address Book.

Copy that WAB file to a floppy disk or somehow get it over to your laptop. From there you can import it into that machine's copy of OE by using the File ➤ Import ➤ Address Book (WAB) command. Then you'll have all your contacts on both systems.

How Can I Get the Data from My Address Book out into Some Other (Any Other) Program?

The best technique to try is to use the CVS file format, which is also known as a delimited text file. The file (text only) contains each address book entry on a line by itself with the "fields" from each entry separated by commas. This common file format can be imported by most database, spreadsheet, and—hopefully—other e-mail programs, should you need to get your contacts out of the Address Book and into something more useful.

To create a CVS file from the Address Book, heed these steps:

1. Choose File ➤ Export ➤ Other Address Book.

2. Choose "Text File (Comma Separated Values)" from the list.

3. Click the Export button.

4. Enter a filename.

   The files are saved in the My Documents folder, unless you use the Browse button to find another spot for them.

369

5. Click the Next button.

6. Use the CSV Export dialog box to choose which fields from each contact you want included. Obviously if you haven't filled in all the information for each contact you'll want to un-check some things; only put check marks by those fields you use, such as First Name, Last Name, Name, E-mail Address—which is about it for me.

7. Click the Finish button.

The file is created and contains the information you wanted (from Step 6) for each contact.

8. Click the Close button, then close whatever other windows are in the way.

 You can view the resulting file using the Notepad application.

Note that the first line of the file is the "header" describing each field. For example:

```
First Name,Last Name,Name,E-mail Address
```

This is followed by the names of the contacts from your address book, each on a line by itself, as in:

```
Dan,Gookin,Dan,dgookin@wambooli.com
Bill,Gates,Bill,billg@microsoft.com
```

(And so on...)

Blank fields appear as a single column, as in the first line above. And there you have the common delimited file format, or CSV as Microsoft refers to it. Remember that just about any database, spreadsheet or other type of organizational program can typically read this file format.

Can I Print the List of Contacts in a Group?

Certainly! Just remember to select the group in the Address Book, then in the Print dialog box, choose All instead of Selection. (That's the biggest mistake I typically make; choosing All prints the names and vital stats of everyone in the group, while choosing Selection prints information for only one contact.)

Will They Think I'm Cool or That I'm a Dork If I Use That vCard Thing?

Welcome to the dumbest name of any Microsoft product. VCard is a business card that is sent via e-mail. So, let's say you have all this stuff about you that you'd like to send to people, you can make your own business card and then send it as an attachment. "Hi, my name is Dan. I'm 6 foot tall, I have long brown hair, I'm a Libra, and I love long walks on the beach..." you get the idea. The information can be like this or strict business information that is boring and dull, such as name, address, phone number, fax number—basically all the information you fill in when you make a new contact in the Address book.

I Want a vCard!

To create your own business card in the Address Book you must first create an Address Book entry for yourself. Have you done this yet? It's typically one of the first things I create. I give myself the nickname "me," which I use to carbon copy myself messages. A handy tool, so create a new contact for yourself if you haven't already:

1. Choose File ➤ New Contact.

2. Fill in all the blanks in each of the sections, such as Name, Home, Business, Personal, Other. You get the idea.

3. Click OK when you're done filling in the information.

   Now that you have an entry for yourself you can create the vCard:

4. Select yourself from the Address book.

5. Choose File ➤ Export ➤ Business Card (vCard).

6. Use the Save As dialog box save your card.

 I recommend keeping the options in the Save As dialog box as they appear: the vCard name is your name plus the `.vcf` extension—good. And the card is saved in the My Documents folder—also good.

7. Click the Save button.

To use the vCard, simply attach it to any outgoing message you create. Be aware, however, that not all e-mail programs display the vCard information as you see it in OE; with some e-mail programs the vCard merely appears as a text file attachment.

371

Any Way to Automatically Include a vCard with All My Messages?

You can preset a vCard to be included with all your e-mail. Here's how to do that from the main Outlook Express window:

1. Choose Tools ➤ Options.

The Options dialog box appears.

2. Click the Compose tab.

The bottom part of the window deals with Business Cards. Yippee!

3. Put a check mark by "Mail."

4. Choose your personal contact information from the drop-down list.

(You created this contact in the previous section.)

5. Click OK.

 The "News" option in the dialog box allows your vCard to be attached to any USENET news messages you send. If you're like most people, then you don't use USENET so there's no point in putting up a signature for that. (And if you do use USENET, then you probably don't want those people having your personal vCard information anyway!)

How Can I Use a vCard Sent to Me to Create an Address Book Entry?

 When you receive an e-mail message with a vCard attached, you'll see a vCard button in the upper right corner of the message window. Click it! That opens the vCard attachment.

 If you see a warning dialog box, choose the option that opens the attachment; do not save it to disk. Generally speaking, vCards are safe and virus-free. This may change in the future and if you ever suspect that a vCard could a virus in disguise, then by all means, don't open it!

After opening the vCard you'll see a Properties dialog box for that person—essentially an Address Book entry. Click the Add to Address Book button to place that person into your address book.

Cinchy.

PART 5

All the Random Tidbits about Configuring Your Computer That You'll Want to Ignore But Shouldn't

25

Say! Isn't that a creaky old DOS program you have there?

A long time ago, in a computer far away (now in a landfill somewhere), there was an operating system known as DOS. Funny, but today "DOS" is mostly used to stand for *Denial Of Service*, a type of nasty attack on an Internet server or website. It's still pronounced *dos* (with the short O, as in *boss*). But the older term DOS stood for *Disk Operating System*. Specifically, it was MS-DOS, the Microsoft Disk Operating System, the bane of every PC user in the world—and *the* reason for Windows coming into being.

Windows ended the DOS nightmare when Windows became the PC's main operating system in the mid-1990s. You see, though it was unpopular and suffered from many irritating limitations, DOS had a boatload of software available for it—so much software, that you can pretty much bet that if an organization has been around for a dozen years or longer, that there's probably some old, dowager DOS software chugging along somewhere in some basement computer. Or—the subject of this chapter—the DOS software is struggling along inside the realm of Windows XP.

Rather than relegate DOS programs to the Island of Misfit Toys, Microsoft kindly blessed Windows XP with a DOS "box" of sorts. It's called the Command Prompt window, and it offers up a text mode environment in which many DOS programs can dwell. Oh, and if you're a *super dooper* user, then you can also use the Command Prompt window to control the computer. But that's a heavy-duty subject beyond the bounds of this book's slender binding.

DOS Mysteries Unraveled and Command Prompt Secrets Explored:

- Using the Command Prompt window
- Making the Command Prompt window prettier
- Checking for older-program compatibility

In the future I may provide supplemental documentation on using the Command Prompt window—stuff beyond the basic information provided in this chapter. You can find this documentation by visiting my website, www.wambooli.com.

What's the Point of the **Command Prompt Window?**

I suppose that there are two reasons for having a Command Prompt window. The first is to provide a place for older DOS programs to run. A happy place, a familiar place, but most importantly a *safe* place. You see, older DOS programs tended to run AMOK! DOS programs don't share resources like Windows programs do, so a DOS program believes it "owns" the whole computer. That's about as dangerous as letting a 4-year-old helm an RV and having him try to parallel park.

The second reason for having the Command Prompt window is that it provides a powerful way of controlling your computer and managing your files. Using the command prompt, you can copy, move, delete, rename, and otherwise mess with files, create folders, *plus* manage some system information. Of course, that takes an iron will, determination, and the ability to spell correctly, which is why I'm glossing over it in this chapter.

I Need to Run a Program at the Command Prompt, Where Do I Start?

Here's how to open a Command Prompt window:

1. Click the Start button.

2. Choose All Programs.

3. Choose Accessories.

4. Choose Command Prompt

And the window opens, as shown in Figure 25.1. Note the important parts, which are easier to describe by pointing to them in the figure than by having me wallow through several dull paragraphs.

Figure 25.1 Behold the Command Prompt

The command prompt displays a pathname. That shows you which folder the Command Prompt window is using.

This isn't really a Keyboard Master tip, but you can also start a Command Prompt window by pressing Win+R to summon the Run dialog box, then type in CMD and press Enter. CMD is the name of the Command Prompt program. (You can also type in the word COMMAND, which was the old DOS name for the command prompt program.)

Now That I've Opened a Command Prompt Window, How Do I Close It?

The best way to close a Command Prompt window is to type EXIT at the prompt and press the Enter key.

Of course, you can always close the Window by clicking its close button. But if you attempt to do that while a DOS program is running, you'll see a warning dialog box telling you, basically, that what you've done is a no-no. It's always best to quit a DOS program, then close the window.

I Have an Older DOS Program I Must Run, How Do I Go About It?

After opening the Command Prompt window, you must follow whatever instructions came with the program. For example, you might be directed to use the CD (change directory) command to focus the DOS prompt on a specific folder. Then you'll have to type in the command to run the program. It's all very specific, which is why I cannot be any less vague here. But I can provide an example.

Suppose you need to use the old DOS Edit command:

1. Start the Command Prompt window.

2. Type EDIT at the DOS prompt.

If you make a mistake, use the Backspace key to backup and erase.

You can type DOS commands in upper, lower, or mixed case.

3. Press the Enter key.

And the Edit program runs.

If you made a typing error, then you'll see one of the infamous DOS error messages. It says that what you typed is not recognized as a command. Okay. Shed your embarrassment and try again.

4. To quit the Edit program, choose File ➢ Exit from the menu.

At this point, your DOS window may crash. If so, refer to the next section.

5. Close the DOS window using the EXIT command, as discussed earlier in this chapter.

The only difference between running the EDIT program as covered here and running some other program is that the other program may require you to type in a pathname or use the CD command to change to the program's folder. For example, the instructions may say:

"Log to Drive D and change to the \Games\Doom directory."

To log to drive D, type D: at the command prompt. Typing a drive letter plus a colon at the prompt (then pressing Enter) switches you to that disk drive.

To change to a specific directory (folder), use the CD command followed by the folder's pathname. This is where typing can get really tricky:

```
CD \GAMES\DOOM
```

Of course, if you're adept at typing, you'll find that typing the folder's names after a CD command is quicker than searching for folders in a window and opening them with the mouse—but that only supposes that you know where to go and how to spell it.

If the folder contains a space or its name is longer than 8 characters, then you must enclose the path in double quotes:

```
CD "\PROGRAM FILES\GAMES\DOOM 2\"
```

Beyond that, any specifics should be mentioned in the documentation that accompanies the DOS program.

KEYBOARD MASTER

DOS Keyboard Shortcuts to Know

Here is a smattering of my favorite DOS prompt key command shortcuts:

F3

Repeats the last DOS command you typed. Note that you can use F3 (or the Up arrow key) to recall a command, and then use the Left, Right, Home, and End keys to edit the command line, should you need to.

Esc

Erases the command line and starts over.

Tab

Recalls the name of an address recently typed into a Windows Explorer window. (Of course, unless it's a full pathname, the name recalled will be of little use to you.)

What Does "Cannot Load Command, System Halted" Mean?

The error message basically means that Windows XP tried as hard as it could but was unable to return to the command prompt after your DOS program ran. It's not a big deal; just close the Command Prompt window by using the X close button. Then, if prompted, click the End Now button in the End Program dialog box.

Making DOS Easier on the Eyes

DOS was just plain ugly. No doubt about it. But you don't have to suffer through viewing DOS in an ugly way. No, there are many solutions for putting a better face on the old beast.

Do I Have to Run the DOS Program So Tiny?

The easiest way to adjust the size of the DOS window is to set the DOS text size:

1. Click on the Command Prompt window's Control menu.

Refer to Figure 25.1 to see where it is.

2. Choose Properties.

The Command Prompt Properties dialog box appears, which is a fun place to play, should you have the time.

3. Click the Font tab.

Figure 25.2 shows you what's up with what. Basically you choose a font size from the list, which shows you how the entire window is affected on the screen, as shown in the figure.

4. Choose a font size that makes the DOS window appear larger on the screen.

Use the preview windows in the dialog box to determine your level of happiness.

5. Click OK.

Ah-ha! A question. Do you want this change to affect *all* DOS prompt windows or just the current one?

6. If you want the change to affect *all* windows, choose the option "Modify Shortcut That Started This Window."

7. Click OK.

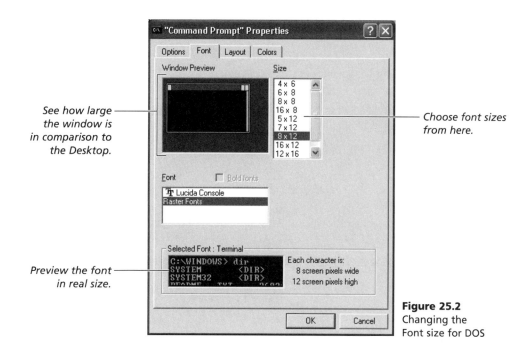

See how large the window is in comparison to the Desktop.

Choose font sizes from here.

Preview the font in real size.

Figure 25.2
Changing the Font size for DOS

What about Running the DOS Program Full Screen, As in the Days of Old?

This trick is really easy: Press Ctrl+Enter. That switches the Command Prompt window to full screen, which is best for playing old DOS games—I mean, er, viewing old Lotus 1-2-3 spreadsheets.

 I must point out that switching to full-screen DOS modem looks very impressive on the monitor, making others think that you really must know your crackers.

To switch back, press Alt+Enter again.

You can also dictate that *all* DOS windows appear in full screen text mode:

1. Click on the Command Prompt window's Control menu.

2. Choose Properties.

3. Click the Options tab (if needed).

4. Click to select "Full Screen" from the Display Options area.

5. Click OK.

Decide whether you want this change for all Command Prompt windows or just the current one. (Refer to the previous section for a description.)

6. Click OK.

379

How Come That Guy Over There Has Such a Colorful Command Prompt Window?

One of the banes of using DOS was that it was boring, just white text on a black background. But then along came various tools and tricks you could use to change the color of your DOS text and background. This became all the rage in 1987, and it can happen again when you learn the secret that your co-workers most likely have neglected:

1. Click on the Command Prompt window's Control menu.

2. Choose Properties.

3. Click the Colors tab.

Ah-ha! Colors! Figure 25.3 shows you what's up, though the dialog box is easy enough to figure out.

On my screen I changed to yellow text on a blue background. I'm stylin'...

4. Click OK.

Again, make the decision to have this be a permanent change or only for the current window.

5. Click OK.

 These changes also affect the colors you see when you view the DOS prompt in full screen mode.

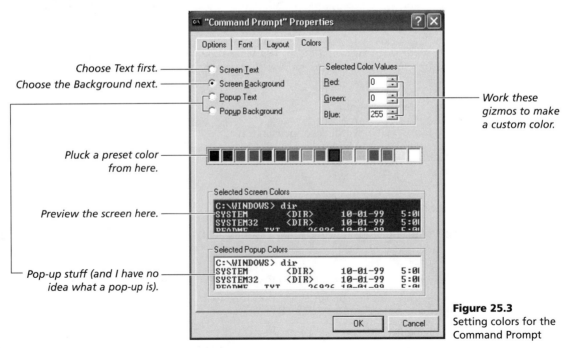

Choose Text first.
Choose the Background next.

Work these gizmos to make a custom color.

Pluck a preset color from here.

Preview the screen here.

Pop-up stuff (and I have no idea what a pop-up is).

Figure 25.3
Setting colors for the Command Prompt

How Can I Be Sure This DOS Program Will Work Anyway?

The sad news is, of course, that not all DOS programs run under Windows XP. Microsoft is trying to tell you something. Basically, MOVE ON. There is help, however. You can try to adjust the compatibility settings for your antique DOS program. This is a process that has no guarantee of success.

1. Locate your DOS program in a folder window.

Browse to the location where you've stored the DOS program.

2. Right-click the program's icon.

3. Choose Properties from the pop-up menu.

4. Click the Compatibility tab.

Figure 25.4 shows the Compatibility tab and the various settings therein.

5. Make settings as needed in the Compatibility tab.

6. Click OK.

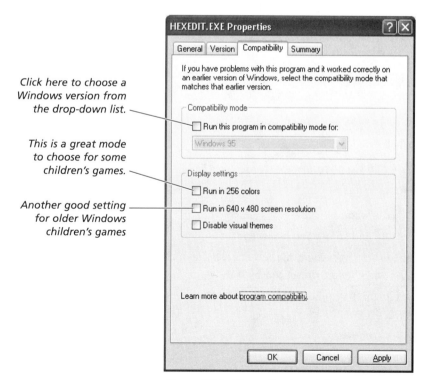

Figure 25.4 Attempting to get this program compatible

My DOS Program's Properties Dialog Box Seems to Lack the Compatibility Tab

Oh. Then you're talking about a *way old* DOS program. My advice: Good luck. Try running the program to see if it works at all. If so, you're blessed. If not, oh well.

What about the Compatibility Wizard?

As a final, last-ditch effort, you can try to run the Compatibility Wizard to check your program, though I personally don't think the wizard is very good. It wasn't able to identify some of my older DOS programs that were, unfortunately Windows XP–challenged. But it's always worth a shot, right?

Alas, there is no central Wizard Location. There should be, like some great ominous castle on a craggy mountain. It would be a place where wizards hobnob and regale each other with fantastic stories over foamy, bubbling brew. But alas, Windows doesn't own that type of creative bone. So you're forced to resort to these mystical steps:

1. Start the Windows Help System.

Press Win+F1 or choose Help and Support from the Start panel.

2. Type `Compatibility Wizard` into the Search box.

In the Suggested Topics area (on the left) you should see one result under "Fix a Problem."

3. Choose "Getting Older Programs to Run on Windows XP."

Almost there...

4. Scroll through the text on the right side of the window until you find "To Run the Program Compatibility Wizard."

5. Click the link, "Program Compatibility Wizard."

And, finally, the wizard runs.

6. Follow the steps in the wizard.

Click the Next button, and so on. You know the drill.

If you're checking for just one program, then choose the option "I Want to Locate the Program Manually," when you're presented with it.

If you're using an old CD, then choose the CD option when presented with it.

Don't let the Wizard disappoint you; Basically it merely tests the settings available in the Compatibility panel, as shown in Figure 25.4. The Wizard does have the merits of testing to see if your program worked, but nothing much beyond that.

7. Quit the wizard when you're sick of it.

Honestly, I'm routinely disappointed—especially because there is no option earlier than Windows 95 for compatibility. But, oh well, it's the fate in store for those of use who can't give up our older DOS programs.

 You know, there's nothing wrong with picking up an older computer, one with DOS still installed, and using that system as a dedicated DOS platform. With proper care and love, a computer can last a long time, at least long enough for you to find a replacement for your old DOS software.

26

True Geniuses Know How to
Manage Disk Drives

All the parts of your computer decided to sneak out of the console one day and have a party at the local Mrs. Fields Cookie store. You didn't know this was happening; you just supposed that your computer had a virus, so you went outside and exercised. But over at The Mall, all your computer's components were having a heated argument:

"I'm most important," said the keyboard. "He touches me all the time! I'm his voice! Without his input through me, none of you would have anything to do!"

The mouse disagreed. "No," it squeaked, "without his input through me he'd never get anything done."

"Oh, bicker, bicker," countered the monitor. "He would pound both of you into the floor if he didn't see the results of your input on my beautiful display. Face it, I *sell* computers."

"Arrogant monitor!" shouted the RAM. "I'm cheap and plentiful, and the rest of you need me to work."

The CPU cleared its throat. "I find all of this amusing," it said in its deep, sonorous voice, "but without my quick thinking, all of you would sit around as dumb and useless as a 5-inch floppy disk."

Then the hard drive had to laugh.

"What do you find so funny," asked the RAM.

"Oh, you all quarrel so well and your relative merit will be eternally debatable. But it is I," said the hard drive, "that the user obsesses over the most. He may buy the computer based on its monitor and CPU. He may use the mouse and keyboard every day. And he may be satisfied after adding more RAM. But for my fellow disk drives and I, his devotion is daily and his attention borders on fanatical. Yup, we are most important."

The disk drives smiled in agreement, ate the last morsel of their Mocha Chocolate Chip cookie, and watched the rest of the computer hardware sulk in silent agreement.

Disk Drive Topics to Obsess Over:

- Finding disk drive information
- Working with Zip drives
- Changing a disk drive's letter
- Mounting a drive to a folder
- Soothing words on disk maintenance

Where Windows Hides All the Useful Disk Drive Stuff

I know where my computer's disk drives are because I've taken off the cover and looked right inside the case. Of course, that doesn't help me work with the drives inside of Windows. No, to do that you need to know the places where you can get at and mess with your disk drives. These may be familiar places, such as the My Computer window, or rather geeky places you probably haven't yet stumbled across.

My Computer: Boring. Yawn.

To see your disk drives in the My Computer window, open the My Computer icon on the Desktop. Figure 26.1 shows the disk drives in that window, though there may also be folders and other junk there.

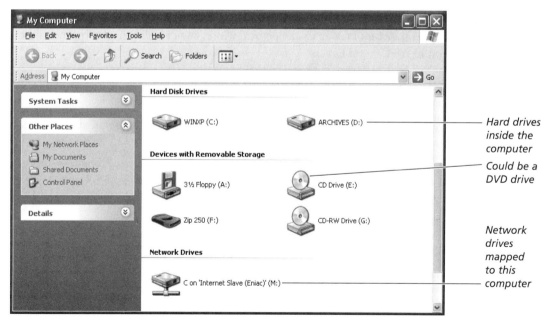

Figure 26.1 My Computer lists your disk drives.

See how the disk drives in Figure 26.1 are organized into areas? Here's how to set up the My Computer window to display things that way:

1.   Choose View ➤ Arrange Icons by ➤ Type.

2.   Choose View➤ Arrange Icons by ➤ Show in Groups.

3.   Choose View➤ Tiles.

To manage the disk drives at this point, you'd have to right-click on a drive and choose Properties from the pop-up menu. That lets you get at some tools or access the drive's hardware or software parts directly. But, as anyone who's been using Windows for any length of time knows, there are other, better ways to get at your disk drive's hardware or software.

Smart Users Know How to Get to the Device Manager

The Device Manager is a central location that lists all your computer's hardware. It's one of the first things I check when I smell hardware trouble. But even when trouble's odious vapors blow not, the Device Manager is a great place for examining your computer's various hardware and software settings.

Here's how to get to the Device Manager in Windows XP:

1.   Right-click the My Computer icon.

2.   Choose Properties from the pop-up menu.

This displays the System Properties dialog box, which you can also display by opening the System icon in the Control Panel.

3.   Click the Hardware tab.

4.   Click the Device Manager button.

The Device Manager window appears, as shown in Figure 26.2. It highlights the six disk drives on my test computer, which are also shown in Figure 26.1.

What you can do in the Device Manager window is view a disk drive's Properties dialog box, where you can change various things—some of which are covered later in this chapter. For now, just consider this yet another spot where Windows hides information about your disk drives.

5.   Close the Device Manager window.

6.   Close the System Properties dialog box.

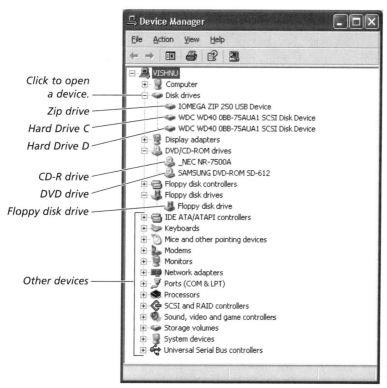

Click to open
a device.

Zip drive

Hard Drive C

Hard Drive D

CD-R drive

DVD drive

Floppy disk drive

Other devices

Figure 26.2
The Device Manager

Only the Most Ingenious Users Know About the Disk Management Console

The final place to visit for messing with your disk drives is the Disk Management Console, which is part of the System Administration nonsense included with all versions of Windows XP. If you've used Windows 95/98/Me, then this is will be something totally new and utterly weird to you.

compmgmt.msc

The first step is to open the Computer Management window, which is one of the Administrative tools. There are five ways I can think of (and millions of ways I haven't thought of) to display this window.

If you've configured the Start panel as I recommended way back in Chapter 6, then choose Administrative Tools ➤ Computer Management from the Start Panel.

If you're using the new "category" style Control Panel, click on the Performance and Maintenance link, then click on Administrative tools on the next screen. Finally, open the Computer Management icon.

If you're using the older style Control Panel, then just open the Administrative Tools icon, then the Computer Management icon.

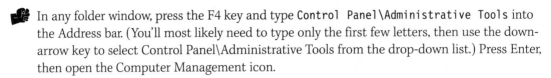

In any folder window, press the F4 key and type `Control Panel\Administrative Tools` into the Address bar. (You'll most likely need to type only the first few letters, then use the down-arrow key to select Control Panel\Administrative Tools from the drop-down list.) Press Enter, then open the Computer Management icon.

Or, the simplest (which I annoyingly save for last): Right-click the My Computer icon on the Desktop and choose Manage from the pop-up menu.

The next step is to choose Disk Management from the Storage category from the list on the left side of the Computer Management window. So it goes like this:

`Computer Management\Storage\Disk Management`

When you've selected Disk Management, you'll see information about the disk drives in your computer, similar to what's shown in Figure 26.3. Your system may not be as involved as mine is (shown in the figure); my system is a multiple boot computer with both Windows Me and Windows XP, as well as DOS and Windows 3.1. It's a crazy example, so I apologize.

There are various and interesting things you can do in the Disk Management window, but this is not the place to discuss them. I'm merely illustrating what the Disk Management window is and how to get there. Later sections in this chapter point out some of the more useful things to do while you visit.

But, dangit—it sure is an impressive-looking place!

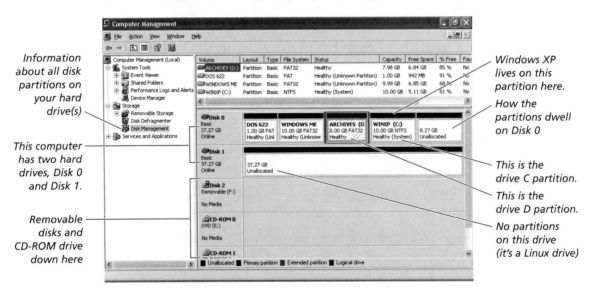

Figure 26.3 Managing disks in the Computer Management window

NERD'S CORNER

Cocktail Party Trivia, Part IX

PHIL: I've never gotten into this disk-partitioning nonsense. What's up with that?

JOHN: Oh, now that I'm sobering up, I remember back in the old days when hard drives were measured in megabytes instead of gigabytes....

LISA: Even today John will mistakenly refer to hard drive capacity in megabytes! He's so cute that way...

JOHN: (Irritated) Right. Early versions of DOS could only access a certain amount of disk space. DOS 2.1, for example, could only access 10MB on a hard drive.

LISA: So if you had a 12MB hard drive, you were screwed out of 2MB.

PHIL: Exactly!

JOHN: No, not really. In that case, you could partition the drive into, say, two 6MB drives. The physical 12MB drive would become logical Drive C at 6MB and logical Drive D, also at 6MB. You could use the entire drive, but you had to divvy it up as Drives C and D.

LISA: It still sounds stupid.

JOHN: It was! Hardware improved faster than software, and soon you would have computers with logical Hard Drives C through H—all partitioned into 10MB chunks because DOS couldn't handle anything larger.

PHIL: Things did get better, right?

JOHN: Certainly. Over time, DOS—and eventually Windows—could handle larger and larger disk partitions. I forget what the limit is today, something like 4,000GB per partition. But the tradition of partitioning disk drives continues. In the case of some computers, it's so that you can have two operating systems (say, Windows XP and Windows 2000) on the same system.

LISA: Or it could be done if you were just used to disk partitions, say you liked putting your games on Drive D?

JOHN: Uh-huh.

PHIL: Or if you were, like, all drunk and decided to have 1,000 partitions on a 10GB drive to remind yourself of the old days!

JOHN: Whatever, Phil.

Some Interesting Disk Tips and Advice

I bought my first disk drive in 1983. It was a 5¼-inch drive capable of formatting a diskette to hold 180K of data. The drive cost me $800. A single 180K floppy disk was $7.95. We've come a long way...

Can I Put My New Zip Disk Drive's Icon on the SendTo Menu?

I love using the SendTo menu. It makes copying or moving files a snap. The typical SendTo menu has the floppy drive listed as well as a CD-R drive (see Chapter 15). But if you've installed a new Zip drive on your computer, it may not be listed. To add that drive, or any removable type of disk drive, to the helpful SendTo menu, follow these steps:

1. First you need to locate the drive, so open the My Computer window.

2. Right-click on the drive.

   Zip 250 (F:)

3. Choose "Create Shortcut" from the pop-up menu.

   Here's where Windows actually—believe it or not—behaves in a logical and clever manner: you cannot create a shortcut in the My Computer window, so you're asked to create a shortcut on the Desktop instead. Very handy.

4. Click Yes.

5. Close the My Computer window.

   And you should see the shortcut icon to your Zip (or whatever) drive on the Desktop. First part's done!

 You can place just about anything on the SendTo menu, not just a disk drive but a folder or even a program. I put the Notepad program on my SendTo menu, which allows me to send unknown files to the Notepad for a quick peek at their contents.

6. Second, you need to copy the shortcut icon to the SendTo menu's secret folder, so right-click on the Start button.

7. Choose Open All Users.

   This displays the Start Menu items shared by all users of your computer.

8. Click the Up button.

   This gets you to the main All Users folder.

9. Open the SendTo folder.

10. Resize or move the SendTo window so that you can see the Zip (or whatever) drive shortcut on the Desktop.

11. Drag the shortcut into the SendTo folder.

Use Figure 26.4 as your guide.

12. Close the SendTo folder.

13. Optionally delete the disk drive shortcut from the Desktop.

Though it's nice to have the shortcut there as well.

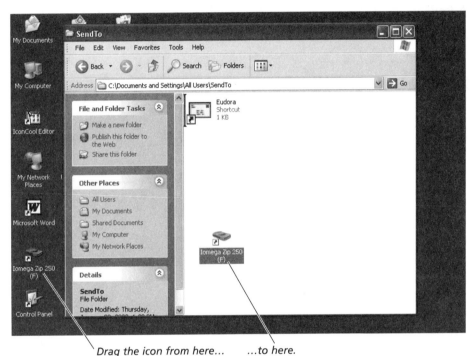

Figure 26.4
Dragging the drive to the SendTo folder

Drag the icon from here...   ...to here.

I Detest That Window That Pops up Every Time I Insert a CD or Zip Disk

Oh, yes. That can be handy—or it can be a pain. But either way, it can be fixed:

1. Open the My Computer window.

2. Right-click on the CD or Zip drive that you want to "fix."

3. Choose Properties from the pop-up menu.

The disk drive's Properties dialog box appears.

4. Click the AutoPlay tab.

Figure 26.5 explains what to do next.

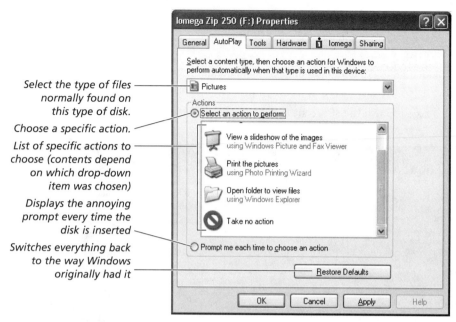

Select the type of files normally found on this type of disk.

Choose a specific action.

List of specific actions to choose (contents depend on which drop-down item was chosen)

Displays the annoying prompt every time the disk is inserted

Switches everything back to the way Windows originally had it

Figure 26.5
Living with AutoPlay and its annoying options

5. Choose a primary content type for the disk.

For example, I use Zip disks primarily to ferry graphics files.

6. Decide whether you want to preset an action for the disk, such as viewing a slide show or merely opening the disk, or whether you want Windows to display the annoying pop-up window to beg for an action every time you insert the disk.

Again, refer to Figure 26.5 to see what to do.

 If you detest the pop-up window, then click to choose "Select an Action to Perform" and then choose "Take No Action."

7. Click OK to close the Properties dialog box.

And, optionally, you can close the My Computer window as well.

I Just Want a Folder Window to Open When I Insert the Zip Disk (or CD)

This is easy to do and, in fact, how I prefer my own computer to behave. And getting a computer to behave, well, that's what life is all about:

1. Open the My Computer window.

2. Right-click on your Zip drive icon.

3. Choose Properties from the pop-up menu.

4. Click the AutoPlay tab.

   Refer to Figure 26.5.

5. From the drop-down list choose "Mixed Content."

   (That's "content" as in "that which is contained," not "to be satisfactory.")

6. Choose "Select an Action to Perform."

7. Select "Open Folder to View Files"

   That's the option you want.

8. Click OK.

   Now Windows will open the disk's root folder window when the disk is inserted.

My Floppy Disk Won't Format

Throw it away.

Why Would I Want to Change My Disk's Drive Letter?

Suppose you have a typical PC with Hard Drive C and DVD drive D. You live a happy existence, content with that setup until…the hard drive is full of MP3 files, graphics, and games. Oh, no!

But it's not a big emergency because you just run out to the computer store and buy yourself a second hard drive. Only after installing it do you realize that you now have hard drives C and D and DVD drive E. But—wait a minute! Your software is still looking for the DVD drive as letter D. Oh no! Again!

The solution for this is to reassign your disk drive letters to something higher. Using the Disk Management window, you can reassign the letter of any disk drive in your system, except for the main boot disk or "system volume." (Yes, this includes extra hard drives as well as any removable drives.)

For example, whenever I first get a computer, I reassign the CD-ROM drive letter to R. I'm fond of giving my Zip drive letter Z. This is okay as long as you make the letter change right away—before installing software that may be confused if you change drive letters after the software has been installed.

So, suppose you've just added the new hard drive, D. Here's how you would change its letter to something else, say… M, or some other letter that won't interfere with other disk drives in your system:

1. Open the Disk Management window.

   Refer to the instructions at the start of this chapter.

2. Right-click on the disk partition you want to change.

   You must be careful here! There is a difference between physical and logical disk partitions. Disk 0 and Disk 1 are physical disks. Each of them contains logical partitions.

In this example, you're looking for Drive D, the new hard drive. But it can be any drive. Just remember that for a hard drive, click on the partition with that drive's letter, such as D or E. For a removable drive, just click on the disk itself either in the top or bottom part of the window. (Removable drives need not have disks in them for you to change their letters.)

3. Choose "Change Drive Letter and Paths" from the pop-up menu.

The Change Drive Letter and Paths for D: dialog box appears. Note that the drive letter is currently chosen.

4. Click the Change button.

The Change Drive Letter or Path dialog box appears, illustrated in Figure 26.6.

5. Select a new drive letter from the drop-down list.

6. Click OK—and keep clicking OK to close all the dialog boxes.

The change takes place after you've reset the computer.

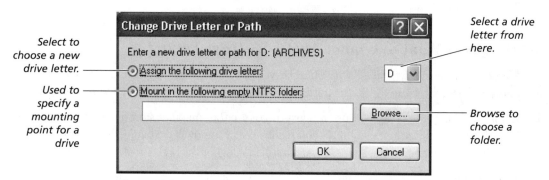

Figure 26.6 Reassign drive letters or mount pathnames here.

I've Put Mostly Graphics on Drive D, but Would Like to Access It from the My Documents Folder Directly. How Is That Possible?

You can assign any disk drive in your system as a pathname, which is an advanced operating system concept, so I'm pleasantly surprised to see such a feature available in Windows. So, for example, you can have all the files on Drive D be accessed through the My Documents folder. Just "mount" Drive D as My Documents\Drive D or whatever, and the files will all be within easy browsing reach.

This operation requires two steps. First, you create the folder in which to mount the disk drive:

1. Open the My Documents folder.

2. Choose File ➢ New ➢ Folder from the menu.

3. Name the folder Drive D (or whatever may be appropriate in your situation).

For example, I store my archives—old documents—on drive D. So I'll call the folder "Archives."

If you want all the computer's users to have access to the drive, then create the empty folder in the Shared Documents folder. Remember that the true path to this folder is `Documents and Settings\All Users\Documents`.

Second, you must tell Windows to mount the disk drive in that folder:

4. Open the Disk Management window.

Refer to the start of this chapter for the specific instructions.

5. Right-click on the drive you want to mount as a subdirectory.

(Such as Drive D, though you can use any drive in your system.)

6. Choose "Change Drive Letter and Paths" from the pop-up menu.

7. Click the Add button.

Refer to Figure 26.6.

8. If you're good, type in the path to mount the drive, otherwise use the Browse button.

Click OK after browsing to the proper empty folder. (And note that you can create a new folder in the Browse for Drive Path window, should you somehow have neglected the first three steps in this section.)

 If you're browsing, remember to browse to the Documents and Settings folder, then your account, then My Documents, then the empty folder.

9. Click OK after selecting the new folder.

That does it. Easy, no?

10. Close the Computer Management window.

11. Open the My Documents window.

 Or open whichever window it was that you mounted the drive in. You'll see the mounted drive appear there in the window, its icon used like a folder. Opening the icon, however, displays the files on that disk drive, which you may find handy.

Archives

The disk drive stays mounted as long as you want it. To un-mount it, work through Steps 1 through 6 above. Then, in the Change Drive Letter and Paths dialog box, click to select the mounting point, such as `WINXP(C:)\Documents and Settings\Dan Gookin\My Documents\Archives`. Then click the Remove button.

 It's possible to mount a disk drive several places on the hard drive. You can have Drive D (or whatever) mounted here, there, everywhere you like. There appears to be no limitation.

General and Routine Disk Management and Chores You Really Need to Do Every So Often

Most of the kiddie books on Windows cover the chores of Defrag and ScanDisk. These are routine disk maintenance tasks you should perform at least once a month. Unlike most people believe, however, doing them more often than that doesn't particularly benefit the computer any, just as cleaning your house every day offers only a marginal benefit over doing it all once a week. (Unless, of course, you're a total slob, but then you probably don't care anyway.)

Why You Should Bother with the Disk Defragmenter (Defrag)

The disk defragmenter is a useful and healthy tool. What it does is clean up some of the slop created by Windows as files are written to disk.

In order to make the best use of disk space, Windows often splits larger files into smaller pieces so that they'll fit on a disk. This is not a bad thing! Because files are more-or-less constantly written to disk and erased by Windows, gaps between the files form. (Windows is constantly writing stuff to disk and erasing these temporary files as it no longer needs them.)

Rather than take time to find contiguous space to store a larger file, Windows just breaks the file up into pieces. It keeps track of where everything is so that when the file is needed it's all reassembled. But on the disk, the file is *fragmented*. Obviously, the process of splitting up and reassembling these files takes time, which degrades disk performance.

NERD'S CORNER

Oh, I Remember...

The first disk defragmenter I used was called the Mace Utilities, after Paul Mace, who developed it. Hard drives had been common on PCs for about five years when Mace developed his disk defragmenter and, as you can imagine, everyone's disk was as fragmented as a mosaic. Mace's software fully defragmented the disk and boosted performance insanely—so much so that the Mace Utilities held the distinction of being the most pirated piece of software for about two years running.

Eventually others figured out the disk defragmentation puzzle. One of the best tools I used was V-Opt from V Systems in San Diego. It was so smart about defragmenting that you could literally pull the plug on the computer while it was defragmenting and not lose a byte of data.

The purpose of the Disk Defragmenter is to reassemble files into contiguous chunks. This speeds up disk performance considerably, especially when the number of fragmented files on a disk approaches 10 percent.

To determine whether or not your hard drive needs to be defragmented, visit the Computer Management window (see the start of this chapter), and choose Disk Defragmenter from the list (see Figure 26.7).

 Defragmenting your drive could take a few hours to do, depending on how badly the drive needs it. It's best not to do anything else on the computer while defragmenting is going on.

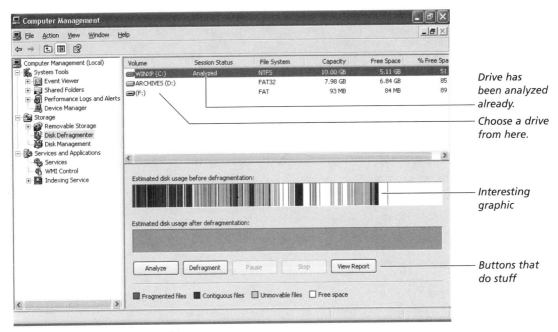

Figure 26.7 Defragmenting a drive

Follow these steps to defragment a drive:

1. Choose the drive from the list at the top of the window.

   You can also defragment a disk by running the Defragmenter directly (All Programs ➢ Accessories ➢ System Tools ➢ Disk Defragmenter), or from the disk drive's Properties/Tools dialog box.

2. Click the Analyze button.

3. Obey the suggestion displayed, whether to defrag or not.

I'm a big fan of clicking the View Report button. In fact, I noticed this last time (after some major file management) that my fragmentation percent was 22! That's pretty bad! So it's off to defrag I go...

4. Click the Defragment button.

> ### You Must Know This: Why Some Files Are "Unmovable"
>
> *Fortunately, the Disk Defragmenter is smart. It recognizes that some files, despite being fragmented, cannot be moved and, therefore, defragmented. These include system files and other files that contain sensitive information, as well as copy-protected files. If those files are moved, they will assume that "something is up" and either not function or sound an alarm that the system has been compromised. So it's best that they're left alone.*

ScanDisk Is Neither Magic nor Hoodoo

The ScanDisk program is used to test a disk for errors and, in many cases, fix them. ScanDisk proves to be a valuable tool, but it's not as good as some of the disk fixing tools you get with the Norton Utilities, for example. (Norton's stuff is generally more thorough and capable than ScanDisk.)

To run ScanDisk, follow these steps:

1. Open the My Computer window.

2. Right-click on the drive you want to check for errors.

You can check all drives except for CD-ROM and DVD drives.

3. Choose Tools from the drive's Properties dialog box.

4. Click the Check Now button.

ScanDisk's less-than-impressive dialog box appears, as shown in Figure 26.8.

> *Choose the "Scan for and Attempt Recovery of Bad Sectors" item for a full disk check, which takes more time.*

5. Click the Start button.

And the drive is checked.

Should anything awry be found, follow the instructions on the screen for how to fix it. Generally speaking, whichever option is suggested is the best one to choose.

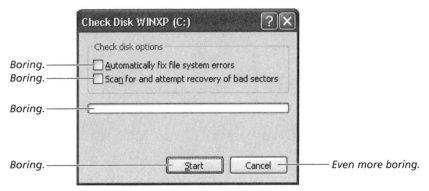

Figure 26.8 ScanDisk. Yawn.

Any Way to Automate These Boring Tasks?

Certainly! The computer is all about automation. And in this book, Chapter 27 is all about automation using the Task Manager. Refer there for instructions on making your disk maintenance tasks automatic.

The Task Manager Nightmare

27

As far as I see it, the biggest drawback to juggling is gravity. Without getting too involved in space-time theory, allow me to say that if gravity were cut in half and if everything moved slowly enough, then anyone could juggle. It wouldn't even be a big deal.

The computer doesn't really care about gravity; it juggles things quite well. It's known as multitasking, or the ability to do several things simultaneously. This was once a big deal with computers—and one of those sour points many people had with DOS. Where DOS could only run one program at a time, Windows allows you to do several things at once. The Taskbar is one place that lets you keep track of what's going on. But the real, secret place is the Task Manager. That's where the power lives. And for you, there is a great benefit to be gained by knowing a few Task Manager tricks that the common computer user is unaware of.

Secrets Revealed and Power Unleashed:

- Finding the Task Manager
- Killing off programs that run amok
- Examining applications and processes
- Watching the CPU meter
- Monitoring and abusing other users

Summoning the Task Manager

The Task Manager is always ready and easy to beckon: Press Ctrl+Alt+Delete, and there it is, as shown in Figure 27.1.

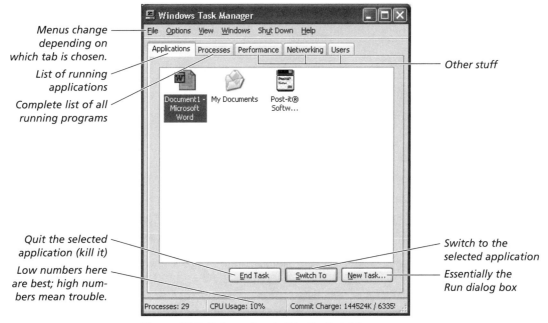

Menus change depending on which tab is chosen.

List of running applications

Complete list of all running programs

Other stuff

Quit the selected application (kill it)

Low numbers here are best; high numbers mean trouble.

Switch to the selected application

Essentially the Run dialog box

Figure 27.1 Noteworthy stuff in the Task Manager window

 The Ctrl+Alt+Delete key combination is, indeed, the handiest way to call up the Task Manager. But if you're just burdened with excess time, you can press Win+R to bring up the Run window and type in taskmgr, *which also brings up the Task Manager.*

Most importantly, the Task Manager tells you what's going on in your computer. In Figure 27.1, you see that three applications are running, Word, My Documents, and the Post-It Notes program. This is also reflected on the Taskbar (which you can't see in the figure, but which would show buttons for all the running applications as well).

NERD'S CORNER

Cocktail Party Trivia, Part X

MARY: *I know, I'm going to guess what you're all thinking: Ctrl+Alt+Delete was the old command that reset the computer back in the days of DOS.*

PHIL: *Yeah, that's what I was thinking.*

JOHN: *Me too.*

LISA: *I'm sorry, I wasn't paying attention. I was reading all the answers to the new Computer Nerd edition of Trivial Pursuit.*

PHIL: *Ctrl+Alt+Delete was known as the...what? Anybody?*

JOHN: *The three-finger salute!*

PHIL: *Correct? Anyone else?*

MARY: *Vulcan nerve pinch.*

PHIL: *Anyone else?*

LISA: *The original name of dBASE II was Vulcan. Who'd have thought?*

JOHN: *Back in the days of DOS, Ctrl+Alt+Delete immediately reset the computer, just like punching a reset button. While it was handy for regaining control of a run-amok computer, it was also abused by many of the primitive DOS users as an alternative method for quitting a program.*

MARY: *That was "bad" of them.*

PHIL: *In Windows, Ctrl+Alt+Delete was used to summon a Close Program window, which you could use to kill off dead or unresponsive programs.*

LISA: *What's the exact difference between a dead program and an unresponsive one?*

JOHN: *In Windows NT/2000, Ctrl+Alt+Delete allowed you to log into the system.*

MARY: *Nice to see that Microsoft is being very consistent with the Ctrl+Alt+Delete key command.*

PHIL: *Eh? No one seems to complain about it.*

LISA: *Forbidden Planet was the first movie to have a soundtrack created using a computer synthesizer.*

When Should I Kill off an Application?

Ding dong, the program's gone. You know the one: you click and nothing happens. Or the mouse makes "tracks" over its window. Dead as a doornail, it is. And just about anyone knows that doornails are pretty dern dead.

Sometimes the Task Manager will tell you that a program is "not responding" and sometimes it won't. In either case, you can kill off the dead application in the Task Manager window by heeding these steps:

1. In the Applications tab, click the dead program's icon.

2. Click the End Task button.

Wait. It takes Windows a while to poke, prod, and finally pronounce a program truly dead.

 The program doesn't need to be dead, by the way. You can quit any program or close any window by choosing its icon and clicking the End Task button. Essentially it's the same thing as the File ➤ Exit command or clicking a window's X close button.

Eventually you'll see the End Program dialog box. It's boring, so I shan't put a picture of it here.

3. Click the End Now button.

And the dead program is no more.

Windows may optionally request that you send a "bug report" to Microsoft, telling them about the problem. Don't.

There's a line of thinking that suggests you restart Windows after removing a dead program. This makes sense: the dead program could still, somehow, be in memory and may cause further problems down the road. So if you have the time, or you just believe it to be a lucky thing to do, restart Windows.

Do I Need to Know the Difference between an Application and a Process?

Application is a Big Picture item. Word is an application. But yet, as you may suspect, running the Word application isn't the only thing the computer does. All the other programs, such as those in the Notification Area, as well as secret behind-the-scenes programs such as anti-virus utilities, they're all referred to as *processes*.

For example, in Figure 27.1, you see that the number of Processes is 29. That means the computer is actually running 29 programs (though processes is a more accurate term because not every process is interactive like a program).

To see the full list of processes, click the Processes tab. You'll see something equally as confusing as what's shown in Figure 27.2.

Choose View ➤ Select Columns to see more trivial tidbits displayed.

Various "programs" running

The program's owner or "thing" responsible for running the program

Percent of CPU time devoted to the process

Memory used by it

Priority information

Enlarge the window by dragging this edge rightward.

Figure 27.2 Processes, processes, processes

The first thing you need to do is say, "Whoa! Look at all the junk!"

The second thing you need to do is note that the list represents *all* running programs on your computer. Yes, even those annoying icons in the Notification area appear in this list—which is one way you can get rid of them. (Alas, you have to know their exact name, and that's the hard part.)

The third thing to notice is the CPU usage. For most applications that will be either zero or, say at times, 10. Unless you have a program that's really busy in the background—a database sort, printing graphics, downloading, music playing, or something intensive—the CPU column should never show any values higher than 10.

As far as the relationship between Applications and Processes, do this:

1. Click the Applications tab.

2. Right-click an icon.

If no icons are open, then start some program, say Notepad or Solitaire.

3. Choose "Go To Process" from the pop-up menu.

Immediately you're switched to the Processes tab and the super secret program that's running your application is highlighted. For example, for the My Documents window (or any folder window), it's the explorer.exe process that controls things. This makes sense because that program is Windows Explorer, responsible for displaying folders on the Desktop.

The purpose of this exercise was to show you the relationship between the applications icons and processes in the Task Manager. But, as you've already noted (second thing above), there are many more processes than applications. That's okay, the computer is, typically, insurmountably busy.

Don't Get Excited about the Priority Stuff

The Base Priority column in the Processes tab shows how much love and attention the computer gives a certain task. (See Figure 27.2.) If you don't see this column, choose View ➤ Select Columns. Then put a check mark by "Base Priority" in the Select Columns dialog box. Click OK.

Processes with High priority get the most attention. Processes with Normal priority get less attention. Windows assigns priorities based on what it feels is best. You can change this, but I can't really think of any advantage to doing so, other than just to say that you've done it.

To change a process's priority, right-click that process. From the pop-up menu choose Set Priority to display a submenu of choices:

Realtime The process gets the most attention, nearly full-time. I can imagine if a team of evil scientists were plotting chemical reactions and needed their program to run almost as if it were the only program in the computer, this would be a good setting.

High The highest level of attention without devoting all of the computer's attention to it.

AboveNormal Just a bit better than normal.

Normal The level of attention that's "fair," where all processes get equal attention. What your mother would insist you set everything to.

BelowNormal Kind of like putting a program into "time-out," the computer continues to pay attention to the process, but not as much as at the Normal level.

Low Maybe once a week the computer will check in with the program and run a few lines of its code.

Again, I know of no advantage to changing the priorities of various applications, but that doesn't mean you can't go into the Task Manager and re-assign priorities just to see how it affects things.

Whoa! The CPU Usage Is Really High!

Danger! The CPU usage is a great indicator of a potential problem in the computer. If the value spikes and stays high—especially if you notice the computer acting sluggish or stupid—then you might have a memory leak. Fortunately, this is a problem easily fixed in the Task Manager window.

First, before you get all spazzy, there is a special process called the System Idle Process. Whenever the computer isn't busy, that process is the one that consumes the most CPU time. On the typical Windows XP system, the System Idle Process displays values that spike out at 98 or 99 percent. That's okay.

Repeat out loud: *The CPU percent for the System Idle Process often spikes out at 98 or 99 percent.*

It is not a problem. However, if some other program is up to, say 78 percent *plus* the computer seems very slow *plus* things are going wrong, you can attempt to kill off the memory hog:

1. Click to select the program that you suspect is hogging CPU time.

2. Click the End Process button.

A warning dialog box appears. A good warning too: you must be certain that this is the program you want to kill off. (As a precaution, ensure that information in other windows is all saved and happy.)

3. Click the Yes button.

The task is gone.

4. Restart Windows.

I heartily recommend the restarting course here. Unlike quitting a program, when you end a process you run the risk that the system may become unstable because you eliminated only one process where the faulty program might be several processes. Be careful! Reset!

I See the CPU Usage Thing Spike When I Open Windows or Do Things

Yes, because that's how the CPU usage thing works. It's a busy indicator, so whenever you use the computer, things happen. A better way to see activity is to use the Task Manager's Performance tab, as shown in Figure 27.3.

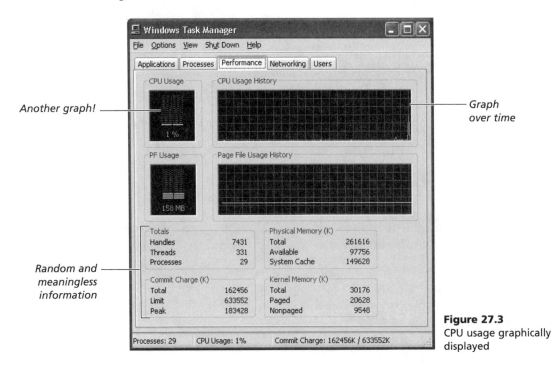

Another graph!

Graph over time

Random and meaningless information

Figure 27.3
CPU usage graphically displayed

Resize the Task Manager's window and watch what happens. Cool, huh? That's because it takes the computer's brain time to think when things change.

Of course, the graph shows you only general CPU usage, not which processes are involved.

Alas, there's really nothing else going on in the Performance tab.

NERD'S CORNER

Page File?

Page files are used by virtual memory, which is how Windows increases the amount of RAM available by swapping chunks of memory out to disk. The more page files there are, the more swapping goes on, which makes things slow down. Alas, the only solution for that problem is to stuff your PC with more RAM.

What's the Difference between the End Task Button and the End Process Button?

The End Task button is on the Applications tab. Clicking that button is the same as closing an application's window. It's the gentle approach, but it also works on dead programs because Windows recognizes that the program isn't responding.

The End Process button on the Processes tab is more lethal. It does not send an "End Task" message to the application. Instead, it merely squishes the program in memory, stopping it from running. This may have adverse consequences, especially if other processes were waiting for that process, in which case you have a larger problem on your hands.

Any Way to Shove the Task Manager Window out of the Way?

Choose Options ➢ Always on Top to remove the check mark there. Otherwise, with a check mark by Always on Top, the Task Manager always hogs the front of the screen.

Oh! So I Can Use the Task Manager to Mess with Other Users on the Same Computer?

In Windows XP it's possible for several people to be logged in at the same time. Whether this is a good or bad thing, I'll leave for you to debate. Whatever you think, by using the Task Manager, you can actually log the others off! Or, more covertly, just snoop around and kind of see what they're doing. Ha! Tickled your curiosity any?

Is Anyone Else Logged into This System?

To see if anyone else is logged into your computer, click the Users tab in the Task Manager window. That displays a list of everyone who's currently logged in—or, more properly, anyone who hasn't yet logged out. Figure 27.4 shows that two other annoying people are logged into my computer.

Me. I'm active.

Other accounts are logged in, but not currently using the computer.

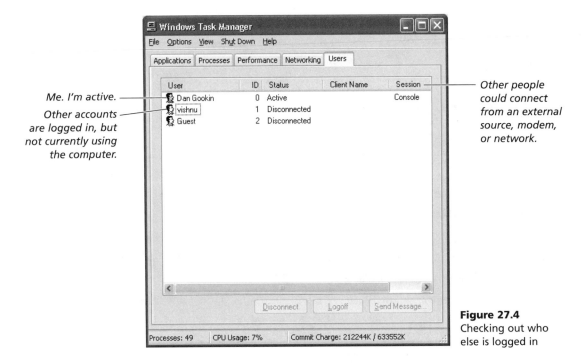

Other people could connect from an external source, modem, or network.

Figure 27.4
Checking out who else is logged in

How Can I Let Others Using the Computer Know That They're Annoying Me?

Suppose you toddle into the den one cold morning. You're wearing your big, fuzzy bathrobe, comfy slippers, and are holding a hot cup of steaming coffee. You sit down to catch up on the overnight e-mail. Jiggle the computer mouse. But, what!? Your teenage son was the last one to use the computer and there's one of his precious games on the screen with the word "Pause" displayed.

Rather than tick him off by quitting the game (or, more honestly, you don't know *how* to quit his game), you just press Win+L to lock the computer and log in as yourself. That's one scenario, but the point is you want to leave the other user a message to tell them to properly log off. Or you can leave them a message on anything, because Windows lets you send messages to any other doofus who's logged into the same computer you are. Here's how:

1. Click the Users tab in the Task Manager window.

2. Select the user you want to write the message to.

Obviously, they must be logged in and visible in the list. If not, then there's no way to send them a message (at least not by using this trick).

3. Click the Send Message button.

A Send Message window appears, as shown in Figure 27.5.

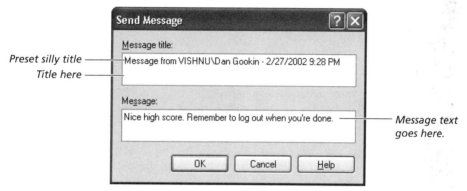

Figure 27.5 Sending another user a message

4. Fill in the Send Message window.

5. Click the OK button.

And the message is sent off.

When that user logs back into the computer, they'll see the message displayed as shown in Figure 27.6.

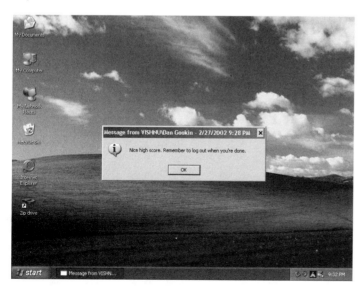

Figure 27.6
How the message appears to the other user

409

Spying on Other Users

So what is that other user doing? Well, you can't tell...exactly. But you can get an idea!

In the Task Manager, click on the Processes tab (shown in Figure 27.2). Ensure that there is a check mark by "Show Processes from All Users." Then, click on the "User Name" heading, which sorts the users in the list alphabetically. Look through the list to find the other user's name listed.

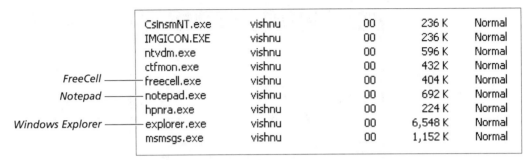

	CsInsmNT.exe	vishnu	00	236 K	Normal
	IMGICON.EXE	vishnu	00	236 K	Normal
	ntvdm.exe	vishnu	00	596 K	Normal
	ctfmon.exe	vishnu	00	432 K	Normal
FreeCell	freecell.exe	vishnu	00	404 K	Normal
Notepad	notepad.exe	vishnu	00	692 K	Normal
	hpnra.exe	vishnu	00	224 K	Normal
Windows Explorer	explorer.exe	vishnu	00	6,548 K	Normal
	msmsgs.exe	vishnu	00	1,152 K	Normal

Figure 27.7 The things the other user is doing

In Figure 27.7 you see a chunk of the list highlighted, which shows what the user Vishnu is doing on my computer. I can recognize three of the programs by name, as shown in the Figure: FreeCell, Notepad, and Windows Explorer. (Actually, Windows Explorer always runs.)

Now there isn't really much good you can do here. Note that I said "good." Theoretically, you could select one of their processes and click the End Process button, but that would be plain mean.

Oh to Be Most Cruel: Logging Someone Else Off

Heh, heh. It's possible to log off another user. There are actually circumstances when this is required, such as when installing or updating new software or whenever Windows tells you that others are logged in and you need to log them out. To log another user off, follow these steps:

1. Click the Users tab in the Task Manager.

2. Click to select the user you want to dispense with.

3. Click the Logoff button.

You're asked to confirm.

4. Click the Yes button.

They're gone!

 There is no warning given if the person you're logging off is still running programs or if they have unsaved data.

OH! SO I CAN USE THE TASK MANAGER TO MESS WITH OTHER USERS...

Heed the above warning, please. Unlike logging yourself out, where Windows warns you should there be any unsaved data, when you log someone else off using the Task Manager there is no such warning. Be careful, lest you raise the ire of the wrathful vengeful person who shares your computer and can do the same unto you.

Finally, Some things You Probably Didn't Know About the Task Manager

Finally, here's a quick round-up of useful and obscure-no-more things you can do in the Task Manager window:

Arranging Windows on the Screen

Like the Taskbar's pop-up menu, the Task Manager's window has some useful commands for arranging windows on the screen. To use them, click the Applications tab, then use the Windows menu to organize the windows on your screen.

 The Windows menu appears only when the Applications tab is selected.

Nifty Shutdown Options

Ah! There's that Shut Down menu. No matter which option you want for turning off, suspending, hibernating, or logging off your computer, it's available in the Shut Down menu.

KEYBOARD MASTER

Shut Down Options

Here are virtually all the Shut Down options via the keyboard courtesy of the Task Manager:

Ctrl+Alt+Delete, Alt+U, B
Stand By (sleep mode)

Ctrl+Alt+Delete, Alt+U, R
Restart

Ctrl+Alt+Delete, Alt+U, H
Hibernate

Ctrl+Alt+Delete, Alt+U, L
Log Off

Ctrl+Alt+Delete, Alt+U, U
Turn Off

Ctrl+Alt+Delete, Alt+U, S
Switch User. Note that Win+L is the easy keyboard option for switching users.

411

28

I Really Want to Impress My Friends and Coworkers with My Knowledge of System Administration

Can You Show Me a Few Tricks Without Boring the Pants Off Me?

So it all comes down to this! One final, hoary chapter on the miscellaneous stuff that remains, which I classify as *System Administration*. Isn't that an important sounding title? Impressive, too. Probably worth another $10K to $15K a year on your annual salary if you can convince the boss that you're adept at "System Administration." And integration. Always add "and Integration" to your title. It means nothing, but it sounds very impressive.

"Yes, I do manicures, pedicures, exfoliation, and integration." See?

The topic of System Administration is typically one that most people ignore—which is why it's always the last chapter in the book! Most of this stuff lies under the tent of "Futzing with the Computer for the Computer's Sake." It's not entertaining. And it's not productive. It's just...boring old System Administration!

Things to Hate, Berate, and Celebrate:

- Discovering the Computer Management window
- Checking error logs
- Working with device drivers
- Increasing disk storage
- Scheduling tasks

The You-Can-Fool-Anyone Tour of Basic Administrative Tools

Like any competent handyman, Windows keeps all its tools in one bag called "Administrative Tools."

 You can set up the bag so that Administrative Tools appears as a submenu off the Start panel. (This is covered in Chapter 6.)

 You can access the Administrative Tools via the Control Panel.

 Or you can, in any folder window, press the F4 key and type `control panel\administrative tools` to see the list.

Here's the list of what you see in the order of importance:

compmgmt.msc
Computer Management This is main window through which you'll do most of the administrative garbage—or at least that's where I've discovered the most useful things.

perfmon.msc
Performance This has some overlap with Computer Management, but it does sport one of the niftiest performance graphs I've seen in Windows. Therefore it ranks up here at the top of the list.

The rest of the System Administration items are pretty much ho-hum for the typical Windows user. Either that or their most useful functions also appear in the Computer Management window:

comexp.msc
Component Services Yeah, I have no idea how this can be useful, though it's fun to open this icon and browse its folders because of all the animation. Quite an impressive display. Useful? Who knows? Who cares? Why bother?

odbcad32.exe
Data Sources (ODBC) If I ever write a screenplay, I'm going to be sure to have the ODBC be the acronym for the huge international crime syndicate that the good guy fights against. "Yes, 007, we've matched you up with Madame Svetlana Chiorney, former head of the ODBC before she converted to the side of good during a religious experience in the Moscow Hilton with agent 009." (She blushes.)

eventvwr.msc
Event Viewer This is fully duplicated in the Computer Management window.

services.msc
Services Again, all the good stuff here can be found in the Computer Management window.

secpol
Local Security Policy This booger appears in Windows XP Pro only. It supports some of the advanced security features offered by XP Pro, such as insisting that users change their passwords every so often, plus network security, information on file encryption, and other cool stuff that makes you wonder why you bought Windows XP Home in the first place.

NERD'S CORNER

CockTail Party Trivia, Part XI

The real reason for Component Services and Data Sources

PHIL: Oh, Dan, you're such a cut-up. Why write about something at all if you don't know what it is?

DAN: But Phil, I do know what those geeky things in the System Administration tools do. I just don't want to waste pages one something I feel most users will never use.

MARY: Who are you to judge, you autocratic scrivening hoodlum?

DAN: Beg pardon?

PHIL: I believe Mary is trying to say, "Prove it, buster!"

DAN: Okay. Component Services are tools used by network administrators to configure and control computers elsewhere on the network. Only if your computer is shackled to a huge network would you need them and, even then, the network administrator is the one who's going to use them.

JOHN: So I can just go ahead and delete all that crap?

DAN: Heavens no! Don't delete anything you didn't create yourself. Dumb question, John.

JOHN: Sorry.

MARY: What about Data Sores?

DAN: You mean "Data Sources," you gin-swilling technocrone. That's support for folks running databases, which is about all I know. Not being a big database user myself, I've found no use for Data Sources. And, no, John, I haven't deleted that stuff from my hard drive.

EVERYONE: Oh.

DAN: By the way, it's been nice conversing with you all these past several hundred pages or so. I do hope that if this book has a follow-on or companion that you'll join me there.

PHIL: What the hell are you talking about, Dan?

MARY: Yeah, talk about drinking too much!

EVERYONE: Ha-ha!

A Quick Visit to the Computer Management Window (Which Will Come in Handy Later)

The Computer Management window is the spot where most of the interesting system administration things take place. Not that it's a place you'll visit every day, just a spot you need to be familiar with. Figure 28.1 shows the typical Computer Management window.

(Refer to the previous section for information on displaying the Computer Management window.)

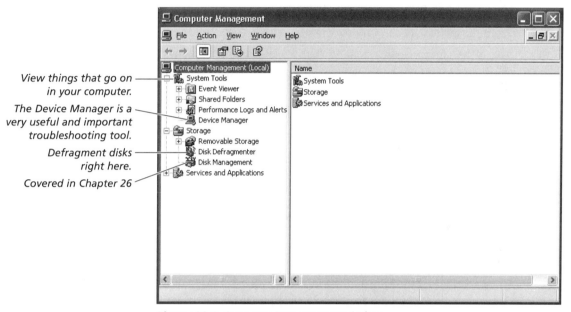

Figure 28.1 Computer Management window

There are many interesting things to do in the Computer Management window, which is why I recommend you know where it is and how to get there. The following sections illustrate a few useful and impressive things you can do in this window.

KEYBOARD MASTER

Quickly opening the Computer Management window

To quickly get to the Computer Management window use the Run dialog box and type in the official filename for that window:

Win+R, compmgmt.msc, Enter

Pressing Win+R summons the Run dialog box. Then type the name of the window, comp-mgmt.msc, *and press Enter.*

What's the Point of Checking the Error Logs?

Windows keeps track of everything it does. For each event, it makes an entry in a log file. The log file itself is basically a text file that states the date and time, what action was attempted, and whether or not that action was successful. Reviewing the logs can be useful in determining what's going on with the computer and fixing various minor problems.

For example, look at some of the logs your computer generates:

1. Open the Computer Management window.

2. From the left side of the window, choose System Tools ➢ Event Viewer ➢ Application.

This is the same area of System Administration that's covered by the Event Viewer application.

The contents of the window may be blank. Or you might see some details, such as those shown in Figure 28.2.

 If the list is blank, consider clicking the Refresh button or pressing the F5 key.

In the figure, you'll notice that there was an "application hang" on December 10, 2001. Double-clicking to open that item explains things in more detail.

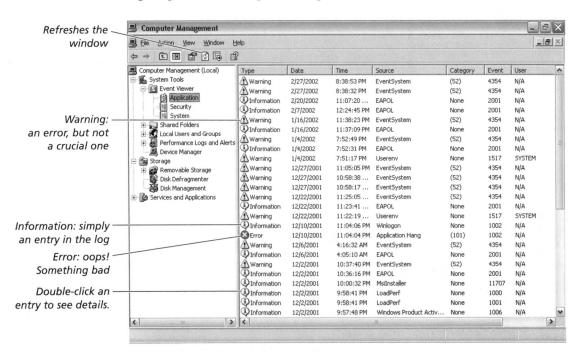

Figure 28.2 A typical Application event log

Refreshes the window

Warning: an error, but not a crucial one

Information: simply an entry in the log

Error: oops! Something bad

Double-click an entry to see details.

3. Choose the System item under the Event Viewer.

The System Log contains events generated by Windows itself. One thing you may notice in there, especially if your computers are not on a large network, are various warnings or errors about the W32Time event.

W32Time is a network service Windows XP runs to synchronize all the computers' clocks on a network. To make this happen, your computer must be connected to a Windows XP network that includes a *Time Server*. If not, then you get the error. (And you can read this information yourself by double-clicking one of the errors in the log.)

Obviously if the W32Time event is causing errors or warnings, and those errors bug you, then you can disable that service. That can also be done in the Computer Management window:

4. Click to select Services in the Services and Applications part of the Computer Management window.

5. Scroll through the list until you find Windows Time.

6. Click to select Windows Time.

You'll see a description of what it does displayed in the window. Yes, this is the same program that's creating the warning entries in the event log. And, yes, you can turn off this service and prevent the errors from happening again in the future. (This is *really heavy* system administration stuff!)

7. Double-click to open the Windows Time service.

You'll see the Windows Time Properties dialog box, as shown in Figure 28.3.

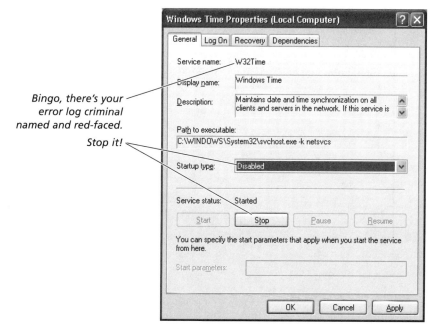

Figure 28.3
Disabling a service

417

8. Choose Disabled from the Startup Type drop-down list.

    That disables the service the next time the computer starts. Otherwise, had you just clicked the Stop button, the service would stop but then start again the next time the computer started.

9. Click the Log On tab.

    You must also disable the service for your hardware configuration, which is listed in the bottom of the Log On tab in the dialog box.

10. Click the Disable button.

11. Click OK.

    And, hopefully, the W32Time thing will not be bothering your error log in the future.

This run-through of checking a log and fixing a problem is rather simplistic. The problem was obvious because the error message stated specifically which service was screwing up. On a non-networked computer, it's a common and predictable problem.

On your own, you can use the Event Logs to help determine what's a problem in the computer and, hopefully, pinpoint where the solution lies. One way to do that is to review each event in the log: double-click the event to open it, then use the dialog box (Figure 28.4) to scroll through the list.

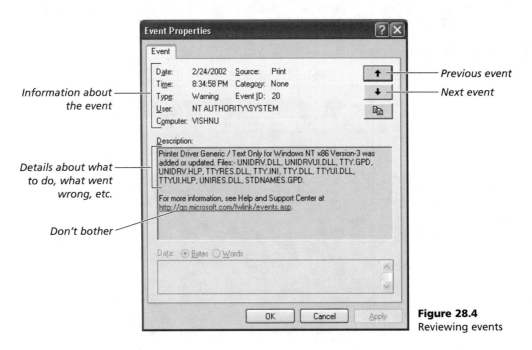

Figure 28.4
Reviewing events

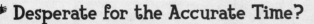

Desperate for the Accurate Time?

What time is it anyway? The only entity with the time, money, or ambition to answer that question is the U.S. Government, which has set up various and sundry clocks around the country that keep track of the "official" time. Windows XP has the gears within it to connect to one of these official timekeepers and update your computer's clock to something more accurate than your garden sundial or Uncle Vern's antique pocket watch that he swears is the most accurate thing in the known universe.

To sync up your computer's clock, open the Control Panel's Date/Time icon. In the Date and Time Properties dialog box, click on the Internet Time tab. Then click the Update Now button. Windows forays out into the Internet (though you may have to connect to the Internet first, before you click the Update Now button), and synchronizes the computer's clock to some more accurate clock somewhere else.

You can also click on the "Automatically Synchronize with an Internet Time Server" check box to have all this done automatically, such as when you're sleeping or out sneaking a cigar while your wife is visiting her sister's.

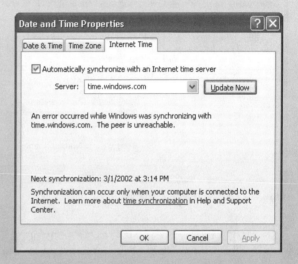

Yes, the Device Manager Can Help You Troubleshoot Your System

One of the keenest items in the Computer Management window is the Device Manager, shown in Figure 28.5. It lists all the hardware in your system, which is nice—and a good thing to remember. But more importantly, the Device Manager will flag certain hardware that's misbehaving.

If any bum hardware does show up, you'll see it flagged in the Device Manager window with a little yellow circle. Inside the circle is an exclamation point (!), which tells you that such-and-such a device or piece of hardware is malfunctioning. If you double-click to open the malfunctioning device, it's Properties dialog box typically tells you what's wrong and how to fix it—making you appear to be a genius, but it's really the computer doing all the work.

You can also view the Device Manager from the System icon in the Control Panel: click the Hardware tab, then click the Device Manager button.

419

Hardware in your PC

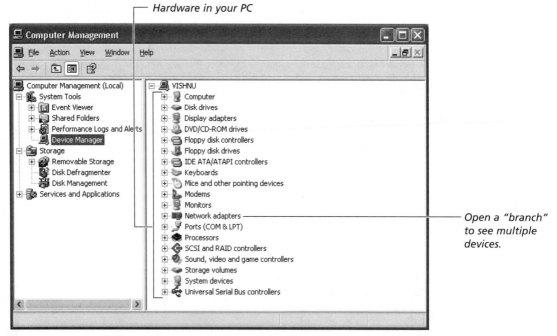

Open a "branch" to see multiple devices.

Figure 28.5 The Device Manager

 KEYBOARD MASTER

Summoning the Device Manager

This is my favorite keyboard shortcut of all time, very impressive to show your fellow Windows XP users:

Win+Break, Right-arrow, Right-arrow, Alt+D

The Win+Break key combination summons the System Properties dialog box. (Note that the Break key is the same as the Pause key.) Pressing the Right-arrow key twice switches to the Hardware tab. Pressing Alt+D "clicks" the Device Manager button. Very keen.

Installing a New Driver Often Helps Cure Hardware Ills

One common thing to do in the Device Manager is to install a new driver (software) for your hardware. This could be because either the existing driver is no longer compatible or perhaps—and this does happen—Windows loses track of your driver and you must reinstall it. For example, say the display suddenly switches to the "dumb mode" of 640x320 pixels with only 16 colors. In that case, you'd need to reinstall the video driver to get things back to normal.

Here are the generic instructions for reinstalling a driver:

1. Open the Device Manager window.

2. Open the branch containing the device needing a new driver.

If it's a bum device, then the Device Manager will have it open and flagged with a yellow circle automatically for you.

3. Double-click to open the device itself.

For example, to replace a video driver, you first open the Display Adapters branch. Then you double-click to open the NVIDIA GeForce2 GTS (or whatever) video adapter installed in your computer.

The device's Properties dialog box is displayed.

4. Click the Driver tab.

Figure 28.6 illustrates a window typical of what you'll see. Replacing the driver is done by clicking one of the four buttons, as shown in the figure. Well, actually, there are only two buttons that count:

Update Driver Choose this option to install a newer version of the driver, one that's either already installed on your hard drive, downloaded from a website, or on a removable disk.

Roll Back Driver Choose this option to restore a previously installed driver should a newer driver make things act weird in your computer.

5. Click the proper button, per the advice in the figure and mentioned above.

6. Follow the instructions on the screen.

Eventually the new driver will be installed and you can go back to using your computer as you once did.

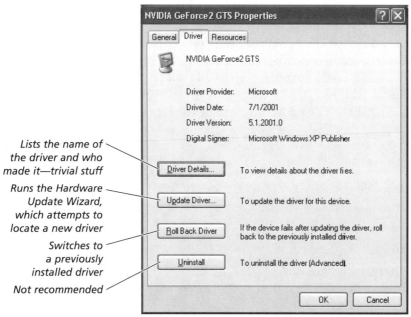

Lists the name of the driver and who made it—trivial stuff

Runs the Hardware Update Wizard, which attempts to locate a new driver

Switches to a previously installed driver

Not recommended

Figure 28.6
Changing or updating a device driver

There is really no need to install or update device drivers unless something is wrong with your computer or the manufacturer strongly suggests that you update. In fact, the only time I've done this is when a device stops working or gets flagged with the yellow circle in the Device Manager window.

To check for new drivers, visit the website for the hardware manufacturer. You can get there by typing the name of the hardware into a search engine, such as Google. Then, when you're at the manufacturer's site, check for Drivers, Downloads, or Technical Support to locate new drivers.

Do not pay for new drivers! Hardware manufacturers owe it to you to support their products. If you have to pay for a new driver, then you're looking in the wrong place; drivers should be free. If the manufacturer is stubborn and refuses to give away their drivers, then have their hardware un-installed and buy your stuff from someone else.

Anything Cool I Can Do with the Local Security Policy?

secpol

The Local Security Policy icon appears with the Administrative Tools only in Windows XP Pro. It contains categories of various security things, dos and don'ts, and configuration options, that let you control how people use the computer. There's nothing in there that's particularly difficult to understand, nor are there any hidden treasures or secrets.

The best way to use the Local Security Policy program is simply to browse through it and examine the various options and settings. To change a setting, double-click it and work the dialog box that appears.

As with the majority of advanced or technical things, the settings mostly apply to computers chained to an advanced network. For a single user, messing with the Local Security Policy is a waste of time.

Any Tips on Increasing Disk Storage?

Until they invent the disk drive capacity stretcher (not $199, not $149, but available now for three low, low payments of just $39.99) you'll have to rely upon some old and trusted techniques for increasing your disk storage—yet another aspect of System Administration. I have three suggestions:

First, buy a second hard drive. They're cheap. They store lots of information. And if your PC is equipped with a USB or Firewire (IEEE 1349 port), you can easily add as many external disk drives as your lust demands.

And then, of course, the secret to having a second hard drive is to use it! I'm shocked at how many people already have a drive D (or E) and just forget to use it. Also see Chapter 26 for information on mounting hard drives as folders, which makes them really handy to use.

Second, consider archiving some of your stuff from the hard drive off onto Zip disks or CD-Rs, as well as using Windows XP's "blue" compressed files. Refer to Chapter 14, which is all about archiving.

Third, clean some of the crap out of your disk drive. Rather than have you in your mere mortal wisdom determine what's crap and what's worth keeping, Windows comes with a handy Disk Cleanup utility to do the job for you. Here's how to run it:

1. From the Start menu choose All Programs ➤ Accessories ➤ System Tools ➤ Disk Cleanup.

2. Optionally choose the drive you want to clean up from the drop-down list and click OK.

   Choose Drive C or whichever hard drive has Windows XP installed on it. (This step doesn't appear if your computer has only one hard drive.)

   Windows examines the drive, looking for files it can utterly do away with.

3. Work the dialog box to choose which types of files you want to remove.

For example, in Figure 28.7 you can see that roughly half a megabyte of junk is stored in the Recycle Bin—an easy thing to clean and get back a ton of disk space. Refer to the sidebar "Dan's Useful Descriptions of Delete-able Disk Detritus" for more information.

4. Click OK. And your disk drive is scoured of the junk you don't need to make room for more junk you do need.

Options for uninstalling parts of Windows, programs, or System Restore information

Golly!

Select an item here.

View its description here.

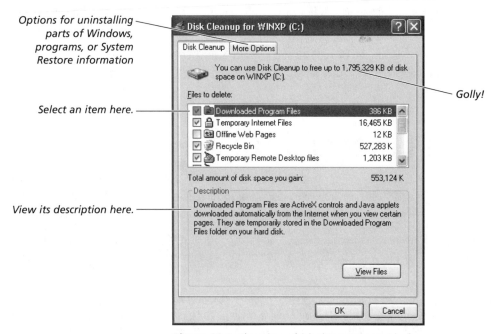

Figure 28.7 Choosing which things to get rid of

Dan's Useful Descriptions of Delete-able Disk Detritus

The list of things delete-able in the Disk Cleanup dialog box (Figure 28.7) can be confusing. Here are my descriptions and advice for each category:

Downloaded Program files *No, these aren't files that you've downloaded, but rather small programs or plug-ins that Internet Explorer itself downloads. They're okay to delete because IE has already installed them.*

Temporary Internet files *This is the "cache" used by IE, saved graphics images and stuff from web pages that make those pages load all the faster on second viewing. Deleting these files is only a temporary fix; the files will fill up again quickly as you go back onto the Internet. (To regulate the amount of storage used by Temporary Internet Files, choose Tools ➤ Internet Options in IE. In the Internet Options dialog box, General tab, click the Settings button to adjust the amount of disk space used by temporary files.)*

Offline web pages *Any Web page you've downloaded or linked to for later viewing— something few people do, so this item may not even appear in the list.*

Recycle Bin *Where deleted files are kept, free to delete—providing you don't feel you have anything that requires eventual recovery. (You can set the amount of storage the Recycle Bin uses by right-clicking its icon on the Desktop and choosing Properties from the pop-up menu. You can set the amount of storage that the Recycle Bin uses as a percentage of the entire disk's storage space.)*

Temporary files *These are files created by Windows and other programs, files that you assume the computer would be smart enough to clean up when it's not done with them, but no, they hang around and use up space needlessly. (Please do not attempt to delete these files on your own; only delete temporary files with the Disk Cleanup utility.)*

Compress old files *This is an interesting option that uses "blue" compression to shrink down the amount of disk space used by files you don't access that often—an excellent item to set. It doesn't actually delete anything, but it will help the bottom line of disk space.*

Other things *There's a collection of miscellaneous items in the list to check, various log files and information used for disaster recovery and whatnot—nothing to go into too much detail over, so if you feel like checking the rest of the items, go ahead.*

System Administration While You Sleep: The Task Scheduler

The Task Scheduler is a nifty little program that lets you run a specific program (a "task") at any time you specify. For example, you can configure Disk Cleanup to run every Saturday morning at 3:00 AM. Or you can configure an enemy's computer to bleep every hour on the hour. Anything you want, any time you want, just by using the Task Scheduler.

 Only users with password-protected Administrative status can use the Task Scheduler.

Where the Task Scheduler Lives

The Task Scheduler is a special window, just like Dial-up Networking or the My Computer window. It isn't a folder, but rather a place you go to create new tasks or edit (disable, enable, modify) existing tasks.

You get to the Task Scheduler by choosing All Programs ➢ Accessories ➢ System Tools ➢ Scheduled Tasks. (I'm quite surprised that this option isn't available in the Administrative Tools window/menu.) Figure 28.8 shows a typical Task Scheduler window. The window lets you review existing tasks, checking out whether or not they've run recently and how often they're scheduled. You can create new tasks, edit or delete existing tasks.

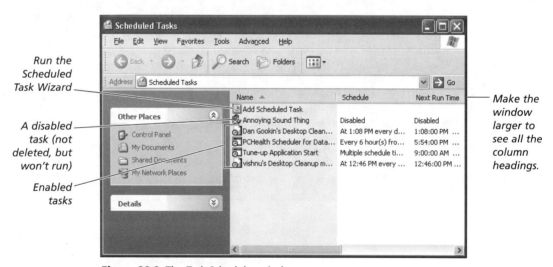

Figure 28.8 The Task Scheduler window

Yes, I Want My Computer to Automatically Run Disk Cleanup Every Morning at 3:00 AM

No matter what the task (though running Disk Cleanup every so often is a nifty idea), here are the steps you take:

1. Open the Task Scheduler.

2. Double-click the "Add Scheduled Task" icon to start the Scheduled Task Wizard.

3. Click the Next button.

4. Choose Disk Cleanup from the list of programs.

Not all programs are shown in the list. Generally speaking, you want to run programs that can be configured to behave automatically or run by themselves. Interactive programs, obviously, cannot run without your input so there's no point in scheduling them to run automatically.

5. Click the Next button.

6. Choose Weekly from the list.

Or select whatever interval you'd like to use for running the program. Optionally you can type another name for the program into the box.

7. Click the Next button

8. Enter 3:00 AM into the box

 You can click to select the hour, then type 3. Click to select the minutes, then type 00. Click to select AM/PM and type A or P to reset that value as well.

9. Choose Saturday.

10. Click the Next button.

All tasks in Windows must be run as a specific user. In this case, your logon name is specified as the user who runs the program. (And you must be an Administrative level user to do this.)

11. Enter your password twice.

You must do this or the task will not run.

12. Click the Next button.

13. Click the Finish button.

You'll see your task listed in the window, titled "Disk Cleanup" or whatever name you gave it.

Will the Program Really Run at 3:00 AM Every Saturday?

Yes, providing that the computer is on at that time. Tasks you create will not turn the computer on. They will "wake up" the computer should it be sleeping, but the computer must be on (or sleeping), not off (or hibernating) for the task to run in the middle of the night.

How Can I Be Sure That the Task Runs Properly?

The best thing to do after creating a task is to test-run it to see what happens. After all, not every task runs automatically, so there may be some adjusting required. Here's how to do that in the Scheduled Tasks window:

1. Right-click the task you want to test.

2. Choose Run from the pop-up window.

Now what you see take place would be what happens when the task runs automatically. So if the program's window just sits there waiting for your input, that will be what happens when the task runs. If you need the task to be fully automatic, then you must determine if there's a way to make it do things automatically.

3. Observe what happens.

This requires insight so:

If nothing happens then it could mean that you didn't enter a proper password when setting up the task. A quick check of the Event Viewer/Security logs will confirm this. A "Failure Audit" appears if you attempt to schedule a task without a proper password-protected Windows XP account.

If the task runs, but requires input, then more information is needed for the task. In the case of Disk Cleanup, you'll need to specify a "command-line option" to get it to automatically do its task. In this case, the command is /sagerun. Here's what you need to do:

a. Double-click to open the task in the Scheduled Tasks window.

b. In the task's dialog box, Task tab, edit the Run command box to contain all the options necessary to run the task automatically.

In this case, you need to add the text /sagerun after the text already in the Run dialog box. It should look like this:

```
C:\WINDOWS\SYSTEM32\cleanmgr.exe /sagerun
```

c. Click OK.

d. Re-enter and confirm your account's passwords.

e. Click OK.

Test the task again after modifying it to ensure that it runs completely automatically.

One of the tasks you might consider scheduling is the Disk Defragmenter. Alas, that program cannot be automated in Windows XP.

For programs beyond what Windows offers, such as the Norton Utilities, instructions for letting the programs run automatically are usually given in the manual. If there are specific programs in Windows you're concerned about automating, you can e-mail me at dgookin@wambooli.com and I'll do my best to see if the program can be automated and which options would be available for that.

NERD'S CORNER

Where the Hell Did "Sagerun" Come From?

The only question you probably have—and it's bugging you—is how the heck did I discover the /sagerun option for the Disk Cleanup program? It's true that /sagerun is undocumented; at least it's nowhere to be found in the help system.

So, knowing that such things exist but also that Microsoft doesn't let anyone know about them, I found the program file, CLEANMGR.EXE, on the computer and disassembled it (which is against the End User License Agreement, by the way). As a programmer myself, it was easy to find the hidden options available to the Disk Cleanup program and, after testing a few of them, I figured that /sagerun was the best for a routine disk cleanup check.

INDEX

Note to reader: **Bolded** page numbers refer to definitions and main discussions of a topic. *Italicized* page numbers refer to illustrations.

SYMBOLS

TELL US WHAT YOU THINK!

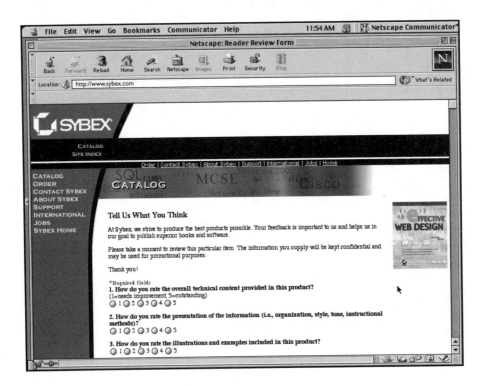

Your feedback is critical to our efforts to provide you with the best books and software on the market. Tell us what you think about the products you've purchased. It's simple:

1. Visit the Sybex website
2. Go to the product page
3. Click on **Submit a Review**
4. Fill out the questionnaire and comments
5. Click **Submit**

With your feedback, we can continue to publish the highest quality computer books and software products that today's busy IT professionals deserve.

www.sybex.com

SYBEX Inc. • 1151 Marina Village Parkway, Alameda, CA 94501 • 510-523-8233